2022

To Sophie
Happy late birthday
An intellectual biography
of an Australian (one
CPA member)

The Work of History

historian to an
intellectual historian

xxx

D1810675

Peter Beilharz is Professor of Critical Theory at Sichuan University. He is founding editor of *Thesis Eleven*.

Sian Supski is a freelance researcher, and Adjunct Research Fellow in Sociology at La Trobe University. She is an editor of *Thesis Eleven*.

The Work of History

Writing for Stuart Macintyre

Edited by Peter Beilharz and Sian Supski

MELBOURNE
UNIVERSITY
PRESS

MELBOURNE UNIVERSITY PRESS
An imprint of Melbourne University Publishing Limited
Level 1, 715 Swanston Street, Carlton, Victoria 3053, Australia
mup-contact@unimelb.edu.au
www.mup.com.au

First published 2022
Text © Peter Beilharz and Sian Supski
Design and typography © Melbourne University Publishing Limited, 2022

Text design by J & M Typesetting
Cover image: Stuart Macintyre, in his office at Melbourne University, 28 September 2004. Picture by Cathryn Tremain, Fairfax images.
Printed in Australia by McPherson's Printing Group

A catalogue record for this book is available from the National Library of Australia

9780522878608 (paperback)
9780522878615 (ebook)

Picture Acknowledgements

Burke and Wills photo: *The Australian* newspaper, photographer Simon Schluter
Martha Macintyre and Jessie Macintyre: family photos
Marcus Clarke Annual Lecture, Athenaeum Library: Athenaeum Library, photographer Janine Eastgate

Contents

Preface · viii

Contributors · xi

Introduction: The Work of History · 1
Peter Beilharz and Sian Supski

Part 1   Communism · **19**

1   What happened in the 1970s? · 21
    Geoff Eley

2   Stuart Macintyre and British communism · 27
    Kevin Morgan

3   Stuart Macintyre and Australian communism · 47
    Terry Irving

4   Militant: Stuart Macintyre and Paddy Troy · 65
    Bobbie Oliver

5   Writing communist history · 81
    Ann Curthoys

6   Professor and comrade · 85
    Peter Love

Part 2   Australia: Foundations · **89**

7   On Stuart's 'Victorian Visionaries': Gender, race and
    contested colonial liberalisms · 91
    Marilyn Lake

8   Stuart Macintyre's new province for labour history: · 106
    Arbitration, the Labor Party and Federation
    Frank Bongiorno

9   Collaborating with Stuart · 122
    Sheila Fitzpatrick

10 Departments and discussions · 127
    Stephen Knight

Part 3   Historians   131

11   A biographer's journey of revelation: Stuart Macintyre on   133
     Ernest Scott
     Joy Damousi

12   Scrutiny, context and power: Stuart Macintyre on   149
     Australian historians
     Sean Scalmer

13   Taking note   165
     Diane Kirkby

Part 4   Postwar Australia   171

14   'A very liberating experience': The historical repositioning of 173
     postwar reconstruction
     Nicholas Brown

15   Winners and losers   190
     Rob Watts

16   History and the 'social science project'   207
     Tim Rowse

17   Labour colleagues   224
     Phillip Deery and Julie Kimber

Part 5   General histories   229

18   Writing the Cambridge 'Australia'   231
     Alison Bashford

19   Things as they are   235
     Kate Darian-Smith

20   Companions   249
     Graeme Davison

21   The making of a trans-Tasman bubble   266
     Len Richardson

22   Oceanic connections   271
     Philippa Mein Smith

Part 6   Public works   277

23   The sentimental deficit: Australians and their Constitution   279
     Carolyn Holbrook

24   Stuart Macintyre and the 'History Wars': Compassionate   296
     histories and compassionate historians
     Anna Clark

25   Universities   311
     Simon Marginson

26   Stuart Macintyre as colleague   329
     Patricia Grimshaw

Part 7   Conclusion   333

27   What true believers need: Understanding Labo(u)r   335
     Liam Byrne

28   Response   353
     Stuart Macintyre

Epilogue: What if?   357
Peter Beilharz and Sian Supski

Appendix: The work of supervision   360
Bibliography   366
Index   383

Preface

The idea for this book has been circling for a while. As one of us wrote in opening a book of essays collected in 2014, Stuart Macintyre had, along with Bernard Smith, left footprints in the sand for many of us. What is striking about this kind of claim is the extent of its applicability. So many of us are in debt to Stuart Macintyre, intellectually and personally. Yet his personal modesty has meant that while the works are standard references, there has hitherto been little public discussion of what might be called the Macintyre Effect.

We floated the idea with Nathan Hollier, who was enthusiastic. Then we tried it out on Stuart, who was more reluctant. He was the rarest of academic creatures, the scholar indifferent to the cult of self-promotion. His engagement with this project was warm but detached. The editors and contributors take sole responsibility for its contents.

We asked Frank Bongiorno and Joy Damousi to act as project advisers, and thank them for their wholehearted efforts to make it work, both as tribute and as innovation. We sincerely thank our authors, who got it. They understood the need both to appraise and to add, to give this book its value in recognition of Stuart and to offer a contribution to Australian historiography in its own right. We thank Martha Macintyre, not least for help with photographs. We thank the MUP crew, Nathan Hollier, publisher and CEO, our editor Catherine McInnis, Duncan Fardon, publishing assistant, and Karen Gillen, indexer. We also thank our fastidious copy-editor Cathryn Game.

Finally, we thank Stuart Macintyre, for a life of inspiration and support, for good spirit and example. We thank him for leading us in the work of history.

Peter Beilharz and Sian Supski
Melbourne, 2021

Stuart Macintyre died on 22 November 2021, while this book was in production. He was able to read the materials in manuscript and to write a modest response. We deeply regret missing the opportunity to hand him the finished volume and to say thank you, one last time.

PB & SS
Melbourne, 2022

Contributors

Alison Bashford is Director of the Laureate Centre for the History of Population at the University of New South Wales. She co-edited *The Cambridge History of Australia* with Stuart Macintyre, and her most recent book is *The New Worlds of Thomas Robert Malthus: Rereading the Principle of Population* (with J.E. Chaplin; 2016).

Peter Beilharz is Professor of Critical Theory at Sichuan University, and is affiliated with Yale, Leeds, La Trobe and Curtin universities. He founded *Thesis Eleven* in 1980. He has published thirty books, most recently *Circling Marx* (2020) and *Intimacy in Postmodern Times: A Friendship with Zygmunt Bauman* (2020).

Frank Bongiorno studied under Stuart Macintyre at the University of Melbourne in 1989 and 1990. Stuart supervised his Honours thesis, and they have subsequently collaborated on other projects. Frank is Professor of History at the Australian National University. His books include *The Eighties* (2015).

Nicholas Brown is one of the many who have benefited from Stuart Macintyre's generous, tolerant and wise PhD thesis examination. A Professor of History at the Australian National University, he was working with Stuart and others on a study of J.G. Crawford. His works include *Governing Prosperity* (1995).

Liam Byrne is the author of *Becoming John Curtin and James Scullin* (Melbourne University Press, 2020). In 2018 he began work with the Australian Council of Trade Unions, and in 2019 was appointed its historian. He writes here in a personal capacity.

Anna Clark is a historian at the University of Technology Sydney. Stuart Macintyre supervised her PhD thesis, which looked at contests over Australian History education, and invited her to contribute some of that research to his book, *The History Wars*. Her most recent book, *Making Australian History* (2022), is a study of Australian historiography.

Ann Curthoys is a historian. She is Professor Emerita at the Australian National University and Honorary Professor at the University of

Sydney and the University of Western Australia. Her most recent book is *Taking Liberty: Indigenous Rights and Settler Self-Government in Colonial Australia, 1830–1890* (with Jessie Mitchell; 2018).

Joy Damousi is Professor of History and Director of Humanities and Social Sciences at the Australian Catholic University and Redmond Barry Distinguished Professor at the University of Melbourne. Her most recent publication (as General Editor with Phillip Dwyer) is *The Cambridge World History of Violence* (four volumes, 2020).

Kate Darian-Smith was a colleague of Stuart Macintyre at the University of Melbourne for more than two decades, where they co-taught Australian and world history and collaborated on history projects. She is Professor and Executive Dean, College of Arts, Law and Education, University of Tasmania.

Graeme Davison is an Emeritus Professor of History at Monash University. With Stuart Macintyre and John Hirst he co-edited *The Oxford Companion to Australian History*. His most recent books are *City Dreamers: The Urban Imagination in Australia* (2016) and *Hugh Stretton: Selected Writings* (2018).

Phillip Deery is an Emeritus Professor of History at Victoria University who specialises in Cold War history, and his most recent book is *Spies and Sparrows: ASIO and the Cold War* (2022). He and Julie Kimber have worked with Stuart in the Australian Society for the Study of Labour History for more than a decade.

Geoff Eley is Professor of History and German Studies at the University of Michigan, Ann Arbor. His most recent book is *Nazism as Fascism: Violence, Ideology, and the Ground of Consent in Germany, 1930–1945* (2013). He is writing a general history of Europe in the twentieth century.

Sheila Fitzpatrick is Distinguished Service Professor Emerita at the University of Chicago and a professor at Australian Catholic University. Her most recent book is *White Russians, Red Peril: A Cold War History of Migration to Australia* (2021), and her next, *The Shortest History of the Soviet Union*, will be published in 2022.

Patricia Grimshaw is Professor Emeritus in the School of Historical and Philosophical Studies at the University of Melbourne, where she taught subjects in Australian and American history and Gender Studies for several decades. She wrote and co-edited a number of books and articles in these areas, and served in administration in the school and the Faculty of Arts.

Carolyn Holbrook first met Stuart Macintyre in 1994 when she was a junior bureaucrat on the Civics Expert Group secretariat. Stuart later co-supervised her PhD thesis at the University of Melbourne. Carolyn is a historian and ARC DECRA Fellow at Deakin University. Her books include *Anzac: The Unauthorised Biography* (2014).

Terry Irving, radical historian and educator, is Honorary Professorial Fellow at the University of Wollongong. His books include *The Barber Who Read History: Radical History Essays* (with Rowan Cahill) and *The Fatal Lure of Politics: The Life and Thought of Vere Gordon Childe*. He was editor of *Labour History*.

Julie Kimber teaches history and politics at Swinburne University of Technology. She and Phillip Deery worked with Stuart in the Australian Society for the Study of Labour History for more than a decade. She has edited book collections and conference proceedings on Australian labour history and has written, most recently, on Dexter Daniels for the *Indigenous Australian Dictionary of Biography* with Charlie Ward.

Diane Kirkby is Professor of Law and Humanities at University of Technology Sydney and Professor Emeritus at La Trobe University. She works across several fields of history and is editor of *Labour History*. Her latest book, *True-blue Internationals: Navigating Region and Race on the Long Voyage to Seafarers Rights*, will be published in 2022.

Stephen Knight, an Oxford graduate, worked in English at Sydney and then at the University of Melbourne (1987–92), when he moved back to Britain until retiring in 2011 and returning as an Honorary Research Professor to Melbourne. He has published on medieval literature and on popular literature, especially crime fiction and the myth of Robin Hood.

Marilyn Lake is Professorial Fellow in History at the University of Melbourne, where she taught Australian History with Stuart between 1984 and 1987. Her recent books include *Drawing the Global Colour Line* (co-authored with Henry Reynolds; 2008) and *Progressive New World: How Settler Colonialism and Transpacific Exchange Shaped American Reform* (2019).

Peter Love is a retired Politics academic from Swinburne University. He has read most of Stuart Macintyre's work, has prescribed some of his books as set references for his subjects and has reviewed a number of them. His own works include *Labour and the Money Power* (1984).

Simon Marginson is Professor of Higher Education at the University of Oxford. He previously worked at Melbourne and Monash universities. Simon works on global, international and comparative aspects of higher education, global science, higher education in East Asia, and higher education and public goods.

Philippa Mein Smith is Emeritus Professor of History and Ahorangi Tauhere at the Ng i Tahu Research Centre, University of Canterbury, Christchurch, Aotearoa New Zealand. Twice resident in Australia, first to undertake a PhD at the Australian National University, she lives in New Zealand and researches trans-Tasman relations.

Kevin Morgan teaches politics and contemporary history at the University of Manchester and first met Stuart in 1994 when he was sorting out the previously inaccessible British Communist Party archives. Kevin's interest in communist history has resulted in a number of publications, including *Communists in British Society 1920–1991* (jointly, 2007).

Bobbie Oliver is an Honorary Research Fellow at the University of Western Australia. She is the author of many books and articles on labour history. Her most recent publication is '"No place for tourists": Deaths on Western Australian construction sites', *Labour History*, no. 119, November 2020.

Len Richardson was, in the early 1970s, a PhD student at the Australian National University where his work on the labour movement in Wollongong during the Great Depression was supervised by Bob Gollan. He taught New Zealand and Australian history at the University of Canterbury, and his research interests continue to focus on Australasian labour movements.

Tim Rowse is a historian who has been reading Stuart's work and talking to him about shared interests since 1977. Tim's primary topic of research, since the early 1980s, has been the relationship between Indigenous and non-Indigenous Australians. He has also written on the history of the social sciences in Australia and about the life and work of H.C. ('Nugget') Coombs.

Sean Scalmer is a Professor of History at the University of Melbourne. Stuart Macintyre was one of the examiners of his PhD thesis (in 1997), and Stuart has acted as a great adviser, supporter and sometime collaborator in the years since. Sean's latest book is *Democratic Adventurer: Graham Berry and the Making of Australian Politics* (2020).

Sian Supski is a cultural sociologist who works as a journeywoman researcher. She has written two books, *A Proper Foundation: A History of the Lotteries Commission of Western Australia* and *It was Another Skin: The Kitchen in 1950s Western Australia*. She is an editor of *Thesis Eleven*. Sian was a visiting scholar at the Stellenbosch Institute for Advanced Study in 2015 and is affiliated with Sichuan University. She is Adjunct Research Fellow, La Trobe University.

Rob Watts is Professor of Social Policy at RMIT University. He completed his PhD in history at the University of Melbourne (1979–84). His first book was *Foundations of the National Welfare State* (1987). His most recent book is *Criminalizing Dissent: The Liberal State and the Problem of Legitimacy* (2019).

Introduction: The Work of History

Peter Beilharz and Sian Supski

Stuart Macintyre was one of the leading Australian historians of our time. The breadth and quality of his work is exemplary, from labour history in Britain and then Australia to social and general history, social justice, civics and education. He was well known as an enabler, as one who made things happen, as supervisor, editor, adviser and general dynamo. He was a leading figure of the Melbourne History School but also went his own way. He was a superb writer, a stylist who combined involvement and detachment. There is much of the Protestant ethic to his example. History here is central, professionally and in everyday life; but it is also work, and can best be understood as the work of gathering evidence and summoning argument, of memory and discernment, of text and archive that make the work of writing possible, and worth reading. All of which begs the question: how do we work intellectually, and what might our legacy be? Such is the purpose of this book: to appraise his work by looking back, in order to look forward.

What is the work of history? Marx famously differentiates between the mode of research and the mode of presentation that might be most appropriate to our work. This is by no means an approach explicitly followed by practising historians, although the distinction may be useful. The sources we use act as guides and correctives to our thinking, but we also are given to the detection of patterns and the construction of narratives. How did Stuart think? Work? Write? What are the modes of investigation and presentation that drove his work?

What are the models of labour history and general history in these hands? This is not a *Festschrift*, conventionally defined, where the invited scholars are licensed to give the subject a nod before bolting off elsewhere on their own. We have asked our contributors to explain and appraise a book or theme from the work of Stuart Macintyre. We invited them to address those in the know but also to be mindful of a general audience and newly emerging generation. We asked them to engage with Stuart's work and to add something new, or of themselves. These are the results.

Who was Stuart Macintyre? Some details of his life and work will help us begin.

Stuart Forbes Macintyre was born in the Melbourne suburb of Kew in 1947. He attended Scotch College and then the University of Melbourne (BA 1968—a good year), Monash, MA 1971, and St John's College, Cambridge through to 1975, PhD. In 1971 he married Margaret Geddes. In 1976 he married the social anthropologist Martha Bruton. The couple had two daughters, Mary and Jessie. From 1977 to 1978 Stuart was Research Fellow at St John's College. Via a year at Murdoch in Western Australia during 1979, he returned to the University of Melbourne in 1980, spending two years (1982–83) on the Social Justice Program at ANU. Returning to Melbourne in 1984, he rose to the position of Ernest Scott Professor in 1990 and Laureate Professor from 2002 until retirement in 2014. As these years passed, they were diarised more and more in terms of committees, councils, academies and public and civic duties and activities. At first a reluctant controversialist, he was to become a keen advocate of history, for example with Anna Clark, and of the social sciences, and of civics in general (as Carolyn Holbrook shows in this volume). Stuart died in Melbourne in November 2021.

The extent of his writing is difficult to map. An almost full list is appended at the end of this book. There are close to fifty books and endless papers, essays and articles. Some highlights are as follows. Across this expanse, invariably our preferences here in this introduction will be personal and selective.

Stuart's first monograph was *A Proletarian Science*, quickly followed by *Little Moscows* in the same year (1980). *Militant*, his life of Paddy Troy, appeared in 1984 and *Winners and Losers* in 1985. His fourth volume of the Oxford History of Australia, *The Succeeding Age 1901–42*, appeared in 1986, followed by *The Labour Experiment* in 1989. *A Colonial Liberalism* was published in 1991. His study of Scott, *A History for a Nation*, was published in 1994; *The Reds*, the first volume of the history of the Communist Party of Australia (CPA), in 1998. The first of five editions of *The Concise Cambridge History of Australia* appeared in 1999. A history of social sciences in Australia, *The Poor Relation*, appeared in 2010, and his history of postwar reconstruction, *Australia's Boldest Experiment*, in 2015. The second volume on the CPA, *The Party*, followed in 2022. As readers can see from the bibliography, there is a swathe of shared and co-edited books, essays and articles. Stuart was a man taking notes, always reading, writing, researching and engaging, responding and supervising (eighty thesis supervisions, at a rough count; how many examinations?).

As we read through Stuart's work, and that of the contributors commissioned to write for this book, some patterns and emerging trends suggest themselves. We discern eight areas of interest, by way of introduction, and follow them with personal conclusions. These are as follows: liberalism, the dominant ideology, and its counterpoint in Marxism; communism, both in Britain and in Australia; labourism and, separately, labour history; history from below, and then above; lateral views from the edges, including trans-Tasman and the west; work across the humanities and social sciences; and lastly, voice and style.

First, let us begin with liberalism, here considered together with the Marxism with which Stuart himself began. Origins matter. Australia has been called a liberal nation. This may be taken to refer

to the party political dominance of the Liberal Party and its predecessors. More substantially, it refers to the hegemony of liberal
patterns of thinking and habits of working in this world.

Liberalism has a long and rich intellectual history.[1] The lineage
that runs from J.S. Mill to Keynes and subsequently Whitlam travels
via significant radical currents usually known as social, or new, liberalism. This stream is keen to identify the negative effects of markets
and to seek to ameliorate them. It is another world from that of
neoliberalism, which from the 1980s was known in Australia as the
province of the new Right or by the tag of economic rationalism.
Across these and other variants liberalism becomes the default
language and mentality of settler capitalist experiences such as
Australia.

Some of Stuart's most innovative work takes on this legacy in
Australia, from colonial liberalism to postwar reconstruction. But
Stuart's intellectual formation was influenced rather by Marxism,
and especially by the 1970s enthusiasm for structuralist Marxism
associated with Louis Althusser. In Australia, this move was led by
the Left Tendency of the Communist Party—the Carlton branch—
and its journal *Intervention*, where enthusiasm for Althusser and other
continental innovations came together with a prescribed need to
write a version of Lenin's *Development of Capitalism in Russia* for
Australia. The Althusserian moment may now be seen as a detour,
which raises the interesting question of what Stuart retained from
this tradition in his own writing of history. Sean Scalmer identifies
the concern with totality as enduring, and, Kevin Morgan suggests,
the interest is less in modes of production than in social formations
that frame public and private life. Geoff Eley adds to this sense that
Althusser was a moment of correction, rather than an immense
historical revolution. What becomes clear as we read across the path
of Stuart's work is that its theoretical curiosities remain, even if
embedded rather than in the foreground.

As Marx said of labour, it disappears into its object, the
commodity, here the essay or book. In a different setting, Stuart's
future biographer will need to address more fully these puzzles to do

with ways of thinking. Certainly the young Stuart was taken by the ideas of historical materialism. Structuralism arrived as a corrective to the more naïve insistences of humanist Marxism: that it was easy to change the world if you really wanted. It offered a powerful surge for historiography, via the work of the *Annales* School and then world systems analysis. This coincided with the ongoing impact of Marx and Freud, Saussure in linguistics, Levi Strauss in anthropology and beyond, and with the three-year period in which Martha Macintyre was working as Edmund Leach's librarian at King's College, while Stuart was friendly with many young Marxists and other more senior anthropologists such as Jack Goody.[2] Structuralism was in the air. In retrospect, it may be that Stuart was intuitively closer to scholars like Stuart Hall and Raphael Samuel. The guiding point, as Hall said to one of us in Melbourne in 1983, was likely *The Eighteenth Brumaire* more than *Capital*. Althusser was the Marxist least friendly to the work of history; but this did not prevent his influence in the field, although the towering figure of the *paterfamilias* was rather E.P. Thompson.

These scuffles among Marxists may seem comical in retrospect: noises off rather than the main game. Liberalism was always more widespread, more pervasive and protean. Liberalism is capable of social engineering and reform, but it is also marked by masculinism and, as Marilyn Lake reminds us, the racism of whiteness. Liberalism has long been caught up with individualism, more particularly what C.B. Macpherson called possessive individualism, or what Castoriadis torched as the cult of rational mastery. This critique of liberalism is in stark contrast to the abstract fantasies of social contract theory, where solitary individuals somehow come together only for their mutual protection. In contrast the tradition of sociology, like Marxism, begins with the social: there are only ever masses of suffering sentient human beings. Liberalism nevertheless remains hegemonic, as Tim Rowse established forty years ago in *Australian Liberalism and National Character*.[3] In Canberra and in everyday life, liberalism still rules. In Australia, its best radical representatives would include H.V. Evatt and H.C. Coombs.

Are liberalism and Marxism then at all compatible? Essentially, or ontologically, no. One starts from the individual, the other the social. Practically, or historically, yes, for each of us combines different elements and contradictions in thinking. And it may well be that across the life work of an historian such as Stuart Macintyre there is a gentle slide or process of accommodation, as the narration of the nation is impossible to engage outside this liberal hegemony. The critics of professors themselves become professors, or at least they become used to liberalism. As several of our contributors remind us, no scholar is singular in their choices of influences or inspirations. Our patterns of thinking and intuition are all mixed up. And as Marx also insisted, he himself was not a Marxist; he also began as a liberal. The notion of a Marxism worn lightly also has purchase in Australia. The most striking parallels in antipodean radical scholarship here would be V.G. Childe and Bernard Smith, where Marx remains one key influence among others, this perhaps submerged as the life proceeds.

The second theme we draw attention to here is communism. Communism needs to be differentiated from Marxism: it has the historicity of state power, above and beyond the history of ideas or the history of the organised socialist movement before 1917. Stuart's first two books took on the case of British communism.

A Proletarian Science, signed off in Cambridge in 1978, enters into and constructs the life worlds of the autodidacts, students and teachers of Marxism and its literature between the wars. This is labour history as social history, yet it also anticipates the long arc, the overarching interest in education, which is to return rather later in Stuart's work with reference to the universities. Its companion, *Little Moscows*, is signed off in Fremantle in 1980. Still interwar in focus, it relates the cultures of working-class self-activity, self-defence and proletarian pride of places like Mardy and Lumphinnans and the Vale of Leven. These radical communities were taken to be exemplary of the world around but had not attracted sustained historical work of engagement until this book. The interest in working-class self-activity then connected to the life of Paddy Troy in *Militant*, and continued to influence Stuart's later work on Australian radical lives in communist and labour circles.

Next came the history of communism in Australia, *The Reds* and later *The Party*. Gramsci famously claimed of the Italian case that to write the history of communism would be to write a history of its people. This may be more emphatically true of Italy, given its popular–national history, than any other, but it has some pertinence in Australia too. Communism is understood here as culture or whole way of life, at least as it represents this sector of Australian life. *The Reds* (1998) and *The Party* (2022) are archivally driven, determined by the incredible volume of files including those gathered by police and security agencies as well as by their own documentary industriousness; communists used up a lot of paper, and helped generate a lot of paperwork.[4] Communism was at the least a significant minority movement in Australia, in the labour movement and trade unions; arts and culture; and in civil society and its struggles, including those for the rights of colonised and Indigenous peoples.

More than this, as Stuart signalled, it was also a distinct type of party. From its formation it was internationalist, as much concerned with issues in China or Yugoslavia, Moscow or Rome as Fishermen's Bend or Port Kembla. If we were to refer, as we often do these days, to matters of identity politics, it becomes clear reading this work how much the identities of these ordinary folk were caught up not only with locality but also with global events and more, with particular moments in world history, Sheepskins for Russia through to Pig Iron Bob and the war in Vietnam and so on. The world was bigger than their backyards. This is a world we have lost, or one that has been transmuted into global tourist itineraries.

The Reds was completed in Melbourne, its acknowledgements closing with thanks to Martha, who had shared the experience of CPA membership with him, although she knew better when it came to the spell cast by Althusser.[5] It was to take Stuart twenty years to get to volume 2, partly because life and other pressing matters got in the way, partly because of the extent of the materials available, which continued to expand. Some sense of the earlier extent of materials can be gained from the bibliography of Beverley Symons, constructed with Stuart and Andrew Wells in 1994—way back![6] Stuart was the kind of traditional historian for whom everything must be read, primary and secondary alike. Volume 2, *The Party* spreads out into institutional and political forms—international, as the party was by its scope of networks, yet local in its activities and commitments.

As Terry Irving observes, the CPA did indeed head into the mainstream, and this is apparent both in the early history by Alastair Davidson, published in 1969, and in Stuart's two volumes, where the hegemony of the Soviet experience was both to orient communists to the world and to distract their local patterns of thinking. The irony here is that both these histories, the Davidson and Macintyre alike, close on the cusp of the 1970s, before the last gasp of the CPA as it fuelled argument for the most significant development of the period, the ALP–ACTU Accord. The New Left had some influence here, not least with its enthusiasm for political economy and later, industry development policy. After the 1980s, when the ALP–ACTU Accord arrived as it were out of thin air, it took some time to become clear that this was also a communist initiative.[7] Communists may well have exerted undue influence in national politics, only now in clearly reforming or corporatist rather than revolutionary directions.

This brings us, third, to labourism. Communism in Australia always manoeuvred around the Labor Party, and was often inflected by labourism. Stuart shows how Stalinism cast a significant shadow on the CPA, although this kind of claim begs the question of the content of local or ordinary Stalinism in places as diverse as France and Australia. Labourism, like liberalism, was a stronger cultural current in *The Labour Experiment*.[8] Stuart observes, in league with W.G. Spence, that around 1909 the labour movement seems to dominate the community as the twentieth century opens; as it closes, even by the 1960s, the programs that had brought labourism into existence and sustained it from 1900 to 1950 seemed finally exhausted.[9] Then, the political economy of labourism seems finally to be closing, under influence of Hawke and Keating.[10] Labourism in the Anglo world had been defined as the defence of the interests of workers and their families: men in the labour market, women allegedly at home.[11] In everyday talk the vocabularies of socialism, labourism, communism, social democracy and democratic socialism were all mixed up. Stuart here shows exemplary clarity of terms and conceptual precision in thinking. What was Labor's program? 'From its origins right up to World War II, I would characterise it as a labourist, masculine form of state intervention in a semimature capitalist economy.'[12] (Note well: every word is made to count.) This gave way momentarily to the prospect of what he emblematically called 'The short history of social democracy in Australia'—Whitlam, a promise rather than an enduring achievement of something beyond labourism.

Fourth, labour history has especially since the 1960s often taken the view from below. This is not identical with labourism as a political form or field of discourse and practice. Rather, the vitality of labour history in the hands of Stuart and his generation reflected the broader enthusiasm for the creativity of social history understood as the realm of everyday life. Everyday life, community studies, ethnography, the categories of experience were to be measured against those of theory. This reminds us of Thompson, not Althusser, but it refers not only to consciousness but also to activity, to the transformative practices of everyday life. This is where, for example, the Katoomba Reds come into the story. Bruce Milliss, a leading activist, was a loyal communist into the 1950s and a strong local advocate in the Blue Mountains of the school Oslo lunch movement. Communists were full of surprises, in terms of the popular cartoon images of espionage and subversion.[13]

This much in Stuart's work clearly indicates the pertinence of the view from below. But the social formation is bigger than that, and the historian cannot afford to be one-eyed. Capital is a relation, so that attention must also be paid to the captains of industry, Essington Lewis, Australia Unlimited and the Millions Club. Later in Stuart's work the line of vision is elevated—from above, or via mediation of third classes, not least those new liberals who were nation-builders from Deakin and Higgins through to Coombs and Whitlam. As Stuart summarises the optic in opening *The Succeeding Age*, he is not convinced that the view from below invalidates the concern for political processes. 'We may learn much from reconstructing the full range of social relations and the texture of everyday life, but we will not understand the popular experience unless we recognize the effects of structures of power.'[14] Power and culture go together. Worlds of labour open onto other worlds, both near and far.

What would it mean to write the history of the nation? The optic opens further from labour and then social history. These progressively larger questions are addressed in this volume by Frank Bongiorno, Joy Damousi and Kate Darian-Smith. They reach back, before invasion, and out, to the question of the nature of the Australian experiment. They also serve to remind us that Stuart was keenly aware of the work of others: history is also historiography. As the picture becomes progressively bigger, the more elongated became Stuart's engagement with other labourers in the vineyard. The work of history is collegial and collective, just as it is also driven by strong individuals.

For fifth, as mentioned above, labour history from the 1980s engaged in Stuart's hands with the idea of social formation, or totality. Social formations are implicitly national, but they are mediated together via the world system of imperialism. Class actors are often plural and may be elsewhere. This is indicated later in the interest in labour and in capital and those middle-class progressives who mediated the difference, such as Higgins and the project of arbitration, where the reliance on the unit of the household opens onto all manner of issues to do with class, gender and age of individuals, addressing the question: who on all these social levels are the actors? This would necessarily mean taking in individual as well as collective forms of action. To step aside from or attempt to place individualism is not to ignore individuals but to foreground them in this way. In contrast to the populism of his predecessors, who focused on the people or the people and their enemies, Stuart opened the door to third and other parties and groups. As he puts it with precision on the sleeve notes to *The Succeeding Age*, his is a narrative history 'which draws on the experience of diverse individuals to illustrate larger patterns, and which traces links between social, economic and political processes'. Such an approach, as he says, demands that the historian must tell a story with a purpose.

Sixth, while the prominence given to colonialism formally defers to nation state and nationalism after Federation in 1901, its larger and smaller units remain, in the interest in empire and imperialism and in regions and states. Whatever Federation means, everyday life is still acted out in cities with long colonial cultures—think only, still, of Sydney versus Melbourne—and at the same time is overdetermined by the distant hearts of empire in London and Washington DC, as well as by what happens in Jakarta and Beijing. Stuart also keeps one eye on the trans-Tasman and the other facing the west: Western Australia on one side, Aotearoa New Zealand on the other. And there are more influences here: Shann and Bolton on the west, Olssen and Belich to the east. Bobbie Oliver connects to the experience of the west, Philippa Mein Smith and Len Richardson to the further east. In terms of Stuart's own origins, these sensibilities reach back to Lenin's *Imperialism* and Fitzpatrick's work on the British Empire. The continent we call Australia always needs to be located among these sturdy yet shifting tectonic plates.

Seventh, Stuart's work retains an uncommon spread across interests more directly aligned with humanities as well as the social sciences. The curiosity in social sciences follows on the interest in reform and liberalism, for its actors were also often housed in the project called sociology across the Anglo world. But this is not only sociology as a zoological category—what the others are doing—as in the work of Bruno Latour and Steve Woolgar on scientists.[15] There is an implicit preference for historical sociology in Stuart's work, given his interest in its core concerns, power and culture. History nevertheless is the preferred field of operation. Sociology in Australia has always been marginal as an academic discipline, although it has been a hardy perennial further afar, in demography, health, agriculture and statistics. Until recently history may have been the national narrative; we had history wars rather than cultural wars.[16] In Stuart's terms, the social sciences were the poor relations in the Australian academic scene. Sociological narratives have revived more recently on the Left as political claims concerning intersectionality. Metanarratives, whether of social liberal progress or stubborn independent nationalism, have been destabilised by the effects of the postmodern, cultural relativism, by regimes that claim to be post-truth, and by the contraction of the public sphere, the militarisation of Australian history, the truncation of the high school curriculum and the radical transformation of universities.

Are we then after Enlightenment? Not yet, as Simon Marginson hopes, nor yet after the better part of what universities might still stand for. Together with Stuart Macintyre, we may still stand for the residual importance of disciplines as skills and understandings that we work in and against. Immanuel Wallerstein's conclusion, in *Open the Social Sciences*, suggested co-appointments as one useful way to moderate the negative effects of disciplinary policework.[17] Stuart, for his part, insisted that disciplines are not silos (silos are serviceable instruments but poor metaphors) and they are porous. All of us, sociologists included, cannot avoid history and historicity. Always historicise.

Eighth, and last for our purposes here, there is the question of voice and style. Stuart writes like Fred Astaire dances. Many of the contributors to this volume observe that Stuart combines lapidary style with direct and clear voice, mastery of well-chosen detail and clarity of narrative, but this is not just the routine punchy Anglo defence of clarity, as in Orwell. He chooses the fact that matters. Consider, for example this hook on the first page of *The Boldest Experiment*: in 1939 'Most households in Sydney and half of those in Melbourne were made up of tenants ...'.[18] The sentence evokes a whole, frugal way of life. But there is more. Literary device is common in his prose. Stuart is always happy to talk about Carlyle, Stern, Peacock; Barnard Eldershaw, Devanny or Waten. Reminding of the tropes of discourse surveyed by Hayden White in *Metahistory*, he thinks with symbol, as in *The Reds*, and *The Party*, terrific single-term titles that condense a whole world of experience by conferring dignity on its subjects before you even open the book in your hands. In the case of *Militant*, there is something like word painting at work. As Alison Bashford tells, we learn from Stuart the importance of the single-clause sentence. Powerful it is! Or, *commas go home*!! He knows the power of suggestion—Bonegilla, working the associations of the senses: 'The pervasive smell of sheep fat and eucalyptus remained long in the memory.'[19] His employment of vignettes, as Sheila Fitzpatrick and Joy Damousi show, conveys something indicative of the world of Brian Fitzpatrick, Professor Scott or of the colonial liberals' stuffed shirts. You feel as though you know the actors, or at least their types. Then, as Ann Curthoys puts it in these pages, Thucydides emerges as the submerged trope for the party as tragedy, not necessarily in the epic sense but at least in the sense that our deeds and hopes always go awry. Tragedy can also be ordinary.

Such richness of prose and generosity of insight are apparent in his engagement with the *enfant terrible* Robert Hughes. Hughes liked to skewer his opponents and was skewered in return. Not by Stuart, this even though Hughes was taken by other historians to be a poacher. Evoking Gibbon, in review of *The Fatal Shore*, Stuart indulges Hughes's willingness to cast convictism as the Gulag:

> Consider the full measure of Hughes' achievement. The story of convict transportation spans eighty years. It moves from Georgian Britain to more than a dozen places of settlement ... Its complex institutions were devised and modified by a host of administrators. The origins, experiences and responses of its 160 000 victims defy the most elaborate taxonomy. The book evades none of these complexities, yet not once in six hundred pages does it strain the reader's attention.[20]

This could be a description of Stuart's own effect. Stuart read, and wrote, for gain rather than loss. If tragedy looms large here, so does comedy. His humour was sparing, perhaps, but when it arrived it was timely. He had a keen eye for the small absurdities, or ironies of everyday life, as when a horse called Russia takes the Melbourne Cup in 1946.[21] Finally, for those who follow, the question of late style may come into play in appraising Stuart's work. How did he achieve, for example, the majesty of *The Boldest Experiment*? Nicholas Brown takes us to this door and invites readers in. The final invitation comes from Liam Byrne, who takes us full circle and forward, here with the labour movement, the origin and a major legacy of Stuart's life's work.

As Graeme Davison tells, these are stories of companions and companionship, and as Pat Grimshaw, Phillip Deery and Julie Kimber, Peter Love, Diane Kirkby, Stephen Knight and others here explain, they are stories of open collegial support and collaboration. Stuart had the gift of gentle confidence, which made it possible for him to be unconditionally generous. Encyclopedic, discerning, he was also a democratic personality. A scholar among us, taking notes and sharing them, with ideas and enthusiasms, urging us on, expecting us always to do better and ever helping us to do so.

To close on a personal note. One of us (Sian) first met Stuart Macintyre in 2004, not long after completing doctoral work. Stuart was in Western Australia to deliver a lecture at the Old Hale School, which sits behind parliament. I had never been inside this building before. It is the site of the first boys' school in Perth, one of a few remaining colonial buildings in that precinct. Bobbie Oliver reminds me that it is now the Museum of the Constitution. I do not recall the lecture title, but it was likely on the History Wars, or perhaps arbitration. I introduced myself to Stuart after the lecture. He was generous and curious, and asked about my own research. It was a brief encounter.

Ten years later, after I moved to Melbourne and was working as a freelance researcher, I had the opportunity to interview Stuart about his creative process. I was working on an ARC research grant on creativity led by Peter Murphy and Simon Marginson. We arranged to meet for the interview in the University of Melbourne staff club (another colonial building).

Again, Stuart was generous. His answers were considered, and there were even a few laughs. I was in awe, meeting in this way with one of Australia's pre-eminent scholars, now able more fully to engage. When I now re-read the transcript of that interview I am struck by Stuart's clarity of purpose. Here is a working historian who has always sought to resolve intellectual questions on problems and ideas that are ambiguous or problematical. He sits with the archives, absorbs the texts, thinks with the questions and problems, then decides. 'How do I tell this story? Where do I begin? What do I need to say, and what do I need not to say?' This is the key to Stuart's work. He was a grand storyteller. Even throughout the interview it was possible to see him weaving a story, creating sense and producing understanding that makes the reader (or interviewer) think about knowledge differently. Throughout his work he challenges us to think differently about something we thought we knew, or he reveals to us something that is wholly new. This was Stuart's gift.

The other (Peter) began a relationship in correspondence with Stuart into the 1980s, coincidentally with the arrival of the journal *Thesis Eleven*. Years later the journal was to be one of the first platforms to celebrate his work: number 95, 2008.

In 1987 Stuart was pivotal in securing me a postdoctoral fellowship at the University of Melbourne. This was a moment in which I was about to give up research, given the double teaching load in the polytechnics and the responsibilities of a young family. It was a turning point in my career, or maybe the point at which it became possible. At Melbourne I co-taught—or at least audited—Stuart's new course on colonial liberalism. It was brilliant, unanticipated timing, as I was working on the project that became my most important early work, *Labour's Utopias*. He even launched the book for me, in the company of Whitlam, after Whitlam had, on being invited himself to launch it, deferred to Stuart as the authority in the field. Stuart then commissioned and entitled the best review essay I was ever to write, 'Elegies of Australian communism'.

When he loaned me the draft for the *Concise History*, *sans* conclusion, as my reference book to teach Australia at Harvard in 1999, I asked my American students each to write the conclusion for him and for me. It was a small gift in return, sent back across the globe in a padded bag. As other contributors here observe, and for each and all of us, Stuart became a constant adviser and inspiration, perpetual reader of manuscripts and general oracle, or encyclopedia, and quiz master. There was always more to come.

To travel full circle here, what then is the influence of Stuart's work? Unlike historians who sit with the Owl of Minerva, he was willing to speak of the present, not just the past. His work is both involved and detached, political and scholarly at the same time or by turns. When controversy called, he stepped up, added context, the longer story and its nuances, and called for judgement and debate. He varied the common distinction: he showed, but he also told. He interpreted, as well as entering into the fibre of the historical moment, its forces and personalities. There is so much here to learn from and to build upon. This is the space in which past, present and future bleed together and fuse. Such is this legacy and its challenge.

Notes

1   Michael Freeden, *The New Liberalism*, Oxford University Press, Oxford, 1986; Michael Freeden, *Liberalism Divided*, Oxford University Press, Oxford, 1986; Steven Seidman, *Liberalism and the Origins of European Social Theory*, University of California Press, Berkeley, 1983; W.H. Greenleaf, *The British Political Tradition*, Methuen, London, two volumes, 1983; James Kloppenberg, *Uncertain Victory: Social Democracy and Progressivism*, Oxford University Press, New York, 1985; Peter Clarke, *Liberals and Social Democrats*, Cambridge University Press, Cambridge, 1978; Stefan Collini, *Liberalism and Sociology*, Cambridge University Press, Cambridge, 1979.

2   Alex Golub, 'Encountering anthropology: An interview with Martha Macintyre', in Nicholas Bainton, Debra McDougall, Kalissa Alexeyeff, John Cox (eds), *Unequal Lives: Gender, Race and Class in the West Pacific*, ANU Press, Canberra, 2021, pp. 472–3.

3   Tim Rowse, *Australian Liberalism and National Character*, Kibble, Melbourne, 1978.

4   Peter Beilharz, 'Elegies of Australian communism', *Australian Historical Studies*, vol. 23, no. 92, 1989, pp. 293–306; 'The end of Australian communism', *Thesis Eleven*, no. 27, 1990, pp. 54–62.

5   Stuart Macintyre, *The Reds: The Communist Party of Australia from Origins to Illegality*, Allen & Unwin, Sydney, 1998, p. xii.

6   Beverley Symons, with Stuart Macintyre and Andrew Wells, *Communism in Australia—A Resource Bibliography*, NLA, Canberra, 1994.

7　　Max Ogden, *A Long View From the Left*, Bad Apple Press, Melbourne, 2020.

8　　Stuart Macintyre, *The Labour Experiment*, McPhee Gribble, Melbourne, 1989, p. 4.

9　　Ibid., p. 62.

10　Ibid., p. 65; Peter Beilharz, *Transforming Labor*, Cambridge University Press, Sydney, 1994.

11　Peter Beilharz, 'The Australian Left: Beyond labourism?' in Ralph Miliband (ed.), *The Socialist Register 1985/6*, Merlin Press, London, and see Beilharz, *Transforming Labor*.

12　Stuart Macintyre, 'The short history of social democracy in Australia', *Thesis Eleven*, no. 15, 1986, pp. 3–14.

13　Stuart Macintyre, *The Party*, Allen & Unwin, Sydney, 2022, p. 151 (proof copy).

14　Stuart Macintyre, *The Oxford History of Australia*, vol. 4: *1901–1942: The Succeeding Age*, Oxford University Press, Melbourne, 1986, p. x.

15　Bruno Latour and Steve Woolgar, *Laboratory Life*, Princeton University Press, Princeton, 1979.

16　Peter Beilharz, 'Australian civilization and its discontents', *Thesis Eleven*, no. 64, 2001, pp. 65–76.

17　Immanuel Wallerstein, *Open the Social Sciences*, Stanford University Press, Stanford, 1996.

18　Stuart Macintyre, *Australia's Boldest Experiment*, NewSouth Publishing, Sydney, 2015, p. 1.

19　Ibid., p. 406.

20　Stuart Macintyre, 'Hughes and the historians', *Meanjin*, vol. 46, no. 2, 1987, p. 244.

21　Macintyre, *The Party*, p. 9.

Part 1

Communism

Chapter 1

What happened in the 1970s?

Geoff Eley

On setting foot in Emmanuel College, Cambridge, where I had arrived in January 1975 to take up an academic appointment, literally the first person I met was literary scholar and film theorist Colin MacCabe, who whisked me off instantly to the Marxism seminar, where that afternoon Ben Brewster was presenting a paper. What followed greatly exceeded my eclectically acquired familiarity with Marxist theory. I remember a classroom of dauntingly earnest students seated at ranks of desks, diligently taking notes from a fearsomely learned disquisition on the problem of commodity fetishism that passed me by completely.[1] This was my induction into the highly theoreticist Marxism of the Cambridge Left in the middle 1970s. Clearly, there was much homework to be done.

Helping me get started was a locally produced pamphlet by two members of the Cambridge Communist Party, Stuart Macintyre and Keith Tribe, *Althusser and Marxist Theory* (1974). Having encountered Althusser so far mainly as a warning issued from hostile quarters, I welcomed this elucidation of why exactly his thinking might matter.[2] Kevin Morgan has discussed this broader intellectual–political context with admirable succinctness, so I shall confine myself to a few personal recollections. Much Marxist debate of the time focused

around base–superstructure ideas and their reductionist insufficien-
cies. These were central to the dilemmas of social historians too, with
their robust understanding of the sovereignty of the economy, the
patterning of material life and the associated class relations, whose
explanatory primacy seemed, 'in the final instance', always assured. In
my own case, I was looking for an improved theory of ideology, one
that could illumine the popular success of mass-political appeals
without having to presume an interest-based model of social explanation. This was where Althusser's retheorising of ideology came to
the rescue, far less via the argument about ISAs (ideological state
apparatuses) than through his concept of interpellation. That
approach, it seemed to me, was better attuned to the experiential
dynamics, self-contained logics and independent efficacy of particular
political appeals and rhetorics than the materialist analytics the available social histories allowed. It seemed capable of capturing both
ideology's 'relative autonomy' and its 'structural determinations', in
the watchwords of the time.

Not just in the universities but also in a wide variety of settings,
the mid-1970s were a time of extraordinary flux. Fresh and challenging ideas were in the air. In my own case, that meant Gramsci,
whose reception climaxed around 1977, closely followed by
Raymond Williams, whose 1973 article 'Base and superstructure' was
a constant point of reference, leading to *Marxism and Literature*, again
in 1977. Althusser's influence preoccupied British Marxists, doing
more than anything else to release thinking about ideology from its
impedance in ideas of 'false consciousness', just as Poulantzas'
complicated treatments of state, political power and social classes.
Furthest reaching of all, new feminisms were impossible to ignore.
Foucault was starting to trouble the assumptions. *Screen* and film
theory became an important hub. Finally, Stuart Hall and the
Birmingham Centre for Contemporary Cultural Studies came into
focus, notably with *On Ideology*, while Ernesto Laclau's *Politics and
Ideology in Marxist Theory* also appeared (each likewise in 1977).

Excitingly if disconcertingly, these discussions battered the edges
of an older materialist consensus. If acutely alerted to the base and

superstructure dilemmas, however, most Left social historians persisted in a rethought structuralist idiom, particularly when less active in theory debates *per se*. So this 'Althusserian moment' was less a bubble that burst than a vitally enabling break with hampering habits of thought. It was far less a passing phase (like emerging from rehab or shedding a skin) than a hard-won stocktaking that not only showed a way forward but also left many fertile traces.[3] This is what Kevin describes, I think, in his account of Stuart's superb couplet of books from this period, *Proletarian Science* and *Little Moscows* (each 1980). They contained richly grounded empirical–analytical labours that presumed the simultaneous work of theory (and vice versa), whether that generative back and forth was directly visible on the page or not. Moreover, that conversation between history and theory occurred best in definite collective settings.

On reaching Cambridge, I wanted to start something like the Oxford Social History Seminar, which since the later 1960s had been a main gathering place for Left-oriented social historians. No sooner had I put this into motion (partly with the help of David Blackbourn) than one of those Oxford convenors, Gareth Stedman Jones, arrived in Cambridge too, with an appointment in King's, where we now launched the aforesaid Social History Seminar. Shortly afterwards, Stuart joined as third member of a trio. Meeting once a week throughout the academic year, this seminar became a place of intensely engaged intellectual life, where changes in the discipline merged to other kinds of radicalism, from leftist politics to the generational militancy of a certain marginal or subaltern status. As graduate students, research fellows, part-time teachers and non-tenured lecturers, all in our twenties and early thirties, we had neither support nor standing in the Cambridge History Faculty, virtually none of whom ever graced the weekly meetings.[4] What I recall most about the seminar was its rare intensity of intellectual community.

That verve came not from the seminar alone but from a larger overlap of scenes. These included the Marxism Seminar in Social and Political Sciences (SPS) already mentioned; the interdisciplinary

'Women and Society' course just created in SPS, run by a collective of faculty, graduate students, non-academic professionals and community workers, some with formal university affiliation, others not (including Martha Macintyre); a very vibrant social history of medicine scene at the Wellcome Centre; and so forth. A collective *esprit* carried across these sites that was non-hierarchical, self-consciously egalitarian and purposefully democratic. Well attuned to the micropolitics of the seminar room, it was intensely preoccupied with the relationship between intellectual work and political action, whether inside the university, inside one's academic discipline, inside the community or inside society at large. Leftist faculty formed a regular lunch group that under one hat organised public lectures as the Tawney Society (one year we had visits from Tony Benn and a Partito Communista Italiano senator), and under another formed a caucus in the local AUT (Association of University Teachers).[5] It was all borne by the conviction that thinking, learning, writing, personal life and politics all belonged together. Indeed, the whole point was to work against those separations. The huge paradox, of course, was the surrounding location: this politics of knowledge, this democracy of knowledge, was being imagined inside one of the least democratic of institutions, one of the most ivory-towered in the country. But the intimacy joining intellectual work to social relationships, personal life and politics was an accomplishment that cannot be gainsaid.

'Politics' here meant not only the nationally, globally and officially organised institutional arenas of public political action but also the micropolitical settings and practices through which we try to engage those larger or more abstract relations inside our local or everyday lives. My best friendships have presumed this sense of political intimacy—not just between individual persons but also between politics and life, between politics and the mundane practices and relations that texture the ordinariness of what we do. That is what I remember about our friendship in the 1970s. In Stuart's case, there was an avowedly oppositional quality too, a certain sensibility, a propensity for making good trouble, along with his quietly impassioned manner of doing it. Then came another bundle of characteristics: a shrewdness, an always on-call critical faculty, a generosity, a sense of humour, not to forget that permanently ingrained work ethic. At the core was an axiomatic, default under-standing that one's historical work is predicated around a politics of knowledge and the associated guiding convictions. For anyone with leftist or progressive inclinations, becoming a historian in the 1960s and 1970s required a self-consciousness of such a kind. You had to name your assumptions and starting points and be explicit about the nature of the interests structuring and driving your relationship to your topic and the questions you wanted to bring. In other words, moving your relationship to your historical work, defining the ground of your intellectual life, was a set of ethical and political imperatives. In this there was an important recognition that in doing your historical work important things, politically and ethically, were at stake.

This was the flavour of the 1970s. It is how I remember the Cambridge years of my friendship with Stuart. The countless happy times my then partner Eleanor and I spent with Martha, Stuart, Mary and Jessie were entirely continuous with everything I have described. In this rather fleeting but expansive moment, we wanted—and came close to having—something like an integrated life.

Notes

1   Among many other talents, Ben Brewster was Althusser's English translator, including *For Marx*, Allen Lane, London, 1969, and *Reading Capital*, New Left Books, London, 1970.

2   I had recently attended a Birmingham WEA-sponsored day conference on popular culture, whose featured speaker, Edward Thompson, cuttingly slapped down a carefully respectful graduate student interlocutor with slightly mysterious allusions to baleful influences from Paris. Althusser was already being invoked as the enemy of right-thinking intellectual work by a broad front of socialist–humanist, marxological, sectarian and Thompsonian opinion.

3   This is a friendly corrective to Kevin's description. See Barry Hindess, 'The Althusserian moment and the concept of historical time', *Economy and Society*, vol. 36, no. 1, 2007, pp. 1–18; E. Ann Kaplan and Michael Sprinker (eds), *The Althusserian Legacy*, Verso, London, 1993; Geoff Eley, *A Crooked Line: From Cultural History to the History of Society*, University of Michigan Press, Ann Arbor, 2005, pp. 90–102.

4   Faithful participants included: Jane Caplan, Raj Chandavarkar, David Crew, Jennifer Davis, Karl Figlio, Biancamaria Fontana, Jim Gillespie, Kim Howells, Joanna Innes,

Ludi Jordanova, Susan Pennybacker, Alastair Reid, Eve Rosenhaft, Keith Snell and others.

5   One recurring issue in the AUT was the encroachment of private health insurance, which we doggedly opposed. During one memorable meeting, Stuart's patiently reasoned defence of the National Health Service provoked an apoplectic interruption from the then Smuts Professor Eric Stokes (a neoliberal *avant la lettre*), whose anger all but launched him physically across the room.

Chapter 2

Stuart Macintyre and British communism

Kevin Morgan

I

In 1973, the History Group of the Communist Party of Great Britain (CPGB) carried out a survey of its rapidly expanding membership. Among the new recruits was Stuart Macintyre, who the previous year had arrived in Britain to write a PhD at Cambridge. Stuart's replies included his thesis working title, 'Understandings of Marxism in Britain 1917–1940', and summarised his view of the practice of leftist history as he embarked upon it. 'I feel quite strongly that the Group should concentrate on work of significance for a Marxist understanding of social formations, rather than the populist or uncritical admiration of "our history".'[1]

Seven years later Stuart published two landmark texts on British Marxism that helped to open up the subject as a subject and remain key reference points today. Had he had another questionnaire to fill, he would not by this time have answered in quite the same way. Nevertheless, this early statement of intent, as forthright as it must have seemed, does also hint at the conflicted and paradoxical character of the enterprise he had undertaken. This is also the measure of

Stuart's achievement. His work already showed a penchant for the biographical sketch that illuminated the intersecting milieux through which the individual passed without ever simply disappearing within them.

As a scholar and an activist, Stuart also trod a path between different milieux, loyalties and expectations: between different political generations, between engagement and the academy, between communism and the wider Left, and between Cambridge seminars and the old industrial Britain in which the subjects of his writings lived on to voice claims to their own history. For all these reasons, this earliest phase of Stuart's career is approached through the wider interactions within which he himself might have situated it.

In the first instance, there was 'our history' versus 'social formations'. To those who read the comments, the first phrase would have signified the Our History pamphlets, which by the early 1970s were the History Group's only real sign of life. The second phrase, at least for cognoscenti, would also have had an automatic association: with the Left Bank communist philosopher Louis Althusser, with whom the idea of social formations was synonymous. Although Althusser's proved a moment of Warholian transiency, his structuralist Marxism at this time exercised a powerful attraction for a younger generation of whom Stuart was one. With this as its juxtaposition, 'our history' also had a wider connotation: that of the recreation of the corporate experience of movement or of party without relating these to the 'full social formation' that—to the Althusserian—encompassed economic, political and ideological practices.[2] 'Our history' in this negative construction was epitomised to the point of caricature by the prevailing Communist Party histories. To Eric Hobsbawm, by now the undisputed doyen of the History Group, these were histories of the regimental type that inspired and uplifted but never asked a difficult question.[3]

Hobsbawm wrote no regimental histories, nor had his generation of Marxist historians offered much in the way of a critical history of the twentieth-century Left. As communists they had been bound by powerful institutional ties, and even as these were

transition for Clan
against clan
Stuart Macintyre and British communism   29
to popular front

weakened or severed post-1956 they still showed remarkably little interest as historians with the modern labour movement. Stuart too did not envisage an institutional party history. Nevertheless, his designated period of 1917–40 was one of Marxism's infrangible entanglements with the would-be party monopoly of Third International communism. This was not a social formation in the Althusserian or any other sense. It was a tradition and a claim to leadership that principally engaged the historical energies of those who identified with some variant of the ideals it reputedly embodied, distorted or betrayed. It always was, in some sense, 'our' history.

For Stuart's generation, it was at least past history in a way it could not be for Hobsbawm's. Nevertheless, Stuart's was a research topic freighted as almost no other with the legends, anathemas and taboos that our history signified. To its left-wing detractors, Althusserianism was a cult of abstraction unabashedly inimical to the work of history. Another of the older generation, E.P. Thompson, fired off a fusillade of invective that linked it with a generation detached as never before from the practice of organised mass politics. Even within the communist parties, Thompson maintained, the Paris and Oxbridge *lumpen-intelligentsia* inhabited their own intellectual ghettos.[4]

The CPGB and its History Group were not, however, one of these. Stuart's subjects, unlike Thompson's, had not yet vacated the historical stage, whether as an institution or as a cadre of veteran functionaries and activists who as informants, interlocutors and 'worker-intellectuals' were anything but deferential in respect of their own history. There were no Oxford or Cambridge histories of British communism. Despite the differences in scale, these were nevertheless experiences that Stuart might later have called upon in turning to the histories of larger collectivities like the nation. That is another good reason for dwelling for a moment on the interplay of the work of history and collective and institutional memory before turning to the two key texts on British communism that Stuart published in 1980: *A Proletarian Science*, a reworked version of his PhD thesis, and a study of the localised bases of communist support, *Little Moscows*.[5]

II

When James Klugmann died in 1977, the CPGB was left without an official historian. A communist from the early 1930s, Klugmann was a trusted in-house intellectual who, at the time of his death, had taken twenty years to cover the first six of the party's history. He had also come to see the gulf in expectations between the party elders who oversaw his drafts and a critical reading public who increasingly included communists themselves. Hobsbawm's withering verdict was that he had avoided all the crucial questions of Communist Party history and failed entirely to penetrate the CPGB's public façade. Reissued in his 1973 collection *Revolutionaries*, Hobsbawm's preferred alternative was to entrust the history to professional historians who were prepared to rattle a few skeletons.[6]

There was no lack of younger historians willing to supply the want. With the upsurge of interest in Marxism in and around the universities, the History Group's membership had almost tripled since the early 1970s. Theoretically and substantively, interests ranged far beyond 'our history' with conferences on Lukács, Gramsci and Althusser in 1974 and on pre-capitalist societies in 1975. As the decade went on, there was nevertheless a decided shift to the home terrain of communist and labour movement history. Already in 1976, the half-centenary of the British General Strike was one contributory factor. Friendly exchanges with the History Workshop movement also encouraging shared interests like the oral history projects whose most obvious subjects were now the post-Edwardians who had built the interwar labour movement.[7]

Within weeks of Klugmann's passing, a weekend conference and book of essays on party history were already planned. There followed plans for oral history interviews (Stuart proposed an inventory of them) and discussions aimed at securing access to the party archives. In terms of theory, methods, sources and conclusions, communist history opened up briefly as a primary field of enquiry: so much so that a History Group member researching Bengali trade unions resigned because the group seemingly catered only for 'certain aspects of British labour movement history'.[8]

Stuart had by this time completed his PhD and returned to Britain to work upon the project that became *Little Moscows*. His supervisor had been Henry Pelling, whom he recalled as the very last person to engage with communism as 'ideology and lived commitment'.[9] Although Pelling's works included the CPGB's first academic history, its notoriety as the archetypal Cold War narrative had only been rekindled by its recent reissue in paperback. Even so, in an age enthralled by theory, Pelling had a salutary regard for the archive and an empiricist's eye for the spongy generalisation. Moreover, while it precluded any prospect of a master–pupil syndrome, the unlikely pairing did rather bear out Neal Wood's claim of how in Britain bonds of profession or education combined with a culture of mutual forbearance to counteract tendencies to a closed-off communist microsociety.[10] Pelling thus saw to it that Hobsbawm was one of Stuart's examiners, and doubtless also steered him to the Cambridge *Historical Journal* for the first of two early published research papers. The other appeared as an Our History pamphlet; few could have told from the internal evidence which was which.[11] At Cambridge there was also a fortnightly social history seminar convened by Geoff Eley and Gareth Stedman Jones that did not in the least replicate the recession into homegrown labour history. The latter's 'Pathology of English history' had also had an important influence on Stuart, with an alertness to the 'poverty of empiricism' among the credentials that he brought to the table vacated by Klugmann.[12]

Stuart would afterwards have much occasion to reflect on the dilemmas of a public political history. What were the connections between past history and present politics? What was the role of historical narrative in both affirming and interrogating collective memory and identity? How did one navigate a past still embodied in structures that could release or withhold research materials and in actors able to inform and contest their own rendering into history? Even setting aside these interactions, how could one establish the relations between the social, economic, political and ideological dimensions of these histories? Did a political subject imply a political history such as Pelling would have recognised? And if one were to maintain these institutional boundaries, how were the acknowledged complexities of gender, class, ethnicity and place to be accommodated within them?[13]

One could ask these questions of a state or national polity such as Australia. One could also ask them of a political party, and Stuart was now caught up in a collective enterprise that was assiduous in doing so. When the planned conference on CPGB history took place in May 1978, Stuart's was one of the four main papers, and he was also designated editor of a symposium by younger specialists earmarked for publication on the CPGB's sixtieth anniversary in 1980. The contributors included both communists and other leftists such as the socialist feminist Sue Bruley. In terms of major published work, Stuart's independent projects would prove among the few that actually came to fruition. Nevertheless, the historiographical challenges they confronted were ones very much encountered in common.

All agreed that there was no further mileage in regimental history. Beyond this there were two basic lines of approach. The first was that adopted by the Italian communist party (PCI), at this time the largest of the non-communist world and one with a special appeal to intellectuals as seemingly the most supple, strategically minded and politically intelligent. In respect of the PCI's history this was demonstrated by the provision of general scholarly access to the party archives and the commissioning of an arm's-length multi-volume history by Paolo Spriano. Unencumbered by direct political oversight, Spriano confronted just those 'difficult' aspects of party history that Klugmann had systematically disregarded. For critical-minded communists, the PCI's was the example for others to follow and, at the History Group conference, was the focus of another of the principal papers by Donald Sassoon.[14]

The debit side was that this was a narrowly political history and somewhat conservative in its methodology. Sympathetic commentary noted the top-down focus on apparatus, policy and internal debates and the discounting of issues of ideology, political culture and social base—and the multiple forms of differentiation that these necessitated. Sassoon's *Strategy of the Italian Communist Party* (1981) was of a similar character. Its strong chronological thrust derived from published party texts and a preoccupation with the party line that only the PCI's Gramscian aura allowed to be dignified as strategy. For reform-minded communists, such an approach had an instrumental rationale inasmuch as a reckoning with past successes and failings was seen as the condition of their party's renewal on a sounder and less compromised basis. The results were vastly superior to the older party histories, but were nevertheless an advance upon them rather than a new departure.[15]

There was no hard and fast division with the second approach. Its key text was Gramsci's dictum that 'to write the history of a party means nothing less than to write the general history of a country from a monographic viewpoint'. Everybody cited it, including Sassoon, and it could indeed be taken as a general rationale for communist party history.[16] Even so, it was congruent with a wider conception of social formations that implied a communist history that was neither introspective nor self-referential but fed into counter-narratives of national history through the counter-hegemonic elements of contestation and resistance. Gramscian notions of the national-popular could also imply a nationally bounded conception of the totality of social relations that later scholarship would bring sharply into question. What primarily stands out is nevertheless an outward-looking disposition that was particularly attractive in the case of smaller parties like the CPGB whose claims upon traditional political historians were evidently not inexhaustible.

Within the context of British Marxist historiography, this was also more akin to the histories with which Hobsbawm and Thompson's generation had made their reputations. The difference was they had always stopped short of the 1917 watershed. Stuart himself referred to it as a 'pre-modern' agenda relating to the formative years of working-class politics. 'Work of similar quality has not been done on the factory-based, twentieth-century working class, whose industrial and political movements have so far been left to more orthodox labour historians.'[17] This was rather more than just a searching and self-critical version of the older party history. It also helps explain why Stuart's work was so commended by the historians of Hobsbawm's generation like John Saville and Victor Kiernan.

One of Althusserianism's standard-bearers, Barry Hindess, wrote later that one of the lessons he learnt from its unrelenting pursuit of rectitude was the 'academic virtue of toleration'.[18] Another possible lesson, for a historian such as Stuart, might have been a wariness of theory disconnected from actuality, or ruling over it as some distant colony sunk in positivist stupor. By 1977, in any case, the Althusserian bubble had burst. Hindess and Paul Hirst, having published *Pre-Capitalist Modes of Production* in 1975, followed it with an auto-critique precipitate even by the standards of the Marxist tradition. Stuart, on the other hand, did not update his early excursions into synthetic reasoning and steered clear of the quicksand of passing controversy. There must indeed have been many readers of *A Proletarian Science*, like the present one, who would never have dreamt of the author's past Althusserian enthusiasms. Nevertheless, these may still be registered as part of the context in which the project first took shape.

Seemingly, Stuart offered only one published exposition of his theoretical concerns once he reached Britain. This was a text co-authored with the economic historian Keith Tribe and delivered as a talk to the CPGB's Cambridge branch. Althusserianism as usual appears there as an antidote to the 'humanism' of the post-1956 New Left. More specifically and iconoclastically, Christopher Hill, among the most revered of the earlier generation of British Marxist historians, is singled out as a cautionary example of a crude and unsustainable determinism giving way to the abandonment of historical materialism altogether.[19]

Stuart was lucky that Thompson had no copy to hand as he erupted his way through 'The poverty of theory'.[20] Nevertheless, he was already much closer to Thompson and Hill than any of them might at first have appreciated. What Thompson first of all saw in Althusser was the mode of production understood at an almost

esoteric level of abstraction. The same was also true, in a more positive sense, of Hindess and Hirst. Stuart, on the other hand, was drawn
by Althusser's notion of the social formation. This was conceptual-
ised in terms of discrete levels of economy, politics and ideology,
which Althusser allowed a relative autonomy of each other. To Perry
Anderson, this represented a pre-eminently historiographic advance
that Thompson had occluded by conflating it with the mode of
production. 'The concept of social formation was initially introduced as a forcible reminder that the diversity of human practices in
any society is irreducible to economic practice alone.'[21] One might
wonder why all the fuss to be reminded of what the entire non-
Marxist world believed anyway. Relative autonomy licensed the
compartmentalisation of traditional historiography, and if Sassoon
found his way through Althusser to a contained political history,
Pelling had already got there without going via the rue d'Ulm
(École normale supérieure).[22] Stuart, however, was not writing this
sort of history, and his 'problematic' centred on the intersections
between the economic, political and ideological. Althusserianism was
a passing phase, but it did signify both release from determinism and
acknowledgement of the crucial role of ideology in the Marxist
understanding of social formations.

The principal outcome was *A Proletarian Science*. The unre-
flecting reader (I was one) was swept along as by a Christopher Hill
writing of more recent times. How little there was of this quality
that you could read on British communism. The anticipated book of
essays never appeared. Another of Klugmann's generation was swiftly
and pre-emptively appointed official historian by the CPGB leadership. She alone had access to the archives—which in any case she
hardly used—and in a book that did not appear until 1985.[23] Only
the second of the two critical approaches to communist history was
at this time really practicable in Britain. This in broad terms was
Stuart's approach, and in adopting it he published the two books that
now stand almost alone as an enduring record of this whole brief
ferment of activity.

III

The principal showcase for the CPGB's counter-hegemonic cultural politics was the annual Communist University of London (CUL). History featured prominently, and the year that Stuart first attended in 1977 the History Group offered a course on 'new work in British working-class history' for which two alternative progams had been proposed. Stuart featured in both, either specifically on Marxism or more broadly on the 'varying influences of Marx, Liberal radicalism, Ruskin etc, the emergence of diverse currents of thought (Marxist, Labourist, Fabian, etc)—their different analyses of society and methods of political expression'. Stuart's own strong preference was for the latter. 'Speaking for myself, I find "Socialist ideas and the labour movement, 1880–1929", far more exciting than Marxism between the wars and would be very keen to have *that* as a topic.'[24]

This might have been a curious diffidence regarding the subject of his own forthcoming book. In reality, it was an indication of how broadly he conceived of it. The manuscript of *A Proletarian Science* was completed the following year. Stuart described its dual objective as being to capture the social basis and the changing doctrinal character of British Marxism. Four chapters and an introductory overview dealt with the first of these, and the other chapters discussed diverse matters of doctrine, including economics, politics, historical materialism and the dialectic. Whether socially or ideologically, the material is constantly ranging beyond its ostensible boundaries. Even at its most abstruse, Marxism as Stuart approached it is not abstracted from history but recovered through the sources on which it drew, the value systems with which it interacted, and the social and political agency of those who espoused it. A Quentin Skinner might have seen this as necessary context for the thinkers who truly mattered. Stuart's more democratic instinct was that beliefs held seriously, and involving the heroic commitments to self-education that he so graphically depicted, also deserved to be taken seriously. The study could not have been based on institutional archives, and few readers will regret it. With a sense of freedom that was also the recognition of necessity, Stuart deployed the more imaginative strategies of the new social history and fashioned his subject from the widest range of sources, notably including the myriad traces of the print culture in which the aspiration to a proletarian science was so richly documented.

Some reviewers thought Stuart's title unnecessarily restrictive; Stuart conceded that it might seem to some a storm in a teacup. But it also represented a challenge to complacencies of the 'Labour's Forward March' type.[25] Stuart rejected both the 'genetic' character of a labour history fixated on the seemingly successful and the 'linear historical process' by which it was held to prevail. Pelling's was just such a conception of the labour mainstream; against such teleological readings Stuart contended that the modern labour movement was the outcome of a far more uneven historical process that involved the ebb and flow of multiple political currents.

Marxism mattered as both an inalienable component of this tradition and the principal alternative to it: precisely the strategic options between which British Marxists had been torn for almost a century. In the case of communism in particular, the choices seemed ambiguously poised between what easily slipped into a non-linear pluralism or eclecticism and a brusquely counter-linear narrative culminating in the CPGB and the works of Lenin. Stuart saw the danger of implying a single stream of social protest that would 'merely revive a new genetic reading … as a radical counterpart to the conventional one'.[26] He offered no facile resolution, nor did he simply discount considerations of effectiveness or 'success'. The Marxists he brought back to life had been all too ready to call upon Comrade History as the final arbiter in their favour. Few socialists, however, can write of the history of their own movement without some sense, if not of winners and losers, then of those who should have won and lost. If in this instance one was not always sure whom to side with, the result was a sense of complexity and creative tension through which readers of quite varying perspectives could find some common ground or language—exactly as the Left itself was broadly, sometimes inchoately constituted.

Marxism in Britain. 1917–1933. Stuart both proposed these demarcations and simultaneously brought them into question—just as the communists themselves had formed a separate party and then immediately sought affiliation to the Labour Party. Klugmann would have recognised Stuart's binaries of Marxism and 'labour socialism', which he would have labelled reformism. For Stuart these were 'relatively systematic ideologies', and he set out their defining characteristics with exemplary clarity. Where labour socialism clearly implied a sort of party destination, Marxism in theory also corresponded to the CPGB and beyond it to the Comintern. Stuart's premise was unambiguous: in this period 'there was no alternative understanding of Marxism to that of the Communists'.[27]

This did suggest a counter-mainstream with its own backwaters, like the ailing Marxist sects that Stuart summarily dismissed. He nevertheless had a sharp eye for locality and variation. He reached out to currents like guild socialism that could not be confined within his own ostensible boundaries. He registered how a popular Marxism flourished in wide sections of the labour movement, not as a holistic worldview but as a component of something less systematic.[28] Was this the complicating factor of labour Marxism, or *marxisant* labour? Should it be seen as the rejection, dilution or wider dissemination of the Marxism *in stricto sensu* that Stuart differentiated from labour socialism? In the 'conjuncture' of the 1970s, or latterly the Corbyn years, its very diffuseness seems less a backwater than a congenital feature of the British political landscape.

Still more ambiguous was the structuring device of 1917. Nothing in Britain alone could have recommended it. For all within the communist tradition, it meant the unity of theory and practice embodied in a before-and-after watershed and wrenching forward by the example of Bolshevism. One could hardly be a communist without this sense of the new advancing on the old. In *A Proletarian Science* it is represented organisationally by a bolshevised party model combining mass work with the advantages of democratic centralism. It also represented doctrinally a displacement of the groping efforts of the working class autodidact as the precondition of a necessary advance in Marxist ideology. With a mildly Maoist inflexion Stuart even describes it as a rectification. In chapters on the dialectic or the state, the logic of 1917 is that of the extrication from a political and theoretical cul-de-sac and engagement with the problems of the modern world.

This might have been the condescension of posterity; in reality, it reads more like an act of historical recovery in the spirit of the older historians' work on the Levellers, the Paineites or the Blanketeers. Some of the strongest work in current labour history cuts across the dividing line of 1917, as Stuart himself urged in the case of a movement like syndicalism.[29] Despite his own nominal date range, he followed this logic in *A Proletarian Science* in dealing at least as fully with the pre-1917 period. In a brilliantly evocative chapter like the one on literature and education, he thus disposed of the CPGB itself in a couple of pages. More than that, he described how consolidation into party, and into Marxism as a party worldview, came at the expense of 'diversity of organisation, strategy and social thought', of plurality, of overlap and of 'a general openness of debate that were largely lost after 1918'.[30]

These seem notably benign formulations. Stuart's master's thesis had been on John Strachey: old Etonian, scion of England's 'intellectual aristocracy' and pre-eminent exponent of the Marxism of the 1930s.[31] Strachey broke with the CPGB in 1940, which might have suggested Stuart's original thesis end date. But as this was pulled back to 1933, like the other end of the rug that now pre-dated 1917, communism as a product of the public schools and universities was pushed to the margins of his account.[32] Had he had to single out a hero, he might have been the self-taught working-class polymath Tommy Jackson, for whose centenary Stuart also co-authored an Our History pamphlet. This does record how Jackson described his encounter with Lenin and Leninism as a truly revelatory experience. Nevertheless, of all of those who found it so, no other leading communist remained as firmly and defiantly embedded in the language, culture and institutions of the older working-class Marxism.[33]

Whoever personified the catharsis of rectification, they found no such empathetic treatment in Stuart's writings. Might one describe this as an elegiac quality? Sassoon recalls the attraction of history's big battalions: 'Why spend the best years of your life on a small party not many people care about?'[34] The logic seems compelling; but as the old industrial Britain went the same way as the stockingers and handloom weavers there is also a very different sensibility that one may perhaps describe as Thompsonian. It is no surprise that Raphael Samuel, who would vividly recover the 'lost world' of British communism, was among the admirers of Stuart's writings.

Hobsbawm saw the study of plebeian ideology, 'thanks largely to Hill', as one of the achievements of his own generation of Marxist historians.[35] *A Proletarian Science* not only continued the tradition but also stumbled on the same conundrum of the relation between different types of social activity that Hill had not resolved and Althusser had only formulated differently. This at least was Stuart's verdict as to the main limitation of his own account. He saw it as a gap between his chapters on Marxism's social, political and economic basis and those on its specific ideological configurations. He had skilfully crafted a *tour de force* of the social history of ideas, but he was troubled that the ideas themselves continued to appear as if driven by internal lines of filiation and adaptation.[36]

Could a totalising history of social formations ever be written in a monographic form? One possible answer was the synoptic local study. Stedman Jones and John Foster were among those seeking to reach beyond the limits of a corporate labour history, and although diverging sharply in their theoretical premises both also used the method of the local or regional study.[37] The importance of such variations was recognised in *A Proletarian Science* and was consistent with its concerns with ideology as 'practised in a material form within working-class communities'.[38] Stuart had therefore included thumbnail sketches of communist strongholds in South Wales and the west of Scotland, and now added to these a third such case in the Fife coalfield. The result was his book on the Little Moscows as a structuring theme allowing him to explore the interplay of work-place, domestic relations, politics and the local state at the level of the small-scale community.

As he worked on the project, the political clouds were dark-ening. Hobsbawm announced the halting of Labour's Forward March; the PCI was doing no better, Eurocommunism had clearly had its moment, and in Britain the day was dawning of Thatcherism's 'great moving right show'.[39] One straw in the wind was what Stuart described as a 'fast-growing corpus' of revisionist histories that discounted the idea of political radicalisation between the wars.[40] This was another face of what he called the 'Whig interpretation of labour history';[41] remembering the Little Moscows might have been a way of contesting its inexorability. Stuart, however, made little of the argument. Instead, he offered a 'counter-factual' rationale for the study of atypical cases: one that acknowledged their exceptionality as a way of isolating what it was exactly that set them apart. The infer-ence might have been drawn that this did not so much challenge revisionism as sit alongside it as militant obligato. Politically, it proved far from congenial to some CP veterans, who questioned the assumption of distinctiveness and urged the importance of wider patterns of class and community activism.[42]

Unlike *A Proletarian Science*, *Little Moscows* has no concluding evaluation but only an epilogue leaving larger political questions undisturbed. Superficially, it is in any case a more clearly delimited piece of work with well-defined political and economic boundaries. Politically, 'interwar' meant post-1917 and the influence of the Russian Revolution; economically, it meant the rending crisis of Britain's staple industries, which was precisely why thoughts might turn politically towards the USSR. Elsewhere in Europe, examples of a localised mili-tancy of distinctly pro-Soviet cast can be traced through to 1956 and far beyond. In Britain, the Thatcher years would see renewed forms of counter-hegemonic politics at the level of the local state and the evoking of the Little Moscows as a precedent. These are not, however, connections made in Stuart's text, which defines his subject as one 'contained' within the interwar period.[43]

But as the further sequel would demonstrate, it was only the contingencies of circumstance and commitment that were contained in this way. A key finding of *Little Moscows* was that it was almost impossible to specify the economic or social conditions that made for a militant stronghold. The one remaining variable was politics— or, more precisely, political activism and the agency of militants moved by communist beliefs and commitments. Stuart thus identified a real if limited transformation of locality with a political process of permeation or mobilisation of existing social forms. He also echoed Hill in associating it with the image of a world 'turned upside down'.[44]

But if this was the key variable, there was no reason why it need be confined to interwar Britain or the politics of locality. Every communist and Labour College militant, Stuart had written, was in some sense 'striving to build a Little Moscow'. So of course were other militants, pursuing activist commitments that could move through different phases and environments across their lifetimes. Stuart therefore urged labour historians to move on from their institutional fixations to the 'actual social dynamics' of labour movements and how men and women were drawn into such life-defining commitments.[45] The Little Moscows offered one such variant of the phenomenon, but only one. Others included shopfloor networks, 'factory fortresses', communist-led unions and numerous other forms of community and ethnic mobilisation. Militants driven from the Little Moscows animated new movements in other parts of the country: just as those radicalised by student communism dispersed into their professions, into white-collar unions, and into academic clusters like the historians that now included Stuart himself.[46]

There were therefore questions still to follow up. *Little Moscows* took from the study that preceded it a subject and a theme that Stuart had had no scope to develop there. In just the same way, *Little Moscows* itself opened up further lines of enquiry without yet fully pursuing them. 'Such was the force of institutionalised consensus that it was easy to believe that change flowed from the centre and from the ruling elites who seemingly controlled the course of events.'

This, however, was an illusion, for if mainstream labour moved at all it was due to the 'vigorous tributaries and turbulent eddies that feed it and impel it onwards'. These again are Stuart's words; they might have had a place in *Little Moscows* in connecting interwar militancy with Labour's electoral breakthrough in 1945. But as it happens, they are from his study of the Fremantle militant Paddy Troy, which built upon the logic of *Little Moscows* in 1984.[47] Despite the shift in geographical focus, there is much to be said for reading these three key texts of communist history together—and in the sequence in which they were written.

Already when the first two appeared, Stuart was back in Australia. The CPGB marked its sixtieth anniversary, not with the projected book of essays but with an illustrated brochure by another of Klugmann's contemporaries and fellow party workers. More auspiciously, there also appeared in 1980 Francis and Smith's acclaimed history of the South Wales miners, demonstrating how an institutional format could be stretched to accommodate the new social history agendas. That, however, had depended on the unearthing of rich archival seams under the patronage of 'kindly' institutional custodians.[48]

There was no chance whatsoever of a CPGB history being written under similar conditions. In *Little Moscows*, Stuart left a pioneering exercise in micro-history and abiding reference point for the study of 'local communisms'. In *A Proletarian Science*, he left a classic work of empathetic reconstruction and a testimony to the political engagements on which it drew. He would return to the communist party as historical subject, and to the challenge of a history of an institution that would not just be an institutional history. But this was a different party in a different country, and in different political times that the Left historians of the 1970s could not even have imagined.

Notes

1   CPGB questionnaires, 1973, in Labour History Archives and Study Centre
     (henceforth LHASC), Manchester, CP/Cent/Cult/7/1. For my understanding of
     the CPGB, I draw extensively on the papers in Manchester deposited by the group's
     secretary, John Attfield. I am also indebted to several of Stuart's British
     contemporaries for comments on the text and/or their recollections of the 1970s,
     namely Jon Bloomfield, Sally Davison, David Howell, Alastair Reid and Willie
     Thompson.
2   Stuart Macintyre, 'Radical history and bourgeois hegemony', *Intervention*, no. 2, 1972,
     pp. 47–73.
3   Eric Hobsbawm, 'The Historians' Group of the Communist Party', in Maurice
     Cornforth (ed.), *Rebels and Their Causes: Essays in Honour of A.L. Morton*, Lawrence &
     Wishart, London, 1978, p. 30.
4   E.P. Thompson, *The Poverty of Theory and Other Essays*, Merlin, London, 1978, p. 376.
5   Stuart Macintyre, *A Proletarian Science: Marxism in Britain 1917–1933*, Cambridge
     University Press, Cambridge, 1980; *Little Moscows: Communism and Working-class
     Militancy in Inter-war Britain*, Croom Helm, London, 1980.
6   E.J. Hobsbawm, 'Problems of communist history', *Revolutionaries: Contemporary
     Essays* [1973], Quartet Books, London, 1977, pp. 3–10.
7   Paul Thompson's oral history classic, *The Edwardians*, had been published in 1975.
8   This was Stephen Gourlay, whose thesis on 'Trade unionism in Bengal before 1922'
     was completed in 1983 and is now accessible online; see Gourlay to John Attfield, 8
     March 1977, CP/Cent/Cult/8/6.
9   See Stuart's obituary, 'Henry Pelling (1920–1997)', *Labour History*, no. 74, 1998, pp.
     190–2.
10   Neal Wood, *Communism and British Intellectuals*, Gollancz, London, 1959, p. 24.
11   Stuart Macintyre, *Imperialism and the British Labour Movement*, Communist Party
     History Group, London, 1975; 'British labour, Marxism and working-class apathy in
     the 1920s', *Historical Journal*, n.s. 20, 1977, pp. 479–96. Despite the different
     publication dates, both were actually written before the first of them appeared.
12   See Stuart's reflections in 'What is history? Historiography Roundtable', *Rethinking
     History*, vol. 22, no. 4, 2018, pp. 515–16.
13   For these observations, I am prompted in part by Stuart's own 'Response' to recent
     works of the 'new political history' published in *Australian Historical Studies*, vol. 25,
     1993, pp. 398–402.
14   Donald Sassoon, 'How the Italian Communist Party approached its own history',
     Our History Journal, vol. 4, 1979, pp. 1–4; also Franco Andreucci and Malcolm
     Sylvers, 'The Italian communists write their history', *Science and Society*, vol. 51, no. 1,
     1976, pp. 28–56.
15   In 1979 Sassoon edited a selection of Palmiro Togliatti's writings for the communist
     publishers Lawrence & Wishart. This now seems by far the last gasp of an older
     practice than the beginning of a new one, and it is telling that Sassoon's study was
     originally published in Italian under the title 'Togliatti and the Italian way to
     socialism'.
16   See Antonio Gramsci, *Selections from the Prison Notebooks*, trans. and eds Quintin
     Hoare and Geoffrey Nowell Smith, Lawrence & Wishart, London, 1971, p. 151.
17   Stuart Macintyre, 'Some recent labour history', *Historical Journal*, vol. 22, no. 3, 1979,
     pp. 729–30.
18   Barry Hindess, 'The Althusserian moment and the concept of historical time',
     Economy and Society, vol. 36, no. 1, 2007, p. 13.

19 Stuart Macintyre and Keith Tribe, *Althusser and Marxist Theory*, privately published, Cambridge, 1974.

20 I have written about Thompson's closeness to Hill in my article 'As everlasting yea, a no: Agency, necessity and *The Making of the English Working Class*', *Contemporary British History*, vol. 28, no. 4, 2014, pp. 457–76.

21 Perry Anderson, *Arguments Within English Marxism*, Verso, London, 1980, pp. 67–8.

22 For the Althusserian imprint, see Peter Beilharz, 'Socialism and culture: An interview with Donald Sassoon', *Thesis Eleven*, no. 98, 2009, pp. 117–18.

23 Noreen Branson, *History of the Communist Party of Great Britain 1927–1941*, Lawrence & Wishart, 1985. There was, however, general agreement that Branson had been sought to address the more 'difficult' questions of party history in a way that Klugmann had been unable to.

24 Papers on CUL 1977, including undated note from SM, LHASC, CP/Cent/Cult/7/3.

25 This was the title of the commemorative Labour Party history by Francis Williams, which Hobsbawm in 1978 implicitly evoked in his lecture 'The forward march of labour halted?'

26 Macintyre, *Proletarian Science*, pp. 1–4.

27 Ibid., chs 1–2.

28 Ibid., pp. 24–5, 36.

29 Macintyre, 'Some recent labour history', p. 725.

30 Macintyre, *Proletarian Science*, chs 1–2.

31 For which see Wood, *Communism*, pp. 83–4.

32 Compare notably with Gary Werskey, *The Visible College: A Collective Biography of British Scientists and Socialists of the 1930s*, Allen & Unwin, London, 1967.

33 Vivien Morton and Stuart Macintyre, *T.A. Jackson: A Centenary Appreciation*, Communist Party History Group, London, 1979.

34 Beilharz, 'Socialism and culture'.

35 Hobsbawm, 'The Historians' Group', p. 44.

36 Macintyre, *Proletarian Science*, pp. 235–6.

37 See Stedman Jones's *Outcast London*, 1971, and Foster's *Class Struggle and the Industrial Revolution*, 1974.

38 Macintyre, *Proletarian Science*, pp. 1–2.

39 Hobsbawm's 'Forward march of labour halted?' and Stuart Hall's 'The Great Moving Right Show' appeared in the CPGB's theoretical journal *Marxism Today* in September 1978 and January 1979 respectively. Stuart's 'Red strongholds between the wars' appeared in the March 1979 issue.

40 Stuart Macintyre, 'Some recent labour history', *Historical Journal*, vol. 22, no. 3, 1979, pp. 726–7.

41 Macintyre, *Proletarian Science*, p. 3.

42 Idris Cox, 'Communist strongholds in inter-war Britain', *Marxism Today*, June, 1979, pp. 191–2; also Attfield to Joseph Melling, 8 April 1981, CP/Cent/Cult/9/7. From his joining the CPGB in the mid-1920s, Cox had been a leading communist activist and organiser in South Wales.

43 Macintyre, *Little Moscows*, p. 20.

44 See Stuart's comments on the Little Moscows in *Proletarian Science*, pp. 43–4.

45 Macintyre, *Little Moscows*, p. 19.

46 I am drawing here on Kevin Morgan, Gidon Cohen and Andrew Flinn, *Communists and British Society 1920–1991*, Rivers Oram, London, 2007. This could be seen as taking the logic of *Little Moscows* but extending it to the many environments across the decades in which communists could seek to assume such roles.

47   Stuart Macintyre, *Militant: The Life and Times of Paddy Troy*, Allen & Unwin, Sydney, 1984, pp. 220–1.
48   Hywel Francis and David Smith, *The Fed: The History of the South Wales Miners in the Twentieth Century*, Lawrence & Wishart, London, 1980.

Chapter 3

Stuart Macintyre and Australian communism

Terry Irving

What might it mean to write a history of communism in Australia? One can imagine conservatives treating the Communist Party as an enemy of the liberal capitalist West, and Leninists seeking to draw lessons from its history in order to assist future anti-capitalist movements.[1] Even an ostensibly neutral institutional history of the party might end up, in a backhanded way, affirming the rightness of liberalism and representative government to the extent that its story revealed the political system's consistent stymying of the party's attempts to compete with it.

Stuart Macintyre's studies of Australia's communist history fall into none of those categories. In fact, when thinking of those studies it is not helpful to think in terms of categories. Over the span of years in which they were written, from the early 1980s to the publication of *The Party* in 2022, Stuart shifted his focus, highlighting different aspects of Australian communism's history and different explanations for its pathos and romance.[2]

He has several persistent themes, however. One of them is Stalinism: how its grip tightened on the Australian party; why party members accepted its dogma and discipline; how the party leadership suppressed discussion of Stalinism after 1956; and how the party under new leadership became one of the most independent in the international communist movement. Stalinism, however, is not his only theme because communist history is not co-extensive with Stalinism, as Stuart understood. On the first page of *The Reds*, he explains that his attraction to the history of communism began when he was caught up in the campaigns and causes of the 1960s: 'Both as a historian and a participant, I responded to the aura of the communist tradition. For the best part of the 1970s, as the currents of twentieth-century history eddied and then turned, I joined with others who sought to empty the Stalinist cargo from the revolutionary vessel.'[3]

There is a tacit recognition in this statement that the history of communism is not the same as the history of the Stalinist party. It is also the history of the revolutionary vessel, that impulse in the working class for self-emancipation from capitalism. Starting from this perspective, more communist histories might emerge. One would deal with the many strands of revolutionary politics, a history that reaches back at least to the formation of the Communist League in 1847; another would astonish by disclosing the continuing evolution of the communist idea since the international system of parties based on Bolshevik principles collapsed at the end of the 1980s.

These possible histories are imbricated in Stuart's formation as a political person and his writing of communist histories. In his youth he was nudged towards the Left by his Labor-voting mother and the example of his local Labor member of parliament, Jim Cairns, a socialist and leader of the anti-Vietnam War movement. As an undergraduate at Melbourne University, Stuart joined the Labor Party; while tutoring for the Department of History in 1971 he resigned from Labor to join the Communist Party, because, as he told the Melbourne student newspaper, the communists had better links with working-class struggles.[4]

In the Communist Party's Carlton branch he was associated with other young, university-educated revolutionaries who were dissatisfied with many features of party policy, in particular its failure to define the Labor Party as one of the main pillars of Australian capitalism, and its preference for union-led industrial work rather than rank-and-file insurgency at work.[5] In 1972, with some of these comrades, he established *Intervention: A Revolutionary Marxist Journal*, which aimed to reinvigorate Marxism in Australia through economic and historical analysis.[6] In his only contribution to the journal before he left for doctoral studies in Cambridge, he demolished the 'radical nationalist' tradition in Australian history, concentrating especially on the work of former communists Robin Gollan, Russel Ward and Ian Turner. Through its empiricism and failure to think structurally, he argued, this historical tradition actually cemented bourgeois hegemony.[7] This was his Althusserian moment, which he ruefully admits in the acknowledgements to *The Reds*.[8]

While at Cambridge, Stuart divested himself of the more abstract elements of Althusserianism, a process described by Kevin Morgan in chapter 2, but he retained Althusser's belief in the relative autonomy of the 'ideological level'. This became the basis of his respect for the particularity of the 'idiom of Australian communism', and his capacity to analyse its 'doctrinaire pragmatism', in *The Reds*. Soon, he would make further intellectual adjustments. At the end of the 1970s, when he returned to Australia after a second period in Cambridge, this time as a research fellow, the Australian party was in terminal decline. Its failed strategy of a 'Coalition of the Left' signalled the exhaustion of the party's contribution to revolutionary politics. As a vehicle for the creative interaction of Marxism and working-class struggles its licence had expired. In 1979, Stuart joined the Labor Party, as did many disillusioned communists in these years.[9] All his subsequent writing on Australian communism bears the stamp of this political decision.

Stuart's serious engagement with writing the history of Australian communism began in the early 1980s. In 1979 he spent a year lecturing at the new Murdoch University in Western Australia. A few years earlier, while tutoring at Murdoch, he had heard Paddy Troy, a communist and former local union leader, speak at a public meeting. He met Paddy Troy's son, Patrick Troy. In 1981 Patrick Troy was coordinating a Social Justice Project through the Urban Research Unit at ANU, where Stuart would spend two years as a research fellow attached to the project. Out of these moves and connections came his first two books on Australian history, *Militant: The Life and Times of Paddy Troy* and *Winners and Losers: The Pursuit of Social Justice in Australian History*.[10] Meanwhile, in 1980 his books on British communism, *Proletarian Science* and *Little Moscows*, appeared.

There was certainly some continuity of approach between the British and Australian books of those years as well as some differences. During an interview in 2018 he was asked about his interest in labour and the political system, and whether class inequality was a primary inspiration for his work. He replied:

> My first two books were exercises in a particular kind of labour history—one inflected by Marxism and social history. Class inequality and exploitation was certainly a major concern, one arising from my involvement in the New Left, and I'd always been interested in the study of politics, though the theories of class with which my generation worked extended to other social relations.[11]

I think this suggests that the differences were greater than they were. The biography of Paddy Troy, the communist secretary of the Fremantle union of dockworkers for twenty-five years, continues *Little Moscows'* interest in local communism and worker militancy. But in *Militant* Stuart looks beyond the uniqueness of the local, its atypical status, to affirming that in the labour movement change comes from the 'vigorous tributaries and turbulent eddies' that drive the mainstream forward. So Fremantle's history could be generalised, but at the same time the 'turbulent eddy' had to be analysed by examining the specificities of Australian working-class militancy. Where did its vigour come from? Answer: its questioning of capitalism's destruction of 'basic human values'—quite a Marxist inflection. Stuart then sketched the characteristics of the militants: they were formed in the 1930s Depression, self-educated, 'proud of their occupational skills, intensely class-conscious, suspicious of all compromise', and aware of their historical mission. The communists were only a part of this turbulent minority.[12]

Moreover, the weakness of this militant tradition had to be noted. When its energy was expressed through trade unionism, the limits and possibilities of industrial struggle were revealed. So this was not a romantic and unqualified endorsement of militancy, but it is a genuine expression of admiration, and it surfaces again in *The Reds*. In fact, the connection between Stuart's thinking about communism at this time and his later work is also apparent in *The Party*. One of the themes in that book is the tension created in the party by different generational experiences. There were chasms of personal and collective understanding separating communists who joined in the depressed 1930s, the confident mid-1940s and the affluent 1960s. Stuart rehearses the conflict between the first and third of these generations in *Militant*.[13]

Winners and Losers might not appear from its subject matter to be relevant to this discussion, but in its use of contemporary Marxist theories of the state and its emphasis on the role of the oppressed in the fight for social justice, it acted as another bridge between Stuart's British and Australian writings on communism. The key idea was the ambiguous role of the state in social justice history. The state was partly constituted by the struggle of the oppressed for social justice and partly an impediment because of its 'fiscal crisis' and its exercise of social control through the welfare system. Controlling and receiving welfare in this system produced a complication in the class structure, the appearance of a new middle class and a new welfare class, in symbiotic relation to each other and cutting across the labour–capital class divide. Nonetheless, in the struggle for social justice the oppressed were always active and, in the end, it was their agency and power, harnessed through the labour movement and often articulated by social liberals, that determined progress towards social justice.[14]

In the 1980s, Stuart's academic reputation grew quickly as he published notable books on colonial liberalism in Victoria, and—a high distinction—a volume in *The Oxford History of Australia*. He also published in 1988 a short survey of the parliamentarist tradition in Australia's labour movement.[15] This book was described by a reviewer in the Marxist journal, *Thesis Eleven*, as 'sober and engaged'.[16] Obviously, his commitment to the Left was continuing, but he was also widening his research interests and lifting his standing in the profession. In 1990, he became a professor in Melbourne University's Department of History—the powerhouse of academic history in Australia. By 1991, when the Search Foundation invited Andrew Wells and Stuart to write the history of the Communist Party,[17] he was a progressive historian who had successfully impressed the gatekeepers of mainstream history, of history defined as one of the liberal arts, an art for ruling, as well as a scholarly discipline.

Meanwhile, changes in the Communist Party had taken it, as one critic alleged, 'into the mainstream'.[18] It had been ditching bits of its Bolshevik cargo for more than two decades. It had welcomed the departure of supporters of the Chinese and Russian versions of communism from its ranks and had adopted a charter of democratic rights to guide its own governance and to reassure Australians of its nationalist credentials. It had theorised and then supported the Accord between unions, business and the state introduced by Labor in the 1980s, thus opening the way to neoliberalism.[19] Australian communism was painfully shedding its Stalinist carapace. When the pain became too much it died, but not before it began to take liberalism seriously. It had become pluralist and constitutional. To forestall further defections to the Labor Left, the few remaining members dissolved the Communist Party into the New Left Party and set up the Search Foundation.

Both sides—the liberal remnants of the Communist Party and Stuart—had changed during the 1970s and 1980s, drawing closer to each other in the process. What united them was a common interest in understanding Stalinism and then separating it from the militant or communist tradition in Australia. The remnants wanted a progressive historian with unchallengeable mainstream credentials to write the history of communism as they saw it, a movement as much made by its Australian setting as by Stalinism and therefore deserving recognition as a force for Australia's improvement. They wanted respectability for their former party. As for the historian, Stuart said in 2019 that it is futile for historians to pretend to be neutral:

> So, in my own case … I take topics that I have an attachment to, but I still don't know where I stand in relation to them, or there are bits of them that puzzle me, and I want to know more. The idea of political neutrality I think is very hard to sustain, but to interrogate your own expectations and assumptions is very important.[20]

What puzzled Stuart was how a universal model of the infallible party—the Leninist model—was grafted onto Australia's history and traditions and why it took so long for it to be rejected.[21] Reading his two volumes on the Communist Party, we can easily imagine him pondering his expectations and assumptions about the radical strand in Australia's past and its relationship to communism.

In *The Reds*, this is how Stuart concludes an account of the genesis of the cult of the communist leader: 'Stalin's dark shadow falls as a curse across the entire history of communism.' By 'entire' he means to include Australia. He opens *The Reds* with this statement:

> Stalin undoubtedly bears responsibility for millions of deaths by execution or starvation, but to attribute these atrocities to one man and his -ism is to pass over the clear symptoms in earlier communist practice and absolve a movement that hailed him as the architect of socialism and leader of world revolution. Any history of communism must ask what made Stalin possible and why it was unable to find a lasting alternative to his methods.

In *The Reds* and *The Party*, Stuart is determined not to absolve Australian communists and their party from Stalinist practices. He closes *The Reds* by insisting that the communist project, which 'nurtured tyranny within its emancipatory scheme', was therefore 'deeply flawed'. In every communist, whether leader or cadre, the will to tyrannise was internalised; it was what made Stalinism possible. To break with Stalinism was to break from communism.[22]

And yet ...? Such a sweeping condemnation is modelled on the complete identification of party members with their party, their unquestioning acceptance of its twists and turns, their absolute faith in the wisdom of their leaders, and their uncritical carrying out of the party line. It depends on the model of communism as a disciplined monolith. No doubt there were members of the Communist Party who acted as if this were true. But for many others there was a day-to-day communist life in which that monolith was not omnipresent. And there is evidence in *The Reds* that Stuart understands this. In fact, the story he tells is not one of members characterised by 'docile obedience' but of 'activists inclined to communism by a spirit of rebellion—determined, headstrong and refractory men and women who did not easily receive orders'.[23] Speaking in 2020 at an event to mark the centenary of the formation of the Communist Party, Stuart said, 'Communists were dedicated but they were also rebels, attracted to the party because it channelled their rebellious instincts.'[24] Sometimes the channelling did not work. Hence the expulsions, although these were never as common as the resignations, the disaffections and the 'falling away' of comrades.[25] And those who remained often did so by focusing stubbornly on their own social practice in workplace or community to the neglect of party campaigns required by the needs of international communism. These were the 'ordinary' communists, loyal but also conflicted, true believers with misgivings.[26] Looking back on his years in the party, Stuart expressed his 'intense admiration' for comrades such as these—the majority, in his experience—for they had 'dedicated their lives to human betterment'.[27]

When Stuart accepted the invitation from the Search Foundation it was to write the history of the party, not of communism in Australia. This he has done, in two exemplary works of history, but at the end of the second he makes a veiled reference to the distinction between 'ordinary communists' and the party's Stalinists: 'The temptation in writing communist history is to attribute all that was rewarding and admirable to communists while reserving censure for communism as an ideology and organisation. It is a false dichotomy.'[28]

What if there were no dichotomy but just a lot of ordinary comrades with reservations about the ideology, their leaders and communist regimes, but who persisted with the tasks of organising in the hope that their local efforts for human betterment would contribute to a movement for revolutionary change? There are many examples of them in Stuart's books, including Paddy Troy in Fremantle, Jean Blackburn in South Australia and Shirley Andrews in Victoria. Most of the ordinary communists never reached their level of contribution. They were more likely to be found as stalwarts of the local progress association or parents organisation or women's group, as I recall from my childhood growing up in a communist household in the 1940s and 1950s.

It was the others, the party-focused zealots, of course, who defined the party to itself, to its would-be allies and to its enemies. It is these men and women, from whom the leadership of the party came, who are the focus of Stuart's argument about Stalinism, and it was to explain their acceptance of Stalinist methods of control—both inside their party and in its dealings with outside organisations—that he embarked on the project that became *The Reds* and *The Party*. In the ethnographic sections of his books, he convincingly illustrates the processes involved in creating this way of thinking. He quotes Jean Devanny's statement in her memoir that obeying party orders gave her 'a sense of consecration', of being set apart for a higher purpose, and 'a wonderful feeling of belonging'. He notices the way party propaganda ascribed 'transformative qualities' to routine party tasks such as selling the party newspaper on the streets. He is particularly attentive to the role of language in constructing the communist identity: 'Communist rhetoric codified an understanding of politics that enclosed its practitioners within the certainties of language.' While outsiders commented on the impenetrable jargon of party propaganda, the leadership defended it vigorously. Critics of the use of jargon were often charged with 'bourgeois intellectualism'. Party classes were exercises in mechanical learning, schematic and rigid, until the 1960s at least. In a particularly revealing section on the party's reception of the news of the 1930s 'show trials' in the Soviet Union, Stuart explains how the 'brutal language' ('exposure, liquidation and annihilation') of the 'class against class' period 'functioned at first as political hyperbole', but by the time of the purges in the mid-1930s these terms had 'desensitised those who used them to the atrocities they licensed'.[29]

What is the relationship between communism and the traditions of Australian radicalism? In 1969 Alastair Davidson published the first scholarly history of the Communist Party in Australia (CPA). A comparison of his book with Stuart's helps to answer this question.

Davidson's study of the CPA sets out to be an example of Marxist political history. It sees communism as the expression of the contemporary stage of class struggle history, the stage of proletarian revolution against capitalism. But it is also Marxist political history of a particular kind, one that makes rationality and will—each understood as socially constructed, not as attributes of individuals— as central to the explanation for what happens in history. Davidson sharply distinguishes this kind of Marxism from economic determinism. In his view, the Australian Communist Party should be understood as attempting to fashion a collective proletarian will and to insert an alternative communist reasoning into politics. But in the Australian case, the fashioning was clumsy and the insertion was mechanical. Nothing went smoothly in the 'dialogue between local exigencies and central orders'. According to Davidson, those central orders from the Comintern fatally drew communists 'away from Australian traditions into an alien tradition, which made the CPA inappropriate in Australia'. But there was a moment of historic redirection. The idea of a radical tradition in working-class politics became a triumphal theme in CPA propaganda during and after World War II as the party grew and when its leaders imagined themselves in a future People's Government, a 'united front from above' with the Labor Party. And coincidentally, according to Davidson, this was when the Communist Party began 'a stumbling, groping, limping move back to Australian traditions, with the weight of past errors on the party's shoulders'.[30]

There is nothing of this kind of Marxism in the theoretical underpinnings of Stuart's two books. When Stuart and Andrew Wells wrote the introduction to the first of Beverley Symons' bibliographies, they presented the Communist Party's claim to be a force of anti-capitalist struggle (at least until the 1970s) as an accurate picture of the party's activities.[31] By the time of *The Reds*, the account is more nuanced: the anti-capitalist thrust in party policy is clear in the class-against-class period of the early 1930s, but thereafter until the late 1960s the party is best understood as a hostage to Soviet foreign policy. The party is no longer anti-capitalist except in its own estimation. As the question of how the party succumbed to Stalinism becomes central to Stuart's account, anti-capitalism fades from view. In the index there are no entries for capitalism, class or working class.[32]

I do not want to push this point too far. The 'times' have to be taken into account. Stuart published his books thirty years (the first volume) and fifty years (the second) after Davidson. By that time, communism in its Leninist/Stalinist form was well and truly dead. Stuart has two ways of thinking about this trajectory. In the first, as expressed in *The Reds*, it was killed as much by its own inanition as by the hostile actions of the 'free world'. But now we live in different times, and in 2019 he provided a view of the demise of communism that glances towards political economy. In a lecture entitled 'From Bolshevism to populism: Australia in a century of global transformation', Stuart sees communism as a response in the early twentieth century to 'poverty and insecurity', to 'hunger, deprivation and economic crisis'. It died because capitalism after World War II stabilised and widened the horizons of working-class families.[33]

When Davidson envisaged the Communist Party limping back to relevance after jettisoning the alien Soviet aspects of communism, he hoped to find a revolutionary mojo in Australian working-class history. Stuart, having broken with the radical nationalist tradition of historical writing, has an opposite expectation. Notwithstanding that the party recruited many members who were 'inclined to communism by a spirit of rebellion—determined, headstrong, and refractory men and women', when Stuart looks at the non-communist history of the working class, he sees only organisations, specifically the 'trade unions and the Labor Party whose pragmatism bound their deliberations to the logic of the market and the ballot box'. Moreover, to the extent that the Communist Party involved itself with those organisations, it lost its revolutionary zeal. This idea is found at the beginning of *The Reds*: the more successful the party was in claiming the 'oppositional practices' of the trade unions, the more it was 'assimilated'. And at the end: by 1939, the party's range of 'public activities' made it part of 'civil society'. It still contested 'exploitation and injustice … but it did so from within'. Then, in the 1940s, having adopted the policy of a united front from above with the federal Labor government, it championed the 'peaceful transition to socialism' along a parliamentarist road. After a short but disastrous turn to adventurist industrial struggles in the late 1940s, it tried (but failed) in the early 1950s to resolve the disjuncture between its espousal of revolution and its non-revolutionary activities, which gave it a place in Australian politics and society.[34]

What is the explanation for Stuart's unwavering expectation that as the Communist Party put down roots in civil society it became less revolutionary? Why is engagement with the 'oppositional' practices of trade unions expected to result only in the assimilation of communists to the capitalist social order? There is a clue to the answer in Stuart's discussion of the effect on party policy of the 1942 decision to pursue the united front above: it resulted in the Communist Party 'setting aside much of what distinguished revolutionaries from reformists'. In fact, this distinction runs right through his treatment of Australian communism, but its centrality is established in chapter 2 of *The Reds*. Titled 'What was to be done?', the chapter places the formation of the Australian party as an effect of the struggle in European socialism between parliamentary social democracy and Leninism, the former equated with reformism and the latter with revolutionary politics. Stuart's summary of Leninism is masterly, but in the absence of a discussion of the revolutionary opponents of Leninism, the model of revolutionary politics associated with him—Bolshevism—stands in for the whole revolutionary tradition in socialist politics. And so Stuart sets the course for an analysis of Australian communism. Its model of revolution is imported, and after 1928 so also is its model of the revolutionary party with its top-down leadership and monolithic culture. The consequence is that whatever strategy or policy demanded by the Comintern is by definition revolutionary; whatever openings for communist activity provided by civil society—even if warranted by the history of Australian working-class radicalism—must by default lead to reformism.[35]

In this model of revolutionary politics, the communists in Australia were damned if they did and damned if they did not: they were in error if they applied the Comintern's 'universal model' because it was 'grafted onto their own country's traditions'; they were also in error if they followed those traditions and opted for the ballot box and/or trade unionism's role in the 'management of discontent'.[36]

This model works perfectly for understanding Australian communism in terms of its party. It was the party's understanding of revolutionary and reformist politics because it was the Comintern's, based on a particular reading of previous European socialist history and the international security needs of the Soviet state. It is Stuart's because he is writing the history of the Communist Party. In this sense only was it an appropriate model for Stuart to use.

Sometime in the future another historian will sit down to write an account of communism's Australian history in which the role of the party will not loom so large. New themes will be in their mind. For one thing, they will be curious about all those communists who were outside the party because they could see that its model of revolution would damage socialism, politically and intellectually. Some of them would have been among the 100 000 Australians who passed through the party. Stuart writes: 'The various causes taken up by ex-communists form an integral part of communist history.' Tracing their impact on Australian life will be difficult but not impossible for those who retained or built a public presence. Stuart refers to some of them. In fact, Stuart was one of them—as I am. There is a story to tell about non-party communism.[37]

Another theme will be how to place the communist *party* moment in the history of Australian radical politics. Obviously, this history begins before the formation of the party, and just as obviously it will not regard socialist politics as exhausted by an analysis of the conflict between capitalist-state-smashing revolutionaries and state-accommodating Labor reformists. This history would take a radical approach to working-class formation, by focusing on the thousands of episodes of informal worker mobilisation charted by Michael Quinlan. It would reveal those moments in the nineteenth century when working men and women campaigned for bottom–up radical democracy—in New South Wales in the 1840s; in Victoria in the 1870s; in New South Wales in the 1890s. It might decide that the labour movement was not just a political movement of trade unionists but also—and more importantly—a movement of democrats, most of whom were trade unionists. It would follow their attempt to impose popular rule on Labor politicians through the mechanisms of caucus, pledge and conference. A redeeming feature perhaps in the history of Australian reformism? It would move onto the 1910s when rebellious workers on strike refused to take the advice of their Labor and union leaders to return to work and submit to arbitration. Then into the decades of the Communist Party, where it would follow this rebellious anti-political and anti-capitalist spirit as it expressed itself in different sections of the workforce and through movements seeking justice for gender, sexual and racial oppression. Finally, into the post-party era, where it would deal with the horizontalist 'politics of the squares', of the left-wing populism of Podemos, Sanders and ... what? Eco-communism perhaps?[38]

Stuart closes his second volume in 1970 just as the framework for understanding communism moved beyond the stale argument of revolution versus reform. When he suggests in the epilogue that a separate history would be required to make sense of the new policies and practices of the Communist Party in its last two decades, I think he recognises this. The questions confronting revolutionaries in that period were not always new, but their rediscovery was only possible once the endless banality of the argument over reform versus revolution had been pushed aside by the collapse of the communist states and the recomposition of the working class. There was a return to thinking about prefigurative politics, about the state as a site for the struggle between capital and the working class (Childe had suggested this in 1919), about 'slow movements' against consumerism, and the 'everyday' forms of resistance to capital. There were experiments in the practice of resistance: work-ins, worker cooperatives, workers' control of management, and intentional communities.[39]

These are big themes, and they would certainly require a different kind of approach to the history of communism. The historian who undertook such a task, however, would need to adopt not just the standard of Stuart's superb scholarship but also his extra-scholarly principles. What I like best about his two volumes on Australian communism is the insight they provide into enthusiasms and moral judgements not required by any professional or careerist need. In the final paragraph of *The Party*, Stuart writes about those communists who remained when the party was wound up: men and women who had found a purpose in carrying out party tasks in order to make a better life for their fellow workers. The pathos of Communist Party history aside, Stuart's books are humanist, progressive and socialist. In their intention to provide civic instruction based on those principles, they update the tradition of historical writing laid down by the great British liberal historians of a century ago.[40]

Notes

1   As in Tom O'Lincoln, *Into the Mainstream: The Decline of Australian Communism*, Stained Wattle Press, Sydney, 1985.
2   Stuart Macintyre, *The Party: Communism in Australia, Heyday and Reckoning, 1940–1970*, Allen & Unwin, Sydney, 2022.
3   Stuart Macintyre, *The Reds: The Communist Party of Australia from Origins to Illegality*, Allen & Unwin, St Leonards, 1998, p. 1.
4   Sadia Schneider, 'The Australian New Left: A study in historiography and social change', BA Honours thesis, Department of History, University of Melbourne, 2013, p. 33, reporting her interview with Stuart Macintyre.
5   Winton Higgins, 'Reconstructing Australian communism', *The Socialist Register 1974*, Merlin Press, London, 1974, pp. 151–88, provides a sympathetic account of the theoretical basis and political perspectives of what came to be known as the 'Left Tendency' in the party. See also O'Lincoln, *Into the Mainstream*, pp. 153–6.
6   *Intervention* continued until 1988.
7   Stuart Macintyre, 'Radical history and bourgeois hegemony', *Intervention*, no. 2, 1972, pp. 47–74.
8   Macintyre, *The Reds*, p. xii.
9   Schneider, 'The Australian New Left', pp. 44–5.
10   Stuart Macintyre, *Militant: The Life and Times of Paddy Troy*, George Allen & Unwin, Sydney, 1984; Stuart Macintyre, *Winners and Losers: The Pursuit of Social Justice in Australian History*, Allen & Unwin, Sydney, 1985.
11   Australian Historical Association Early Career Researchers blog, 13 June 2018, https://ahaecr.wordpress.com/2018/06/13/qa-with-stuart-macintyre/ (viewed 1 June 2021).
12   Macintyre, *Militant*, pp. 220–1.
13   Ibid., p. 209.
14   Macintyre, *Winners and Losers*, chs 3, 4 and 5, and Conclusion.
15   Stuart Macintyre, *The Labour Experiment*, McPhee Gribble Penguin, Melbourne, 1988.
16   Christine Ellem, 'Labour in the margins: Reconsidering *The Labour Experiment*', *Thesis Eleven*, no. 95, 2008, p. 138.
17   In *The Reds*, pp. x–xi, Macintyre thanks Wells for his contribution, after explaining that the Search Foundation first invited Wells, who then persuaded Macintyre to join him in the project. Other responsibilities prevented Wells contributing to the writing of the book.
18   I am thinking of O'Lincoln, *Into the Mainstream*.
19   Damien Cahill, *The End of Laissez-Faire? On the Durability of Embedded Neoliberalism*, Edward Elgar, Cheltenham, UK, 2014; Elizabeth Humphrys, *How Labour Built Neoliberalism: Australia's Accord, the Labour Movement and the Neoliberal Project*, Brill, Leiden, 2018.
20   Stuart Macintyre, from a discussion with fourth-year History students at the University of Melbourne, April 2019, https://blogs.unimelb.edu.au/shaps-

research/2021/01/12/stuart-macintyre-in-conversation-with-history-honours-students/ (viewed 18 June 2021).

21 Macintyre, Introduction, *The Party*, p. 2 manuscript version.

22 Macintyre, *The Reds*, pp. 363–4 for 'dark shadow'; p. 3 for the long quotation; p. 413 on nurturing tyranny.

23 Ibid., p. 415.

24 Stuart Macintyre, 'One hundred years of the CPA', *Hummer*, vol. 14, no. 1, 2020, p. 42.

25 Macintyre, *The Party*, ch. 1, p. 12 manuscript version, for the expulsions following the Soviet invasion of Finland, and ch. 4, p. 2 for expulsion of supporters of an all-party government.

26 For 'ordinary communists', see Phillip Deery, 'American communism', in Norman Naimark, Silvio Pons and Sophie Quinn-Judge (eds), *The Cambridge History of Communism*, vol. 2: *The Socialist Camp and World Power, 1941–1960s*, Cambridge University Press, 2017, p. 664, and the review of this volume by Jeffrey Burds in *American Historical Review*, vol. 124, no. 2, 2019, p. 597. It is important to distinguish ordinary communism from 'ordinary Stalinism', an idea that refers to the rigidity of democratic centralism as the defining feature of non-Soviet communist parties, as in Ronald Tiersky, *Ordinary Stalinism: Democratic Centralism and the Question of Communist Political Development*, Allen & Unwin, London, 1985. The idea of ordinary communism has much in common with Sheila Fitzpatrick's *Everyday Stalinism: Ordinary Life in Extraordinary Times: Soviet Russia in the 1930s*, Oxford University Press, New York, 2000. See also Peter Beilharz, 'The end of Australian communism', *Thesis Eleven*, vol. 27, 1990, p. 56, who distinguishes 'local Stalinism' from ordinary communism.

27 Macintyre, 'One hundred years of the CPA', p. 42.

28 Macintyre, Epilogue, *The Party*, p. 14 manuscript version.

29 Macintyre, *The Reds*, pp. 243, 348, 350, 379.

30 Alastair Davidson, *The Communist Party of Australia: A Short History*, Hoover Institution Press, Stanford CA, 1969, pp. xi, 183; Alastair Davidson, 'Writing the history of a CP', *Australian Left Review*, vol. 1, no. 27, 1970, pp. 81–2.

31 Beverley Symons, compiler, with Andrew Wells and Stuart Macintyre, *Communism in Australia: A Resource Bibliography*, National Library of Australia, Canberra, 1994.

32 Andrew Wells and Stuart Macintyre, 'Introduction' to ibid., pp. viii and ix.

33 Macintyre, *The Reds*, p. 2; Stuart Macintyre, 'From Bolshevism to populism: Australia in a century of global transformation', *ANU Historical Journal*, vol. 2, no. 1, 2019, pp. 212, 215.

34 Macintyre, *The Reds*, pp. 52, 415, 418, 419; Macintyre, Introduction, *The Party*, p. 24, manuscript version, and chapter 3, p. 4.

35 Macintyre, ch. 3, *The Party*, manuscript version, p. 4; Macintyre, *The Reds*, ch. 2.

36 Macintyre, Introduction, *The Party*, manuscript version, p. 2; radical US sociologist C. Wright Mills coined the phrase the 'management of discontent', using it in several of his works, including his *New Men of Power* (1948).

37 Macintyre, Introduction, *The Party*, p. 18 manuscript version.

38 Michael Quinlan, *The Origins of Worker Mobilisation: Australia 1788–1850*, Routledge, New York, 2018; Terry Irving, *The Southern Tree of Liberty: The Democratic Movement in New South Wales before 1856*, Federation Press, Sydney, 2006; Sean Scalmer, *Democratic Adventurer: Graham Berry and the Making of Australian Politics*, Monash University Press, Melbourne, 2020; Terry Irving, 'William Astley (Price Warung) and the radical invention of the Labor Party', in Rowan Cahill and Terry Irving, *The Barber Who Read History*, Bull Ant Press, St Peters, NSW, 2021; Terry Irving, 'Rebellious workers:

Insubordination and democratic mobilisation in Australia in the 1910s', in Peter Sheldon, Sarah Gregson, Russell D. Lansbury and Karin Sanders (eds), *The Regulation and Management of Workplace Health and Safety: Historical and Emerging Trends*, Routledge, New York, 2021; Rodrigo Nunes, *Neither Vertical nor Horizontal: A Theory of Political Organisation*, Verso, London, 2021.

39   Terry Irving, *The Fatal Lure of Politics: The Life and Thought of Vere Gordon Childe*, Monash University Press, Melbourne, 2020, ch. 11; Mike Makin-Waite, *Communism and Democracy: History, Debates and Potentials*, Lawrence & Wishart, London, 2017, discusses communism's 'democratic deficit' in order to revive radical politics through participation in the state.

40   Macintyre, Epilogue, *The Party*, p. 16, manuscript version; Victor Feske, Introduction, *From Belloc to Churchill: Private Scholars, Public Culture, and the Crisis of British Liberalism, 1900–1939*, University of North Carolina Press, Chapel Hill, 1996.

Chapter 4

Militant: Stuart Macintyre and Paddy Troy

Bobbie Oliver

In 1988, when I was a tutor at Murdoch University, the School of Social Inquiry where I worked had a custom of honouring past lecturers by retaining name plates from their office doors and displaying them on a board in the staff common room. Among the names was that of Stuart Macintyre. I had met Stuart the previous year when he spent a week at the University of Western Australia (UWA) as a guest lecturer while I was tutoring in Tom Stannage's first-year Australian history unit. At that early stage of my academic career, I was a sponge, soaking up everything I could learn about Australian history, for I was very new to the field. I became something of a 'groupie', attending all of Stuart's lectures and tutorial sessions in that week. When my doctoral research took me to the eastern states, I visited Stuart at Melbourne University and spoke with him about my thesis. He would later become thesis examiner, referee and mentor as I progressed from student to lecturer, and he retained an interest in my work, for which I am grateful. We shared a passion for labour history, and each of us had a long-time involvement with the Australian Society for the Study of Labour History.

Stuart had been appointed a lecturer at Murdoch University in 1979; formerly, he spent a year as a tutor there in 1976. While in the west, he became deeply interested in the life and work of Paddy Troy, a trade union secretary and a member of the Communist Party of Australia (CPA). The result of his interest was *Militant: The Life and Times of Paddy Troy.*[1] *Militant* was Stuart's third book, and it remains his only full-length biographical study of an individual. In that sense, the book is unique among his many authored and edited works. Researching Paddy's life, along with his time at Murdoch University, gave Stuart an appreciation of Australia's western third that is rare among eastern states historians. For example, Stuart commenced his volume of *The Oxford History of Australia* with brief biographies of five Australians, two of whom lived most of their lives in Western Australia, albeit having originated in New South Wales. Of the other three, one was from Tasmania, a state similarly neglected by many Australian historians.[2] Stuart wrote that these five 'vignettes', as he termed them, contained several common themes, including 'mobility', whether around a state, across the country or even over-seas.[3] In contrast, his biography of Paddy Troy is very much grounded in the west and in particular the port of Fremantle.

I believe that a biographer must engage with their subject in order to write good biography. Sometimes that engagement is nega-tive and highly critical, but most often it is positive, springing from interest in and even admiration for a particular person. What attracted Stuart to Paddy Troy as a subject worthy of biographical research? No personal motivation is mentioned in *Militant*, but the lines he wrote fourteen years later when introducing his major study of the CPA, *The Reds*, might have applied equally to his reasons for writing about Paddy.

The interest that led me to this subject began ... when I was a postgraduate student. Like many of my generation, I was caught up in the radicalism of the 1960s. A whole range of campaigns and causes ... led me to communism. Both as a historian and a participant, I responded to the aura of communist tradition. For the best part of the 1970s, as the currents of twentieth-century history eddied and then turned, I joined with others who sought to empty the Stalinist cargo from the revolutionary vessel.[4]

Then there was the attractiveness of the character himself. Long before Stuart wrote *Militant*, Paddy Troy had become an institution in Fremantle. Who would not be intrigued by stories of the place he occupied in the community? 'There was talk of taking C.Y. O'Connor off his pedestal and putting Paddy there,' according to one old timer. O'Connor was the engineer who designed Fremantle Harbour and made it accessible to ships by blasting out the sandstone bar that blocked the entrance. Consequently, he was quite a local hero in Fremantle. Who could this person be who was so revered that he might replace O'Connor? Other Fremantle residents said, 'Paddy is better known than the Town Hall clock but he doesn't strike quite as often', or 'Paddy was like a lord walking around Fremantle; everybody knew him and everybody was almost lifting their hat to him'.[5]

Militant is also the story of Fremantle when it was a working-class town peopled by wharfies, dockies and seamen, and of the Fremantle Harbour during its heyday before industry moved to North Wharf. There are many pen portraits of Fremantle scattered through its pages, beginning with the bustling port to which Captain Troy brought his family during World War I (a 'labouring community' with most of the inhabitants working 'on the wharves or in allied transport, mercantile or service industries' and living in 'simple houses, made of limestone, brick or timber, with iron roofs').[6]

Although the gentrification of 'Freo' began in Paddy's lifetime, with young professionals beginning to see the attraction of stone cottages,[7] preparation for the America's Cup defence in 1987 speeded this process up considerably. Fortunately, this occurred after the value of heritage buildings was recognised, and the grand old warehouses and commercial buildings (now occupied by Notre Dame University, upmarket apartments and the like) were saved. But the working-class ethos of Paddy Troy's Fremantle was lost forever. The remaining limestone cottages have been renovated and added to, and carry a price tag far beyond the means of the average worker. The historic sheds on Fremantle Wharf have been converted to markets to cater for tourists.

Stuart never met Paddy, although he heard him speak at a public meeting in 1976.[8] By all accounts, Paddy was a commanding platform speaker, with a wide vocabulary, and that may have been what first piqued Stuart's interest in him. Paddy died in 1978, the year before Stuart was appointed lecturer at Murdoch University. About 1500 people attended his funeral service, and, as his daughter Hazel Butorac has recalled, many posthumous honours were bestowed upon him, including the naming of a pilot boat in 1985.[9]

Paddy left few personal records, partly as a result of having to bury papers during the communist purges of the 1940s and 1950s, partly by choice. He destroyed a lot of personal papers after his wife Mabel died. When Stuart began researching *Militant*, he was relying upon the testimony of family, friends and former colleagues, 'supplementing them wherever possible against the documentary record'.[10] Strong family support, in particular, aided the project. Paddy's son Patrick Troy encouraged Stuart to embark on the biography. He made enduring friendships with Paddy's children.

Biographical writing is never easy, especially when your subject left few personal papers, his life is recent history, and there are many living relatives, friends and colleagues—both admirers and detractors—who are likely to present conflicting views. Fortunately, Paddy had recorded several interviews after his retirement. Stuart discovered that he was a 'skilful raconteur with an eye for detail and an ear for the striking phrase [who] recorded the names and events that shaped his life as accurately as he could'.[11] Wherever Stuart was able to check Paddy's account with reliable documentary evidence, he found the former to be consistently accurate, including such details as the wage he was paid or the name of a ship that he worked on, as much as fifty years earlier. Paddy also kept detailed union minutes, and maintained the union records in good order. The thoroughness of the research is evident throughout the book, but the narrative is never swamped with detail. It maintains a good pace, resulting in a story well told.

Stuart's knowledge of Australian history and the CPA resulted in *Militant* being much more than the story of one man and his family. The book is appropriately subtitled *The Life and Times of Paddy Troy*. Paddy's life provides a lens through which to view the society of his day. Today, it is hard to imagine what becoming and being a communist meant in the Cold War world. Stuart's description of what confronted Paddy in making this decision shows how difficult it was to make a public stand as a communist in Western Australia in the 1930s, and even more so in a country town like Geraldton. Stuart writes:

> In the circumstances of the Depression there were young men and women all round Australia who made the same choice [as Paddy] … At the time they made their commitment, the choice required courage and dedication. In an isolated place like Geraldton the choice would have been particularly difficult. Paddy must have thought long and hard before taking the decisive step … There were many people in the town who considered it an act of folly or worse … So far as they understood communism, they understood it as a purely destructive creed, tearing things down. For a local man to appeal to international examples, and to proclaim class warfare and the need for revolution, was an act of heresy.[12]

When he made this momentous decision in 1934, Paddy was still living at home. His was a close-knit, Irish Catholic family. At one time, as the oldest son, he had been destined for the priesthood. There were bitter domestic rows, although the Troy family never abandoned him—unlike some families when a son or daughter declared themselves communist. While some of the community turned their backs, others went out of their way to maintain friendship, out of respect for him personally. This would continue throughout his life.

Stuart's narrative unfolds a story of discrimination and over-coming disadvantage. Paddy was sacked from a mine site at Youanmi after encouraging the men to strike because, he claimed, poor safety practices led to a miner's death. He was one of the first to be arrested and imprisoned when the CPA was made illegal during World War II; his wife Mabel experienced severe hardship during his imprison-ment, and his children were bullied at school because of their father's unpopular beliefs. Mabel never forgave the party for their neglect of her and her children while Paddy was in jail.[13]

Despite these setbacks, Stuart observes, Paddy did not appear to suffer the same doubts as other communists and sympathisers—even concerning the Nazi-Soviet Non-Aggression Pact, which was so shattering to some that they withdrew from the party, or, like James Normington-Rawling, adopted such unorthodox views that they were expelled.[14] Vere Gordon Childe, a communist fellow traveller who never joined the party, was so depressed by the pact that he considered suicide.[15] Paddy was much more pragmatic. Stuart writes:

> Paddy's unswerving attachment to the Soviet Union … stemmed ultimately from his experiences in the Depression. In his rejection of a social order which allowed the sanctity of private property to override human needs, he identified with a country which had overthrown capitalism and was building socialism. He accepted in full the claims that the USSR made about the ending of exploitation and the build-ing up of a new order in which all benefited. He embraced its ideology and accepted the discipline it imposed on its adherents.[16]

In both *Militant* and *Reds,* Stuart details the nationwide repres-sion of communists during the early years of World War II. This was most severe in Western Australia, largely because of an ambitious detective sergeant of police named Ron Richards, whom the communists called 'the black snake' or 'Ron the Con'. Richards later moved to Canberra, where he became deputy director of ASIO.[17] Richards, then head of the Special Branch in Perth, was a drinking companion of WA party secretary Bill Mountjoy. Foolishly, Mountjoy trusted Richards, even believing that the police would tip them off if a raid was planned. He was greatly mistaken. Paddy was sentenced (along with Kevin Healy and Arthur Rudkin, editor of the CPA paper *Worker's Star*) to three months hard labour on a charge of publishing information that might be useful to the enemy.[18]

After his release from prison, Paddy found work as a casual with the Coastal Dock Rivers and Harbour Works Union (CDRHWU or 'dockies'), beginning a lifelong association with the union that was a poor cousin to the famed Fremantle Lumpers (wharfies). The dockies union had formed at Fremantle in 1911, drawing its membership from several waterfront occupations: ship repairers and painters, dock workers, harbour construction workers, crews of harbour vessels, watchmen, riggers and others, which were employed in the private and public sectors, and with a range of differing pay and conditions.[19]

In simple but stark prose, Stuart describes the appalling conditions that made the casual section of the workforce particularly militant but were also circumstances that made the men receptive to joining a union:

> They were mostly working for a group of employers, the shipowners, who had demonstrated with their ruthless treatment of the seamen during the strikes in the 1920s that they were prepared to grind their employees for the last penny. Much of their work, particularly the handling and cleaning out of noxious cargoes, was back-breaking toil ... [T]he casual yard consisted largely of men who couldn't or wouldn't work permanently for one employer at the same task. The need to stand in the yard each morning brought the men together and enabled them to discuss their experiences. And finally, Fremantle was a very compact port in

which it was easy to gather union members together for a meeting.[20]

It was to reforming this industry that Paddy would devote his life and earn the respect of Fremantle and, clearly, of his biographer. He became a paid official in 1945 and union secretary in 1948.

Stuart's narrative depicts the early post–World War II period as a turbulent time when unions, formerly constrained by wartime controls, demanded increased pay and better working conditions in return for their sacrifices during the war. Western Australia's industrial base was still small, as Stuart states: 'Apart from the waterfront, Collie [coal mines], Kalgoorlie [gold mines] and the State [Railway] Workshops, there were few places employing more than a hundred workers.'[21] Yet militant unions made progress as the union power base began to shift from the declining AWU to industrial unions such as the Amalgamated Engineers, the Collie Miners, the Locomotive Engine Drivers and the waterside workers; separate lumpers' unions had now merged under the title of the Waterside Workers Federation.

Unlike many militant union leaders, Paddy became a master advocate in the Arbitration Court and used it skilfully to improve his members' pay and conditions. He soon gained a reputation for eloquence, as exemplified by one particular case. The margins paid to harbour construction and maintenance workers had been fixed in 1923. In 1947, fighting for increased margins, Paddy pointed out that men who had built the harbour

> are in the cemeteries in Karrakatta and Fremantle. Even some of the wooden piles have been pulled up and concrete ones have been put down. The very strong jarrah has been worn away by the action of the sea. The only thing that has remained constant is the marginal rate of the workers that built them. They are still on 6-shilling and 9-shilling margins.[22]

Stuart demonstrates how Paddy's reliance on the legal arbitration system exacerbated divisions in the CPA and annoyed CPA leaders from the eastern states (such as Sam Aarons, J.B. Miles and Ron Hurd). According to Miles, 'there is no such thing as a Communist or Bolshevik in Western Australia'.[23]

This was manifestly unfair, given the treatment WA communists had suffered during the war. It also ignored Paddy's enduring loyalty to the party. According to Stuart, the main bone of contention was Paddy's generally good relations with the wider labour movement and his preference for arbitration, rather than direct action, to resolve industrial disputes. Despite his orthodoxy, as the 'leading Communist trade unionist' in Western Australia, Stuart concludes, Paddy was blamed for the 'Western Australian exceptionalism' that so offended party leaders in the east. Ultimately, pressure from the new state secretary of the Seamen's Union, Ron Hurd, and Sam Aarons pushed the dockies to take more militant action. This resulted in more strikes and spelled the end of the dockies union. The union was de-registered in the Arbitration Court in 1952.[24] Unfortunately, in trying to steer a middle course, using the Arbitration Court and resorting to strikes only when employers or the court remained obdurate, Stuart indicates, Paddy failed to satisfy either his party's leaders (who thought he wasn't militant enough) or employers (who thought he was too militant).

In the ensuing carve-up of the dockies union, Paddy retained only the ship painters and dockers, and the watchmen.[25] Later, after further amalgamations, a new union, the Maritime Workers Union of Western Australia, was registered in 1968. This was at the beginning of a wave of union amalgamations, in the early 1970s—well before Bob Hawke's drive for twenty 'super unions' across Australia.

Paddy's struggle to save the dockies and then build the new WA branch of the Ship Painters' and Dockers Union took place during the zenith of union power in Australia. Union density (the proportion of the workforce that was unionised) reached 63 per cent of the workforce in 1953, from there declining to 50 per cent by 1983.[26] It was the era of closed shops—workplaces where no non-unionist would be employed—and award clauses that gave preference to employment of union members, encouraging employees to join unions. While Paddy did not live to see union density plummet from just over 50 per cent in the late 1970s to the current figure of about 17 per cent, he evidently saw it coming. Stuart analyses the membership decline in the maritime unions from mid-century:

> [In the 1950s] as shipowners began replacing their ageing fleets, they introduced larger vessels which required fewer seamen. On the wharves there was increasing mechanisation, with pallets and unitised cargo preparing the way for roll-on roll-off methods and containerisation in the 1960s. The newer, more modern vessels did not require the same maintenance as the older, coal-burning steamers and hence did not provide the same volume of work for dockies ... New ways of treating rust with sandblasting and spray-painting equipment had a similar effect on employment ... Simply to maintain a union whose membership seldom rose above 200 and sometimes fell as low as 130 was a constant struggle.[27]

In the 1950s, the wharfies alone could boast a membership of 2000. Twenty-five years later, the entire inner harbour workforce was barely half that number.[28]

While Stuart concentrates on Paddy's struggles to retain union strength and maintain his own position, it is clear that this dilemma was shared by waterfront union officials in the context of the declining harbour workforce. There was also a depressing political reality that deeply affected Paddy—and, indeed, most in the labour movement: in the 1960s and most of the 1970s, conservative governments triumphed at both the WA and federal ballot boxes. Paddy believed that the Liberals were nothing more than a 'clique of capitalists'.[29] He made a practice of writing their name as '£iberals', and found their continued success in elections incomprehensible. Their policies set the scene for the privatisation of many public facilities and the mass deunionisation of the workforce in the last two decades of the twentieth century.

As Stuart writes,

> In his own State [Paddy] found it ... hard to accept the emergence of a highly successful style of conservatism, that of David Brand and Charles Court, who orchestrated the massive capital investment in mining and industrial projects. Labor's earlier supremacy had rested on the encouragement of labour-intensive public works and primary industries. They were trumped by the postwar Liberals whose strategy was to encourage international participation, negotiate contracts with overseas purchasers [exemplified by the industrial complex at Kwinana and the Pilbara iron ore industry] and pursue development at any cost ... The new materialism was wholly repugnant to Paddy and he found it hard to understand how so many of his fellow-citizens who benefited hardly at all nevertheless succumbed to its allure. While the benefits were reaped by the ruthless, many more owed their jobs to the new enterprises or were caught up in the search for capital appreciation and consumer pleasures. They formed the constituency of the new conservatism. And Paddy, who was always astute in his assessment of the mood of his own union members, underestimated its strength.[30]

I have quoted this passage at length because it subtly describes a change in Paddy's life as well as the changes on the harbour and in the fabric and ethos of Fremantle. Paddy, the reader sees, is no longer in full control. Embittered by the continued electoral successes of the Liberal Party, inculcating into society values that were anathema to him, by his late fifties, Paddy is shown sympathetically as being less able to rebound, to be proactive in a hostile environment.

Like many working men of his generation, Paddy did not long survive his retirement. The stress of his lifestyle as a union official had already caused him to suffer numerous health problems. Retiring in 1973 aged 65, he yielded to Mabel's wishes and purchased a house in Safety Bay, south of Fremantle. Only two years into their retirement, Mabel died suddenly. Paddy remarried a year after her death, but died following an unsuccessful operation in 1978. Dying at only 70 years of age, he remained true to his maxim that he would 'wear out rather than rust out'.[31]

There is an expectation that biographies will end with an assessment of the subject's achievements and life—as if authors have to justify writing about them. In weighing Paddy's contribution to history, Stuart asks: 'How would he have assessed the significance of his life?' He imagines that Paddy would have seen himself as 'a working man who, to the best of his ability, endeavoured to uplift the lives of his people'.[32] He did not run one of the state's powerful unions; he remained loyal to a marginalised political party even when all that it stood for had been discredited by revelations of the excesses of the Stalinist period; he never entered parliament or gained a title. Yet, as Stuart reminds us, to assess Paddy's importance in history by these standards is 'to slip too easily into the conventional vocabulary of the big battalion'.[33] He argues that the real forces of change come not from major political parties or captains of industry but from the turbulent eddies that feed the mainstream.

This apt observation has much wider implications for historians, and not merely biographers. Sometimes historical subjects are neglected or ignored because they aren't 'mainstream'—the numbers of people involved are deemed to be 'insignificant', perhaps—but this should not be so. As Stuart writes,

> More generally, Paddy represents a distinctive strand in the Australian labour movement, that of the militant. In his case militancy took the form of communism but the tradition extends further than that … Again, Paddy's activities as a trade unionist offer an insight into the limits and possibilities of industrial organisation. He joined an industry that was poorly paid and insecure, and left it transformed.[34]

Using a light touch that is neither hagiographic nor condemnatory, Stuart is able to depict Paddy as both a zealot and an ordinary human being. Because of their devotion to the party, communists have frequently been depicted as one dimensional fanatics. Paddy certainly was zealous, and he was stubbornly loyal to a doctrine that he accepted in his youth and continued to hold for the remainder of his life. But he was also prepared to use tools not normally associated with communism to 'uplift the lives of his people', including the mechanisms of arbitration and democratic elections.

Although Stuart had abandoned communism before he wrote *Militant*, he was able to depict, sympathetically and realistically, the life of a man who remained loyal to the party. Paddy Troy's biography therefore is a testament to the best labour scholarship: balanced, carefully researched and contextualised. Paddy's story is the story of many men in the first half of the twentieth century in Australia, whose early working lives were blighted by the Great Depression. It is also the story of the Coastal Dock Rivers and Harbour Works Union (CDRHWU), a small, inconsequential Western Australian union that Paddy turned into a militant organisation, and of the old, working-class port of Fremantle before it became gentrified.

Many of the features of Stuart's writing about Paddy Troy illustrate points he made twenty years later in the Introduction to his edited collection, *The Historian's Conscience*, a book that arose from the bitter disputes of the early 2000s, termed the History Wars:

> If it is the fundamental duty of the historian to tell the truth, then that scarcely exhausts the obligations that arise when we work with the past. The choice of subject, fair dealing with the work of others, attention to context, humility in the exercise of judgement and recognition of what cannot be known—these are just some of the responsibilities a researcher incurs. The mediation between past and present is a profoundly moral activity. Of all the faculties of the historian, a good conscience is indispensable.[35]

Elsewhere in that book, one of the contributors, Alan Atkinson, quotes Stuart as stating, 'while historians might disagree on such points, [as the numbers of Indigenous deaths on the frontier] "at the very least we expect to find sympathy and compassion for the victims"'.[36] The attention to veracity, fairness, sympathy, compassion, humility and avoidance of speculation are all evident in the writing of *Militant*. The last lines are devoted to Paddy's funeral in 1978 and the tributes that flowed in from many quarters.

> The service was held at the Fremantle crematorium and attended by more than 1500 people. Next day a smaller group of relatives and union officers took the ashes by tug out to the Gage Roads and scattered them on the water. The death notices—five columns of them—cards, letters and telegrams all testified to his standing. Parliamentarians, trade unionists, employers' representatives, the TLC and the ACTU sent their condolences. The Mayor, Councillors and citizens of Fremantle [paid tribute to] 'a most sincere man who had a great love for our city and who was loved by its people in return'. The Communist Party of Australia proclaimed him an 'outstanding, revolutionary, workers' leader' … A trade unionist expressed the belief that 'God has something more for you to do somewhere'.
>
> A wharfie put it more succinctly: 'Sleep well, Paddy, the long shift is over.'[37]

Despite locals' predictions that he would replace C.Y. O'Connor, there is no statue to Paddy Troy in Fremantle. I came to Western Australia before the big 'gentrification' of the early 1980s—long enough ago to remember the vestiges of a working-class town, such as the footbridge over the railway line (now replaced by pedestrian crossings). Stuart knew that Fremantle, as it still existed, at least in part, during his time at Murdoch University, and his skilful pen evokes many images of the port as it once was, when Paddy Troy was not just a pilot boat but one of the best known men in town.

Notes

1   Stuart Macintyre, *Militant: The Life and Times of Paddy Troy*, Allen & Unwin, Sydney, 1984.
2   Stuart Macintyre, *The Oxford History of Australia*, vol. 4: *1901–1942: The Succeeding Age*, Oxford University Press, Melbourne, 1986, pp. 1–24.
3   Ibid., p. 22.
4   Stuart Macintyre, *The Reds: The Communist Party of Australia from Origins to Illegality*, Allen & Unwin, Sydney, 1998, p. 1.
5   Macintyre, *Militant*, p. 181.
6   Ibid., pp. 3–4.
7   Ibid., p. 190.
8   Ibid., p. 224.
9   Hazel Butorac, 'Paddy Troy, 1908–1978', in Bob Boughton, Danny Blackman, Mike Donaldson, Carmel Shute and Beverley Symons (eds), *Comrades! Lives of Australian Communists*, Search Foundation in association with the Australian Society for the Study of Labour History, Sydney, 2020, pp. 135–8.
10 Macintyre, *Militant*, p. 224.
11 Ibid.
12 Ibid., p. 39.
13 Ibid., p. 62.
14 John Pomeroy, 'Rawling, James Normington (1898–1966)', *Australian Dictionary of Biography*, National Centre of Biography, Australian National University, https://adb.anu.edu.au/biography/rawling-james-normington-11492/text20495.
15 Terry Irving, *The Fatal Lure of Politics: The Life and Thought of Vere Gordon Childe*, Monash University Press, Melbourne, 2020, p. 296.
16 Macintyre, *Militant*, p. 59.
17 Macintyre, *The Reds*, p. 398.
18 Macintyre, *Militant*, p. 61.
19 Bobbie Oliver, 'Conflict on the waterfront: Fremantle Dock Workers and "new unionism", 1889 to 1945', *Studies in Western Australian History*, vol. 31, 2016, pp. 159–72.
20 Macintyre, *Militant*, pp. 74–5.
21 Ibid., p. 137.
22 Ibid., p. 95.
23 Ibid., p. 139.
24 Ibid., pp. 140–2.
25 Ibid., pp. 145–6.
26 Michael Crosby, *Power at Work. Rebuilding the Australian Union Movement*, Federation Press, Sydney, 2005, p. 43.
27 Macintyre, *Militant*, pp. 147–8.
28 Ibid., p. 199.
29 Ibid., p. 190.
30 Ibid., p. 190.
31 Ibid., p. 185.
32 Ibid., p. 220.
33 Ibid.
34 Ibid., p. 221.
35 Stuart Macintyre, 'Introduction', in Stuart Macintyre (ed.), *The Historian's Conscience: Australian Historians on the Ethics of History*, Melbourne University Press, Melbourne, 2004, pp. 4–5.

36 Alan Atkinson, 'Do good historians have feelings?', in Macintyre, *The Historian's Conscience*, p. 17.

37 Macintyre, *Militant*, p. 223.

Stuart with his father, Forbes Macintyre, 1948

Stuart with his brothers, Clem, and Sandy, 1958

Stuart and Margaret Geddes, his first wife, 1970

Stuart and Martha in Carlton, 1971

The Macintyre family at The Knott, Cambridge, 1975

Stuart with his daughter Jessica, Margaret River, Western Australia, 1976

Stuart and Martha on their wedding day, Fremantle, 1976

Stuart, in Melbourne, reading *The Age* in the back garden, Brunswick West, 1981

Stuart with Henrietta Probert, his daughters Jessica and Mary, and their dog Dipper, Kew, 1985

Stuart, John Hirst, Graeme Davison—Oxford Companions, 1998

Stuart c 2008, Melbourne

Stuart, Marcus Clarke lecture, Athenaeum Library, 2016

Stuart speaking at a function for the Heritage Council of Victoria, 2016
(Photograph by Andrew May)

Chapter 5

Writing communist history

Ann Curthoys

In some ways, Stuart Macintyre's life and work parallel mine. We were both born in the early postwar years, he in April 1947 and me in September 1945. We were both part of the boom in university enrolments in the early 1960s, and both completed History honours, he in Melbourne in 1968 and me in Sydney in 1966. We both completed PhDs in history and became academic historians, although never at the same institution at the same time. In our historical work, we both focused on Australian history set within a larger world or imperial context, and we have both written about Australian historiography as well as Australian history. Furthermore, we both spent brief periods in the Communist Party, I in 1964–65 and he in the early 1970s. While we have written on many other subjects, we have both attended to communist history, Stuart especially in *Militant: The Life and Times of Paddy Troy* (1984), *The Reds: The Communist Party of Australia from Origins to Illegality* (1998) and now his new book, *The Party* (2022), and me in co-editing two books on Australia's Cold War, publishing several essays and now completing a book on Paul and Eslanda Robeson's visit to Australia and New Zealand in 1960, which entails considerable communist history. From this common interest and background, I want to explore Stuart's contribution to communist history and, through it, to Australian and indeed international history.

I read *The Party* in 2021. It was in pre-publication form, a set of eleven long pdf chapters with an introduction and an epilogue. This is a late career book, based on the extensive research, thought and experience of a lifelong working historian, arriving as it does twenty-three years after *Reds* and thirty-seven years after *Militant*. A great deal of work has been done along the way, and many other books and essays in Stuart's career have influenced this one. The result is a detailed, comprehensive and eminently readable book. This is an even-handed yet spirited account of the trials and tribulations of Australian communism, its extraordinary history, its failures and its achievements. While it covers both internal party politics and the CPA's relations with Australian society and the world beyond it, its most striking dimension is its discussion of internal strife, as communists struggle to manage both their loyalty to the Soviet Union and their day-to-day local activism. The discussion of the Australian party reaction to Krushchev's Secret Speech of 1956 and to the Sino-Soviet split of the early 1960s, to take just two examples, is riveting. There is plenty of historical judgement—and it will come as no surprise to most readers that Stuart is highly critical of the party's loyalty to the USSR—yet we can remain interested in, and often sympathetic with, the party members who respond so variously to these and similar crises.

Although I began by pointing out our commonalities, there is a major difference in our life histories that affects the way Stuart and I approach communist history: I was brought up in the Communist Party and Stuart was not. When I write about communist history, I am constantly trying to match it against my own childhood and teenage experience (I left soon after my twentieth birthday). I wrestle with filial loyalties, school and undergraduate university experiences, memories of my parents' many communist friends, and a sense of limited—inevitably skewed—insider knowledge. When I read particular details concerning communists in the 1950s and early 1960s, I have the feeling that I *know* these people. As I write and think about communist history, then, I need historical accounts that are not saturated with such concerns, and I turn to Stuart's work and that of others such as Phillip Deery for an independent assessment of those same times.

I see *The Party* as an exemplary work of Thucydidean history. By this I mean that this is a history that focuses on public life and the drama of politics and war in the tradition established in the fifth century BCE by one of history's founding great practitioners, Thucydides. In *Is History Fiction?* (2002), John Docker and I describe Thucydides' great *History of the Peloponnesian War* as 'fast moving, precise, directed, decisive, carefully structured and highly analytic, deploying a strict chronological method where the recording of events can be organised year by year, season by season'. We draw attention to the famous set speeches in the *History* and the way in which they present divergent views as powerfully as possible, and we discuss the ways in which the *History* 'moves towards its conclusions of disillu-sionment for the author, and massive failure in the war for Athens'. We conclude that, in its juxtaposition of episodes and its aesthetic shape, Thucydides' *History of the Peloponnesian War* is a tragedy.[1]

It seems to me we can describe *The Party* this way too: it is clear, analytical and chronologically organised, and gives space to contesting views both within the party and between it and its oppo-nents. Although some space is given to the impetus the party gave to certain political campaigns, from unionism to peace to Aboriginal rights to women's rights, it is above all a tragedy, of high ideals, misplaced loyalty, personal failings, at times of dishonesty and skull-duggery, a meditation on political imagination, ambition, fantasy and failure. In the epilogue, Stuart writes perceptively,

> Party members were as varied in their personal qualities and
> as subject to the vagaries of human nature as lesser mortals.
> It was the party that brought them together, trained them in
> the practical tasks of political activism, lifted their sights
> beyond national boundaries, provided them with opportu-
> nities for education and cultural engagement, sustained and

inspired them. In doing so it also made heavy demands, imposed an ideology that was not open to question, required them to suppress misgivings and blinded them to the reality of communist regimes.[2]

Even when Stuart is having fun with some of the antics of the historical characters who people his story of Australian communism, then, there is something sombre about *The Party*. It is a book we can learn from, not only about the past but also about the nature of the political choices we face in the present. In the end, it made me think not only about communists and communism but also about the importance of our work as historians as we attempt to understand the tumultuous and contradictory world we live in.

Notes

1   Ann Curthoys and John Docker, *Is History Fiction?*, UNSW Press, Sydney, 2002, pp. 34–44.
2   Stuart Macintyre, *The Party: Communism in Australia, From Heyday to Reckoning, 1940–1970*, Allen & Unwin, Sydney, 2022, p. 407.

Chapter 6

Professor and comrade

Peter Love

'My burgeoning interest in history ... had its basis in political engagement.'[1] Stuart Macintyre traced the course of his own attachment to history as a vocation, as well as his progression through New Left enthusiasms to a broader concern for greater equity and justice as organising principles in our civic experience.

Along with his lengthy publications record and active engagement on numerous editorial boards and professional committees, Stuart's work expanded to encompass matters that extended beyond academic disciplinary boundaries to cognate public issues, where his historical perspective informed sound political judgement. He served on both social sciences and humanities academies, advisory committees for the Australian Research Council and cultural policy for the Victorian Ministry for Planning. Both the National Library of Australia and the State Library of Victoria appointed him to their respective councils. He was added to judging panels for literary prizes such as the National Library's Harold White Fellowship, the *Age* Book of the Year, the Victorian Premier's Literary awards and the Redmond Barry Award, and chaired the Prime Minister's History Prize judging panel. He served on the councils of Victoria University of Technology, the University of Melbourne and Ormond College.

Stuart's professional eminence was also expressed in his work chairing the Inquiry into School History for the Commonwealth Department of Education, the National Centre for History Education and History Council of Victoria. He was appointed an auditor for the Australian Universities Quality Agency and a member of the Victorian Qualifications Authority. He also worked on developing indicators for Research Excellence in Australia and the UK. His work has been acknowledged in visiting appointments to several Australian and New Zealand universities, culminating in the prestigious Chair of Australian Studies at Harvard.

His contribution to the public sphere in Australia was officially recognised in the award of a Centenary Medal in 2001, and more substantially in his nomination as an Officer of the Order of Australia in 2012. By then, his public profile as an eminent historian had been widely recognised and affirmed by his frequent public addresses on contemporary issues that had historical resonances. Matters surrounding the Australian Constitution, its historical roots and present implications were the subject of numerous chapters, articles and public addresses.

The most famous of his roles in national debates was precipitated by his book with Anna Clark, *The History Wars*.[2] For some time there were heated polemics over the matter of Australia's historical foundations and development. These were a proxy war of the wider cultural struggles between established liberal/social democratic ideas, which faced a ferocious assault from neoliberals who launched a conservative mobilisation across most aspects of contemporary Western societies. In the Australian case, much of the cultural war was focused on its colonial origins, particularly the history of Indigenous people and their treatment by European colonists who were, variously, said to have 'settled' a *Terra Nullius* or 'invaded' a land belonging to an ancient culture. The arguments and the abuse raged for some time when Macintyre and Clark published their well-informed, measured but robust account of the turbulent squabbles that surrounded accounts of Australia's history. The conservative assaults on the history profession in universities and schools had disfigured public discussion and debates within institutions. Our authors offered a defence of the modern research and scholarship that dared to question the conservative certitudes of these renewed historical narratives. This was an outstanding case of a historian as public figure defending the civilised, intellectual foundations of his discipline and arguing for their centrality to the cultural principles of a civilised nation.

In *Winners and Losers* Stuart explored the historical development of the search for social justice in Australia.[3] Considering the role of law in the early convict colonies, he looked at how that regime set a pattern for the rule of law that was to follow. He tracked the struggles to democratise land ownership, the campaign for a fair wage and the right to work. He explored attempts to reach full employment, assure social welfare and construct a ladder of opportunity. The idea of common citizenship was hardly adequate to the emerging claims for special treatment by mobilised identity groups and how public policy moved beyond the established doctrine of common citizenship.

In the end, Stuart established seven theses about how complex the structures and processes of reform are in the modern Australian state. They represent his assessment of the challenges facing the pursuit of social justice. While there are libraries of works on social reform, Stuart's short and succinct catalogue establishes the developing role of reformers, their opponents, the state and its numerous instrumentalities in shaping the possibilities of a fairer, more stable nation. This is not simply another academic treatise; it is a deeply scholarly text that all people engaged in political activity should consider for the public good.

Stuart's later, more substantial account of *Australia's Boldest Experiment: War and Reconstruction in the 1940s* is a monumental work that eclipses all previous work on the subject.[4] He digs deeply into the role of World War II in stimulating the idea that it would be prudent (and implicitly optimistic) to plan for a postwar world that managed the transition from war to peace in a manner more successful than the aftermath of World War I. In exploring the range and dimension of the planning he shows how the various dimensions of social well-being were addressed in a systematic manner that addressed the present needs of the community and made provision for a more stable, prosperous and equitable community within the constraints of constitutional requirements, legislative authority, economic constraints both domestic and international, and the scope of the political imagination of the planners.

Stuart lays out the complexities and tensions within and between each area to be reformed, details the wider context of a world move towards Keynesian reconstruction and casts a clear and sober eye over the results. *Australia's Boldest Experiment* is a book for Australians to review now, how comprehensively we might reform economy and society in line with the same type of civilised and sophisticated blueprint that the planners gave a postwar Australia. It is also a secular hymn of praise to political and public service planners of the day, such as Coombs, Curtin, Chifley, Dedman and, in the 1950s, Menzies. Stuart gave us not only a superb work of scholarly research and writing but also an account of our history that may well inspire ambitious political visions of similar scope and effectiveness.

Stuart Macintyre showed how we can learn from history much that pertains to our current discontents. As a Professor of History he tirelessly professed history to his national community and showed beyond dispute that history can have seriously productive civic purposes. All this while behaving like a comrade.

Notes

1   Stuart Macintyre, 'True for the moment', in Bain Attwood (ed.), *Labour Histories: Robin Gollan, Stuart Macintyre, Verity Burgmann, Peter Beilharz, Raelene Francis*, Department of History, Monash University, no. 17, 1994, p. 20.
2   Stuart Macintyre and Anna Clark, *The History Wars*, 3rd edn, Melbourne University Press, Melbourne, 2013.
3   Stuart Macintyre, *Winners and Losers: The Pursuit of Social Justice in Australian History*, Allen & Unwin, Sydney, 1985.
4   Stuart Macintyre, *Australia's Boldest Experiment: War and Reconstruction in the 1940s*, NewSouth Publishing, Sydney, 2015.

Part 2

Australia: Foundations

On Stuart's 'Victorian Visionaries'

Gender, race and contested colonial liberalisms

Marilyn Lake

The impact of historians' work is evident across a range of professional activities that include teaching, research, writing and supervision, but it is sometimes as journal editors that they also exercise a major influence on the direction of historical debate. I had reason to be personally grateful when the editorship of Australia's premier history journal, *Historical Studies*—soon renamed *Australian Historical Studies* (*AHS*)—changed hands in 1986. On the recommendation of Professor Greg Dening, Stuart Macintyre took over the editorial reins. He then unilaterally—or so it seemed to me—overturned the decision of his predecessor to reject my first major academic article.

The subject of the article, 'The politics of respectability: Identifying the masculinist context', was new. It proposed the need for a history of masculinity and in particular of 'men pursuing their "masculinist" interests as men'. It also suggested some of the ways in which gender dynamics animated major political movements, ranging from feminism to socialism to nationalism. 'It is time', I declared on the first page, 'that gender became a central category of all historical analysis.'[1] Thankfully Stuart was receptive to this theoretical intervention, which would be published as a contribution to the series 'Historical Reconsiderations' initiated a few years before by a previous editor, John Hirst. When he read the first version of my article, Stuart immediately grasped the argument and encouraged me to state my thesis up front instead of leaving it buried, as it was, in the body of the text. As an editor, Stuart was a key historiographical 'influencer' and, as it turned out, he was also prescient. Recent Taylor and Francis statistics for AHS suggest that 'The politics of respectability' has had 1849 'views'. Later reprinted in a number of different historical anthologies, it also became one of the journal's most widely cited articles.[2]

Stuart was appointed to the University of Melbourne as lecturer in history in 1980. As a junior colleague I was fortunate to get to know him at Melbourne, first in 1984, when I was appointed a full-time tutor in Australian history and again between 1986 and 1988 as Ashworth Lecturer in Social Theory, based in the gender studies program in the History Department. When he was appointed the new editor of *Historical Studies* I appealed to him to review his predecessor Paul Bourke's decision not to publish my submission. I was hopeful, because they were clearly very different kinds of historians. Stuart was young, radical, open-minded and alert to the new intellectual challenges posed by feminist scholarship. The extent of his engagement with the concept of gender as a category of political analysis and his delight in exploring different historical modes of masculinity became fully evident with the publication of *A Colonial Liberalism: The Lost World of Three Victorian Visionaries* in 1991, which—unusually for the time and especially for political history—listed 'masculinity' as a major index entry.

A Colonial Liberalism has continued to be an inspiration to numerous historians pursuing a variety of projects across the decades since. It has shaped my thinking at various times in a number of different ways, most recently when writing my study of trans-Pacific Australian/American progressivism, which built on Stuart's emphasis on the novelty of Australia's self-governing liberal democracies. 'We are too habituated to liberalism', he writes in his first chapter, 'to appreciate the radical novelty of its constitution of the individual as a social actor and of society as a voluntary association of sovereign individuals.'[3] Stuart also declared an interest in 'lived experience' and political subjectivity. Of his three subjects he wrote: 'Their liberalism was no tepid orthodoxy, it was a consuming passion.'[4]

A Colonial Liberalism critiqued the conventional idea that Australian liberalism was a derivative, dependent, British politics and insisted that we pay attention to the distinctiveness of the 'local habitat'.[5] When researching the friendship between the leading Victorian liberal Alfred Deakin and the Californian-born Harvard philosopher Josiah Royce, who met in Melbourne in 1888, I was struck by Royce's interest in the novelty of 'new communities' and the dynamics of the 'voluntary association of individuals', an interest that would continue to preoccupy him and inspire his book, *The Philosophy of Loyalty* (1908).[6] 'Organization, if it succeeds,' Royce concludes in an article written for *Atlantic Monthly* soon after his visit to Australia, 'does so by virtue of the loyalty of the individuals, and the result must be in general normative and progressive.' Royce was impressed by the progressive, innovative politics of Australia's colonial self-governing communities and their 'socialistic' tendencies. 'No English community elsewhere has sought to govern itself in just the way here exemplified,' he writes. 'Here are pure democracies, with what an American must unhesitatingly call strongly socialistic tendencies.'[7]

In *A Colonial Liberalism* Stuart offers an account of progressive political thought in Victoria through the public and private lives and political visions of three key figures: George Higinbotham, editor of the *Argus*, later Attorney-General and then Chief Justice; David Syme, proprietor of the *Age* and ardent proponent of tariff protection and land reform; and Charles Henry Pearson, English history lecturer and journalist, Victorian Minister for Education and subsequent author of the influential work of prophecy, *National Life and Character: A Forecast*. In their different projects all were passionate, reforming, radical democrats. Not all liberals were democrats, Stuart notes, but the liberal insistence on equal rights led inexorably towards equality in political rights.[8]

Repulsed by the English class system and hereditary social hierarchies, all three colonial democrats believed in the equality, dignity and rights of manhood—and that (white) working men were entitled, equally with aristocrats and property owners, to the rights of men. 'Self-government is perceived to possess a double meaning,' observes Higinbotham, 'individual and political, each exhibiting the closest correlation with the other; and in proportion to a man's self-control is observed to be his capacity to be entrusted with political power.'[9] The self-controlling, self-disciplined liberal political subject was indubitably a (white) man. 'Gender', as Stuart noted, 'was a crucial feature of this liberal discourse'; liberalism was 'a masculine doctrine'.[10]

One of the delights of all Stuart's political histories is his deft pen portraits—mostly humorous, often affectionate—of his main subjects. In *A Colonial Liberalism* he offers extended biographies of his three main characters with gender depicted as a key dimension of their characters and political subjectivities. Higinbotham was often described in his time as feminine in feeling and fussy in his grooming. His grandchildren waited outside his door to accompany him to breakfast: 'he would appear, pink of cheek, smelling of soap and eau-de-cologne, and shake out the whitest of handkerchiefs to put in his breast pocket'.[11] But in his professions of politician and judge he exercised the requisite manly independence and masculine mastery. 'The great moral idea of liberalism,' observes Stuart, 'was manliness, and the vocabulary it employed to mark out the attributes of a fully developed individual—the language of independence, honour, chivalry, resolution and mastery—enshrined masculine qualities.'[12] Higinbotham conceived of government as a manly pursuit, although he was also one of the first colonial liberals to support women's suffrage.

David Syme's masculinity was of a more austere, stern and domineering kind. At home he was a forbidding and distant father. In the office he ensured that the *Age* operated as an instrument of his will. He laid down the direction of the leading articles and indeed determined every aspect of the paper. His control was absolute and peremptory, and he was unforgiving of failure. 'When David Syme sat in his office each evening to read proofs,' Stuart writes, quoting his biographer, 'he struck out every fanciful adjective and ornamental phrase. The language he wished to see in his organ was "strong, terse and virile".'[13] Syme's idea of independence was defined by 'patriarchy and property': 'to be manly was to be strong, resourceful, reliable, a good provider—the truly independent man sat at the head of his table and carved for his wife and children—and above all, masterful'.[14]

Charles Pearson, who wrote some of Syme's opinion pieces, was more like Higinbotham in presentation: courteous, refined, more effeminate in style. But he shared with both Higinbotham and Syme a radical respect for the manliness of Australian working men, and all three radical democrats believed that the status of white Australian manhood must be preserved through immigration restriction. In their view the ideal of democratic equality necessitated racial exclusion. It was their very passion for equality and democracy that led them to become crusaders—in the press, the parliament and the Supreme Court—for the exclusion of Chinese immigrants. The passion for Chinese exclusion was arguably one of the constitutive features of the colonial liberalism practised by Stuart's 'Victorian visionaries'.

By pointing to the 'creative contribution of nineteenth-century Australians' to the political theory and practice of liberalism, Stuart rightly insists that 'colonial liberalism' be understood as a product of its 'local habitat' with its distinctive circumstances, history and political traditions. A key dimension of that local habitat, absent from Stuart's account, was the arrival from the 1850s of thousands of Chinese immigrants to the Victorian goldfields. By 1857 around 45 000 or one-sixth of the Victorian population had been born in China.[15] The first Immigration Restriction Act was passed in 1855 but repealed under British pressure. As Attorney-General in 1865, Higinbotham drafted a new Chinese Immigrants Statute, which provided for the regulation and segregation of Chinese colonists and expressly prevented a Chinese immigrant 'notwithstanding that he holds a miner's right or business license' from voting for the election of members of mining boards, a local act of disenfranchisement that anticipated legislation at the colonial level in 1881, when Chinese Australian men were barred for the first time from voting in Victorian elections.

That year the Victorian government passed a Chinese Influx Restriction Act to stop Chinese immigration—imposing tonnage restrictions on incoming ships and a poll tax of 10 pounds—together with an amendment to disenfranchise Chinese men already resident in Victoria, who, together with other adult male colonists, had been entitled to vote at municipal and parliamentary elections since the enactment of manhood suffrage in 1856.[16] Supporters of the discriminatory legislation explained its necessity in terms of the Chinaman's complete ignorance of 'Caucasian civilization'; his low standard of living; and, as an inherently servile and docile race, Chinamen, it was said, lacked the manly capacities of independence and autonomy necessary for participation in democratic self-government. Chinese colonists were incapable of acting autonomously, it was said, because they were controlled by 'headmen'. They 'voted to order' and 'voted simply for the candidate who was in favour of the headman'.[17] In other words the Chinese were not considered to be manly men. Race as well as gender was a crucial feature of this colonial liberal discourse. Or, to put it another way, the gendered dynamic of radical colonial discourse—and its concept of manliness—was racialised.

One of the most eloquent supporters of immigration restriction legislation was Charles Pearson, a recently arrived English colonist, Fellow of Oriel College, and former Professor of History at King's College, London. He had been elected in 1878 to the Legislative Assembly of Victoria, which as 'the most prosperous, the most energetic, and, as I think it is supposed, the most ambitious of the different colonies' was looked upon, he was pleased to tell the parliament, 'somewhat as the New England states used to be looked upon in America—as a community with a sort of preternatural sagacity'.[18]

Victoria was ambitious for its Anglo-Saxon democracy, which Pearson had already celebrated in his contribution to the English volume, 'On the Working of Australian Institutions', in *Essays on Reform*, in 1867.[19]

In his speech in support of the 1881 legislation, Pearson cited the newly circulating knowledge of China's vast population—some 400 million people—who if allowed to migrate freely would surely swamp the small colonial settlements of Australia:

> The population of China was nearly 400 000 000, and the mere natural increase of that population in a single year would be sufficient to swamp the whole white population of the colony. Australia was now perfectly well known to the Chinese; communication between the two countries was thoroughly established; and, in the event of famine or war arising in China, Chinamen might come here at any time in hordes. He had read the Bill with greatest satisfaction, and he considered it reflected great credit on the government.[20]

Pearson's observations about Australia now being 'well known to the Chinese' and the possibility of 'famine' driving their hordes to swamp the white population of Australia echoed—and probably depended on—statements set out by leaders of the politically active local Chinese community, two years before, in *The Chinese Question in Australia*. Written by Lowe Kong Meng, Cheok Hong Cheong and Louis Ah Mouy, it was published in Melbourne in 1879 and widely circulated. There they write:

> When we heard, about five and twenty years ago, that there was a great continent nearly half as large again as China, and containing only a few hundreds of thousands of civilized people … that it was rich in the precious metals and very fertile; and that it was only a few weeks' sail from our own country, numbers of Chinese immigrants set out for this land of promise … China had 2 000 000 square miles of

territory and 400 000 000 of people. Australia comprises an area close upon 3 000 000 square miles and it contains no more than 2 100 000 white people and a few thousand blacks. In our land, millions of men, women and children … yes millions … have died of starvation during the last year.[21]

Pearson's parliamentary warning about Chinese 'swamping' the white population of Australia drew on Chinese colonists' writings and would be reproduced twelve years later in his influential work of prophecy, *National Life and Character: A Forecast*, a book that would in turn be held high by Australia's first Prime Minister, Edmund Barton, in the first federal parliament, in 1901, when he spoke in support of the Immigration Restriction Bill.

When Chinese Australians refuted the racist arguments of advocates of immigration restriction they styled themselves as both subjects of the Chinese empire and would-be British colonists— 'cosmopolitan in spirit and sympathy'—and argued for their universal 'human rights' on a number of grounds: as Christians, as civilised peoples and in terms of the precepts of international law. 'God hath made of one blood all nations of men,' they write, and they emphasise the similarity between the lessons of the Scriptures and Confucian principles—'the sublime precepts of Confucius and Mencius'—especially in support of the ideals of reciprocity, mutuality and respect for strangers. They also invoke the same principle of reciprocity when quoting the law of nations and international treaties.[22]

Lowe Kong Meng and his fellow authors insisted that the treatment of the Chinese in the Australian colonies contravened international law as outlined by the 'illustrious Vattel', who had declared that the obligation of a state to render justice to all others was 'a perfect obligation', of strictly binding force, at all times and under all circumstances. The obligation entailed a right, a perfect right, a reciprocal right: 'The freedom to come and go, to trade and settle'. Their booklet was informed by a sense of bewilderment and injustice:

In the name of heaven, we ask, where is your justice? …
Where your enlightenment? Where your love of liberty?
Where your respect for international law? … what has
become of those sublime and lofty sentiments of human
brotherhood and cosmopolitan friendship and sympathy
which are so often on your lips, and are proclaimed so wise-
ly from pulpit, press and platform?[23]

Having been forced into a cosmopolitan mode of existence by
Western powers who said, 'in effect "We must come in, and you *shall*
come out. We will not suffer you to shut yourselves up from the rest
of the world"'—these Chinese colonists now demanded, in reciprocal manner, a cosmopolitan understanding of human
rights—common to all civilised peoples of the world—to overcome
national and racial exclusions.[24]

In response to this cosmopolitan insistence on 'common human
rights', radical colonial liberals—led by Higinbotham, Syme and
Pearson—became ever more strenuous in their espousal of national
sovereign rights. An intercolonial conference was planned for Sydney
in mid-1888 to enact new uniform legislation to restrict the entry
of Chinese to all Australian colonies. In the midst of preparations for
the conference, two ships, *Afghan* and *Burumbeet*, arrived in
Melbourne carrying several hundred Chinese passengers, many of
whom were returning from filial visits to China and carried British
naturalisation papers. Regardless of their naturalisation or prepared-
ness to pay the poll tax, there was immediate opposition to their
landing. Leading the campaign was Syme's newspaper, the *Age*,
which repeated the Californian cry: 'The Chinese must go.'[25]

Later in the month the *Age* editorialised: 'It should be clearly
understood that treaty or no treaty we are legally entitled to exclude
any contribution to our population which we object to, and that we
intend to exercise that right by excluding the Chinese.' And the
reason for excluding the Chinese? 'It is quite impossible that two
races so dissimilar should live together on the lines of equality which
have been laid down in these colonies.'[26] Equality demanded racial

exclusion. All passengers were prevented from landing by the executive decision of the Victorian government—in which Alfred Deakin was Chief Secretary—an act characterised by political opponents as neither democratic nor liberal but as 'arbitrary and high-handed' and by the Chinese community leader and minister of religion, Cheok Hong Cheong as a 'coup d'état'.[27]

The validity of the government's decision was tested in a legal challenge issued in the name of one of the Chinese passengers. In *Chung Teong Toy v. Musgrove*, the Supreme Court of Victoria in a majority decision rejected the government's argument that it had a sovereign right to exclude aliens from its territory as an act of state. The majority argued that the Victorian government's authority was 'limited'. Under its Constitution Act, the colony of Victoria 'enjoyed a perfect scheme of local government, limited to its internal relations'. Victorian democrats—such as Higinbotham, Syme and Pearson—preferred to speak not of 'local' government but of 'self-government', a status they would later invoke to argue their sovereign right to racial homogeneity.

For the government, Higinbotham argued that the right to exclude unwanted aliens had been conferred by the system of self-government in Victoria.[28] There was 'an apprehension on the part of Her Majesty's government for Victoria', he said, 'that a large influx of Chinese into the colony was imminent, and in the opinion of the Minister and the Government, such influx should be prevented, and no further Chinese … should be allowed to enter Victoria'. The right to prevent aliens from landing, he said, 'appears to be necessarily inherent in the Sovereign power of every civilized society occupying a territory within defined limits'. More particularly, the 'right and duty of guarding it are recognized in the kindred institutions of the United States of America'. With the grant of self-government this republican right had been conferred on the responsible government of Victoria.[29]

When the Collector of Customs, Musgrove appealed against the Supreme Court decision to the English Privy Council, that august body held that the colony of Victoria did indeed have the right to exclude unwanted immigrants. Ironically, Higinbotham's radical claim to Victorian sovereignty was vindicated by a British court of appeal. The case of *Toy v. Musgrove* has been described by Zelman Cowen as unique in the law reports in providing 'an elaborate examination of the scope and nature of responsible government' and an unparalleled opportunity for Higinbotham to expound his brand of colonial liberalism.[30] In a move that would become common in Australian history, sovereignty was claimed in the service of racial exclusion.

In their campaign for human rights without distinction and freedom of movement, the Chinese Victorians were supported by a number of other white liberal colonists, such as William Shiels and Henry Wrixon, who deplored the discriminatory basis of recent Victorian legislation. Political historian Geoff Serle called them 'old-fashioned liberals', but from the contemporary perspective of multiculturalism they now look like the true visionaries, rather than their nationalist, racist opponents.[31] In 1881, when the government disenfranchised Chinese Australians, lawyer and politician Henry Wrixon denounced 'the novelty' that parliament 'might disfranchise any nationality they did not like'. 'The Constitution', he stated, 'provided that every man, wise or foolish, ignorant or learned, should have a vote, and he maintained that that principle should be carried out.'[32]

The protest at racial discrimination and restrictions on freedom of movement continued when the colonial governments introduced new uniform legislation following the intercolonial conference in Sydney in 1888. One of the provisions of the new Victorian law was to further restrict Chinese movement between Australian colonies by requiring resident Chinese to obtain special permits to show at all colonial borders. Leading liberal and future Premier William Shiels—and like Higinbotham and Pearson an ardent proponent of women's rights—was outraged. To impose 'special disabilities' on one section of the community was an innovation of 'a particularly grievous character'. Surely such reactionary developments were at odds with an advanced liberalism. 'Was this not a revival of a practice which was utterly barbarous, and which abrogated one of the dearest rights of citizens—perfect liberty of locomotion,' he asked parliament. Surely, insisted Shiels, 'the first duty which the Legislature should demand and insist upon receiving from the government of the day is that its acts, especially against foreigners—against weak defenceless foreigners—should be within the confines of legality'.[33]

Chinese colonists expressed their outrage in similar terms. In a 43-page 'Remonstrance to the Parliament and the People of Victoria', signed by nine committee members and chairman Cheok Hong Cheong, they characterised the new legislation as neither liberal nor civilised but 'barbarous'. They made a lengthy case for their status as civilised people, listing Chinese cultural and intellectual achievements, but in the end recognised that the real issue was not a dispute about the status of an ancient civilisation but the modern preoccupation with race. The Chinaman was denied 'common human rights', they noted, because he differed from the European in the 'colour of his skin'.[34]

Stuart addressed the 'limitations of colonial liberalism' in Victoria in a final chapter of *A Colonial Liberalism* he called 'Reconsiderations'.[35] There he points to the failure to extend full civil and political equality to women: 'The liberals replaced patriarchy with domesticity and left intact the gender qualities that sustained the marital union, along with the gendered characterization of the public world, the individual and his capacities.'[36] The most 'basic' limitation to the colonial liberal vision was, however, colonists' refusal of recognition of Aboriginal peoples as first nations, the original possessors of the country. The colonial liberals thought of themselves as settlers, he noted, when they were in fact invaders. 'The persistent refusal to recognize that theirs was a conquest society … was an evasion far reaching in its consequences. The Aborigines are the absent centre of colonialism.'[37]

Although Stuart also refers to 'Pearson's warning of the teeming Asian hordes' and growing anxieties about the racial purity of the nation, the voices of the activist Chinese colonists and those parliamentary liberals who supported them in arguing for a more liberal liberalism, one opposed to the oppression of foreigners and racial discrimination, are absent from *A Colonial Liberalism*. Yet the indefinite article of the title invites us, I think, to consider other kinds of colonial liberalism than the version espoused by the democratic radicals Higinbotham, Syme and Pearson, an arguably more progressive liberalism which rejected the argument that equality meant exclusion and democracy necessitated discrimination. In their advocacy of the rights of mobility and the idea of human rights without distinction, Chinese colonists and their white liberal supporters anticipated an internationally oriented multicultural democracy that would become the dominant Australian ideal of the late twentieth century. But in the 1880s it was the nationalist version of liberalism that won the day. The issue at stake for the colony, said Pearson, was the 'national existence' of the people of Victoria.[38]

The story of *A Colonial Liberalism* comes to an end in the late nineteenth century before the national existence of the Victorian people was realised with Federation and the inauguration of the Commonwealth of Australia. In a final section on 'Masculinity and nationalism', Stuart noted that as 'the nation assumed a sacral significance, membership was redefined to demand specific qualities'.[39] Indeed the new Commonwealth of Australia became a self-declared 'white man's country' that enshrined a white man's 'standard of living', as Stuart explores elsewhere in his histories of industrial arbitration and the labour movement.[40] Alfred Deakin, as the first Attorney-General of the Commonwealth of Australia, explained the necessity of racial exclusion to the new federal parliament in these terms: '... it is nothing less than the national manhood, the national character and the national future that are at stake'.[41]

In *A Colonial Liberalism* Stuart offers a sympathetic, rich and memorable account of the radical visions and gendered subjectivities of three leading colonial democrats: George Higinbotham, David Syme and Charles Pearson, and 'their need as men to achieve mastery of their circumstances'.[42] In so doing, he illuminates the ways in which the imperatives of white nineteenth-century radical manhood, their need as men to achieve mastery—including over national borders through the White Australia Policy—shaped Australian nation-building in the decades to come.

Notes

1   Marilyn Lake, 'The politics of respectability: Identifying the masculinist context', *Historical Studies*, vol. 22, no. 86, 1986, p. 116; Joan W. Scott's 'Gender: A useful category of historical analysis' was published later the same year in *American Historical Review*, vol. 91, no. 5, 1986.

2   See Marilyn Lake, 'The politics of respectability: Identifying the masculinist context', in Gillian Whitlock and David Carter (eds), *Images of Australia*, University of Queensland Press, St Lucia, 1992; Marilyn Lake, 'The politics of respectability: Identifying the masculinist context', in Susan Magarey, Sue Rowley and Susan Sheridan (eds), *Debutante Nation: Feminism Contests the 1890s*, Allen & Unwin, Sydney, 1993; Marilyn Lake, 'The politics of respectability: Identifying the masculinist context', in Penny Russell and Richard White (eds), *Pastiche: Reflections on Nineteenth-century Australia*, Allen & Unwin, Sydney, 1994.

3   Stuart Macintyre, *A Colonial Liberalism: The Lost World of Three Victorian Visionaries*, Oxford University Press, Melbourne, 1991, pp. 15–16, quoted in Marilyn Lake, *Progressive New World: How Settler Colonialism and Transpacific Exchange Shaped American Reform*, Harvard University Press, Cambridge MA, 2019, p. 2.

4   Macintyre, *A Colonial Liberalism*, p. 15.

5   Ibid., p. 12.

6   Marilyn Lake, 'The brightness of eyes and quiet assurance which seem to say American: Alfred Deakin's identification with republican manhood', *Australian Historical Studies*, vol. 38, no. 129, 2007, pp. 34–7.

7   Royce quoted in Lake, *Progressive New World*, pp. 1–3, 45, 62.

8   Macintyre, *A Colonial Liberalism*, p. 27.

9   Ibid., p. 27.

10 Ibid., p. 207.

11 Ibid., p. 24.

12 Ibid., p. 34.

13 Ibid., p. 196.

14 Ibid., p. 97.

15 Marilyn Lake and Henry Reynolds, *Drawing the Global Colour Line: White Men's Countries and the International Challenge of Racial Equality*, Cambridge University Press and Melbourne University Press, Melbourne, 2008, pp. 15–45.

16 Ibid., p. 35.

17 Marilyn Lake, 'The gendered and racialised self who claimed the right to self-government', *Journal of Colonialism and Colonial History*, vol. 13, no. 1, 2012, pp. 11–12.

18 *Victorian Parliamentary Debates*, Legislative Assembly, 24 June 1884, p. 231.

19 C.H. Pearson, 'On the working of Australian institutions' in *Essays on Reform*, Macmillan, London, 1867, pp. 191–216.

20 *VPD*, Legislative Assembly, 4 October 1881, p. 220.

21 Lowe Kong Meng, Cheok Hong Cheong and Louis Ah Mouy, *The Chinese Question in Australia 1878–79*, F.F. Bailliere, Melbourne, 1879, pp. 5–9.

22 Marilyn Lake, 'Chinese colonists assert their "common human rights": Cosmopolitanism as subject and method of history', *Journal of World History*, vol. 21, no. 3, 2010, pp. 383–4.

23   Lowe Kong Meng, Cheok Hong Cheong and Louis Ah Mouy, *The Chinese Question*, pp. 29–30.
24   Ibid.
25   Lake and Reynolds, *Drawing the Global Colour Line*, pp. 39–40.
26   *Age*, Melbourne, 17 April 1888.
27   Ibid., p. 40.
28   Macintyre, *A Colonial Liberalism*, p. 177.
29   *Victorian Law Reports*, vol. XIV, Supreme Court, Chung Teong Toy v. Musgrove, pp. 378–9.
30   Gwyneth Dow, 'Higinbotham, George (1826–1892)', *Australian Dictionary of Biography*, Melbourne University Press, Melbourne, vol. 4, 1972.
31   Geoffrey Serle, *The Rush to be Rich: A History of the Colony of Victoria 1883–1889*, Melbourne University Press, Melbourne, 1971.
32   *VPD*, Legislative Assembly, 10 November 1881, p. 700.
33   *VPD*, Legislative Assembly, 6 December 1888, p. 2369.
34   Lake and Reynolds, *Drawing the Global Colour Line*, p. 43.
35   Macintyre, *A Colonial Liberalism*, p. 203.
36   Ibid., p. 207.
37   Ibid., p. 211.
38   Marilyn Lake, 'Equality and exclusion: The racial constitution of colonial liberalism', *Thesis Eleven*, vol. 95, 2008, pp. 20–32.
39   Macintyre, *A Colonial Liberalism*, p. 213.
40   Stuart Macintyre, *The Labour Experiment*, McPhee Gribble Publishers, Melbourne, 1989; Stuart Macintyre and Richard Mitchell (eds), *Foundations of Arbitration: The Origins and Effects of State Compulsory Arbitration, 1880–1914*, Oxford University Press, Melbourne, 1989.
41   Lake and Reynolds, *Drawing the Global Colour Line*, pp. 139–40.
42   Macintyre, *A Colonial Liberalism*, p. 197.

Chapter 8

Stuart Macintyre's new province for labour history

Arbitration, the Labor Party and Federation

Frank Bongiorno

In 1976 Stuart Macintyre returned from Cambridge to teach at Murdoch University in Perth. The university was only beginning its second year of teaching, and Stuart was not yet 30. Up to that time, all his research work had been in British history. As Stuart looked around sun-drenched Perth, wondering how he 'fitted into this place', he did what many Australian intellectuals and academics before him had done in their effort to find a window onto the national soul. He read Henry Lawson and Joseph Furphy. 'I discovered after all I would be an Australian historian.'[1]

There was a broadly national context and purpose in much of Stuart's work as a historian since the late 1970s. He explained that his 'burgeoning interest in history' as an undergraduate at the University of Melbourne had 'its basis in political engagement'.[2] It was therefore not surprising that as an Australian who studied British history at Cambridge but then decided to work in Australia as a historian of Australia—and one with Stuart's belief that understanding history was essential to productive engagement with politics—he would gravitate to writing about the nation's foundational political values and institutions.

This chapter is concerned with Stuart's writings on Federation, the Labor Party and arbitration, with a focus on the formative period of the making of the Commonwealth of Australia: the era between 1890 and 1914. Interestingly, Stuart never wrote a book specifically on any of these topics. We need to go to general histories, co-edited collections, scholarly articles and public lectures to build up a picture of Stuart's understanding of these matters, including the relationship between them. Even while he pursued other historical interests, Stuart returned to these subjects repeatedly in the period between 1978 and 2004. Sometimes, as in the case of the centenaries of Federation, the federal Parliamentary Labor Party and the federal arbitration system, the impulse was commemorative. But there was also a substantial engagement with the history of the labour movement, the Labor Party and the arbitration system in the 1980s that had nothing to do with such memory work. Indeed, Stuart's preoccupations with these subjects need to be placed in the wider context of his concern with how Australia has been made and transformed through the dynamic interactions of structure and agency. His research on the social sciences, the universities, postwar reconstruction and even the Communist Party, while beyond the scope of this chapter, were also very much a part of this concern with how a distinctively Australian national modernity came about.

Stuart's preoccupation with the foundations of the Australian nation occurred at a time in the 1980s and 1990s when those values and institutions were called into question and, in some cases, either destroyed or changed beyond recognition. As he remarks in an elegiac conclusion to his little book *The Labour Experiment*, the Hawke Labor government had presided over extensive dismantling of the policies that the labour movement had helped to craft over almost a century. He noticed that, up to that time (1989), the labour market had been an exception to this extensive deregulation, 'though it remains to be seen whether the arbitration system can stand alone as a single tree where once there was a forest. If it falls too, the political economy that the Australian labour movement helped to establish will have finally ended.'[3] Within a few years, he had his answer, even if vestiges of the old system would survive the industrial relations changes of the Keating Labor and Howard Coalition governments.

Stuart emerged in Australia in the 1960s and early 1970s as a New Left intellectual. Active in the Communist Party in Britain, where he joined others in seeking 'to empty the Stalinist cargo from the revolutionary vessel', he gravitated to Labor on returning to live in Australia permanently.[4] He did so at a time when Labor was on the verge of one of its unusual decades of political dominance. But as his commentary at the end of *The Labour Experiment* indicates, these Labor governments would not be like those of the past. They dismantled many aspects of the country's institutional legacy of the Federation era, even as they claimed to be pursuing Labor tradition.[5] Compulsory arbitration, tariff protection, state paternalism: the values and institutions of the protective state came under fierce political criticism and intense pressure from within the Labor Party, as well as from critics on a Right invigorated by the free-market temper of the times.[6]

Stuart was by no means unique as a former communist seeking to engage with and influence mainstream labour politics in the 1980s.[7] But as the decade unfolded, the hopes with which the Left set out were more commonly disappointed than fulfilled. As he would point out in an address to a Labor Party National Conference in 1994, pragmatism was not enough, compromise was dangerous if divorced from principle, and traditions needed to be renewed: 'True believers need beliefs.'[8] Yet it is testament to Stuart's creativity as an intellectual, citizen and historian that he was able to find a way through these pressures via an extraordinary body of historical and historically informed writing, teaching, public speaking and public service, an effort that never lost sight of Marx's insight that the point is not only to interpret the world but also to change it.

Arbitration, Labour and liberalism

'The things that interest me in teaching and writing, I now see,' Stuart explained in the mid-1990s, 'are those things to which I have a strong attachment (that is my filial piety) and an unresolved ambiguity (that is the oedipal element).'[9] Stuart's interest in arbitration drew on both impulses. It was a distinctively Australian—or Australasian—solution to the problem of how to manage relations between capital and labour. It appealed to his attachment to Australia and his admiration of the efforts Australians had made to bring social justice to the heart of their social order. Stuart's background in British labour history, where he encountered a state less involved in the market, a union movement less enamoured of state interference in its affairs and, in its formative period, a Labour Party less able to envisage gaining control of the state to support its goals, led him to ask novel questions about arbitration.[10]

His starting point was Brian Fitzpatrick, whom Stuart had heard speak at Melbourne University late in the life of the famed Melbourne economic historian and public intellectual. Fitzpatrick had treated arbitration as the means by which 'beaten unionists could be induced to accept their lowly status'.[11] While the Marxist in Stuart admired Fitzpatrick's capacity to bring class analysis to his account, he was dissatisfied with this interpretation.[12] Stuart asked a more fundamental question, one that had rarely if ever figured in the historiography: why did labour assume that it could 'employ its electoral strength to wrest the state away from the control of its enemies and use it to bring about a new economic and social order?'[13] It is hard to miss that those such as Stuart who had come to the Labor Party from the non-ALP Left were asking similar questions about their own political involvement in the 1980s.

Stuart's *Winners and Losers: The Pursuit of Social Justice in Australian History* is in many ways a long answer to that question. Stuart shows that a mixture of British custom—a moral economy—had combined with the early and extensive involvement of the state in economic and social life, the activities of social movements and the efforts of the occasional visionary individual to encourage a habit of turning to government for assistance and support.[14] When he came to examine compulsory arbitration, he found that both the labour movement and the liberals who helped to create that system had few qualms about relying on the state—not only to resolve industrial disputes but also to lay the foundations for a peculiarly Australasian welfare system that relied on supporting the wages of the male breadwinner to protect the family from the cold chill of capitalism.

If there was filial piety here—a quiet pride in an Australian institution—there was also ambivalence. The latter found expression in Stuart's account of the role of liberals in initiating arbitration. As Stuart himself put it, his own radical politics 'were formulated as a rejection of liberalism', and his earliest writing in Australian history vigorously criticises bourgeois academic history's liberal assumptions.[15] 'The academic study of history', declared the 25-year-old Marxist in the journal *Intervention*, 'begets dissenting liberalism.' And he makes it clear that he does not rate it highly as either the basis for history or politics.[16]

By the mid-1980s, Stuart was still preoccupied with liberalism, but his attitude to it had softened. Now, he credited liberals with having played the most influential role in the emergence of compulsory arbitration in Australia and New Zealand. Support for this 'new province for law and order', as the second president of the Commonwealth Court of Conciliation and Arbitration, Henry Bournes Higgins, had called it, was a product of liberals' aspiration to harmonise relations between capital and labour. Their efforts occurred against the background of the 1890s strikes, as well as the depression of the 1890s: they wanted to stabilise a settler capitalism revealed as vulnerable to the external shocks of plunging commodity prices and capital investment. Stuart's remained a class analysis rooted in the conditions of settler capitalism; the legacy of his Marxism was clear enough, as well as a debt to the recent work of Donald Denoon.[17] The character of the economy, the balance of class forces and their expression in politics helped explain when legislative innovation occurred and the shape that it assumed in different places. The unions were too weak to create arbitration. Employers were too divided to stop it. Factions of capital involved in pastoralism, mining and transport were opposed to giving a weakened labour movement a leg up via state intervention, but urban manufacturers saw advantages in such a system, not least in protecting both them and their workers from unfair competition. For Stuart, arbitration emerged out of the agency of neither capital nor labour: the process displayed the 'relative autonomy of the state'.[18]

The common feature was rather the role of the colonial liberals. It was their understanding of the circumstances they encountered—especially growing class antagonism and industrial conflict—that resulted in arbitration courts and wages boards. In the face of rising class conflict, national tension and racial fear, their liberalism became less confident in the efficacy of its own rationalism and more preoccupied with using state power to control irrational and harmful impulses that they worried might tear society asunder.[19] The institutional structures that emerged reflected this evolving civic ideology.

Stuart was accordingly sceptical of the role of the unions and the Labor Party in creating arbitration. Here, he was entering a long-running debate—one that by the 1980s had run its course—about whether Labor ought to be considered a 'party of initiative' and its opponents 'parties of resistance'.[20] In the case of arbitration, Stuart thought the Labor Party too lacking in influence in most jurisdictions to have played a determinant role and the unions insufficiently committed before 1900 to have been the critical force in bringing it into existence. He did not argue his line dogmatically: he recognised that in the case of New South Wales, Labor exercised some influence in the establishment of the system at the turn of the century, even allowing that the Oxford-educated new liberal Bernhard Wise was the chief architect. But Stuart argues forcefully that Labor was unable to initiate or even substantially shape the system. In the Commonwealth, it was the Free Trade government of George Reid, supported by conservative Protectionists, who would eventually bring a long-running and contentious process to fruition in 1904. Stuart did concede to the rising power of Labor in the years before World War I, culminating in the first majority Labor government in

1910, a role in consolidating a system that was otherwise under pressure from both employers and the High Court.[21]

None of this was ever quite settled; the arbitration system remained contentious, with conservatives and employers seeking to undermine its ability to promote union organisation and improve wages and conditions. But there was also opposition on the Left, among some socialists, unionists and syndicalists. For Stuart, a new balance of class forces inevitably produced a new politics of industrial relations. But for most of the century, there was never a balance of forces sufficient to destroy the system.[22] The concept of path dependence was only beginning to take off when Stuart was writing in the 1980s, but Stuart was essentially grappling with an example of it without using the theoretical concepts that were emerging in a body of theory now called historical institutionalism. But his Marxist concern with the central role of capitalist development and class provided him with tools for explaining both innovation and stasis.

Stuart was ambivalent about arbitration for other reasons than its origins. He stressed its masculinism. Stuart was himself the father of a young family by the 1980s, and his early writings on arbitration return repeatedly to its protection of the interests of the male breadwinner and its role in reinforcing an existing sexual division of labour. Here, Stuart was drawing on an emerging body of feminist scholarship.[23] But he was equally influenced by Francis Castles's concept of the 'wage-earners' welfare state'.[24] Stuart's account of arbitration and the labour movement emphasises that centring the male breadwinner wage had powerful implications for the subsequent history of the welfare state, rendering 'superfluous any large-scale supplementation of market outcomes' via the kinds of universalist measures associated with European social democracy—such as generous provision of public housing or health care.[25] Instead, the wage-earner's welfare state sought to modify market outcomes to support the breadwinner and his family through a living wage. In *Intervention* in 1977 Stuart contrasts 'Laborism', based on the organised working class and preoccupied with defending those interests through the wage system, with a vague and eclectic socialism that had come to the early Labor Party from petit-bourgeois intellectuals.[26] But in the following decade he also came to contrast labourism, understood as the foundation for the Labor Party over its longer history, with a more expansive social democracy that he believed had been trialled belatedly by the Whitlam government and strangled at birth by the end of the long boom and the return to conservative government.

There was a final reason for Stuart's ambivalence about arbitration. He believed it was a poor instrument for achieving its ostensible purpose of protecting the living standards of the working class. In the end, he thought arbitration had not significantly altered the 'distribution of economic rewards'. The efforts of employers and judges to hamper the arbitration system—and the departure from the living wage concept towards a stress on the capacity of industry to pay—undermined the capacity of the court to support good wages and conditions. In the end, wage levels tended to be regulated more by the cycles of the capitalist economy than by state intervention. More generally, tariffs, arbitration and a parsimonious system of social security were unable to insulate Australia's commodity-based economy from the powerful shocks that an unstable international economic order meted out in the years between the 1890s and the 1940s, and again from the mid-1970s.[27]

In later work on arbitration, such as his long chapter on the history of federal arbitration in a 2004 centenary collection he edited with the economist and arbitration commission deputy president Joe Isaac, Stuart the seasoned academic examined the impact of political interference, legislative change, judicial decision-making, staffing, accommodation and the play of personality on the workings of the system. The evocation of those who ran the system is rich: Higgins 'had known the pinch of poverty but not the sweat and grind of manual toil, the aching limbs and shortened breath—his hands were smooth'. And there was a preoccupation with the detail of how institutions worked: 'During conciliation, the jackets came off, cigarettes were lit and participants addressed each other by their first name.' That is the kind of concern with personal and institutional detail that one might expect not only of a historian at the height of his powers but also perhaps a former departmental head and present Dean of Arts—one who had now spent a significant part of his career combining historical research with university administration and committee work. Still, Stuart attends to the big picture: arbitration was 'a bold experiment and distinctively Australian institution'.[28]

Federation, the Labor Party and democracy

Stuart was sceptical about the influence the labour movement and the Labor Party had been able to exert over Australia's political economy. Part of the problem was its precocity: Labor was in government in Australia—even majority government—while still barely tolerated in many other Western countries.[29] Labor had no choice but to confront difficult social questions decades before its counterparts elsewhere. It did not withstand that strain particularly well.

Labor precocity, for Stuart, helped account for its ideological narrowness. It became captive to deeply entrenched ways of seeing the social order, embracing the settler capitalist enthusiasm for racial exclusion with notable enthusiasm, and relying on a moral economy that upheld the rights of the male 'wealth-producer' but had little to say on behalf of anyone else. The policy experimentation of European social democracy held little attraction. In the state jurisdictions, where it would have more electoral success, it became closely identified with state-sponsored development and a 'spoils to the victor' form of politics that won votes but also produced cynicism and corruption. In the more sophisticated industrialised economy of the postwar era, this politics was overwhelmed by non-Labor administrations prepared to hitch their wagon to big business.[30]

One factor that limited Labor's ability to implement its goals was the federal Constitution. The Australian Federation was the product mainly of bourgeois politicians, some of a conservative stamp. The Constitution that emerged from these proceedings did not reflect the more radical version of democracy being championed by the early Labor Party. Stuart narrated the process by which, at citizens' and people's conventions such as those at Corowa in 1893 and Bathurst in 1896, radical democratic and republican interventions by the isolated labourite, socialist or republican were deflected by those of a more conservative, imperialist and pragmatic bent.[31] Still, Stuart's account of Federation is one marked by contestation, contingency and personality. He resists the 1950s and 1960s habit of reducing the federal movement and the Federation process to a struggle between interest groups. At the same time, he departed from radical–nationalist interpretations of Federation as a capitalist plot to ensnare the working class, as well as the revisionist argument of the conservative republican historian John Hirst that it was a miraculous expression of democratic popular sovereignty.[32] This left a narrow space for interpretation that was both distinctive and persuasive.

The result is an interpretation of Federation notable for its scholarly subtlety and pertinence to the politics of the 1990s, as well as being prescient about the wider dangers for democracy of the stoking of popular prejudice against 'politics' and 'politicians'. Written mainly at the invitation of various organisations, institutions and the editors of essay collections and journals in the period leading up to the Centenary of Federation, Stuart used his writings on the subject to develop a broad interpretation of the character of Australian democracy:

> The antagonism to politics and politicians is a vein running through Australian political history … It seems to surface episodically at moments of social distress and national strain. It produces short-lived campaigns to clean up politics, fiercely antagonistic to the politicians who are blamed for the shortcomings of representative democracy, with an energy that is then absorbed back into the political parties whose shortcomings generated the discontent.

Stuart argued that this disillusionment with democracy, dismissed as a hunting ground for venal, corrupt and self-serving politicians, was in place in the very earliest years of self-government in the mid-nineteenth century and rooted in its horse-trading style.[33] Also developed in his work on liberalism is an account of Australian political culture that deserves a far wider influence than those that have stressed the political culture's fundamental utilitarianism above all else.[34]

As in his explanation of the origins of arbitration, Stuart emphasised the role of liberals and relative paucity of labour influence on the arrangements eventually agreed. Nonetheless, he still finds a significant role for the Labor Party, and for radicals in general, in his story. While the *Australian* in 'Australian Labor Party' signalled the strength of that party's commitment to nationalism, that party's hostility to the 1891 draft constitution would help prove fatal to the movement early in the decade. Labor combined with the emerging Free Trade leader and rival to Henry Parkes, George Reid, to veto further moves by that colony towards federation. At critical junctures in the road to federation during the 1890s, such as at the convention in the border town of Corowa in 1893, the marginalisation of radical and republican voices by more conservative forces continued the isolation of the labour movement from the federal movement and loosened federalists' embrace of popular sovereignty.[35]

Crucially, Stuart's close study of the tactics and rhetoric of key leaders of the federal movement showed that they had fostered support for their cause by impugning their own profession of politics and pretending that federation would only be achieved by 'the people' if they shunned 'the politicians'. Stuart was not impressed by this populism. In reality, the process of achieving federation was in essence political, its leaders were practising politicians, and the whole effort was one to create a national political system where there had previously been six separate, rival and barely connected colonies. Not only did Stuart see this sleight of hand as hypocritical but also he argued that it involved an appeal to that popular prejudice against political democracy which, as we have seen, he regards as a deeper strain in the culture. These politicians, with their attenuated understanding of popular sovereignty, invoked 'the people' in their rhetoric, and they provided the method by which citizens could elect representatives to a convention and then have a say, through a referendum, on a draft federal bill. But in resorting to the vote, they also created a mythical and disembodied 'people' who were supposedly 'capable of an altruism that they themselves could not achieve'.[36]

Stuart's dissection of popular prejudice against politics is prescient of the crisis in which we now find ourselves. What is Scott Morrison's appeal to his 'Quiet Australians' if not a reprise of the populism of federal leaders? Rather like the outpourings of John Quick, Edmund Barton and George Reid, but without the substance of their achievement, is it the appeal of a man whose career has been almost entirely in politics, who seeks to exploit the notion that real Australians do not engage in that business? And what is Trumpism, or the prime ministership of Boris Johnson, if not a similar kind of anti-political politics, based on the illusion that they were not truly politicians but some other species of being?

As in his mature work on arbitration, Stuart's on Federation is rich in personality and ideas, incident and language. It is also a contested and even counterfactual history. There is a sense that things might have worked out differently—notably in the form of a more democratic Constitution. (He appears to have been less engaged with the possibility that it might not have happened at all, although he saw the prospect that it might only include the south-east given the hesitations in Queensland and Western Australia.)[37] In a lecture to mark the centenary of the 1898 referendum in Victoria, for instance, he noted that while the majority for 'Yes' was clear, David Syme at the *Age* as well as the liberal government of George Turner hesitated to support the draft federal bill, not convinced that it was in the interests of their colony until Deakin probably persuaded them otherwise. Moreover, H.B. Higgins, Labor and the unions were hampered by their lateness in launching the 'No' case.[38]

The vision of a republic, hanging by the most tenuous threads in the 1890s but in the political mainstream a century later (and he was involved with the Australian Republican Movement), haunts Stuart's account of Federation. He was unable to share Hirst's sunny account of the federal movement because Stuart was much more conscious of the ways the federalists had policed the boundaries of their movement, to ensure that radicals and republicans, no less than Chinese and Aboriginal people, were outside the charmed circle.[39] At the end of his account of the Corowa conference, Stuart echoed E.M. Forster on democracy by giving two cheers for Federation. But he clearly wanted Australians to remember it, and he bemoaned their habit, in line with the strain of hostility to politics and politicians in their culture, of erasing their political and civic endeavour from collective memory and commemorative culture, as well as the marginalisation of such activity through shifting historiographical and intellectual fashion.[40]

The restrained applause can be extended to much of what Stuart found in the Australian labour movement and to the institutions devised (as he argued) by liberals to respond to the challenges it posed to the established order. The first federal Labor Caucus, he concluded in the centenary history of the Federal Parliamentary Labor Party he co-edited with Labor Senate Leader John Faulkner, 'was broadly representative of the labour movement … a white brotherhood that was exclusive in its composition and outlook, and which nevertheless aspired to a more decent, democratic and equal Australia'.[41]

Still, Stuart's sympathies with Labor and the Left extended through his adult life. Stuart was active in the Australian Society for the Study of Labour History, serving as president and one of its review editors. He numbered many Labor politicians among his friends and could be seen handing out how-to-vote cards in his suburb of Brunswick: a Melbourne working-class bastion that has gentrified as professionals such as history professors made their home there. Labor and Greens now compete for allegiance in such suburbs, but Stuart's own sympathies and interests remained rooted in his ambivalent identification with the cultures of labourism, socialism and liberalism explored in his historical work. These were the ingredients of his own political ideals and civic identity, and they were accompanied by a gentle patriotism that found expression in public service and historical scholarship rather than jingoism and flag-waving. I recall much that Stuart taught me as an undergraduate, but I have never forgotten his comment in an honours seminar that even while we might deprecate the influence of nationalism, many of us feel the hairs standing up on the backs of our necks when our allegiance is engaged.

Stuart was never shy of drawing attention to Australia's success. The 'black armband' that is supposedly essential attire for 'leftist historians' never attracted him much. Stuart knew too much Australian history to be able to overlook the country's notable success of recent decades, its growing wealth, the rise of educational opportunity, the greater equality of women and First Nations people, and the success of multiculturalism—and all while recognising democratic decay, policy failure, worsening economic inequality, declining public provision and environmental destruction.[42]

I never asked him, but I imagine that Stuart would also have offered two cheers for Australia. This is the only response that any intelligent and civilised citizen should offer even the happiest of lands this side of the millennium.

Notes

1   Stuart Macintyre, 'True for the moment', in Bain Attwood (ed.), *Labour Histories: Robin Gollan, Stuart Macintyre, Verity Burgmann, Peter Beilharz, Raelene Frances*, Monash Publications in History, Department of History, Monash University, Clayton, Vic, 1994, p. 24.

2   Ibid., p. 20.

3   Stuart Macintyre, *The Labour Experiment*, McPhee Gribble Publishers, Melbourne, 1989, p. 65.

4   Stuart Macintyre, *The Reds: The Communist Party of Australia from Origins to Illegality*, Allen & Unwin, St Leonards, 1998, p. 1.

5   Peter Beilharz, *Transforming Labor: Labour Tradition and the Labor Decade in Australia*, Cambridge University Press, Cambridge, 1994, p. 78.

6   The standard account is Paul Kelly, *The End of Certainty: The Story of the 1980s*, Allen & Unwin, St Leonards, 1992.

7   Sean Scalmer and Terry Irving, 'The rise of the modern labour technocrat: Intellectual labour and the transformation of the Amalgamated Metal Workers' Union, 1973–85', *Labour History*, no. 77, 1999, pp. 64–82.

8   Stuart Macintyre, 'Who are the true believers?', Manning Clark Labor History Memorial Lecture, delivered by Stuart Macintyre at the ALP National Conference, Hobart, 28 September 1994, *Labour History*, no. 68, 1995, pp. 155–67.

9   Macintyre, 'True for the moment', p. 27.

10   Peter Mandler, 'Taking the state out again: The social history of modern Britain', *Journal of Interdisciplinary History*, vol. 22, no. 3, 1992, pp. 465–76.

11   Brian Fitzpatrick, *The British Empire in Australia: An Economic History 1834–1939* [1941], Macmillan, South Melbourne, 1969, p. 195.

12   Stuart Macintyre, 'Neither capital nor labour: The politics of the establishment of arbitration', in Stuart Macintyre and Richard Mitchell (eds), *Foundations of Arbitration: The Origins and Effects of State Compulsory Arbitration 1890–1914*, Oxford University Press, Melbourne, 1989, pp. 178–80.

13   Macintyre, *Labour Experiment*, p. 11.

14   Stuart Macintyre, *Winners and Losers: The Pursuit of Social Justice in Australian History*, Allen & Unwin, Sydney, 1985.

15   Macintyre, 'True for the moment', p. 27.

16   Stuart Macintyre, 'Radical history and bourgeois hegemony', *Intervention*, no. 2, 1972, p. 58.

17   Donald Denoon, *Settler Capitalism: The Dynamics of Dependent Development in the Southern Hemisphere*, Clarendon Press, Oxford, 1983.

18   S.F. Macintyre, 'Labour, capital and arbitration 1890–1920', in Brian Head (ed.), *State and Economy in Australia*, Oxford University Press, Melbourne, 1983, p. 104. See also Macintyre, '"Neither capital nor labour" and "Holt and the establishment of arbitration: An Australian perspective"', *New Zealand Journal of Industrial Relations*, vol. 12, no. 3, 1987, pp. 151–9.

19   Stuart Macintyre, *A Colonial Liberalism: The Lost World of Three Victorian Visionaries*, Oxford University Press, Melbourne, 1991, pp. 187–93.

20   For a recent revisiting of this debate, see Linda Courtenay Botterill and Alan Fenna, 'Initiative-resistance and the Australian party system', *Australian Journal of Politics and History*, vol. 66, no. 1, 2020, pp. 63–77.

21   Macintyre, 'Neither capital nor labour', pp. 191, 196.

22   Macintyre, 'Labour, capital and arbitration', pp. 110–11.

23   For example Edna Ryan and Anne Conlon, *Gentle Invaders: Australian Women at Work 1788–1974*, Thomas Nelson, Melbourne, 1975, and Marilyn Lake, 'Historical reconsiderations IV: The politics of respectability: Identifying the masculinist context', *Australian Historical Studies*, vol. 22, no. 86, 1986, pp. 116–31.

24   Francis G. Castles, *The Working Class and Welfare: Reflections on the Political Development of the Welfare State in Australia and New Zealand, 1890–1980*, Allen & Unwin in association with Port Nicholson Press, Wellington and Sydney, 1985.

25   Stuart Macintyre, 'The short history of social democracy in Australia', *Thesis Eleven*, no. 15, 1986, p. 5.

26   Stuart Macintyre, 'The concept of class in recent labourist historiography: Early socialism and labor', *Intervention*, no. 8, 1977, pp. 79–87.

27   Macintyre, *Labour Experiment*, pp. 47, 51.

28   Stuart Macintyre, 'Arbitration in action', in Joe Isaac and Stuart Macintyre (eds), *The New Province for Law and Order: 100 Years of Australian Industrial Conciliation and Arbitration*, Cambridge University Press, Cambridge, 2004, pp. 62, 86–7, 97.

29   Macintyre, *Labour Experiment*, p. 65.

30   Ibid., p. 61.

31   Stuart Macintyre, 'Corowa and the voice of the people', *Canberra Historical Journal*, n.s., no. 33, 1994, pp. 2–8; Stuart Macintyre, 'After Corowa', *Victorian Historical Journal*, vol. 65, no. 2, 1994, pp. 98–111; Stuart Macintyre, 'The idea of the people', in David Headon and Jeff Brownrigg (eds), *The People's Conventions: Corowa (1893) and Bathurst (1896)*, Papers on Parliament no. 32, Special Issue, Department of the Senate, Parliament House, Canberra, December 1998, pp. 76–9.

32   Stuart Macintyre, 'The fortunes of Federation', in David Headon and John Williams (eds), *Makers of Miracles: The Cast of the Federation Story*, Melbourne University Press, Carlton, 2000, pp. 3–17.

33   The wider argument is articulated in Stuart Macintyre, '"A parcel o'rogues in a nation": Australian attitudes to politics and politicians', 2002 Reid Oration, unpublished lecture in possession of the author, pp. 12–13.

34   Hugh Collins, 'Political ideology in Australia: The distinctiveness of a Benthamite society', *Daedalus*, vol. 114, no. 1, 1985, pp. 147–69.

35   Stuart Macintyre, 'Federation and the labour movement', in Mark Hearn and Greg Patmore (eds), *Working the Nation: Working Life and Federation, 1890–1914*, Pluto Press, Annandale, 2001, pp. 11–25.

36   Macintyre, 'The idea of the people', p. 77.

37   Stuart Macintyre, 'Some absentees from Adelaide', *New Federalist*, no. 1, 1998, pp. 16–17.

38   Stuart Macintyre, 'Victorians and Federation: The first referendum of 1898', unpublished lecture in possession of the author, delivered to the Royal Historical Society of Victoria, 26 May 1998.

39   Macintyre, 'Some absentees from Adelaide', p. 17.

40   Stuart Macintyre, 'Introduction', in Alfred Deakin, *'And Be One People': Alfred Deakin's Federal Story*, Melbourne University Press, Carlton, 1995, pp. xxvii–xxviii.

41   Stuart Macintyre, 'The first caucus', in John Faulkner and Stuart Macintyre (eds), *True Believers: The Story of the Federal Parliamentary Labor Party*, Allen & Unwin, Sydney, 2001, p. 29.

42   Stuart Macintyre, *A Concise History of Australia*, 5th edn, Cambridge University Press, Cambridge, 2020, pp. 322–8.

Chapter 9

Collaborating with Stuart

Sheila Fitzpatrick

When I first collaborated with Stuart, what astonished me was the extent to which he inhabited the world of his subjects.

The occasion was a collected volume, based on a 2006 conference in Melbourne, which we were jointly editing for Melbourne University Press.[1] The subjects of our collaboration were two Australian historians: Brian Fitzpatrick and Manning Clark. Given that Brian Fitzpatrick was my father and Manning Clark a family friend whom I had known since childhood, I had a lot of personal connections with our subject matter. Re-reading my correspondence with Stuart during the editing process, I see that I assumed quite an authoritative tone on interpretive issues involving Fitzpatrick, based both on private knowledge and recent research in the Fitzpatrick papers and those of others in his circle in the National Library of Australia. That authoritativeness must have been to some extent a façade. Over four decades of living outside Australia, my Australian memories had dulled.

When, a few years later, I sat down in my visitor's office at the University of Sydney to start writing a memoir of my childhood, my first impression was that if I wrote down absolutely everything I could remember on every trivial aspect of my life up to 16, from great-aunts' gardens to AMEB exams, it might just stretch to a long essay.[2] So, while I may have tried to convince Stuart that I was an authority on Brian Fitzpatrick and, to a lesser extent, Manning Clark, my private reaction was quite different. It was not just that I recognised that Stuart, as an Australian historian of rare breadth and erudition, knew their milieu better than I did. What was startling was that Stuart actually seemed to know them better as people, too.

In our editorial correspondence, the thing that seemed to be bothering me most was Stuart's suggestion that Fitzpatrick, in contrast to Clark, had fallen into total obscurity. This was partly, no doubt, a difference of temporal perspective. I, as a young adult, had had the painful feeling that my father's lifework, as historian and civil libertarian, had come to nothing, and that seemed to be confirmed by what I gathered (from a distance) of Australian (non-)reaction to his death in 1965. Then, on my first visit to Australia for fifteen years at the end of the 1970s, in Canberra in the wake of the Whitlam years, I was astonished to find that he had apparently achieved a posthumous renaissance as a minor hero/martyr of the Left. It perhaps had not occurred to me that this renaissance was as a colourful radical character rather than as a historian, or that what remained filed in my mind as contemporary Australian opinion was now almost thirty years old. Stuart, in any case, politely resisted my pressure on the 'obscurity' issue, not significantly shifting his position ('obscurity' became 'comparative obscurity'). It was only when I came back to Australia in 2012 and had a look at some Australian history syllabi that I saw how right he was.

Readers of our separate chapters in *Against the Grain* might be forgiven for thinking that the author with a personal understanding of Fitzpatrick was not the one who shared his last name but Stuart Macintyre. My piece, 'Brian Fitzpatrick and the world outside Australia', was a rather impersonal exploration of what access (in terms of publications) Fitzpatrick—and others of his generation, especially those without the financial means to travel—had to reliable information about the world outside Australia; it was based mainly on archival research in the Fitzpatrick papers in the National

Library, only occasionally supplemented by memory of what books were on our shelves at home. Stuart's lead essay, 'The radical and the mystic: Brian Fitzpatrick, Manning Clark and Australian history', on the other hand, was a vivid double portrait based not just on extensive research but also on what seemed like a comfortably intimate *knowledge*—all the more powerful for being presented so unpretentiously—of two unusual individuals and their relationship. There were things in Stuart's article I did not know (I left home for university in 1958 and Australia for graduate school in the UK in June 1964; my father died in September 1965), notably the intensity of his search for paid academic employment in the last decade of his life and the strength of the feeling of defeat that accompanied his failure ('My own situation is that I see no future,' Brian wrote to Clem Christesen in 1957). Stuart's evidence came from various archives (*Meanjin*'s, in the case of the quotation), but when he wrote about these matters, it was in the tone that might be used for talking, sympathetically but not uncritically, about one friend to another. I remember crying when I first read this passage, and I cried again this time.

One of the things Stuart captures about Brian, which I do not think was clear even in Don Watson's excellent life of him,[3] was Brian's strong sense of loyalty and a quixotic private code of honour that, unlike most people, he stuck to. Thus, when the first volume of Manning's *History* came out, Brian's private opinion of it was low ('the book may last for some time as a picture of Manning, may all the muses except Clio bless him,' he wrote to an intimate), but according to his rules, it would have been dishonourable to make any public criticism of the work of a friend, especially one who was already under attack from the Right, so he never said this in public. (It would be the same story a few years later with Clark's *Meeting Soviet Man*.) Stuart reports this sympathetically, but there is also a degree of sympathy in his account of Manning's non-reciprocation, notably in his somewhat duplicitous handling of Brian's job search, assuring Brian of his support but actually, behind the scenes, giving lukewarm to negative assessments.

It would be easy for a historian to skewer Manning on this kind of thing, but that is not Stuart's way. He may comment slightly waspishly that, in the effusive elegy he delivered after Brian's death, 'Manning was ... interring Brian in the mausoleum of his own concerns',[4] but at the same time he manages to convey Manning's elusive combination of high-flown generosity and petty meanness, of overblown rhetoric and real insight. When, on that 1979 visit to Canberra, Manning delivered an impromptu version of his elegy on Brian to me, I warmed to him and recognised the impulse as generous, even if at another level I did not believe a word of it.

A few years before I returned to Australia to live in 2012, I started tentatively reconnecting with the worlds of Australian history and Australian academia with which I had had little contact since undergraduate days. It is generally quite a tricky business dealing with a senior scholar from another field and another academic culture who is trying to find her way in yours—but not for Stuart. He was a wonderful resource of knowledge and research tips for me, totally without 'this is my turf' touchiness or any sense of awkwardness at, in effect, mentoring an equal. He simply seemed to enjoy talking about things he was interested in to somebody who was interested in learning. Sometimes, in our periodic lunchtime conversations at University House when I came down to Melbourne on a visit, he would say he had to look up a source, and the information would be duly dispatched by email within a day. But usually his huge store of knowledge about people and their networks and interactions (both historical and contemporary) was immediately accessible. He talked in the same way, with his characteristic grasp of detail, easy assurance and lack of malice, about people who were historical personae and those who were our academic contemporaries, so that the normal line between a historian and his subjects seemed to become diffuse and permeable.

When Stuart recently reviewed a book of mine in the *Australian Book Review*, he told readers, accurately and in surprising detail, who I was. Reading the review, I heard the same voice that, in my first years back in Australia, had told me who everyone else was. I was very pleased to find that I had acquired my own entry in the card index of Stuart's mind, next to Fitzpatrick, Brian, and Fitzpatrick, David, since he keeps the living and the dead in the same file. Stuart noted in his review (with approval or perhaps just factually—with Stuart you cannot always tell) that in the years away I had shown no interest in Australian history but was now trying my hand. Try as I may, however, I will never be able to equal Stuart's encyclopedic grasp of the historical actors and their historian-interpreters, or emulate his ability to make them live together in a single universe of the mind.

Notes

1   Stuart Macintyre and Sheila Fitzpatrick (eds), *Against the Grain: Brian Fitzpatrick and Manning Clark in Australian History and Politics*, Melbourne University Press, Melbourne, 2007. The conference was one of a series held at the University of Melbourne in July 2006 and funded by a Distinguished Achievement award granted to me during my tenure at the University of Chicago by the Andrew W. Mellon Foundation. Justified under the rubric of US–Australian intellectual cross-fertilisation, the conferences were also in effect a celebration of the 65th birthdays of Katerina Clark (Manning's daughter; professor at Yale University) and myself, most of them covering our respective scholarly fields of Soviet history and Soviet literature and involving our US postgraduate students and scholarly collaborators. The two conferences dealing with Australian history were 'Australian visitors to the Soviet Union in the 1930s–1950s', and 'Brian Fitzpatrick, Manning Clark and Australian history'. 'Australian visitors' also produced a collected volume: Sheila Fitzpatrick and Carolyn Rasmussen (eds), *Political Tourists: Travellers from Australia to the Soviet Union in the 1920s–1940s*, Melbourne University Press, Melbourne, 2008.
2   More memories came back after a while. The memoir was published as *My Father's Daughter: Memories of an Australian Childhood*, Melbourne University Press, Melbourne, 2010.
3   Don Watson, *Brian Fitzpatrick: A Radical Life*, Hale & Iremonger, Sydney, 1979.
4   Macintyre, 'The radical and the mystic', in Macintyre and Fitzpatrick, *Against the Grain*, p. 29.

Chapter 10

Departments and discussions

Stephen Knight

As an academic at the University of Sydney from the 1960s on, teaching Literature (English, American, Welsh and medieval European, not just, as the department narrowly called it, English), you might think I would have had little cognition of Stuart Macintyre. But my interest in radical literature, especially in my native Wales, made his 1980 book, from his Cambridge PhD, *A Proletarian Science: Marxism in Britain*, of considerable interest to me—and the flow of Melburnians into the Sydney campus in those days made him a figure of some familiarity.

When in 1986 I—or rather the family—was persuaded to accept the offer of the University of Melbourne's Robert Wallace chair of English Literature (at Sydney we lectured to 600 first-year students in a lecture theatre named for the same R.W., by then the local vice-chancellor), I soon encountered Stuart on a higher floor of the John Medley Building. We had genial conversations and on one occasion even shared presence in a cricket match, but I was by then a little elderly for that kind of thing, and we spent most of our interactive time socially and discussing matters of joint interest.

One of these was my scheme to write, eventually, an account of Welsh fiction in English, which had only started in the later nineteenth century, and a dominant theme of which was the radical politics Stuart had discussed in his PhD. Another shared topic, even more focal for me, was my developing work on crime fiction in Australia, especially the largely ignored nineteenth-century narratives, for which Stuart had a good deal to offer from his research on the early period which would appear in his major—and I suggest in general public terms *the* major—publication, *The Concise History of Australia*. Like his earlier comments, it would be helpful when I wrote *Continent of Mystery: A Thematic History of Australian Crime Fiction* (1997).

But before that there were also university matters to discuss and share, especially after I became head of English in 1989 and then deputy Dean, and Stuart was soon head of History: for him the deanship then only loomed ahead. In general these two large departments—in the austerely academic days before Media Studies and Creative Writing (we called the latter Me Studies)—trundled along amiably, and we were able together to exert some influence on university strategy. We also offered considerable dissent to the damaging innovation of federal Labor, via John Dawkins, imposing new, cost-cutting, employment-oriented structures on the formerly intellectually focused universities, which in Australia had become about as good as any in the world—although perhaps Canada was slightly ahead. In this context Stuart was very helpful, with many comments and explanations when I was writing the critique of this bleak new world that appeared in *The Selling of the Australian Mind* (1990).

Our co-departmental operations were not merely administrative or political. One day, as usual lunching in the genial—if less than sophisticated—staff club, we developed the idea of a shared course named 'The working class in Literature and History'. This would focus on novels from the nineteenth century on and set them in their political and historical contexts. Such a course was not common in English or History programs, and it soon became clear that there were some in both of our departments who thought this sort of operation was below respectable academicism—but as the proponents were the heads, there was for once little the conservatives could do.

The course was available to students in both departments, and began in 1990 with about thirty enrolled. It started internationally with Émile Zola's *Germinal*, from France, then American Jack London's *Iron Heel*, Walter Greenwood's *Love on the Dole*, English, and the Scottish Lewis Grassic Gibbon's *Scots Quair*, Welsh Lewis Jones's *Cwmardy* and George Orwell's *Road to Wigan Pier*, again English. But half the texts were Australian, with *The Working Man's Paradise* by William Lane, Harold Wells's *Earth Cries Out*, Frank Hardy's *Power Without Glory*, *A Poor Man's Orange* by Ruth Park and (I think my favourite) Dorothy Hewett's *Bobbin Up*. A feature I liked especially was that Stuart quite often taught the literary side and I would recurrently talk about the historical context. The students seemed genuinely engaged, discussed matters vigorously and wrote good essays. It was I think a fine course, and I have since—including only last year—heard from several students who found it one of their most interesting experiences.

But the course and our close relationship changed when in 1992, both seeking variety and also having a Euro-language-oriented daughter, I accepted appointment at a new university in Leicester, UK, named for the dubious medieval potentate Simon de Montfort. Stuart and I remained in touch, including when I moved on to Cardiff University, and we met several times over the years when one or the other crossed the globe. I consulted him consistently by the new magic of email on a range of matters, especially relating to earlier Australian authors and their contexts, as well as on the book on Welsh fiction, which appeared in 2004.

When I retired in 2011 we returned to the Victorian capital— the now adult children had bounced back to Australia—and I re-entered the University of Melbourne, as a Vice Chancellor's Fellow and then as an Honorary Research Professor in Literature, mostly supervising postgraduates, using the library and again regularly lunching with Stuart in the unchanged staff club.

His help remained as useful and direct as ever, as I have researched and written on the mid-nineteenth-century *Mysteries of the Cities* series across the world (2012), and on earlier Australia, for a new history of Australian crime writing (2018) and also for several essays and a planned book on Australian fiction before the bush myth. I have also deployed his advice—and indeed quoted his own work—in my return to the genre of socio-political critical essays in *The University is Closed for Open Day* (2019), which also benefited from a Macintyre encomium on the cover.

In all of this activity Stuart was most helpfully informative and the lunches excellent—socially, not gastronomically. As a most welcome addition over thirty-plus years there was the pleasure of listening to Stuart's account of his own research and writing—not to mention all those precise and generally unknown details about the past of local politics and politicians that only Stuart could offer in such rich and revealing detail.

Part 3

Historians

Chapter 11

A biographer's journey of revelation

Stuart Macintyre on Ernest Scott

Joy Damousi

On 23 May 1991, Stuart Macintyre delivered his public lecture as the newly appointed Ernest Scott Professor of History in Lecture Theatre D in the Old Arts Building at the University of Melbourne. The title of the lecture was 'Knowing and Possessing: Ernest Scott's Circumnavigation of History'. I recall sitting in a packed, over-flowing lecture theatre. A heightened sense of occasion and anticipation was palpable, as I took my place among Melbourne's history community, which had assembled in large numbers on a drizzly, cool Thursday evening. My work diary entry for that date suggests there were drinks afterwards. As a junior academic who had only recently completed my PhD (which Stuart had examined four years earlier) I was way too self-conscious to share in the revelry that may have followed deep into the night. Although I do remember the event as somewhat overwhelming, it was at the same time undeni-ably exciting. Everyone knew the significance of the moment: the event marked the arrival of the new Ernest Scott Chair—empty since 1981 when Geoffrey Blainey, who had held the chair since 1977, vacated it in 1982 to become Dean of the Faculty of Arts.

When I arrived in the Department of History at the university a year later, there was clearly a profound sense of how the Ernest Scott Chair and its new occupant had marked a moment in time in the history of the university, the history of the history discipline—and indeed in the history of Australian history.

I begin by mentioning the lecture and the chair appointment because both shaped what would become the basis of Stuart's biography of Scott, *A History for a Nation: Ernest Scott and the Making of Australian History*.

What can we learn from *A History for a Nation* as a biography and itself as a work of history? What threads does Stuart weave into it that not only alert us to the skill and craft of writing biography but also create a wider history through it?

Charting Scott's life, his work and his legacies in a full-scale study, Stuart sets, as one of his aims, navigation through the conflicting representations of Scott by previous scholars. These include those of John La Nauze, the inaugural Ernest Scott Chair in 1956, and Scott's former students, the iconic Kathleen Fitzpatrick, and the doyen of the history profession in the 1960s and 1970s, Manning Clark. In his 1959 Presidential Address at the historical section of the Australian and New Zealand Association for the Advancement of Science La Nauze criticised Scott for the 'thinness of his scholarship'.[1] Fitzpatrick recalled him respectfully, identifying him as a pioneer, although as we shall see she was equally but more gently critical. Clark was bluntly dismissive. In declaring Scott's work free of any originality, creativity or profundity, he effectively doomed his work to the dustbin of history, characterising it as anachronistic, flawed and inaccurate.

This is where it had largely remained until Stuart's biography. Stuart argues that Scott and his work are presented as 'given', without due regard to any systematic analysis or scrutiny of the work itself. Dismissing Scott with hindsight, as La Nauze did in relation to his research, was a 'cruel blow'.[2] Mocking Scott for his scholarship he believed was especially unfair: 'Of all the men who held chairs of history in Australia during the early part of this century, Scott was the most exacting in his insistence that no source be left unexamined.'[3] Scott's reputation, 'once high', now 'languishes'.[4]

There are two further tasks Stuart sets himself in *A History for a Nation*: 'to understand how [Scott] made himself and how he made this history'. As now 'an obscure figure in the lives of others [whose] work is largely forgotten', it is 'necessary to ask how he effaced his own history and how others have effaced the history he made'.[5] In these efforts, he says, 'I have tried to rescue his generation from the enormous condescension of posterity'.[6]

In exploring how Stuart addressed these aims, I have divided this chapter into five themes that tackle the specific questions of the use of sources, methodology and interpretation. It highlights the challenges of biography writing: of drawing character and personality; of the selectivity in sources and methodology; and navigating sensitivities. Two features are especially striking in this work.

The first is not only that Stuart places Scott in his historical context but also that he *explains* that milieu. This is beautifully drawn with detail throughout the biography: the conviviality, self-importance and hubris of the male-dominated worlds of the academy at that time. The Whiggish politics of the day, the British imperial values and the celebration of white Australia is shown as a milieu that is both evoked and explained and analysed. The shifting changes in Scott's thinking and his outlook are captured so that we see a man who changes with his circumstances.

The second striking feature is the discussion that links Ernest Scott and his successor. *A History for a Nation* is perhaps the most personal of Stuart's biographies. Rarely does he adopt the first person in his work, and he seems to have reserved this for his affectionate study of 'Scotty'. There is overt identification with his subject, but it is not uncritical. Stuart is never dismissive out of hand, although he is direct in alerting us to Scott's shortcomings. Stuart demonstrates how understanding Scott's work long after its relevance or academic worth has disappeared can segue seamlessly into an illuminating, eloquent and insightful intellectual history of the mid-twentieth century.

Two biographies in one: 'I became Ernest Scott Professor of History'[7]

Any biography is a dual biography, or two biographies in one: that of the author and the subject. At first glance, judging from his previous works, the subject of Ernest Scott is not a logical or immediately obvious choice of subject. In the decades before tackling the subject of Scott, Stuart had written previously on political subjects. Scott seemed as far removed as possible from Stuart's interest in British left-wing intellectuals, the Australian labour moment and colonial liberals. Indeed, Stuart confesses to being openly dismissive of Scott as an impatient postgraduate tutor. 'His mind was a blunt instrument,' Stuart observed in his firebrand days.[8]

It is of course not a political biography, either: political history is not the overarching framework he employs as he does with other biographies. Already he had published two biographical studies: *Militant: The Life and Times of Paddy Troy* (1984) and *A Colonial Liberalism: The Lost World of Three Victorian Visionaries* (1991). Stuart's appointment to the Ernest Scott Chair in 1990 brought together the biographer and his subject into a perfect match.

Not all biographers reflect on the trajectories of their own careers through their biographical subject. Historians often lament how biographers do not do it often enough. In *A History for a Nation*, Stuart is open, explicit and direct in the comparisons he draws with Scott's times and the conditions under which he and Scott worked. On many levels Stuart notes there are similarities: 'I tread the ground he trod, take part in the rituals he performed, profess what he professed.' But he also identifies the stark differences whereby the contemporary workplace shares no resemblance at all with what existed in the past.[9] The university bureaucracy has changed with the rise of managerialism and bureaucracy and with it the finances of a corporation. Without a university degree or qualification, Scott already stood out at the time. Stuart's steps to the chair through the professionalism of degrees and publications are in stark contrast to Scott's journey. The entire university system has been completely transformed. Scott's extensive activities in the public arena were not altogether embraced by his contemporaries. Today, when academics are now expected to engage fully with government, policy and the media, is a very different world. Access to these in Scott's time was based on male networks and sociability. 'Manners', wrote Stuart, 'were then as important as credentials—urbanity and congeniality were the hallmarks of authority.'[10]

Stuart positions his role and place in the pantheon of historians who have gone before him. But by the time Stuart took the chair, changes were already apace. The unbroken male lineage of the chair, beginning with the appointment of Scott himself in 1913, appeared to continue these traditions seamlessly, but by the 1990s the gender profile of such chairs had not gone unnoticed. Few women occupied chairs in history at the time. But the decade would usher in many changes to the history profession. One of the most significant and enduring was the increasing number of female historians who rose to professorial rank during the 1990s—a cause that Stuart himself championed, advocated and promoted with great conviction and commitment, both within the university and beyond it. The era when well-qualified women such as Associate Professor Kathleen Fitzpatrick, who infamously declared she was not yet 'ready' to occupy a history chair—despite her credentials surpassing those of Scott and many of her peers—belonged to a bygone era.

Turning to such an era, the first challenge Stuart opened for us is that of how a biographer might examine a family and the truth or otherwise of sources. How does a biographer work with contradictory and conflicting evidence? What are the challenges in writing about early life?

We begin by dealing with a problem to test the most adept biographers: that of family secrets.

Secrets and sources: 'three times Ernest Scott set down the details of his ancestry, each time differently'[11]

Scott's early life is intriguing and compelling not only for his inauspicious beginnings but also for the gaps in his story. In Stuart's hand, the challenges that face the biographer are transformed into a quest for piecing together the scantest of fragments.

The opening of *A History for a Nation* begins with the drama of Oscar Wilde's play, *The Importance of Being Ernest*, and the first chapter is named after it. The writing is playful, witty and almost whimsical. Scott's birth and the evidence for it challenges the biographer. Rather than see it as a problem, Stuart takes the opportunity to discuss the demands of writing about a life in which sources are few and conflicting.

One most striking example is the information available about Scott's birth. When Scott marries, his birth is listed as 1867 in Northampton to William and Hannah Scott. On his second marriage in 1915, we are told that Scott records his mother's maiden name as Scott. And in a third entry in *Who's Who* where Scott says in reply to providing (1) Birth, (2) Parentage and (3) Marriage: '(1) as usual; (2) one father, one mother unless I am mistaken; (3) Emmie married me in a fit of absence of mind.'[12] His birth certificate records that his mother Hannah Scott was a housekeeper who lived in Northampton, but there is no record of a father.[13]

The matter of Scott's birth is one that has exercised historians before Stuart, so there is a trail of scholars who had failed in the quest to discover the missing fragments of Scott's life. Percival Serle knew Scott well but not his birthdate. When Serle wrote to his widow on Scott's death, she did not know. Kathleen Fitzpatrick, confronted by the birth certificate, noted that his mother was Hannah Scott and that Ernest had listed William Scott on his birth certificate. Keith Hancock noted that he had been brought up by his grandfather and mother.[14]

So Scott's early life is documented with contradictory and frag-mentary evidence, and there is also speculation about other parts of his personal history. How did Scott, for example, get to write for the *Globe* at a time when it was competitive to enter journalism? There 'is no indication how an obscure provincial novice succeeded in such a fiercely competitive profession, except by his talent', notes Stuart.[15]

We are left wanting to know more, and the suspense of what happens next carries us to the next phase of Scott's life in Australia, again because sources cannot all be fully described.

Emotional lives: 'the unease of the trespasser'

If biographical fragments draw a biographer to speculation, then capturing the emotional life of a subject can be the most elusive of all. Can an inner life ever be captured? On this quest Stuart confronts a dilemma in a 'Dear Reader' moment. How does the biographer manage love letters and intimate communication when they become archival sources? Attached to the letters of Scott is a request from Emily stating that they 'should not be quoted' as she and her husband would 'both have disliked that so much'.[16]

Stuart the biographer asks: 'how can I disregard this injunction?' It is worth quoting Stuart at length to capture his defence for not honouring Emily's wishes: 'I can claim the obligation of the historian to consider all the evidence … I can seek refuge in the salience of Scott's own romance to the historical romance he constructed. I can even point to the use he made of the emotional confidences of his subjects.'[17]

Yet Stuart yields to what he calls the 'unease of the trespasser and unease that all my professional training cannot wholly allay. I can only declare it and invite the reader to complicity'.[18] Still, we are given a glimpse of the intimate playfulness in their marriage. When Emily was at Lorne where she often repaired, Scott wrote seductively: 'Are you very brown?' he asked. 'Like piecrust or cream?'[19] Biographers do not always explicitly discuss omissions and the direct choices made in how and why material is *not* used.

But Stuart does delve into Scott's private world. He shows how life could be very messy indeed. Scott's divorce from his first wife Mabel was complicated and difficult. Over time Scott would not speak her name, as she was known as 'the lady' or 'the person'. For his daughter Muriel, there was 'love and regret'. Scott eventually cut off all contact from them both and began a new life with Emily.[20] When Muriel died in 1924, Scott declared he had only Emily now and that he did not care about anyone else.[21] The cut is sharp, even brutal.

This is not the enduring image of Scott. Stuart seeks to give depth to his personality. He captures a warm family man: 'His nephews and nieces knew a kindly, generous Uncle Ernest with a particular talent for arranging occasions.' They recount the way he would take them to shows with tickets around his neck—issuing them to the children as they enjoyed the dodgem rides. He indulged them with treats.[22]

Emily remains a sketch, and we could have learnt more about her. In his review of *A History for a Nation*, Warren Osmond notes that Emily Dyason is 'in many ways a more interesting figure than her husband'.[23] Emily awaits her own biographer as the details of her here are tantalising but brief. Emily is described in one chapter, but we are keen to hear more about her own life and activities and her efforts to keep Ernest Scott's legacy alive through his contributions.

Making and un-making contributions: 'all his work is largely forgotten'[24]

How can Scott's achievements be summarised? Stuart is at pains to avoid what he sees as caricature in ways others have dismissed Scott's contributions to scholarship. Painstakingly, Stuart explores Scott's methodology, his treatment of historical evidence, his approach to understanding facts. Scott's style and approach was driven by his quest for accuracy: searching for, and knowing, the truth. He favoured exposing the mistakes of others; as Stuart writes, 'throughout his academic life Scott derived particular pleasure from pouncing on the mistakes of lesser historians'.[25] For Scott, a follower of Ranke and the German school of scientific history, making history was a form of creating knowledge in its own right. For him, the primary source was the pathway to the truth. Scott followed this law and Ranke's belief in the objectivity of historical truth, the supremacy of facts over concepts—which led to the erasure of the authorial presence.[26]

Terre Napoléon (published in 1910) provides an excellent platform that allows Stuart to respect Scott's work and the milieu in which it was written as well as directly address its severe shortcomings. Stuart argues that it is a 'remarkably impressive exercise in sustained interpretation'.[27] Further, it carries 'several layers of meaning'. Most important of all these was that it was written within the imperial frame of the early twentieth century,[28] which encompassed many assumptions about Australia's settler colonial past. The underlying beliefs in *Terre Napoléon* are entirely anathema to us today. Australia, as Stuart describes it, is depicted as a 'sleeping continent'. Scott's representation of the land is one without civilisation. His treatment of Aboriginal Australians is abhorrent and repugnant. Stuart notes that while Scott was 'sufficiently prescient to appreciate "the shrivelling touch" of European civilisation' on Indigenous Australians, and condemned atrocities, he was ignorant and contemptuous of the Aboriginal way of life.[29] In Scott's history, Stuart notes that in his discussion of Aboriginal Australians he performs 'a double effacement of the Aboriginal presence, first by denying their resistance to the invasion and second by obliterating all signs of their habitation'.[30]

Context of another kind shapes the path of Scott's *Short History of Australia*. Events conspired to render the book redundant even before it was published. Beginning his writing in 1915 in the middle of the war, *A Short History of Australia* 'is a story of a particular kind of nationality that was achieved when he wrote it'.[31] The timing of writing reflected the period of writing the book, marked as it was by Scott's belief in British imperial values: he celebrated the war and Australia's entry into it. But events overtook it. As Stuart notes, the manuscript was completed in early 1916: 'At the time the AIF was once more in Egypt, withdrawn from the Dardanelles, still to suffer the carnage of the Western Front; at home the illusion of wartime consensus had not yet been shattered in the fight over conscription.'[32] As it would turn out, Scott wrote the Preface 'when he returned proofs to the publisher in England in the middle of the year, just as the first news reached Australia of unimaginable numbers lost in action on the Somme'. *A Short History,* notes Stuart, 'is marked indelibly by the war—most of the first edition, which was printed in England, was lost to German torpedoes in the Mediterranean'. But by the time these copies were replaced, Stuart shows that 'its celebration of filial accord was obsolete'.[33]

Stuart's reading of the work returns us to the contemporary times and how we would now view such contemporary perspectives. 'Several aspects of this narrative strategy jar the reader of modern Australian historiography,' Stuart notes. 'From today's perspective the frontier is a site of conquest and oppression and environmental destruction, but for Scott, it defines what is new and significant … The colonising process, as he saw it, was a drama of men pitted against nature.' There are no women in the story other than 'Mrs John Macarthur', who is the only woman mentioned. For Scott, he describes the 'masculine battle to conquer distance and subdue elements'. Indigenous Australians are shown as passive, unable to fight the might of the explorers or settlers. They are acted upon and have no agency. Occasionally, the writing and understanding by Scott rise above this level, but not often.[34]

Yet paradoxically, at the time when Stuart was writing, in the 1990s, the challenges of postmodernism saw Scott's 'circumstances and practices take on a new significance'. What are these? A 'postmodern attention to the fictive nature of historical prose allows a less censorious approach', Stuart notes.[35] It is worth quoting Stuart's interpretation: 'The playfulness and purple passages, the stylistic subterfuges and the striving for effect, the didacticism, the insistence on truth and the free play of the imagination, bend back towards the textual complexity that is now so fashionable.'[36] Generally, Scott's work is worth analysing because it is 'so much at variance with present practice that it draws attention to the discipline's conventions'.[37]

Moving to Scott's contribution to teaching, Scott did not change the curriculum dramatically—much of it remained with a focus on British history.[38] Without small group teaching, there was a reliance on lectures and books. Students were examined on their knowledge of these texts, and they were required to create a response based on their knowledge of these texts.[39] What made Scott's lectures different? Scott 'captured the attention of his audience with the skill of an accomplished public speaker'. Scott's lectures were a complete entity—unlike previously where lecturers would pick up where they had previously left off. Significantly too they used the latest research: 'unless one does keep abreast of thought and research in a subject, one's lectures must, I think, become flat, stale and deficient in vitality'.[40] Written work consisted of research exercises: setting students problems to examine through primary sources. Scott stressed 'creative scholarship' and not 'passive learning' by asking students to 'read their essays to him and respond to his comments and queries'.[41] Scott deviated from accepted practice at the time by allowing students to take books and notes into the exam so they would not rely on memory.[42]

The most striking feature of Scott's teaching was that he used research essays to teach history to undergraduates.[43] He also revived the Historical Society and saw it as an opportunity to promote 'historical mindedness'.[44] In 1919 Scott restructured the degree to make a clear distinction between the pass and honours degrees.[45] Soon Jessie Webb was appointed to assist Scott in marking essays and examination papers.[46] He was an exacting teacher. Students took no liberties with him, according to Kathleen Fitzpatrick, and they feared him.[47]

At the time, in both teaching and research, Scott sought to promote and advance the discipline, notwithstanding the severe limits of his methods and approaches, to contemporary eyes.

Impact and legacy

On his death in 1939, Scott was lauded for his achievements and contributions. *Table Talk* declared he was 'today acknowledged as one of the greatest of Australia's historians'.[48] Where did his talents lie? He 'was an exceptionally gifted lecturer and became famous as a maker of professors, for at one time, while he himself was still at the University, three other chairs of history in Australia were held by his former students'.[49] Accolades flowed from Scott's colleagues, former students, and public figures.

At the time, Scott's influence and legacy were seen as significant, but these soon waned. His contemporaries were critical of his work and approaches. Stuart notes how 'Against his formidable and vital positive qualities Kathleen Fitzpatrick set a failure of sympathy and imagination'. She also made other observations: 'He was informed and intelligent but not profound.' 'He oversimplified.' 'He could not enter into the otherness of the past, especially the systems of belief that impelled enthusiasts, and he carried empiricism to the point of bigotry.'[50] Manning Clark presented an even less favourable picture: as Stuart notes, he saw a 'a vulgar entertainer, a cynic and a mocker'. Fred Alexander saw Scott's 'excessive fondness for turning a lurid phrase'. Fitzpatrick and Alexander both acknowledged the way Scott as a teacher had shown them 'that the study of history was a means of intellectual discovery and inducted them into its procedures'.[51] But Stuart also lists his shortcomings as they were observed by his contemporaries: '[H]is rhetorical excess, his prejudices, his rush to judgement on the basis of unproblematic "fact", his lack of interest in the epistemological foundations of his discipline, and his well-known dismissal of philosophy of history as "wubbish", came to be seen as deficiencies that the professional practitioner had to overcome for the discipline to advance.'[52]

Stuart chooses to assess his legacy through the contrasting views of his students. For Stephen Roberts, Scott was a 'great teacher who was a slave to duty and who humanised history while making it scientific … His devotion to truth was a religion and that was why his work would live.' Roberts eulogised his work and his influence on him: 'It is difficult to write of a man when one owes him so much and when one admires so greatly that it seems presumptuous to accept an appreciation.'[53] Keith Hancock on the other hand was less fulsome. Acknowledging his debt to Scott, Hancock was respectful but noted that his lectures lacked depth. His own work, notes Stuart, signified a different approach from that of Scott. Stuart describes his work as 'more profound'. Hancock also declined the invitation by Emily Scott to write Scott's biography.[54] The respect of those whom Scott trained as historians, then, were 'qualified' in their praise 'by the awareness of his academic shortcomings'. Astutely, Stuart observes that those who most lauded Scott and his legacy were those from outside the history profession. Teachers, lawyers, diplomats, especially, complimented his teaching.[55]

The replacement of Scott by the 30-year-old Max Crawford also reveals that changes were afoot. Crawford did not radically alter the Melbourne History Department, but he introduced a broader curriculum, as Stuart describes it, a 'more general and philosophical approach to historical education that centred on small-group teaching in tutorials in place of the survey lectures and research essays. They called for more staff with a more professional orientation towards their discipline. They involved detailed calculation of contact hours, extensive discussion with colleagues and repeated drafts until his blueprint was finally ready for implementation.'[56]

Crawford did revive the teaching of Australian history as a separate subject, which he taught in 1945. In 1946, Manning Clark took it over. Clark made clear his view of his predecessors and his teachers, which demanded a break with the past. In a seminar Clark presented on 'some aspects' of historical research in Australia he described such research as 'a wasteland. The available literature was dismissed as slovenly, slapdash, crude and clumsy'. Stuart describes how 'examples were given of the number of errors in standard works by such writers as S.H. Roberts, B. Fitzpatrick and E. Scott'. And 'with this epitaph the old order passed'.[57] Scott's reputation was entirely dismissed. His legacy remained with the Ernest Scott Prize, with the chair and with Scott's library. But the world had moved on, and the profession rapidly expanded in different directions.

In his biography, Stuart restores Scott's past, his world and his mark on history. Stuart reminds us that history is never divorced from its context. But it is also a history of history—its approaches, its deficiencies and understandings articulated by a generation of white men who inhabited the universities in the early twentieth century.

The biographer concludes with a moment of reflexivity in his own earlier dismissal of Scott. In the 1970s Stuart wrote critically of Scott, calling for a 'revolutionary break with the past'. 'Time works its revenge,' Stuart notes ruefully. When he began researching his Ernest Scott lecture, he read the Scott papers in the National Library and was inspired by them, leading him to turn to Scott's publications 'with mounting fascination'.[58] Stuart had himself been on a journey of revelation.

In 2014, Stuart and I again found ourselves in the Old Arts Building at the University of Melbourne brought together by Ernest Scott. This time, twenty-three years after Stuart's lecture, I was co-teaching an honours course with him titled 'The Writing of Australian History'. Ernest Scott's work was featured in the first week of the course under the title 'The Founders'. Scott's *Terre Napoléon* was listed as essential reading. The first exercise for students was a contemporary book review of one of the historians studied, which 'should be contemporary to the period when the book appeared, and it should avoid hindsight: that is, you should write the view according to the circumstances of the period and the conventions of the discipline as they existed at the time'. The purpose of this assignment was to 'foster and apply the skills of historical criticism. The skills involved here are the ability to conduct a close reading of a historical text, to apply critical judgement to its evidence and arguments, to identify and deploy the standards of historical scholarship'. It could be straight from Scott's song book.

The students found the assessment demanding, and few managed entirely to rise to the challenge. Most were exercised by the task of balancing context, text and author within a contemporary frame. It was impossible not to bring to bear contemporary views, they protested. But all found the exercise engaging. Its purpose cut to the very core of what both the author and subject of *A History for a Nation* have aspired to achieve in contrasting ways: critically understanding historical writing within its historical context.

In the classroom, Stuart and I were drawn together to the discipline Scott helped build. In *A History for a Nation*, Stuart reminds us that the discipline will continue to change well after its practitioners and their works have or have not left their mark on their contemporaries and those who followed them. Understanding these works in their context is vital for it provides a necessary history for widening our comprehension of how and why history is written and taught in the way it is and why it is and needs to be everchanging to understand a rapidly complex and shifting world. But this is not the only lesson to be learnt from the story that Stuart tells of Ernest Scott. There is perhaps a far simpler but no less significant one, which is that it is incumbent on us all to ensure that the discipline Scott and Stuart in their own eras have promoted, supported and nurtured continues to be built and ultimately thrives in making sense of and understanding these most uncertain of times, now and in future.

Notes

1   Stuart Macintyre, *A History for a Nation*, Melbourne University Press, Melbourne, 1994, p. 4. All references are to this work unless otherwise stated.
2   Ibid., p. 4.
3   Ibid., p. 5.
4   Ibid., p. 5.
5   Ibid., p. 9.
6   Ibid., p. 211.
7   Ibid., p. 204.
8   Ibid., p. 205.
9   Ibid., pp. 205–6.
10   Ibid., p. 209.
11   Ibid., p. 11.
12   Ibid., p. 10.
13   Ibid., p. 10.
14   Ibid., p. 11.
15   Ibid., p. 13.
16   Ibid., p. 62.
17   Ibid., p. 62.
18   Ibid., p. 62.
19   Ibid., p. 72.
20   Ibid., p. 63.
21   Ibid., p. 68.
22   Ibid., p. 71.
23   Warren Osmond, review of Stuart Macintyre, *A History for a Nation: Ernest Scott and the Making of Australian History*, *Australian Historical Studies*, vol. 26, no. 105, 1995, p. 669.
24   Macintyre, *A History for a Nation*, p. 9.
25   Ibid., p. 38.
26   Ibid., p. 40.
27   Ibid., p. 42.
28   Ibid., p. 42.
29   Ibid., p. 47.
30   Ibid., p. 48.
31   Ibid., p. 73.
32   Ibid., p. 74.

33   Ibid., p. 75.
34   Ibid., p. 78.
35   Ibid., p. 208.
36   Ibid., p. 208.
37   Ibid., p. 209.
38   Ibid., p. 97.
39   Ibid., p. 97.
40   Ibid., p. 97.
41   Ibid., p. 97.
42   Ibid., p. 97.
43   Ibid., pp. 97–8.
44   Ibid., p. 99.
45   Ibid., pp. 99–101.
46   Ibid., pp. 100–13, 114.
47   Ibid., p. 111.
48   *Table Talk*, Melbourne, 29 June 1939, p. 3.
49   Ibid., p. 3.
50   Macintyre, *A History for a Nation*, p. 118.
51   Ibid., p. 118.
52   Ibid., p. 118.
53   Ibid., p. 119.
54   Ibid., p. 120.
55   Ibid., p. 121.
56   Ibid., p. 202.
57   Ibid., p. 203.
58   Ibid., p. 205.

Chapter 12

Scrutiny, context and power
Stuart Macintyre on Australian historians

Sean Scalmer

Stuart Macintyre is justly celebrated for many accomplishments: distinguished works of general and synoptic history; biographies of trade union militants and colonial liberals; histories of communism, of reconstruction, of the social sciences and of the universities. In this Himalayan range, his studies of Australian historians do not immediately loom large. They follow no systematic plan but rather reflect a combination of persistent interest and frequent invitation to contribute. They define no substantial field of scholarly debate, for Australian historians attracted little attention before Stuart's pioneering research and have received little more since.[1] They have not been the subject of sustained discussion, beyond admiring reviews.

Yet these works might collectively be considered as among Stuart's most significant. They constitute an enduring field of passionate and repeated engagement. They have helped to clarify the dynamics and the import of Australian historical writing. They offer possible insights into the trajectory of Stuart's career. They illuminate features of his more acclaimed works. And they provide rich lessons for the contemporary historian.

Stuart's first published academic work was a critical and compelling analysis of Australian historians, 'Radical history and bourgeois hegemony' (1972). Two of his monographs concern Australian historians: *A History for a Nation: Ernest Scott and the Making of Australian History* (1994) and *The History Wars* (2003). Seven of his edited or co-edited books are also directly concerned with Australian historians and so are a score or so of his articles and book chapters. He has taught several subjects directly concerned with these matters at undergraduate, honours and doctoral levels. Among his most recent publications are subtle and engaging studies of the Australian historians Geoffrey Bolton and Ken Inglis and the history of Honours programs in History in Australian universities. For a less gifted and committed scholar, these works alone would constitute a lifetime of honourable achievement. They merit close attention.

In this chapter, I seek to provide such attention. I have three aims. First, to identify the core features of Stuart's distinctive approach and method. Second, to consider how this approach was put to work in a changing context, stretching out over nearly half a century. Third, to place Stuart's own career and conduct against the background of his assessment of earlier work.

Stuart's first academic article was published just after his twenty-fifth birthday. 'Radical history and bourgeois hegemony' appeared in the second issue of the New Left Marxist journal, *Intervention*. That journal symbolised a revived interest in the relevance of Marxism. Apparent political breakthroughs, East and West, had stimulated the search for a deeper revolutionary theory. Italy's 'Hot Autumn' drew attention to the fecundity of Antonio Gramsci's insights. The upsurge of Paris in May 1968 encouraged Australians to turn to Louis Althusser—the Marxist philosopher of the École Normale Supérieure—to chart their next steps. In England, Perry Anderson and his collaborators had cultivated a new awareness of the richness of European Marxism in the pages of *New Left Review*. They had also modelled the possibility that a younger guard might draw on Marxist categories to challenge their elders. In Australia, the journal *Arena* had been launched as a forum for the rethinking of Marxism in 1963; the Communist Party had signalled a new openness with the reshaping of its theoretical journal as *Australian Left Review.*

The young Turk was one of several Melbourne postgraduates who collaborated on the new journal. His first historical essay was sandwiched between intimidating studies of Japanese imperialism and Gramsci and Leninism. It was preceded by an editorial that outlined the journal's central purpose in prose redolent of high Althusserianism: an intention to investigate Australia as a 'social formation' that was both 'grounded in a capitalist mode of production' and 'characterised by quite specific determinations'; a 'theoretical practice' that would help to produce 'knowledge of the social structure' and thereby enable a transformative 'political practice'.[2] In this febrile context, Stuart's investigation of Australian historians took on a sharply critical form.

New Left Review had published Gareth Stedman Jones's evisceration of his elders, 'The pathology of English history', in 1967. This was an obvious inspiration, as was Perry Anderson's 'Origins of the present crisis' (1964).[3] Like Anderson and Stedman Jones, Stuart came not to praise but to bury. History in Australia, as in Britain, was apparently a compound of 'scientistic empiricism' and 'moralism'.[4] The first generation of history teachers at Australian universities had not sought to understand the 'lived past' and had limited their labours to 'moral instruction based on established texts'.[5] Their successors—most notably the following generations of Melbourne professors, Ernest Scott and R.M. Crawford—had reinforced 'bourgeois hegemony' by such devices as an 'inculcation of reverence for the founding fathers' and a preoccupation with 'freedom of the will'.[6] Crawford's explorations of the philosophy of history recognised the limits of empiricism but failed to register the depth and value of the Marxist challenge. His work was 'quite unanalytical' and his system-building a self-evident failure. The professor's liberalism did not survive the rigours of the Cold War. His attempt to develop a new science of History did not outlast a desperate engagement with Hempel and with Wittgenstein.[7]

The radicals who protested the orthodoxy—Brian Fitzpatrick, Ian Turner and his peers—were politically courageous but intellectually stunted. Although Fitzpatrick was the 'first and greatest radical Australian historian', he was also handicapped by an 'untroubled empiricist certainty', a 'conceptual inadequacy' and a limited understanding of 'class struggle'.[8] The academic radicals like Turner were no better. They had narrowed their attention to labour and popular history rather than grappling with the more complicated field of 'class relations'.[9] Their 'undialectical' and 'mechanistic' approach to class offered 'moral outrage' in place of serious social analysis.[10] Neither Fitzpatrick nor his successors had fully grappled with the 'racialist element in the radical tradition'.[11] A new kind of history was needed: based on a new 'problematic';[12] guided by a concern with the 'Marxist concept of totality';[13] devoted to the study of 'class interrelationships and their determining factors'.[14]

The contrast with Stuart's mature work is at first most striking. As a senior teacher and reviewer, he was remarkable for his capacity to deliver fundamental criticisms with a disarming sympathy and gentleness. At twenty-five, his criticisms were unvarnished. The young man was forthright in his proclamation of the necessity of 'arduous consideration of the theoretical problems'.[15] Later, his theoretical interests would be less visible: shaping rather than obtruding from his historical research. Stuart at twenty-five objected to Turner's denial of the 'possibility of a revolutionary intervention into the present capitalist hegemony'.[16] The passing years would leave him less hopeful of the possibilities of fundamental political change.

But the continuities are more significant than the contrasts. Stuart's first published work is animated by three characteristics that would typify his studies of Australian historians in the half-century to come: an unapologetic yet critical interest, an attention to context, and a concern with power. The approach was then unusual, and it elevated his work above conventional scholarly analysis. It enabled a sequence of rich and memorable works: collectively, the most complete analysis of Australian historiography and among the most penetrating studies of any Australian social science.

Stuart's first article was produced just after he had completed an MA on British History at Monash University and just before his departure to Cambridge University, where he would pursue doctoral research on the history of Marxism in Britain. The curriculum at the University of Melbourne had then offered no opportunity for serious study of Australian history. Stuart's frustration at such narrowness is perhaps evident in the initial pages of his 'Radical history', where he observes a tendency in Australian universities to 'weak imitation of the English mother-culture'.[17] The youthful Marxist pursued his Australian studies independently, taking advantage of the resources of the Melbourne department's Jessie Webb Library (now sadly dissolved, in an opportunistic response to budgetary pressures). This was a work of curiosity and political criticism, but it was also a form of protest at the limits of his undergraduate training.

It should not be remarkable that a brilliant young Australian scholar might find the history of their field in their own country of some interest, or that they might consider its leading practitioners worthy of critical scrutiny. Stuart was no radical nationalist—as his assessment of Turner and his peers showed—but he rejected apologetic 'cringing' as much as 'shrill' nationalist strutting.[18] If he rebuffed Crawford's philosophy of history, then he accorded it the respect of his overwhelming demolition. Stuart's attention to the work of Australian scholars implied their significance. While he chronicled the 'acute' tensions between 'Country' and 'Calling' felt by an earlier generation of Australian historians, propelled by ambition and opportunity to make their careers in the metropole,[19] this child of postwar Australia seemed not to internalise such a pull. He felt little need to pursue publications in non-Australian outlets, so as to satisfy others of the excellence of his work. He noted that when earlier historians, such as Keith Hancock, judged 'Australian civilisation' against a 'metropolitan model', they 'ensured it would be found deficient'.[20] From Stuart's early thirties, Australia was his primary quarry. His distinction as a student of historiography was acknowledged internationally, with his appointment as an editor of *The Oxford History of Historical Writing*, volume 4.[21] Yet he overwhelmingly applied these skills to the study of Australian historians. Members of an earlier generation of scholars were typically too deferential of British universities and standards to contemplate such a course. Members of a later generation have been too bewitched by league tables and immediate measures of 'international' recognition.

Inspired by the richness of Marxist scholarship and by Althusser's specific insights, the young Stuart advocated historical studies animated by the 'Marxist concept of totality'. His rejection of economism and idealism was accompanied by a desire to examine 'class interrelationships and their determining factors'.[22] These inclinations persisted even when the trappings of Althusserianism had been laid aside. In a later commentary on the scholarship of fellow New Leftists, 'The making of the Australian working class' (1978), Stuart identified an unhelpful tendency to treat 'consciousness' as the 'ultimate criterion of class'.[23] He urged more careful attention to the construction of a national economy, the character of Australian capitalism and the social basis of racism and imperialism.[24] His prize-winning general history that formed volume 4 of the *Oxford History of Australia, 1901–1942: The Succeeding Age*, reaffirmed a desire to grasp relationships 'in their totality': 'material' practices, 'social' practices, political mobilisations.[25] This granted his narrative accounts an intimidating breadth. But this same sensibility meant that when he turned to the work of Australian historians, he necessarily placed it in a fully realised context.

Stuart's writings on historiography were moored in a deep understanding of their institutional environment. A historian of the Australian university, he was able to illuminate the possibilities and confinements of this place of work: the arduous rounds of teaching, for Australia's first professors of history; the expectation that one might contribute to public affairs; the persistent superintendence of state authorities, including the security services. In his attention to the resources available for research—archives, jobs, scholarships, journals—he was able to trace its growth, its increasingly national perspective and its less gratifying tendency to specialisation.[26]

Stuart went further. In rich analyses of particular historians, he was also able to demonstrate how creative individuals sought to negotiate their changing circumstances, sometimes successfully, sometimes less so. Keith Hancock channelled the expectation that the history professor might explicate Australia's place in a changing world into a compelling essay in national history. His *Australia* (1930) was the work of a young man who had returned to the provinces from the metropole, just as the limits of his homeland had been more starkly exposed. The book was marked by intellectual distance, comparative reach and acerbic insight. The concentrated power of the prose and the coherence of the sustained interpretation reflected the specific purposes of its author; they helped to win *Australia* a significance that would span several generations.[27]

Max Crawford cultivated a 'Melbourne School' of intimidating institutional heft and influence, but in the years of the Cold War he lost confidence in the possibilities of his own intellectual project as he did the prospects of human betterment. His liberalism was compromised under pressure, as he moved from object of surveillance by the security services to a willing informant on his Melbourne colleagues. He ended his career dissatisfied with the changes in the profession that he had helped to make, just as he was regretful of the meagre fruits of his long intellectual labours.[28] The historian fascinated by the 'freedom of the will' was ultimately mastered by circumstances not of his own choosing.

Stuart's capacity to place the historian in their context perhaps yielded the most startling results in his treatment of those writers less fully integrated into the world of the university. Ernest Scott's first researches in history, Stuart demonstrated, owed their blending of von Ranke and romance not simply to the talents of their author but also to the peculiar environment in which they were initiated. Scott was a member of a male dining club, the Boobooks, and it was a convention that members would address their fellows on topics of personal interest and cultural elevation. His more accomplished fellow members could command specialist knowledge of law and science and a deep familiarity with imperial affairs. Scott was but a journalist, and could claim no professional distinction. His first historical studies were initiated in these circumstances. In his use of primary documents to challenge popular misunderstanding (following von Ranke), Scott could make his own claim for expertise. His romantic stories could hold an audience. And in his historical reconstruction of British naval superiority, he could make a bid for his own place at the empire's round table. Scott's lectures to his fellow Boobooks were the first expressions of what would become important contributions to Australian historical research. Their acknowledged distinction, along with his formidable networks, would propel him from journalism into a professorial chair and thence into a central position to shape the field.[29]

Brian Fitzpatrick also combined journalism with history. In a fascinating contribution to *Against the Grain*, Stuart explained why Brian Fitzpatrick's path-breaking contributions to economic and labour history of the later 1930s and early 1940s were stalled in later decades. The reasons lay not so much in a fondness for the bottle (dramatised by his political opponents) but rather a narrowing of opportunities for freelance scholars, a growing conservative mobilisation against radical history, and the unwillingness of apparent allies entrenched in the universities to offer necessary support. In these circumstances, a failure to push ahead could hardly be ascribed to personal weakness. If Stuart's first published assessment of Fitzpatrick's histories evinced an impatience with apparent theoretical deficiencies, his later evaluation demonstrated a compassion born of a deeper understanding of the freelance's difficult circumstances.[30]

Like Scott and Fitzpatrick, Geoffrey Blainey did not follow the established pathway from honours to postgraduate study and thence to junior academic appointment. Although Stuart would be painted by opponents as a shadowy conspirator against his departmental colleague,[31] his writings on Blainey are rather marked by a notable sympathy and respect. Stuart explicitly denied that Blainey was a 'History Warrior'.[32] In 'The making of a school' and *The History Wars* he carefully explained how Blainey's distinguishing features as a writer developed partly in formative years as a freelance historian of business. Blainey was unusual in his tremendous facility, his interest in the power of technology, his attention to resourceful individuals, his chafing against scholarly consensus, his capacity to order a mass of material into a clear narrative, his eye for the illuminating detail and his sheer versatility. He wrote for non-academic readers. These qualities were cultivated in the years before his entry to the academy. As Stuart showed, once Blainey joined the University of Melbourne, they enabled an intellectual contribution of great individuality and achievement, as he assayed major themes in book-length studies of Australian history: mineral discovery, transport, war, the worlds of First Nations peoples before European colonisation. But such qualities also helped to explain a distance and then a disaffection from academic colleagues and, when challenged, a propensity for polemical attack. When Blainey's statements on Asian immigration in 1984 inspired a storm of public and scholarly criticism, Blainey struck back. As he struggled to defend and to entrench his position, the great historian became a 'controversialist'.[33]

Stuart also contextualised Manning Clark's highly individual project. Clark's six-volume *History of Australia* relied on the growing resources made available to the historian from the 1950s. His rewriting of Australia's past was cast in the form of a deliberate 'repudiation of his intellectual inheritance', and gathered inspiration from the parallel explorations of postwar creative artists. His distinctive themes reflected their author's capacity as well as desire to stand a pace or two apart from scholarly convention and from established political tribes. His senior colleagues were at first discomfited by his violation of orthodoxy. But radical historians, such as Ian Turner, were seeking to make sense of Cold War political defeats; they were more sympathetic to his emphasis on individual passions and tensions. And a growing national sentiment in the later 1960s and 1970s—harnessed, symbolised and reinforced by the Whitlam government—provided a receptive environment for publication. Clark, in turn, celebrated the new prime minister and mourned his downfall. Clark's intellectual choices and style won the professor an audience outside the classroom. Right-wing critics—incensed by his defence of Whitlam—excoriated him as the symbol of an ascendant academic Left. But most academics had by this time turned away from his eccentric peregrinations and regarded Clark as irrelevant to their primary concerns. Conservative dismay was matched by academic indifference. Stuart's sympathetic reconstruction helped the reader to understand the peculiarities of the sage from Canberra even as he refused to accept the terms of Clark's sometimes misleading self-conception. And in his capacity to locate Clark against the background of his circumstances, he demonstrated the value of historical approaches the prophet-as-historian had elected to lay aside.[34]

Stuart's deliberate concern with the connections between history and power is evident in the title of his first publication. 'Bourgeois hegemony and radical history' suggested the capacity of the historian to strengthen the hand of the bourgeoisie. His criticism of Ian Turner chided the elder historian for a failure to recognise the 'role of ideas as active forces'.[35] Subsequent scholarship developed the theme and widened its application. In a succession of studies, Stuart carefully documented the position and power of the first generation of academic historians in Australia: controllers of the curriculum in schools as well as universities; prominent in the major cultural institutions of states and Commonwealth; welcome contributors to public discussion in press and on radio. They were respected members of the principal bodies devoted to elite discussion of Australia's place in the world: the Round Table, the Institute of International Affairs. They equipped their students for later careers devoted to government. Their writings recorded the ingenuity of white 'explorers', the evidence of political and material progress, the enterprise of the 'British race'. They thereby validated the British appropriation of Indigenous lands.[36]

The exposure of the academic historian as a handmaiden to the nation's elite was tempered always by a recognition of the limited powers of the professoriate. If academic historians buttressed the authority of the powerful, they fell far short of a capacity to dictate to governments. For all of Keith Hancock's brilliance and lucidity, his historical essay on *Australia* was unable to bump national policy from its settled path.[37] R.M. Crawford's most talented students did not take the values and capacities of the 'Melbourne School' into the broad fields of Australian public life, as he expected, but increasingly plied their trade as members of a growing academic profession.[38] And by the late 1970s, the relationship between the historian and the powerful was being fundamentally recast.

Stuart's 1983 study of 'Manning Clark's critics' was a prescient investigation of the shifting context. Rather than venturing a close examination of *A History of Australia*, the still relatively junior academic resolved to 'say something about the hunters'.[39] Stuart noted that over time academic historians were increasingly prepared to accept the validity of Clark's work 'in its own terms' and reluctant to criticise his *History*.[40] Criticisms were rather increasingly launched from outside the history profession: journalists, amateur historians, sociologists,[41] publishing in the house journals of right-wing think tanks or in the conservative press. The new critics were 'ideologues', anxious to redefine national identity for 'conservative ends'.[42] Their impact on Australian historians would be more fully explored in Stuart's book-length study of 2003 (featuring a chapter by Anna Clark), *The History Wars*.

Written against the background of Keith Windschuttle's accusations of the 'fabrication' of Aboriginal history, *The History Wars* places these conflicts in a longer historical and political perspective. Stuart draws on thirty years of writing on Australian historians to investigate growing public conflicts over Australia's past. He dates the outbreak of hostilities to a series of 'pre-emptive strikes' launched against Manning Clark.[43] In his assessment, these 'History Wars' should be distinguished from the necessary and perennial impulse to rewrite the past. The latter is an accepted aspect of research and debate, regulated by collegial inspection, academic honesty and intellectual fair dealing.[44] The former is animated by a manichean vision and a vigilant resolution against a hateful enemy.[45] It is distinguished by the prevalence of *ad hominem* attack. It is inspired by an anxiety

over the 'politicisation of history', although its prosecutors are themselves 'advocates of a partisan political cause'.[46] Its primary arenas are
'extra-curricular'.[47]

Stuart's analysis of historiographical conflict (and its outcomes)
rests partly upon an assertion of declining academic authority. He
explicitly argues that the influence of academic historians is 'probably weaker now than at any time in the past half century'. He notes
the declining strength of the academic discipline and the growing
confidence of those outside the professoriate to challenge the formal
experts.[48] He emphasises the absence of academic self-organisation
and the limited political clout of professional historians.[49] He stresses
their ill-preparedness to join public controversy.[50] He draws attention to how the mass media has become a new mechanism to
invigilate and discipline research.[51]

Appearing at a moment when the political Right had zealously
indicted the well educated in universities as a censorious and authoritarian 'new class', such an argument was never likely to win universal
acceptance. That Stuart had ascended to the chair at Melbourne, and
that he had held very many high public positions (from membership
of national inquiries to the Council of the National Library of
Australia), left him open to the charge of lacking self-awareness; he
was not obviously less well connected than his predecessors as
Melbourne professor: Crawford, Scott or Blainey. But Stuart's fate in
the aftermath of *The History Wars* certainly reinforced his claims.

On the morning of the book's launch, the *Australian* newspaper
published a feature article that presented him as the 'godfather' of
Australian history; it implied that he had corruptly influenced the
dispersal of Australian Research Council grants. A columnist from
the *Daily Telegraph* alleged that Stuart had improperly used the
stationery of the University of Melbourne in a campaign against
press bias.[52] His critical analysis of the power of a hostile media was
likened to a 'shop steward' seeking to enforce a 'closed shop'.[53] His
writings were rejected as 'vindictive' and 'abusive',[54] reviving the
'pro-Communist' invective of the Cold War. Elaborate attention was
drawn to his earlier membership of the Communist Party, long since

ceded.[55] A later critique raked over Geoffrey Blainey's resignation from the University of Melbourne and presented Stuart as the victor in a vicious game of academic politics that brought him 'power and perks'.[56]

Stuart's response to these attacks was admirable and revealing. In published correspondence with Gerard Henderson, a critic and former classmate, he comes across as unfailingly courteous.[57] He did not retreat from his well-established positions, but neither did he lapse into futile polemics. He remained active in public service. He undertook major new research in Australian history. He continued to consider historiographical problems and to write about Australian historians. He nurtured younger scholars with characteristic generosity. From the distance of two decades, it appears that he barely broke stride.

It is tempting to speculate that his deep study of his precursors might have provided him with guidance on how best to handle such hostile and troubling circumstances. Stuart avoided the dangerous malleability he had discerned in Crawford and Clark. He eschewed Blainey's defensiveness. He recalled the steadfastness of Turner and Fitzpatrick. His political constancy and his calm adherence to his own standards offered inspiration to colleagues. A chronicler of the 'History Wars', he never became a simple partisan. A student of the 'Melbourne School' of history, he maintained its commitment to civic engagement in changed and febrile times.

Had the youthful scourge of the establishment thereby become the defender of orthodoxy? As Stuart himself acknowledged in a personal reflection on the perennial question 'What is history?', published in 2018, 'It is often the case with education that the full effect is felt long after the course is completed.'[58] And in an affectionate portrait of the historian Ken Inglis, published in 2020, Stuart noted that Inglis recognised the value of the intellectual training offered in the 'Melbourne School of History' only years after graduation: an emphasis on primary sources; an openness to exchange between teachers and students; a preoccupation with the purposes of history. Stuart emphasised that Inglis 'carried those virtues with him', throughout a long and rich career. In his emphasis on a later recognition of a valuable inheritance—and in Stuart's insistence that those virtues now 'read oddly in the current lexicon of higher education'—it is possible to identify a strong autobiographical trace.[59]

But this is better seen as an active mining of the past than a passive incorporation by the Establishment. Stuart purposefully extracted the most valuable elements of his Melbourne intellectual inheritance. In a 1985 interrogation of 'The Making of a School', he explicitly drew out his own list of its 'characteristic qualities'. He listed three, differing slightly in emphasis from Inglis: a feeling for the 'larger significance' of the subject, a belief in 'its social relevance' and a 'care in the use of language' to make 'meaning plain'.[60] These qualities were consistent with a radical purpose. Stuart radicalised them. And in combining them with insights drawn from the Marxist tradition, he offered new versions of Australian history and new perspectives on the contributions and role of Australian historians.

Notes

1   Tom Griffiths's *Art of Time Travel: Historians and Their Craft*, Black Inc., Carlton, 2016, is the obvious exception, although it is also notable that of Griffiths's fourteen selected historians, only two overlap with Macintyre's chosen subjects (Hancock and Blainey).
2   'Editorial', *Intervention*, no. 2, 1972, pp. 3–4.
3   Macintyre has noted this influence in his contribution to 'What is history? Historiography roundtable', *Rethinking History*, vol. 22, no. 4, 2018, p. 515.
4   Stuart Macintyre, 'Radical history and bourgeois hegemony', *Intervention*, no. 2, 1972, p. 50.
5   Ibid., p. 48.
6   Ibid., pp. 50, 52.
7   Ibid., pp. 53, 56.
8   Ibid., pp. 58–60.
9   Ibid., pp. 65–6.
10   Ibid., pp. 67–9.
11   Ibid., p. 62.
12   Ibid., p. 72.
13   Ibid., p. 67.
14   Ibid., p. 69.
15   Ibid., p. 48.
16   Ibid., p. 71.
17   Ibid., p. 48.
18   As noted in his review of Robert Hughes's *Fatal Shore*, Stuart Macintyre, 'Hughes and the historians', *Meanjin*, vol. 46, no. 2, 1987, p. 248.
19   Stuart Macintyre, '"Full of hits and misses": A reappraisal of Hancock's *Australia*', in

Keith Hancock: The Legacies of an Historian, Melbourne University Press, Carlton, 2001, p. 41.

20 Ibid., p. 54.

21 Stuart Macintyre, Juan Maiguashca and Attila Pók (eds), *The Oxford History of Historical Writing*, vol. 4: *1800–1945*, Oxford University Press, Oxford, 2011.

22 Macintyre, 'Radical history', pp. 67, 69.

23 Stuart Macintyre, 'The making of the Australian working class: An historiographical survey', *Australian Historical Studies*, vol. 18, no. 71, 1978, p. 248.

24 Ibid., pp. 249–51.

25 Stuart Macintyre, *The Oxford History of Australia*, vol. 4. *1901–1942: The Succeeding Age*, Oxford University Press, Melbourne, 1986, p. x.

26 On how increasing resources underpinned 'a much stronger national perspective': Stuart Macintyre, 'Historical writing in Australia and New Zealand', in Macintyre, Maiguashca and Pok, *The Oxford History of Historical Writing*, p. 425. For critical references to specialisation, see Tyson Retz and Stuart Macintyre, 'The honours conception of history', *History Australia*, vol. 15, no. 4, 2018, p. 808.

27 Macintyre, '"Full of hits and misses"'.

28 An interpretation developed in Stuart Macintyre, 'The making of a school', in *Making History*, McPhee Gribble, Fitzroy, 1985, pp. 3–33. For Crawford as informant, see especially Stuart Macintyre, 'Max Crawford: A casualty of the Cold War', *Overland*, no. 155, 1999, pp. 19–22.

29 Stuart Macintyre, 'Ernest Scott: My history is a romance', in Stuart Macintyre and Julian Thomas (eds), *The Discovery of Australian History 1890–1939*, Melbourne University Press, Melbourne, pp. 71–90; and Stuart Macintyre, *A History for a Nation: Ernest Scott and the Making of Australian History*, Melbourne University Press, Melbourne, 1994. On his absence of expertise, see p. 34.

30 Stuart Macintyre, 'The radical and the mystic: Brian Fitzpatrick, Manning Clark and Australian History', in Stuart Macintyre and Sheila Fitzpatrick (eds), *Against the Grain: Brian Fitzpatrick and Manning Clark in Australian History and Politics*, Melbourne University Press, Melbourne, 2007, pp. 12–36.

31 Keith Windschuttle, 'Stuart Macintyre and the Blainey affair', *Quadrant*, October, 2008, pp. 30–5.

32 Stuart Macintyre, 'The History Wars', *Sydney Papers*, Winter–Spring, 2003, p. 81.

33 Stuart Macintyre and Anna Clark, *The History Wars*, Melbourne University Press, Melbourne, 2003, chapter 5. The quote is from p. 75. See also 'The making of a school', pp. 27–32.

34 Stuart Macintyre, '"Always a pace or two apart"', in Carl Bridge (ed.), *Manning Clark: Essays on His Place in History*, Melbourne University Press, Melbourne, 1994, pp. 17–29. The quote is from p. 20. See also Stuart Macintyre, 'Manning Clark's critics', *Meanjin*, vol. 41, no. 4, 1982, pp. 442–6. On Clark and Whitlamism, see Macintyre and Anna Clark, *The History Wars*, pp. 58–9.

35 Macintyre, 'Radical history and bourgeois hegemony', p. 67.

36 A theme developed most fully in Macintyre's writings on Scott but more generally in 'Historical writing in Australia and New Zealand'.

37 Macintyre, *The Succeeding Age*, pp. 240–1.

38 Macintyre, 'The making of a school', pp. 17–19.

39 Macintyre, 'Manning Clark's critics', p. 442.

40 Ibid., p. 448.

41 For example Malcolm Ellis, J.W. Forsyth, Peter Coleman, John Carroll and Claudio Veliz.

42 Macintyre, 'Manning Clark's critics', pp. 449–50.

43   Macintyre and Clark, *The History Wars*, p. 11.
44   Ibid., p. 218.
45   Ibid., p. 9.
46   Ibid., pp. 218–19.
47   Ibid., p. 78.
48   Ibid., pp. 16, 26.
49   Ibid., p. 15.
50   Ibid., p. 12.
51   Ibid., p. 8.
52   As detailed in Macintyre, 'The History Wars', pp. 78–9.
53   Greg Melleuish, review of 'The History Wars', *Policy*, vol. 19, no. 4, 2003–04, p. 54.
54   Kevin Donnelly, 'Enraged or engaged?', *Review* (Centre for Independent Studies), December, 2003, p. 39.
55   Melleuish, review, p. 54.
56   Windschuttle, 'Stuart Macintyre and the Blainey affair', p. 35.
57   'Correspondence: Gerard Henderson and Stuart Macintyre', *Sydney Institute Quarterly*, no. 34, December, 2008, pp. 21–4.
58   Macintyre, 'What is history?', p. 515.
59   These are virtues that Ken Inglis recognised and that Macintyre appears to endorse, in Stuart Macintyre, 'Going down from Melbourne: Oxford, scholarship, and journalism', in Peter Brown and Seamus Spark (eds), *I Wonder: The Life and Work of Ken Inglis*, Monash University Publishing, Clayton, 2020, p. 58.
60   Macintyre, 'The making of a school', p. 33.

Chapter 13

Taking note

Diane Kirkby

'Prodigious' is the word that springs to mind for Stuart Macintyre's academic output. Understood as meaning 'of extraordinarily large size, extent, power or amount; vast, enormous' in the *Oxford English Dictionary* (the complete thirty-six volumes reduced to two, which I shipped home at the end of my postgraduate studies in the United States), this is the last of four meanings. The others are equated with prodigy: 'causing wonder or amazement, marvellous', also 'unnatural', even indeed 'ominous'. Excluding these last two, we are left with a fair summation of what has been an extraordinary contribution to the writing, teaching, supervision and nurturing of Australian history. The story told among colleagues in Melbourne to explain this productivity is simply that Stuart—while spending long days in meetings, on administration of the department, serving on numerous committees—never stopped writing, even while standing, waiting, at the tram stop. It conjures a vision of Stuart with a trusty biro, perhaps a pencil, more probably a fountain pen—and these days maybe a 'device'—whipping it out of his top pocket to compose a sentence, capture an insight or edit some text. In my experience Stuart could always be relied upon to edit and improve a text. He seemed to be carrying manuscripts, his or somebody else's, in his luggage as inevitably as a toothbrush when we met at airports en route to official gatherings and meetings.

Our association was across several areas of academic life, including service on professional bodies. For a brief period in the 1990s this was as president (Stuart) and secretary (Diane) of the Australian Historical Association. For the last few years it was as deputy president (Diane) and president (Stuart) of the Australian Society for the Study of Labour History. We were two of the international humanities experts on the New Zealand research assessment panel (PBRF) for several years from its foundation in 2003. Our paths started to cross when I accepted a contract as a senior tutor in Legal Studies at La Trobe University in the early 1980s. Located in Melbourne's northern suburbs, the campus was infrequently visited by University of Melbourne staff, some of whom (although I do not recall Stuart being one) expressed the view that they almost needed to pack emergency supplies before embarking on such a long trek. It just meant that we met up instead at the many conferences, seminars, book launches and public lectures that brought together Melbourne's lively inter-university community at the Parkville campus.

Stuart and I both worked in the field of twentieth-century Australian history, particularly on questions of labour, although his was more the political history and mine the social and legal. Occasionally they intersect more directly, as in a focus on the institution of compulsory arbitration, which in the 1980s sparked consideration as it was about to be replaced by enterprise bargaining. Stuart organised a conference with Richard Mitchell from the Melbourne Law School, at which I presented a paper from a feminist perspective. It later became a chapter in their edited book.[1] By then I was on secondment from La Trobe, teaching social history at the University of Melbourne in a temporary replacement lectureship position, while Stuart was Head of Department. His advocacy was instrumental in securing a University Fellowship for Women with Career Interruptions, which enabled me to continue researching at Melbourne when the teaching position ended. That became a turning point in my career, one of the many instances when Stuart used his institutional role to assist junior staff to move their career along. I returned to La Trobe to the History Department and a contract lectureship, which was subsequently converted to a tenured continuing position. There I remained until getting ensnared in the demolition derby of downsizing pogroms now engulfing universities.

The landscape of twentieth-century Australian history is populated with many prominent individuals among whom Stuart found a distinctive place, not just by the quantity of his prodigious output but also with work that was illuminating and wide in its scope. He constantly impressed with his depth of knowledge and elegant turn of phrase. Our shared interest in maritime labour—his on communists in the maritime unions, mine on seafarers and port workers, who were often communists—meant that Stuart was the logical choice to launch my history of the Seamen's Union, at the West Melbourne rooms of the MUA in 2008. That was a memorable event, bringing some legends of the labour movement together to hear a giant of the history discipline. In the course of my research for a forthcoming book on maritime labour internationalists, Stuart's prize-winning study of the Communist Party has been a valuable reference.[2] When I was teaching Australian history to first-year students, his general histories were indispensable aids for lecture preparation. Upper-level, more specialist and honours teaching called on his many studies of welfare and social justice.

Known for his objective, measured approach and narrative style, his books set a standard for a politically engaged scholar interested in individual biography as much as the collectivism of unions. Stuart could write exhaustively about the life of a radical activist like Fremantle dock worker Paddy Troy, yet dispassionately assess (for the *Australian Dictionary of Biography*) leading parliamentarian and jurist Sir John Latham, whose political views clashed with maritime activists willing to challenge at the highest level.[3] Latham, who became Chief Justice in 1935, and famously the sole dissenting judge when the High Court declared the Communist Party Dissolution Act unconstitutional in 1951, is often portrayed as being partisan and

behaving inappropriately in the interest of his class. This is a judgement made not just by prominent New Left critics but also by
distinguished legal scholars who have studied Latham's widespread
clandestine activities. Stuart chose to concentrate on Latham's limitations, portraying him more as lacking the political skills and
creativity needed to 'separate the distinguished' from the simply
'competent'.[4]

Latham figures in my research as the first chair (1950–64) of the
Australian American Education Foundation administering the
Fulbright awards, during its formative years when he was simultaneously chair of the Australian Congress for Cultural Freedom during
the McCarthy era. Stuart's history of the social sciences in Australia
reflected a similar curiosity about higher education in postwar (also
Cold War) Australia.[5] Latham carefully steered the Fulbright board's
alignment to the US agenda while ensuring its avoidance of the
crudeness of McCarthyism, which was unacceptable to academics.
Latham also appears in my more recent research on maritime
workers when, as a Nationalist Party member of parliament, he
served in the anti-labour Bruce–Page government, which tried and
failed to deport militant Seamen's Union leaders in 1925. On that
occasion, too, the High Court's judgement foiled the government's
plans to destroy union militancy. Latham, as Attorney-General and
Minister for Industry in 1928, was the architect of amendments to
the Crimes Act and in strengthening the penalty provisions in the
Arbitration Act. Subsequently, when he joined the bench, he repeatedly maintained that the majority decision of 1925 had been wrong.
Stuart's insight in explaining Latham's actions favouring the ship-
owners who kept him on a retainer during his parliamentary career
as driven not by corruption but from 'a failure to understand militancy except as the result of seditious agitation' captures a complexity
of class politics interweaving judicial intervention, though it may be
overly generous.[6]

With my keen interest in militants and dissidents, comparing
the United States and Australia, sedition and protections of civil
liberties, finding Stuart's lesser known work, which he co-authored

with James Waghorne, has been eye-opening.[7] This is a large field in US legal history but has yet to develop an Australian historiography beyond the legal experts. It provides another example of Stuart's prodigious contribution, which may possibly even be 'ominous' for those in power.

Notes

1   Stuart Macintyre and Richard Mitchell, *Foundations of Arbitration: The Origins and Effects of State Compulsory Arbitration, 1890–1914*, Oxford University Press, Melbourne, 1989.

2   Stuart Macintyre, *The Reds: The Communist Party of Australia from Origins to Illegality*, Allen & Unwin, Sydney, 1998.

3   Stuart Macintyre, *Militant: The Life and Times of Paddy Troy*, Allen & Unwin, Sydney, 1984.

4   Stuart Macintyre, 'Latham, Sir John Greig (1877–1964)', *Australian Dictionary of Biography (ADB)*, National Centre of Biography, Australian National University, https://adb.anu.edu.au/biography/latham-sir-john-greig-7104/text12251

5   Stuart Macintyre, *The Poor Relation: A History of the Social Sciences in Australia*, Melbourne University Press, Melbourne, 2010.

6   Macintyre, 'Latham, Sir John Greig (1877–1964)'.

7   James Waghorne and Stuart Macintyre, *Liberty: A History of Civil Liberties in Australia*, UNSW Press, Sydney, 2011.

Part 4

Postwar Australia

'A very liberating experience'

The historical repositioning of postwar reconstruction

Nicholas Brown

For historians of Australian political, cultural and intellectual realignments—particularly from the perspective of the Left, social policy and reform—the subject of postwar reconstruction in the 1940s has an inevitability about it. That, however, does not make it easy ground. If the 'era' figures as one of the few moments in which the Labor Party had sufficient power, resources and purchase in office to pursue a 'new order' program, it has also prompted close evaluation of that government's caution and compromise. Then there is the question of how, by 1949, the party could comprehensively lose control of an agenda that, refashioned, would serve its opponents so well for the decades of prosperity to come.

This problem was not peculiar to Australia. The lost promise of translating wartime economic planning and social mobilisation into programs to secure the 'four freedoms' of peace and banish the 'five evils' of inequality is a familiar theme. The fate of postwar reconstruction, and its enduring legacy, has been linked to 'one of the most fundamental and important questions in political discourse—how far can the capitalist state reform the economy?'[1] From another perspective, the term has been revived in accounting for an unprecedented extension of state power and associated new knowledge claims, 'everywhere' in the wake of 'total war'—a process that at the time might have added sophistication to characterising established conflicts of class and ideology as the Cold War descended but did little to solve them.[2]

It is not surprising, then, that Stuart Macintyre should have concentrated on this period and these issues in his largest and most honoured book, *Australia's Boldest Experiment*, published in 2015. But what is significant about that study and its place in Stuart's work are the layers of reflection he brings to this engagement. Drawing out those elements—in relation to Stuart's wider interests and contribution, the context of the book, and the challenges it sets for a fresh examination of an established debate—is the objective of this chapter.

Given those 'fundamental questions', postwar reconstruction had featured in Stuart's work at several points before *Boldest Experiment*. In 1985, in *Winners and Losers: The Pursuit of Social Justice in Australian History*, he weighs the extent to which the social and economic policies of the Chifley government between 1945 and 1949 had risen above an ameliorative social security approach to address structural causes of social inequality. His conclusion was not enthusiastic. To a greater extent than British equivalents, core Australian initiatives remained 'heavily reliant on the cooperation of private capital'. At best, they recognised the claims of a rising class of administrators, advisers, planners, social workers, lawyers and researchers, all increasingly professionalised but still effectively agents of the state, and who implicitly looked to the market to provide the 'welfare class' to whom they ministered.[3]

The previous year, in his biography of the militant unionist Paddy Troy, Stuart had traced how quickly a 'postwar reckoning' had begun to turn the prospect of full employment into a wedge to marginalise any more systematic reform of labour markets and conditions. For communists, like Troy, the 'win the war' consensus had few dividends to offer in the 'ebb tide of left advance' by the later 1940s.[4] As Stuart puts it bluntly in *The Labour Experiment*, 'the assumption that the national emergency [of World War II] presented the government with a licence to sweep away all obstacles cannot be sustained'.[5]

These projects were determined critiques, bringing the sharp edge of contemporary methods of class analysis and labour history to bear in placing the 1940s in a longer trajectory. That story centred on the persistence of capitalism, the capitulation of Labor and the always fragile consensus underpinning Australia's distinctive political economy.[6] *Boldest Experiment*, however, provides a different perspective. How might that difference be explained?

This big book presents an equally expansive narrative. It offers immersion into an extensive archive of the state, commentary and community experience.[7] It reaches back into the formative interwar context and out into the international domain that was integral to policy settings and objectives. It encompasses an unprecedented span of social issues, which were drawn, as Stuart notes, into 'the transformative nature of the war, the changes it effected and further possibilities it opened'.[8] This framing is less a reflection of his reinterpretation of the underlying issues noted above in earlier works than of the broader purpose of the book. The 2010s were not the 1980s, and Stuart's work—as this collection overall reveals—always responded to changing political imperatives.

Boldest Experiment has much in common with Stuart's use of subtle portraits to explore the microcosm of cultural conflict within and among individuals through periods of transition (such as the decay of colonial liberalism's ideals of representation into the 'problematic ... social impulses', and the more restricted loyalties of 'place, culture and identity', of its twentieth-century successor).[9] The scale of the book's coverage means that there is relatively little scope to keep as close to personal and professional relationships, and to the values and personalities tested at the thresholds of power and conscience, as Stuart did with Syme, Higinbotham, Pearson and Scott. Even so, he seeks to evoke the 'creative endeavour' of the reconstruction era through the example and explanatory power of several individual figures along with that broader narrative. Those figures contextualise that endeavour and reflect Stuart's concern that such creativity has been too readily taken for granted or subsumed, particularly given the recent capture of the period (like much Australian history) in the valorisation of military conflict alone.[10]

With its focus on the fate of a complex, consuming agenda, driven primarily from within government, *Boldest Experiment* also sits alongside Stuart's work on major policy initiatives, such as his dissection of higher education policy in the 1980s. The link between this policy turn in his writing and Stuart's own professional journey in university administration is raised in several contributions to this present volume. That experience might well have framed the historian's question in relation to core themes of the postwar period: if the new class formations *Winners and Losers* identified were 'to borrow a phrase, present at their own making', was the same true of the institutional context in which they worked? Labor's endorsement of the creation of a new department to address 'the responsibility for planning a peace effort that will be no less effective than the war effort', Stuart shows, was won through divisions over the introduction of conscription on the one hand and a bid for far-reaching constitutional change on the other. But what were the internal dynamics that recast the role and character of the public service that would give carriage to such an effort and the centrality of economic expertise to it?[11]

Such questions have multiple resonances. *Boldest Experiment* mostly implicitly but still defiantly insists that the Hawke–Keating government had no sole claim to heroic 'reconstruction'—a term that, if it remains a Labor lodestar, moves in a far from constant sky (most recently, for example, in packaging an investment fund to support new, post-pandemic national industry and technology).[12] And it is in explaining these differences that the book makes use of central actors as emblematic as much as biographical figures. Those actors reflect Stuart's enduring interest—not only as a historian but also in his sometimes equivocal connection to the party itself—in the tensions of Labor in government 'consolidating power at the time when it claims to be democratising it'.[13] If with reservations in historical assessment and regrets at lost political opportunities, Stuart still finds in those actors an integrity that made those tensions more fundamentally creative than later iterations—including those of the impetuous and truncated Whitlam years, and certainly of the Hawke years—its deregulatory imperatives constituting perhaps the last chop at an inherited political economy.[14]

In concluding *Boldest Experiment*, Stuart endorses H.C. Coombs' reflection in 1993 that World War II had offered Australians a 'very liberating experience'. As Stuart summarises, 'in shaking them from complacency, [Coombs] believed [that the war] increased their self-reliance, capacity and common purpose'.[15] Coombs was, for Stuart, the 'pivotal figure in the history of postwar reconstruction'. Trained in economics, Coombs offered the 'opportunity to move consciously and intelligently towards a new social and economic system', secure from the cruel cycles of capitalism and the fictions of individual choice.[16] His skills and dedication span the book: Coombs was a model of 'equability and reasonableness' and of 'almost romantic idealism and remarkable powers of persuasion'.[17] As Director-General of the Department of Post-War Reconstruction from its foundation in 1943 to 1948, he exemplified transformations and possibilities. He negotiated the risks of public advocacy and the inherent rivalries of personal influence. He drew on qualities of rapport and professionalism that took account of wartime circumstances reaching 'deeply into the fabric of society' yet also offering the prospect of defining and addressing 'new expectations' for peace in fields from town planning and education through to international economic management.[18]

Coombs might have been a 'new class' intellectual—the most prominent among that 'exhibition of economists' who, R.G. Menzies lamented from Opposition, were displacing the authority of parliament and the voice of voters.[19] And certainly there was endurance to his expertise. Moving on to become governor of the Commonwealth and then Reserve Bank from 1949 to 1968, he was aware of the responsibility for managing 'other people's money' but equally of the need to discipline their excessive appetites. Coombs (as Tim Rowse insists) represented a constancy in social democratic critique that went to the central premises of institutional function and the balancing of policy impacts.[20] Stuart seems to endorse Rowse's contention that it was the 'socialising environment' Coombs and his colleagues experienced as the first university-educated but largely self-driven generation edging their way into public administration from the 1930s onwards that shaped much of the agenda of postwar reconstruction. That environment was energised by the 'Keynesian revolution', although it was not simply reducible to the influence of theory or ideology.

As with the patterns of sociability central to colonial liberalism, this group's 'competitive collegial' relationships—refined in lecture halls, meeting rooms, coffee shops, then in offices and corridors—tested claims to knowledge, the role of conventions, the following of protocols, the recognition of lines of authority and responsibility. No small measure of career protection was also involved in 'working out politically appropriate instruments of economic management'.[21] Rowse's title for his biography of Coombs, a 'reforming life', has multiple meanings. A 'complicated man', Evan Jones has argued, Coombs always navigated a 'technocrat/democrat dichotomy', including in the more parallel paths of state and knowledge development over coming decades.[22] *Boldest Experiment* captures those elements in their consolidation, not only as personal attributes but also as explanatory themes. Stuart's account draws out what was at stake in their performance.

Alongside Coombs stands another dominant figure in this book. Ben Chifley, as Coombs's minister, treasurer and prime minister from 1945 to 1949, was a 'frugal, cautious product of the labour movement and deeply imbued with its values'. A 'stranger to progressive intellectual enthusiasms', as Stuart writes, and with a 'distaste for personal publicity', Chifley nonetheless lent his authority to many of the principles and initiatives that meant, in Australia probably more than any other nation, reconstruction was 'attached … to the whole of the government's program and a distinct phase of the country's history'.[23] That association—ironic in itself, given political reservations at the time—reflected another instructive theme in *Boldest Experiment*: imbalances in relations of role and authority between a government and its officials, and resultant spillages into the politicisation of public programs, reflect the institutional weakness of the 'captured' elements as much as the overweening ambition of the captors. Chifley, in some ways a mediating, transitional figure, pushed past his party's divisions and entrenched suspicion of intellectuals, internationalists and economists, or shrewdly translated their ambitious plans 'into the idiom of Labor ideology'. Either way, he extended a 'policy repertoire' in ways that would have enduring influence.[24]

These two men are familiar enough subjects for Stuart. They reflect interests reaching back to labour history: elements of the autodidactic worker in Chifley, his 'homespun' manner matched to a keen 'grasp' of emerging issues and captured in causes admittedly less 'scientific' and more pragmatic than a Paddy Troy or the communists in Scottish textile and mining communities.[25] The knowledge economy institution-building to which Coombs was integral also had some precursors in the increasingly disciplined, critical coupling of 'research and publicity' in the discussion of 'affairs' Stuart traced in the interwar networks and patronage of Ernest Scott.[26] Both formations would prove hard to balance into the postwar decades, but they had nonetheless secured their place. Their coupling here is part of the rich evocation of the distinctiveness of the 1940s.

Perhaps a third actor edges tentatively into this limelight. As prime minister from 1942 to 1945, John Curtin was perhaps too bruised a politician, too trapped by old solidarities and too burdened by the suffering of military conflict to embrace its potentialities for 'liberation' in peace. In his volume of the *Oxford History of Australia*, Stuart has Curtin and Chifley in the 1930s escaping from the 'spent … political efficacy of old Laborism', aware of the importance of integrated social welfare policy and expert economic management but as 'scarcely more than presentiments'.[27] Curtin 'held back' from what remains perhaps the most elusive moment in Stuart's interpretation: what it was that might have secured the broader goals of reconstruction, or nourished citizens' expectations of it rather than leaving them hungry and tempted by lesser fare. Shy and anxious, Curtin rose to the 'fight, work or perish' pressures of wartime and might have just held together a party that (as Stuart quotes Paul Hasluck) 'took to dictatorship as calmly as a man puts on his own shoes'. The challenge of steering political or party coherence into very different postwar demands was another matter, beyond the reach of an exhausted leader.[28] Still, Curtin and Chifley held authority: far from dupes to the expertise they enabled, they stood also for older loyalties—Stuart includes a photograph of the two of them in intense conversation as they stride to Parliament House, reminding readers of the intimate Peter Corlett sculpture based on that image in Canberra's Parliamentary Triangle. *Boldest Experiment* ends with the counsel that 'a people that can throw up leaders with their qualities should honour them'.[29]

For a historian who, as our editors note, 'combines involvement and detachment', there is a striking directness to this salute. Stuart's ostensible target in this last remark (again, pointedly concluding the book) might have been Paul Keating's operatic posturing in 1990 (Curtin 'a trier'; Chifley 'a plodder'). But it underscored his insistence on deeper continuities in Labor's reshaping of Australia. And the 'people' here is an unqualified constituency, as is the imperative to correct what Stuart might elsewhere have termed a 'civic deficit' as a society fails to acknowledge what shaped it.[30] His interest in active, informed citizenship, and in leaders and leadership, is well established, even if the latter is couched (as Stuart would put it) in 'ambiguous attachment': that filial-oedipal dialectic Frank Bongiorno has noted elsewhere in this volume. Here Coombs, Chifley and Curtin evoke something of that complexity, and a time with a distinct poignancy. What is their message?

It is not that they stood alone. *Boldest Experiment* has an extensive cast, evoked in subtle terms, flagging the many elements of creativity in the work of reconstruction. There are the advocates of 'organic' community in regional planning; the engineers and the labourers for the Snowy Mountains Hydro-Electricity Scheme, the former hoping to 'subdue nature', the latter enduring the privatisation of having to live in it, isolated and harried. The newsreels capturing this project's 'sheer mass of concrete and machinery' might be contrasted to the use of other advocates in working with the power of photography and social surveys to convey the desperation endured in slum housing. The 'active public conversation' of the time ran alongside the 'naivety' of young, 'gifted' but relatively inexperienced officers who framed a 'positive approach' to causes both nationally and internationally that at least set principles in play, if not clinching arguments.[31] And the investment of more radical thinkers, such as Brian Fitzpatrick, in reconstruction programs could have the effect of setting back their advocacy for such causes as civil liberty for some time.[32] Yet these three men still highlighted the limitations inherent in these agendas. Most obvious is its gendered character, in its programs, publicity and practice. The imperatives that drove women's mobilisation into supporting the war effort 'in uniform, on the production lines, as breadwinners and household leads' might have generated considerable community interest in building on these precedents but did not necessarily translate into influence in policy priorities.[33] As Stuart shows, several factors contributed to this slippage as one dimension of wider transformations.

There was, for example, often a significant generation gap between those who represented the interests and claims of women and those whose lives were most affected by the employment opportunities, the disruption, even the exploration of sexuality, that came with war.[34] Shaping messages that spanned the divide was a challenge in itself. Despite 'men and women of Australia' being, famously, Curtin's standard evocation, an even more austere masculinism than usual in Australian politics defined his and Chifley's leadership— national government, concentrated in the still rudimentary capital, did little to entice women to Canberra, and Labor had hardly cultivated a profile for the prime ministerial wife, equivalent to that of other heads of state at the time. And while Coombs recognised the importance of such issues as the 're-establishment of women and the needs of the community' in his department's work, that coupling in itself revealed entrenched assumptions. As Stuart notes, one of the most 'outstanding' of the economists to be recruited into postwar planning, Mary Willmott Phillips, had already had her career interrupted by a forced resignation when she married (creating the vacancy that gave Coombs a vital career opportunity). She then found a role in framing for consideration in Post-War Reconstruction a 'constructive population policy', supporting motherhood within a comprehensive program of welfare and employment policy.[35] That, however, was not the message translated into programs offering to return women to lives attuned to ideals of domestic certainty and less threatened by the insecurity of unemployment.[36] Again, reconstruction's pitch, and Labor's stamp on it, had an inbuilt ambivalence.

The challenge of the return to peace for both men and women features prominently in *Boldest Experiment*. The Commonwealth Reconstruction Training Scheme (CRTS) and the Commonwealth Employment Service were established to assist those whose lives were disrupted by military service or economic dislocation. The recognition of the importance of education modelled in the CRTS in particular, Stuart judges, was another innovation with lasting influence, even if caught in 'unresolved differences of purpose'. Were such services a 'benefit', aimed at enhancing opportunities, or 'training', with more narrowly defined applications?[37] Officials debated how to distinguish between questions of eligibility and suitability, given that many of those eligible for assistance had had 'no opportunity of selecting a job or choosing a career' for themselves before the war and were poorly equipped for the task. With regard to suitability, 'something like 1 500 000 men and women will need to be employed in a different capacity from that of earlier years'.[38] Recipients were given the stern counsel that they must return to work as soon as possible:'now you must decide'—even though their lives to that point had left little time or space for decision.[39] Employers were encouraged to make use of aptitude testing and to make allowances for continuing trauma, yet also to be aware that 'war neurosis' was just one aspect of the 'problem of coping with the great and rising incidence of neurosis in the community'.[40] Workplaces had their own concerns: of the strain of new, unskilled placement on conditions that had scarcely improved for more than a decade, or the threat to established structures in the technological change evident in the skills offered to this new infusion.

In addressing these issues, Post-War Reconstruction sought to recognise in 'practically the same terms' the needs of 'men and women'. But while men presented an explicit challenge, evident in increasing industrial tension, for women the issue could seem to be one instead of relative invisibility. As the official journal for demobilisation processes, *Change Over*, observed in December 1946:

> Sixty thousand ex-service women have not relieved the female labour shortage. At first glance they seem to have packed up their uniforms and quietly faded into the hurly burly of the Australian postwar scene. They have not become a readjustment problem. It seems, then, that the majority … are looking after themselves by going back to their pre-war employment, or taking up the management of homes.[41]

The elements of that 'hurly burly' were the other side of Coombs's sense of the 'liberating experience' war had brought to Australia. Still scarred by economic depression in 1939, but at war's end relatively unscathed by the destruction that characterised much of Europe and Asia, the political economy of reconstruction in Australia was limited in distinctive ways.

Boldest Experiment reminds of the range of issues up for consideration at that time: of the extent to which war profoundly changed many aspects of the world in which citizens now oriented themselves. Stuart's emphasis on the inventiveness of policy development sharpens attention to the registers of wider cultural alignments. In 1946, for example, the first issue of a new magazine for youth could introduce a local serial on space exploration alongside another on

'Other places, other people'. A lot of conceptual shuffling was evident in reflections on 'these Indonesians we've been hearing so much about': 'We must be very careful not to blame them too much for their savage cruelty of late, against the Dutch and the British. This has been the work of the Japanese, who have done all in their power to lure the rich Indies away from any friendship with Western races.'[42]

But threaded through Stuart's account is also the steady faltering of the government's capacity to hold, direct and build on such social engagement. Central to his argument is Curtin's reluctance in 1942—at the height of national insecurity and a 'spirit of sacrifice'—to seek through referendum a firmer Commonwealth control over a range of economic and planning powers. Understanding that uncoupling between government, state and people is among Stuart's major contributions in *Boldest Experiment*.

Here again the significance of those three core figures is clear: the difficulties of a Labor government in adjusting to the possibilities of 'democracy', the complexities of a leader seeking to manage the transition between class and welfare policies, and the inevitable compromises for expertise in navigating a reform agenda. The referendum advocated for 1942 was not held until 1944, by which time the government was losing traction.[43] Voters 'delivered an unmistakable rebuff' to Labor's delayed request for a continuation beyond the emergency of war of the capacity to legislate on issues of national reform, given that by then 'the normative principles of reconstruction' were making for increasingly 'restrictive homogeneity'.[44] Whatever consensus had been created over previous years was eroding, in relationships as much as in commitments. By 1947 *Change Over* observed that 'no one will pretend the current mood of all Australians is optimistic': shortages, nervousness, industrial unrest and 'bitterness' set the mood instead.[45] Having committed to a program of public education to enrich citizenship, the ABC became even more self-conscious of having to invigilate what US commentators increasingly termed the highbrow–lowbrow tension: 'Never before in history has there been so much to unlearn for the adult, so much to learn for the child.'[46] As Stuart soberly observes, with atomic bombs so profoundly marking a change of paradigms from the slog of sacrifice to the triumph of modernity, the war ended too soon: 'of all the items that were in short supply' as suddenly Australian citizens faced a world both dramatically changed but resolutely the same, 'patience was the most exiguous'.[47]

Some readers of *Boldest Experiment* have wondered why the book did not give more attention to the long Labor tradition of demanding employment security (highlighted, they suggest, in the 1945 White Paper on Full Employment), or—on the other hand—to the fundamental conflicts between what expert officials such as Coombs pushed for and what politicians were prepared to support.[48] Stuart's point, however, would seem to be that such polarities fall short of comprehending the inherently creative, if chronically limited processes within government, within policy and within relationships that determined what reform then might mean and achieve. As with much of his work, there is an implicit lament for fading prospects of reform in *Boldest Experiment*, but that perception is shaped by a clear sense of what—politically and historically—needs to be learnt from that period and the experiences of those who lived through it. And perhaps, with this book, there is an added dimension to that tendency Stuart has observed in himself. If (invoking Stephen Spender) Stuart confesses to the allure of 'those who were truly great', he also concedes that he usually works with an ambiguity of association to more complex historical figures. There can be a restorative recognition of those he has 'neglected' (the young radical turning away from the 'Melbourne School', for example), or of those he reacted against, while coming to appreciate an inheritance, almost in filial respect for what (in the fullest sense) citizenship can accommodate.[49]

Born in 1947, his father still serving in the air force, Stuart's reflections on his life are framed by an awareness of riding the first cresting wave of baby boomer advantage, which in itself was a complicating factor in the fate of postwar 'new order' idealism. The rising pressures of family formation, coupled to those of immigration, were—as he writes in *Boldest Experiment*—among the first lines in an 'obituary' for the 'policy of economic stability' central to reconstruction planning. The government could not control it all. Stuart is aware of being 'a product' of that momentum, 'impatient with many of its characteristics' if 'deeply grateful for its transformative possibilities'.[50] He also recalls being the fourteen-year-old boy who subscribed to Hansard, a precocious if inchoate fascination with the business of politics coming before a critical engagement with political opinions.[51] If *Boldest Experiment* is distinctive in taking its readers so profoundly inside that business, as generative of rather than simply generated by politics, that is part of the fresh questioning the book prompts.

The reconstruction of the 1940s, as Stuart emphasises, was a product of austerity and the promise that community resources could provide the support for an enhanced experience of social welfare and personal development, premised on the 'integration of work and leisure' as prosperity came.[52] If there was a normative emphasis to this bargain, it was built on a range of national and international commitments to the regulation of the markets that had proved so unreliable in the past, and on breadth of consultation that recognised the depth of enduring social division and sought to work with those who were its subjects.[53] Nearly thirty years on, the circumstances of the Whitlam government—another great moment in a Labor tradition—could hardly have been more different. So also were its instincts and resources, not least in seeking to lift itself above a public service it did not trust and in defaulting to practices that did so much to test conventions of government as evade them. Stuart suggests that it was not simply the prosperity of the 1950s and 1960s which ensured that more remained of 1940s reconstruction than seems to have survived the Whitlam experiment. Such figures as Coombs had a sense of the systems of government because they had worked to build them and understood them as goals in themselves. It was not the same in 1972. And by 1983 such systems were being further radically redefined as 'clients' to direction, and by a new generation of officials and ministers with little time for the past. This gap has continued to widen. Stuart was delighted to be asked to participate in a discussion of *Boldest Experiment* among a group of federal Labor parliamentarians. Their engagement with the book was enthusiastic, but the lessons they were after seemed to relate more to the winning of elections than to the programs that might be taken to an electorate. The idea that some kind of partnership might be cultivated with the community was scarcely raised; absent completely was any consideration of the part the public service might play in framing such an agenda.[54]

Written with a full awareness of that more recent legacy, *Boldest Experiment* is an insistent intervention, in encouraging a measure of 'honour' towards its actors and in reminding us of the political complexity and creativity of what they achieved. If, in these elements of attachment, it is a rather unlikely Macintyre book, that perfectly reflects the more personal aspects of the work it is doing in acting out the 'emancipatory potential of historical consciousness'.[55]

Notes

1 Peter Burnham, *The Political Economy of Postwar Reconstruction*, Macmillan, London, 1990, p. vii.
2 See for example Mark Mazower, 'Reconstruction: The historiographical issues', *Past and Present*, vol. 210, supplement 6, 2011, pp. 17–28.
3 Stuart Macintyre, *Winners and Losers: The Pursuit of Social Justice in Australian History*, Allen & Unwin, Sydney, 1985, pp. 95–6.
4 Stuart Macintyre, *Militant: The Life and Times of Paddy Troy*, Allen & Unwin, Sydney, 1984, pp. 84, 90–1, 106.
5 Stuart Macintyre, *The Labour Experiment*, McPhee Gribble, Melbourne, 1989, p. 5.
6 Ibid., p. 65.
7 Among the major contributions of Macintyre's Post-War Reconstruction project was the extensively annotated guide to relevant National Archives of Australia collections he produced with Graeme Powell: *Land of Opportunity: Australia's Post-War Reconstruction*, National Archives of Australia, Canberra, 2015.
8 Stuart Macintyre, *Australia's Boldest Experiment: War and Reconstruction in the 1940s*, NewSouth Publishing, Sydney, 2015, p. 5.
9 Macintyre, *A Colonial Liberalism*, pp. 193, 214.
10 Macintyre, *Australia's Boldest Experiment*, pp. 3–5, 15.
11 Ibid., pp. 132, 133–7, 266–7.
12 See 'Labor's reconstruction fund', www.alp.org.au/policies/national_reconstruction_fund (viewed 29 March 2021).
13 Stuart Macintyre, interviewed by Susan Marsden, 14 February 2006, NLA TRC 5611, p. 26.
14 See Macintyre, *Labour Experiment*, p. 65.
15 Macintyre, *Australia's Boldest Experiment*, p. 470.
16 Ibid., p. 6.

17   Ibid., p. 110.
18   Ibid., pp. 5, 467, vii.
19   Menzies in D.A.S. Campbell (ed.), *Postwar Reconstruction in Australia*, Australian
     Institute of Political Science, Canberra, 1944, p. 155.
20   Tim Rowse, 'The social democratic critique of the Australian settlement', in Jenny
     Hocking and Colleen Lewis (eds), *It's Time Again: Whitlam and Modern Labor*, Circa/
     Melbourne Publishing Group, Melbourne, 2003, pp. 219–43.
21   Tim Rowse, 'Coombs the Keynesian' in Samuel Furphy (ed.), *The Seven Dwarfs and
     the Age of the Mandarins*, ANU Press, Canberra, 2015, p. 167.
22   Evan Jones, 'Nugget Coombs and his place in the postwar order', *Drawing Board*, vol.
     4, no. 1, 2003, pp. 32–4.
23   Macintyre, *Australia's Boldest Experiment*, pp. 129, 471.
24   Ibid., pp. 471–2.
25   See Macintyre on Chifley in Graeme Davison, John Hirst and Stuart Macintyre
     (eds), *The Oxford Companion to Australian History*, Oxford University Press, Oxford,
     1998, p. 118.
26   Stuart Macintyre, 'Ernest Scott: "My history is a romance"' in Stuart Macintyre and
     Julian Thomas (eds), *The Discovery of Australian History*, Melbourne University Press,
     Carlton, 1995, pp. 86–9.
27   Stuart Macintyre, *The Oxford History of Australia*, vol. 4: *1901–1942: The Succeeding
     Age*, Oxford University Press, Melbourne, 1986, p. 306.
28   Macintyre, *Australia's Boldest Experiment*, p. 109.
29   Ibid., p. 477; see also Stuart Macintyre, 'Labor reconstructs', in Jenny Hocking (ed.),
     Making Modern Australia: The Whitlam Government's Twenty-first Century Agenda,
     Monash University Publishing, Clayton, 2017, p. 194.
30   See Civic Experts Group, *Whereas the People … Civics and Citizenship Education*,
     Australian Government Publishing Service, Canberra, 1994, p. 13.
31   Macintyre, *Australia's Boldest Experiment*, pp. 122, 176, 180, 194, 239.
32   James Waghorne and Stuart Macintyre, *Liberty: A History of Civil Liberties in Australia*,
     UNSW Press, Sydney, 2011.
33   Stuart Macintyre, 'Women's leadership in war and reconstruction', *Labour History*, no.
     104, 2013, p. 66.
34   Ibid., p. 72.
35   Ibid., p. 78.
36   Macintyre, *Australia's Boldest Experiment*, pp. 180–1, 234–6.
37   Ibid., p. 328.
38   Department of Post-War Reconstruction, *Return to Civil Life: A Handbook of
     Information for Members of the Forces on Back to Civil Life*, Australian Government
     Publishing Service, Canberra, 1945, pp. 5–6; Minutes of the Central Reconstruction
     Training Committee, 6 November 1954, ACTU Deposit, Noel Butlin Archives of
     Business and Labour, N21/482, p. 10.
39   Department of Post-War Reconstruction, *Return to Civil Life*, p. 6.
40   Department of Post-War Reconstruction, *Re-establishment and the Employer*,
     Australian Government Publishing Service, Canberra, 1946, p. 5; C.M. McCarthy,
     'The rehabilitation of war neurotics', *Medical Journal of Australia*, vol. 1 (new series),
     no. 26, 1946, p. 910.
41   'Sixty thousand women out of uniform', *Change Over*, vol. 1, no.4, 1946, p. 1.
42   *Pastime*, no. 1, July 1946, p. 5.
43   See for example the portrait of Brian Fitzpatrick in James Waghorne and Stuart
     Macintyre, *Liberty: A History of Civil Liberties in Australia*, UNSW Press, Sydney, 2011,
     pp. 59–60.

44 Macintyre, *Australia's Boldest Experiment*, pp. 269, 473.
45 *Change Over*, vol. 1, no. 6, 1946, p. 2.
46 'This week', *ABC Weekly*, vol. 8, no. 1, 1946, p. 2; see also 'Highbrow–lowbrow war futile', p. 8.
47 Macintyre, *Australia's Boldest Experiment*, pp. 315, 317.
48 See for example Victor Quirk, review in *Economic and Labour Relations Review*, vol. 7, no. 4, 2017, pp. 553–8; Carolyn Holbrook, 'The collaboration of intellectuals and politicians in the postwar reconstruction: A reconsideration', *Australian Historical Studies*, vol. 47, no. 2, pp. 276–94.
49 Macintyre, *A Colonial Liberalism*, pp. 193, 214; Macintyre, 'True for the moment', in Bain Attwood (ed.), *Labour Histories: Robin Gollan, Stuart Macintyre, Verity Burgmann, Peter Beilharz and Raelene Frances*, Monash Publications in History, 1994, p. 25.
50 Stuart Macintyre, André Brett and Gwilym Croucher, *No End of a Lesson: Australia's Unified National System of Higher Education*, Melbourne University Publishing, Melbourne, 2017, p. v.
51 Macintyre, interviewed by Susan Marsden, p. 11; Macintyre, 'True for the moment', p. 20.
52 Stuart Macintyre, 'Labor reconstructs: The 1940s and the 1970s', in Jenny Hocking (ed.), *Making Modern Australia: The Whitlam Government's 21st Century Agenda*, Monash University Publishing, Clayton, 2017, p. 183.
53 Ibid., pp. 191, 195.
54 Stuart Macintyre, conversation with the author, 20 July 2021.
55 Macintyre, 'True for the moment', p. 27.

Chapter 15

Winners and losers

Rob Watts

A consciousness of the history of concepts becomes
a duty of critical thinking.
Hans-Georg Gadamer[1]

Stuart Macintyre's book *Winners and Losers: The Pursuit of Social Justice in Australian History* appeared in 1985, roughly in the middle of a period when many Australian scholars were addressing what they called the 'Australian welfare state'. Between the late 1970s and the late 1990s Australian sociologists, political scientists and policy studies scholars spent a great deal of time trying to make sense of Australia's welfare system. Apart from Stuart, other well-known historians also weighed in.

It was an interesting time for an historian to be reflecting on the idea of social justice, and especially for an historian like Stuart. The spectacular demise of the Whitlam Labor government in November 1975 brought an end to a social liberal triumphalism that had complacently treated the decades after 1945 as providing over-whelming evidence characterising the benefits of Keynesian-style economic management. By 1985 it was clear that if not defunct, the welfare state was in crisis. American and European writers were offering darker accounts, highlighting irremediable structural contradictions set loose by the relations between the 'welfare state' and its capitalist economy.

Equally to the point, Stuart's book appeared just as the Hawke–Keating government had begun boldly to embrace a neoliberal policy frame that involved 'the application of market liberalism as the organising principle and rationale for state action'.[2] This neoliberal project, usefully obfuscated by a social contract called the Accord between the Hawke government and the trade union movement, triggered lively discussion in the 1980s about how the Australian Labor Party understood social democracy and social justice. 'Social justice' also became a key policy term, for example for state governments such as Cain's in Victoria. For a time, social justice was added to administrative documents as the third in a triple bottom line. Social justice remained a keyword well into the Keating years, as the terms of discourse arguably shifted into the language of citizenship and then civics.

The academic caravan moved on. After Francis Castles delivered an obituary for the 'Australian welfare state' in 2000, critical scholars began to stop talking about it.[3] If anyone refers to a welfare state today, this is done more often than not with a wistful glance backwards, before turning to assessing the impact of decades of neoliberal policy change. As for social justice, this category has either been taken up by church groups or displaced by talk of social cohesion and building strong communities or by identity politics. This chapter offers a point of departure for asking how in the 2020s should we read *Winners and Losers* as a history of the 'pursuit of social justice in Australia'.[4]

The framework

Stuart's work as an historian and public scholar began in 1972 and remained unfinished at his death in 2021. My interest in taking up the challenge to write about Stuart and social justice was piqued initially by an interest in making sense of how an historian with a clear, avowed and—even in the 1970s—idiosyncratic affiliation with the Communist Party had somehow made their way from the Department of History at the University of Melbourne through Cambridge University, the Australian National University and back to the University of Melbourne to take up the Ernest Scott Chair in History (1990–2014).

This raises some interesting questions about how Stuart's engagement with the social sciences, and his early Marxism, figured in his work. On the one hand Stuart allowed that 'When I became a historian, the discipline was a more important branch of the social sciences than it is now'.[5] Yet Stuart also acknowledged that his intellectual models included such great narrative British historians as Macaulay, Maitland and Carlyle, while his Australian mentors included Ian Turner, Geoff Serle and Bob Gollan.[6] How did his regard for that strange miscellany of nineteenth-century liberal and conservative historians *and* twentieth-century left-leaning historians align—or become entangled—with his admiration for Marxist historians beginning with Marx, and including Eric Hobsbawm and E.P. Thompson? And how to understand—even though he was far from alone in embracing the Australian Labor Party in the 1980s—his taking a path trodden by other ex-CPA intellectuals and trade union leaders? This thinking led to two questions: how did Stuart intervene as an historian in debates about Australia's welfare state, which he thematised as an inquiry into social justice, and why should we now bother about a thirty-five-year-old book?

To do this I revise Zygmunt Bauman's provocative inquiry into the relationship between sociology and the Holocaust by asking 'what does social justice have to say about social scientists and historians like Macintyre?'[7] It should be said directly that I cannot offer anything like the kind of incisive critical recursivity Bauman brought to bear on his question. This is partly because I cannot claim to know what social justice is in the way Bauman could claim to know the Holocaust. And there is the rub. As I shall argue, neither did Stuart. Yet adopting this strategy highlights the value of confronting questions like: how do social scientists and historians such as Stuart explain or understand the pursuit of social justice historically? I begin from the premise that in the early 2020s we still need to ask how to understand the distinctive moral action of making claims for justice that constitute the pursuit of social justice. How do or should today's social sciences engage that question—and how well? As I will show, this depends to a great extent on the constitutive schemas, logics and modes of understanding or explaining that characterise the practices of social scientists and historians.

This chapter may be treated as an exercise in conceptual history. Kari Palonen notes that conceptual history should best be understood as 'a critique of normative political theory and should therefore be understood as an indirect style of political theorizing'.[8] This approach sustains a critique of normative political theory, which means among other things rejecting the tendency to engage in a search for timeless concepts. This is a disposition that Stuart clearly shares. My reading of Stuart's book is a study of 'texts in context', understood as the study of the changing semantics and pragmatics of concepts in their social and political contexts.[9] I do this in ways that underscore the inevitable diversity of traditions Stuart draws on. As Hans Sluga remarks, 'Our beliefs never form a totality in which the parts are organically and necessarily connected.'[10]

If we treat Stuart's work as belonging to a 'single though multiplex community of discourse', we may see how his work is itself a consequence of his reading of texts by previous historians and other social scientists and theorists.[11] The resultant familiarity produces a knowledge of how various kinds of political or social thought can be stated in historically discovered 'linguistic universes' derived from an eclectic body of modern social sciences, including Marxism.[12] Let me start by putting Stuart's book into its context.

The social sciences and the 'welfare state', 1950–85

When Stuart began to address the history of welfare and the welfare state, he confronted an older liberal social theoretical narrative at work in Anglophone and European scholarship, as well as a more recent critical tradition shaped by Marxist assumptions and preoccupations.

The first generation of welfare state studies in the 1950s and 1960s typically relied on theories of industrialism to account for what was claimed to be a common trajectory of rising welfare state expenditures throughout the developed world. This work argued that all industrialising nations, regardless of their specific historical and cultural traditions, or their contemporary political–economic structures, were on a path to convergence. This industrial society model claimed that modernising societies were driven along a common path of development by a combination of economic and technological growth. As Robert Nisbet reminds us, this was a story framed in terms of a *telos* of inevitable progress by such social theorists as Talcott Parsons and his quasi-evolutionary account of social change.[13] As advocates for this model argued, the very process of industrialisation disrupted traditional family functions (such as caring for the sick or elderly) while the capacity of groups like the very young, the old, the sick and the disabled to secure work was eroded by being embedded in a labour market creating new vulnerabilities. In effect the state more or less was forced to become a welfare state.

This model was open to substantial criticism. By the early 1970s the postwar political compromise that gave rise to the Keynesian welfare state was unravelling fast, especially in the United States and Europe. Neo-Marxists of the 1970s found themselves (although for different reasons) in agreement with neoliberal analysts (back then called the New Right) in concluding that the post-1945 historical compromise between capitalism and democracy was breaking down.

Neo-Marxists in particular pointed to what they saw as a critical gap in the industrialisation model: it had overlooked the conspicuous political struggle over economic resources between classes. Claus Offe highlighted two trends. He claimed that what had been well-defined class politics was being 'deradicalised' and evolving into a new style of competitive party politics in the 1960s and 1970s.[14] Revising Michels's iron law of oligarchy, Offe argued that deradicalisation was the result both of increasingly bureaucratised labour-based party organisation and the electoral pursuit of a larger, more heterogenous base of electors. The result was the erosion of collective working-class identity.[15] On top of that, the growth of welfare state programs dispelled the logic of class conflict structurally intrinsic to the commodification of labour by granting concessions to both capitalists *and* workers, producing 'more economistic, distribution-centred and increasingly institutionalised class conflict'.[16]

Whatever the merits of this analysis, it highlighted a basic conundrum: how could any state in a capitalist social order ever introduce policies capable of meeting human needs, let alone introduce equality of opportunity or outcome? Wouldn't these policies invariably run up against the constraints of the capitalist economic system, a system built as it was, on the premise that some measure of significant inequality in the ownership and disposition of basic economic and sociocultural capitals was a non-negotiable part of the design of any such society? This question reprised important insights from shrewd observers in the 1940s like Michał Kalecki and T.H. Marshall. Both were disinclined to accept that capitalism and democracy could easily coexist. Kalecki presciently asked how long would employers accept the benefits of full employment, especially if it entailed some erosion of their political sovereignty.[17] T.H. Marshall posed a parallel question when he asked whether equality of citizenship could coexist with capitalism, a system based on persistent and irremediable class inequality.[18]

These remarks frame two questions: how does an idea of social justice mesh with neo-Marxist historical and structuralist accounts? How did Stuart address this issue?

Stuart Macintyre on 'social justice' in Australia

As Stuart suggests, his inquiry into the Australian state and its engagement in various social and welfare interventions was conceived of as a history of social justice. He also acknowledged that inquiring into the 'meanings, intentions and outcomes of this protracted endeavour' in the 1980s was possibly unusual in the eyes of both historians and social scientists.[19] He begins by appearing to distance himself from both traditions of inquiry.

Of the 'historian's view', he remarks that historians would be inclined to treat any inquiry into the meaning of justice as making way for an 'imprecise, emotive concern' generating 'slipshod argument, special pleading and humbuggery' to the study of the Australian past.[20] On the other hand, he pointed to a different problem perpetrated by social scientists when he suggested that an 'economist will settle on a given standard of equity and use it to test market outcomes', while a sociologist will want to 'consider the extent to which the educational system satisfies some measure of equality of opportunity'.[21] Stuart seems rhetorically disposed here to rely on a stereotype of the social sciences as disciplines preoccupied simply with measuring quantities—although he clearly knew better.

As I have already intimated, by the 1980s Stuart had available a significant body of sophisticated work, including historical sociology, political sociology and neo-Marxist analyses, which did not conform to the stereotype of either history or the social sciences.

Stuart says that he takes social justice to be an historical phenomenon: 'historically social justice is not a unitary concept'. Second, although this is not the end of the matter, it is clear that Stuart wants to treat social justice as an historical concept that arises 'under specific circumstances and changed as the society changed'.[22] He adds: 'I am … concerned not with what social justice ought to mean but what it did mean.'[23] This is an odd, if symptomatic formulation that warrants further exploration.

In a clear nod to a range of post-Enlightenment traditions, Stuart argues that social justice can become part of a discursive practice 'only when certain historical conditions obtain … [such as the fact that] the imbalances within the society are sufficiently marked and systematic to constitute social injustice'.[24] The legacy of the eighteenth-century Enlightenment's construction of an historical narrative of teleological development is clear when Stuart argues that no idea of justice can emerge from the forms of life developed, say, by Indigenous people as they began occupying the Australian land more than 60 000 years ago.

In terms perhaps reminiscent of Ferdinand Tönnies, Stuart insists that no conception of justice can emerge from the kind of traditional community (*Gemeinschaft*) characterising the social

formations of Indigenous Australians.[25] He says that whatever ethos
the Indigenous people produced, they did not understand the many
Western rules governing kinship relations as products of human
agency and deliberation. The poetics of the great teleological theme
of community giving way to modern (civil) society (*Gesellschaft*) are
clear when Stuart says: '[Indigenous Australians] had no experience
of the faceless and disembodied aggregate that we have created …
They did not draw a distinction between the public and the private,
for their dealings were direct, face-to-face dealings within an
encompassing circle of clearly defined relationships.'[26]

Rather they were doing what they had done since the
Dreaming. Nor were these rules to be best understood in modern or
sociological terms as norms. These days we would say that Indigenous
thinking is different, drawing on an Indigenous cosmology or epistemology. Yet plainly Indigenous politics was also to summon the
language of universal human rights promised but not delivered by
the Enlightenment and its followers. Indigenous peoples were to
return at the end of Stuart's narrative, among the numbers of the
oppressed.

The problem outlined

What is the content of *Winners and Losers*? There are seven chapters
and a conclusion, which will also act as ours here. The book begins
with invasion and the tyranny of law, directed both against
Indigenous people and convicts alike. Politics came to be dominated
by law and both by the lust for the possession of land. The ideology
of Locke came to dominate the land and to justify its dispossession
of indigenous peoples. For those who laboured in the capitalist
economy, the fair wage and right to work became the hope and
slogan, as in Deakin and Higgins. Depression gave way to the hope
of full employment for men as the putative providers for their families after World War II. By the time of the Whitlam government
social justice was rendered as equality of opportunity, this to be
availed by access to health and education via the resources of the
state. Social justice seemed to have become a norm, at least for that

moment in the 1970s. Yet across the two centuries its meanings were varied and diverse, and increasingly adjusted to the relative abundance afforded by the postwar boom for those who worked in the formal economy. Simultaneously other social movements and interests were to make their voices heard. Justice, as ever, was defined against injustice. Social justice was a moving object.

How then does Stuart understand social justice, especially given that he adds that 'if the [social justice] category is to have any analytical vitality, then it needs to be located within the customs and norms of that society'?[27] What does this mean? How is social justice to be the object of inquiry, and how should we understand the idea of norms here?

Stuart early provides an excursus into Marxist accounts of the state and of class society. As he notes, 'The history of all hitherto-existing society, it has been claimed, is the history of class struggle.'[28] He observes too that the social formation set in motion after 1788 was—and is—a 'social order in which one class controls the labour of another, and where the dominant class extends and systematises its advantages into all the corners of social life'.[29] This sets up one problem. How can a conception of social justice emerge within such a social formation, especially given the previous claim that he wants to treat 'social justice' not as some idea grounded in a claim about what it ought to mean (for example, as some abstracted idea such as Rawls's famously Kantian account) but simply what it meant 'as a demand' or what he later calls a 'moral entitlement'?[30] Stuart also wants to insist that social justice 'was pursued not as an ethical category but as a means of altering actual social relationships'.[31]

Staking a claim on social justice, in this way of thinking, seems to be rendered internally to the existing pattern of social relations. When the declared rules of the game are violated, the state can be summoned to bring justice. There is no room for claims to justice here that are not within the normative culture of the social form.

Stuart, however, makes it clear that the state should not be treated as a given or in a structural–functional or reductionist way. Indeed his narrative is situated at the point where 'the ambit of state authority overlaps the claims of moral entitlement'.[32] This is because he says the state is both an instrument for giving expression through the mechanisms of democratic representation 'of the popular will', even as it also 'serves as an instrument of control and coercion'.[33] Here there are obvious resonances with theoretical interventions that emphasised the contradictions of the welfare state producing an ongoing legitimation crisis.

Stuart emphasises two features: 'the state too is shaped by historical processes' while it must also try to solve the 'perennial problem of authority' (or is that legitimacy?). This presents as an issue given that no society, if it relies only on 'compulsion and nothing else could hardly avoid destruction through internecine conflict or paralysis by sullen resentment'.[34]

At this point Stuart seems to revert to a classical sociological position. He has previously committed to exploring the intersection where 'the ambit of authority overlaps the claims of moral entitlement'.[35] How are we to understand the reference to this idea of moral entitlement, especially given his commitment to a classical sociological tradition via a Marxist frame?

We need to pay attention to norms. Stuart allows this when he suggests that one way of resolving the puzzle of why subordinated classes or groups obey those responsible for these relations of subordination is to 'consider the moral norms that prescribe the mutual obligations of the weak and the strong'. As Stuart says, 'These standards of right and wrong are not given by law.'[36] This suggests the legal positivist tradition represented by H.L.A. Hart, which precludes any role for moral ideas or principles in lawmaking.[37]

So, given Stuart's interest both in the 'claims of moral entitlement' and his premise that somehow, in any society characterised by class inequality, there are 'mutual obligations … [between] the weak and the strong', how is this best described?[38] Stuart appeals to a sociological notion of norms while also referring to the Marxist tradition, which emphasises class conflict.

In appealing to the sociological tradition, Stuart claims that what he calls 'notions of obligation and entitlement are deeply embedded in the social fabric and they provide the means whereby people think about and explain the circumstances of their lives'.[39] Certainly conventional sociologists since Durkheim have believed that it is society, which is both the arbiter and the constitutive source of any given society's moral codes, which in turn apparently explains the behaviour of its members. In effect the sociological reduction of morality to a set of norms, and manners that are socially, culturally and historically variable, simply insists that this is what society does, but at the cost of obliterating any other account of moral judgement. Here Bauman offers a valuable, if unintended insight with his sociological explanation of why the Holocaust happened.

Bauman's explanation stresses the malevolent and anti-moral character of the Enlightenment and the concept of civilisation to which the modernising project gave rise. Bauman insists that the rise of scientific social engineering practices and the unreflective consequences of large-scale bureaucracies constrained or destroyed the possibilities of a just society. Even more to the point, Bauman says the Nazi state escaped the conventional social control (that is, moral norms) of German society as it embraced technocratic rationality. As he puts it: 'Having decreed out of court such distinctions between good and evil as do not bear the sanctioning stamp of society, we cannot seriously demand that individuals take moral initiatives.'[40]

There is a high price to pay when sociologists conflate the moral with whatever passes for the idea of social order or society and its norms. Those costs include sacrificing attention to the practice of practical reasoning in ways that are dependent, in part at least, on traditions of moral inquiry and in part on the capacity to exercise our moral imagination and acknowledge the tug of conscience in our judgements. If the Durkheimian (or liberal) view of justice is immanent (or internal), the Marxist view is unhelpful in its dismissive approach to morality. Marxism offers an external view, which has no robust theory of morality at all. The crisis of Marxism, announced by Louis Althusser in 1980, leaves the door open to liberalism to fill this space (although critics of the liberal utilitarian tradition such as John Finnis and Michael Sandel doubt that it can).[41]

Marx may have had an ethics, but Marxism as a tradition has been weak on morality. It seems reasonable to conclude that Marxism, unlike the larger sociological tradition, is unable and unwilling to articulate distinctive moral claims. Equally the greatest failure on the part of organised Marxist parties and movements, especially in the twentieth century, was their inability or refusal to articulate that distinctive moral claim. It is here that Stuart comes into his own, with some powerful insights condensed into a scintillating eight-page concluding essay that matters still thirty-five years on.

Macintyre's conclusion

Winners and Losers closes with seven theses. As Stuart says, the closer he comes to the present the more polemical his tone becomes. They read as follows:

1. Demands for social justice arise in a market society where injustices are no longer based on fixed relationships.
2. The early claims of social justice are formulated as protests against the effects of the market.
3. Characteristically, in this country, social justice is pursued through the representative bodies of the state and institutionalised in state instrumentalities.
4. The ambiguity of the state is sharpened by its assumption of social welfare responsibilities.
5. The search for social justice both reflects and extends conflict.
6. It follows that progress is neither linear nor irreversible.
7. Finally, there is the activity of the oppressed.[42]

Stuart appears to confer upon the oppressed a unique degree of responsibility for rectifying the manifold forms that oppression takes. He says, for example, that it is this activity by the oppressed 'that has determined the fate of social justice'.[43] He adds that this activity of the oppressed is the expression of 'popular expectations of entitlement, commonly held standards of what is fair and what is unfair, which those in authority have had to take into consideration'.[44]

Here Stuart seems to anticipate the development of social movement studies, reflecting a deeper appreciation of the diverse sources of dissent and demands for justice extending the conventional Marxist preoccupation with working-class movements. Social movement scholars foreground the substantial role played by collective movements initiated by people who are not themselves directly oppressed, including children and young people, students and professionals, and civil society organisations. This also seems to allow for the play of moral emotions or moral imagination sourced to and resourced by any number of traditions of moral practice.

Stuart's account of the Australian experience rightly insists on its distinctive features. He does not deny that the demand for social justice in colonial society arose in a market society where injustices were no longer based on fixed relationships such as characterised earlier pre-capitalist societies.[45] However, we should not expect to describe the evolution of the Australian welfare state as if we are dealing with Scandinavia, Germany or the USA. This is because, without downplaying the consequences set loose by a class-based capitalist economy, the kind of market society set up in Australia also enabled the 'creation of a civil society in which all citizens enjoyed certain elementary rights in common' and that 'this was a pre-condition for the pursuit of social justice'.[46]

The early claims of social justice in Australia were formulated as protests against the effects of the market, which come as Stuart insists 'from two directions, from above as well as below'.[47] Here Stuart invokes the growth of colonial liberalism as an important and distinctive feature of the Australian experience, a theme he elaborated later.[48] It was Australian liberals, he says, who were prepared to 'alter the outcome of free competition' as part of a trade-off 'between social justice and social stability'.[49] He draws for example on Alfred Deakin, who in 1903 argued: 'Permanent prosperity can only be based upon institutions which are cemented by social justice. Under the influence of a sense of injustice, of inequality, of unfairness and helplessness, the working population cannot be expected to submit to their lot.'[50]

The role played by Australian liberalism also helps to explain why social justice in Australia is 'pursued through the representative bodies of the state and institutionalised in state instrumentalities'.[51] Against the tendency to treat the state as some kind of monolithic black box tirelessly working to enforce the power of the capitalist system, Stuart insists that the state 'itself becomes a site of conflict' where its 'activities reflect the balance of forces'.[52] When he refers to the 'fiscal crisis of the welfare state', he clearly draws inspiration from the work of neo-Marxists like James O'Connor and Jürgen Habermas.[53] Rather than refer to contradictions, Stuart highlights what he calls the 'ambiguities of the state', which are heightened 'by its assumption of social welfare responsibilities'.[54] As he says, 'the search for social justice both reflects and extends conflict'. This is why Stuart insists that any progress made in achieving social justice 'is neither linear nor irreversible'.[55]

Stuart was writing even as the Hawke–Keating Labor governments (1983–96) were demonstrating the truth of that observation. As Elizabeth Humphrys has argued, the Hawke–Keating governments used their often revised Accord contract with the trade union movement to sponsor a neoliberal makeover with devastating effects.[56] Among its many accomplishments the welfare state was recreated. Welfare payments continued to expand but now, as Loïc Wacquant notes, as part of a 'punitive turn' informed by a 'behaviourist philosophy relying on deterrence, surveillance, stigma and graduated sanctions to modify conduct'.[57]

Looking back thirty-five years later with plenty of critique like Mark Fisher's account of 'capitalist realism' to draw on, what is the legacy of Stuart's account of social justice in Australia?[58]

What Stuart said then—and it matters still—is that politics and political will count more than the lazy critique of scholars pointing to the alleged effects of structural determinants. We still need to talk about winners and losers. What resonates in Stuart's account is an enthusiasm that points to politics. Politics is what we do when we are roused to action by issues we are concerned about, an idea very like John Dewey's liberal account of democracy.[59] For Dewey, a public is a community of strangers, made up of actors who are jointly implicated in an issue but who do not belong to the same social world, which is why they must become organised into a political community if they are to address the issues in question.

Like Dewey, Stuart understands the need for political organisation, skills and resources. This is because the 'outcome of campaigns for greater social justice … depend on the ability of its proponents to mobilise support, not just by lobbying and political manoeuvre but by the widest discussion and debate of social priorities'.[60] This matters in a time when, aside from capitalist realism, many of us agree that representative democracy is in deep crisis. Stuart here seems to suggest that a famous Marxian aphorism requires a tweak: 'Social scientists have only interpreted the world in various ways; the point is to change it.' All the same, as Gadamer tells us, understanding retains its premium. The conversation between historians and social scientists, Marxists and liberals that animates *Winners and Losers* is still worthy of emulation.

Acknowledgement
I would like to thank the two editors of this book for their gentle but firm advice, which added grace, clarity and sense when these qualities were missing.

Notes
1   Hans-Georg Gadamer, 'Rhetoric, hermeneutics and the critique of ideology: Metacritical comments on truth and method', in K Mueller-Vollmer (ed.), *The Hermeneutics Reader*, trans. J Dibble, Basil Blackwell, Oxford, 1986, p. 278.
2   Jonathan Strauss, 'Opposition to the Accord as a social contract in the 1980s', *Labour History*, no. 105, 2013, pp. 47–62.
3   Francis Castles, 'A farewell to Australia's welfare state', *International Journal of Health Sciences*, vol. 31, no. 3, 2001, pp. 537–44.
4   In addressing Macintyre's treatment of the idea of social justice, I focus only on this book.
5   Stuart Macintyre, 'Q&A with Stuart Macintyre', Australian Historical Association Early Career Researchers, 18 June 2018, https://ahaecr.wordpress.com/2018/06/13/qa-with-stuart-macintyre/
6   Ibid.
7   Zygmunt Bauman, *Modernity and the Holocaust*, Cornell University Press, Ithaca, NY, 1989, p. 3.
8   Kari Palonen, 'The history of concepts as a style of political theorizing: Quentin

Skinner's and Reinhart Koselleck's subversion of normative political theory',
European Journal of Political Theory, vol. 1, no. 1, 2002, p. 91.

9 Reinhart Kosselleck and Michaela Richter, 'Introduction: Translation of Reinhart
Koselleck's "Krise"', *Journal of the History of Ideas*, vol. 67, no. 2, 2006, p. 358.

10 Hans Sluga, *Politics and the Search for the Common Good*, Cambridge University Press,
Cambridge, 2014, p. 117.

11 Kosselleck and Richter, 'Introduction', p. 358.

12 Ibid.

13 Robert Nisbet, *History of the Idea of Progress*, Routledge, London, 1994; Talcott
Parsons, 'Evolutionary universals in society', *American Sociological Review*, vol. 29,
no. 3, 1964, pp. 339–57.

14 Claus Offe, *Contradictions of the Welfare State*, Routledge, London, 1984.

15 Roberto Michels, *Political Parties: A Sociological Study of the Oligarchical Tendencies of
Modern Democracy* [1915], trans. E and C Paul, Batoche Books, Kitchener, Ontario,
2001; Offe, *Contradictions of the Welfare State*.

16 Offe, *Contradictions of the Welfare State*, p. 193.

17 Michał Kalecki, 'The political aspects of full employment', *Political Quarterly*, vol. 14,
no. 4, 1943, pp. 322–6.

18 Thomas Marshall, *Citizenship and Social Class: And Other Essays*, Cambridge
University Press, Cambridge, 1950.

19 Stuart Macintyre, *Winners and Losers: The Pursuit of Social Justice in Australian History*,
Allen & Unwin, Sydney, 1985, p. vii.

20 Ibid., p. vii.

21 Ibid., p. vii.

22 Ibid. p. vii.

23 Ibid. p. vii.

24 Ibid., p. x.

25 Ferdinand Tönnies, *Community and Association (Gemeinschaft und Gesellschaft)* [1887],
Routledge & Kegan Paul, London, 1955.

26 Macintyre, *Winners and Losers*, p. x.

27 Ibid., p. x.

28 Ibid., p. ix.

29 Ibid., p. x.

30 Ibid., pp. vii and ix.

31 Ibid., p. viii.

32 Ibid., p. ix.

33 Ibid., p. viii.

34 Ibid., p. ix.

35 Ibid., p. ix.

36 Ibid., p. ix.

37 Herbert Hart, *The Concept of Law* [1961], J. Raz and P. Bullock (eds), 2nd edn,
Oxford University Press, Oxford, 1994.

38 Macintyre, *Winners and Losers*, p. ix.

39 Ibid., p. ix.

40 Bauman, *Modernity and the Holocaust*, p. 210.

41 See John Finnis, *Natural Law and Natural Rights*, Clarendon Press, Oxford, 1980;
Michael Sandel, *Justice: What's the Right Thing to Do?*, Farrar, Straus & Giroux, New
York, 2010.

42 Macintyre, *Winners and Losers*, pp. 139–46.

43 Ibid., p. 146.

44 Ibid., p. 145.

45 Ibid., p. 139.
46 Ibid,. p. 140.
47 Ibid., p. 141.
48 Stuart Macintyre, *A Colonial Liberalism: The Lost World of Three Victorian Visionaries*, Oxford University Press, Melbourne, 1991.
49 Macintyre, *Winners and Losers*, p. 141.
50 Deakin cited in ibid., p. 141.
51 Macintyre, *Winners and Losers*, p. 141.
52 Ibid., p. 144.
53 Ibid., p. 143. See James O'Connor, *The Fiscal Crisis of the State*, St Martin's Press, New York, 1973; Jürgen Habermas, *Legitimation Crisis*, Beacon Press, Boston, 1975.
54 Macintyre, *Winners and Losers*, p. 143.
55 Ibid., p. 144.
56 Elizabeth Humphrys, *How Labour Built Neoliberalism: Australia's Accord, the Labour Movement and the Neoliberal Project*, Brill, Leiden, 2019.
57 Loïc Wacquant, 'Bourdieu, Foucault and the penal state in the neoliberal era', in D Zamora and M Behrent (eds), *Foucault and Neoliberalism*, Polity, Cambridge, 2016, p. 114.
58 Mark Fisher, *Capitalist Realism: Is There No Alternative?*, Zero, London, 2009.
59 John Dewey, *The Public and Its Problems* [1927], Swallow/Ohio University Press, Athens, Ohio, 1984.
60 Macintyre, *Winners and Losers*, p. 144.

Chapter 16

History and the 'social science project'

Tim Rowse

In *The Poor Relation: A History of Social Sciences in Australia*, Stuart states two aims: 'to argue how and why current [higher education and research] policy is mistaken' and to understand 'the reasons for the lesser regard and support for the social sciences'.[1] I will avoid the first of these topics (knowing that Simon Marginson is contributing to this book). To deal with the second I will argue that while the social sciences may have been the 'poor relation' in Australia after World War II, we can find in Stuart's work a richer history of the social sciences in Australia if we widen our understanding of 'social science' to include the formation and propagation of knowledge of society.

Consider Stuart's sketches of the rise of Anthropology and Economics as university disciplines. In *The Succeeding Age* Stuart writes of anthropologists, with Rockefeller funds, shaping Australia's administration of its League of Nations mandate, Papua and New Guinea. Anthropologists addressed an administration convinced of the need to maintain and adapt the village as an institution inherited from the pre-colonial past.[2] At this time, within Australia, economists were also being called upon. They 'were increasingly to be found on statutory bodies and committees of inquiry into areas of public policy, where they found much to criticise. Loan policy, public works, wage determination and the labour market, overseas trade, the tariff, rural settlement, all were weighed in the balance of their specialist knowledge and found wanting'.[3] The economists claimed authority for their insights into economic realities in order to fortify the state against 'the excessive demands that were made of it' by party competition for votes in a liberal democracy.[4] In *Winners and Losers* Stuart writes that the economists' rise as a discipline and profession was marked ideologically by their challenging 'distributive justice' as a value guiding public policy, by their 'deprecating the irresponsibility of the popular approach' and by their propagating 'the new economic wisdom that personal sacrifice was unavoidable and that it was no longer possible to hide behind the skirts of the government'.[5] The economists' 'interpretation of equality of sacrifice' (in the Premiers Plan, for example) 'had an unequal impact on the different groups' in the Great Depression.[6] These passages do not tell a story of the weakness of social science in its relationships with government but of the technical plausibility and civic resonance of recently institutionalised social sciences.

Social sciences as the poor relation

Stuart nonetheless has a point in lamenting that social science has been the 'poor relation' of the physical and biological sciences. The phrase calls attention to an inequity, and *The Poor Relation* is not Stuart's first study of inequity. He begins his essay 'Equity in Australian history' by noticing that 'in the course of arranging their affairs Australians have often appealed to implicit principles of equity'.[7] The word 'principles' is important: only by appeal to some principle can a *difference* be judged an *inequity*. Stuart presents certain differences between the physical and biological sciences on the one hand and the social sciences on the other as inequities. The different foundational grants to the Academy of Science and to the Social Science Research Council in the early 1950s displayed a 'humiliating disparity of fortunes'.[8] And 'as Australian universities expanded in the postwar decades and adapted to the new expectations of research activity, the social scientists fell behind the physical and biological scientists in provision, capacity and standing'.[9] 'Provision' is quantified. 'Twenty per cent of all applications for funding in the first triennium of the Australian Research Grants Committee [founded in 1965] came from the social sciences and humanities, and they received twelve per cent of its funds.'[10]

These sentences present *differences* in esteem and financial support, but to see difference as inequity is to invoke some 'principle' of equity. What is wrong with the social sciences getting less support than the physical and biological sciences?

Stuart argues that we should historicise Australians' understandings of fairness and justice by paying attention to how liberal figures in Australia's public life fixed 'the boundaries within which this conception [that is, 'equity'] could operate'.[11] An important part of fixing the boundaries was to denominate the parties whose relationship with the wider social order was argued to be inequitable: whose circumstances were being compared with what? A political history of 'equity' requires recognition of certain 'disadvantaged groups' or 'client groups' or 'interest groups' (Stuart's terms) demanding to be treated more equitably. Which groups have not got a 'fair go' and have sought redress? The small settler; the wage-earner; 'aged, orphaned and destitute people'; women; the unemployed; Indigenous Australians; the disabled—each of these categories of Australians has, at some time, succeeded in identifying itself as an aggrieved interest.[12] In agitating for 'equity' each has highlighted their difference as a *corrigible* difference of condition—that is, as unfairness that public policy must amend.

In *Winners and Losers* Stuart narrates episodes of asserted inequity and attempts at corrective action: the social justice struggles of convicts, small settlers, wage-earners, the unemployed, those not supported by wage labour, the school-aged, women and Aboriginal people. He highlights changes in the ways that social justice has been conceived, and he traces the effects of public policy solutions on Australian government. The book's succinct conclusion is the best historical conspectus of Australia's political culture that I know. Here he remarks: 'It would have been possible to select a different range of case studies with a much stronger emphasis on present-day priorities.'[13] Is it possible to see *The Poor Relation* as a further case? The social sciences may be seen as 'underdogs' in a knowledge economy that—if only it were fairly structured—would provide them with more resources, building their capacity and elevating their public standing.[14]

There are two reasons not to read *The Poor Relation* as if Australian social sciences were just another aggrieved sector of Australian society identifying itself as disadvantaged and demanding a fair go.

One is that Stuart's respect for what he calls the 'activity of the oppressed' is less plausible when the putative 'oppressed' are social scientists employed by universities—relatively privileged Australians.[15] Indeed, in *The Poor Relation* Stuart's sympathy for the social scientist underdog falters. His narrative makes particular persons (and their egos) visible; in this branch of humanity characters are made from the same crooked timber as in all others.[16] He allows readers to see the social sciences from the standpoint of a sceptical public. Protestations of the utility of social science 'sounded like special pleading', as social scientists, adapting to the increasingly instrumentalist turn in government policy rhetoric in the 1980s and 1990s, had to compete with knowledge workers claiming 'to save lives and effect a digital revolution'.[17] Their claim to serve practical purposes has sometimes 'seemed a thin disguise for empire building'.[18]

The other reason to pause before seeing social scientists (the poor relation) as an ill-treated and aggrieved constituency is that in the very act of representing an inequity we are 'doing' social science. Social science is one source of knowledge of 'oppression', social injustice and social exclusion; when social science is impoverished our discourse about social inequity is incapacitated. A weak social science is thus a society's predicament: underdeveloped self-knowledge, incapacity for critical self-reflection, clueless on correctives. This makes the 'poor relation' a unique case—not simply the latest in a series of cases of constituencies saying they are inequitably treated.

Social scientists' self-representation

In *The Poor Relation*, Stuart depicts social scientists bargaining for resources within a 'triangle', originating in the 1940s, formed by three agents: business (seeking to invest in knowledge-intensive products and services); governments (for whom the promotion of innovation and ensuring a skilled workforce have become increasingly important goals); and universities (increasingly accountable to governments).[19]

Under the stimulus of war ('the sudden discovery of social science as an instrument of the state in a period of extremity'), a Committee on Research in the Social Sciences first met in August 1943.[20] As a standing committee of the Australian National Research Council (ANRC), this voluntary network of academics and senior Commonwealth public servants began to publish *Australian Social Science Abstracts*: 1669 abstracts between March 1946 and September 1950, nearly half of them in Economics. When physical and biological scientists decided to form the Academy of Science in 1951, they excluded the social sciences, and the committee responded by re-forming as the Australian National Social Science Research Council in August 1952 (soon dropping the 'Australian National'). The Social Science Research Council (SSRC) initially consisted of fifty members. Obtaining funding from the Carnegie Foundation in 1953 (until 1959) and from the Commonwealth Government, it incorporated (in the ACT) in 1957.

The SSRC published abstracts (renamed the *Bibliography of Research in the Social Sciences in Australia*) until 1969, and UNESCO recognised it as the national coordinating body for the social sciences. The Commonwealth urged the SSRC to seek non-government donations, like the Academy of Science. In the 1960s, the Myer Foundation became an SSRC donor. In 1971 the SSRC became the Academy of Social Sciences in Australia (ASSA)—emulating the formation of the Australian Academy of the Humanities in 1969.

Stuart shows that social scientists have found it difficult to act corporately, both to do research (multidisciplinary projects) and to lobby for research funds. He points to a strength that has also been a weakness: disciplinarity. Almost to a man or woman, the social scientists in this series of national bodies have been academics, employed by universities to teach, and funded by their universities to do research; each social scientist has worked within a discipline-based department. The social sciences' pattern of development in Australia reinforced disciplines, forming discipline-based associations and founding discipline-based journals. Belonging to a discipline has been a social scientist's foremost vocational identity. The 'paradox' of ASSA (and its predecessor, the SSRC) is that it 'consisted of the country's leading social scientists whose primary obligations lay elsewhere'—obligations intensified by the increasing intramural managerial responsibilities of senior academics since the 1990s.[21]

The ambivalence of 'the discipline' is a leading theme of *The Poor Relation*. On the one hand Stuart firmly defends 'the discipline' as a 'powerfully coherent, durable and adaptive way(s) of advancing knowledge'.[22] He closes *The Poor Relation* with a defence of disciplines as 'repositories of ... specialist knowledge ... modes of investigation and bridges to work done elsewhere'.[23] His plea for 'the discipline' is his critical response to a theory of knowledge production—influential among policy-makers—that highlights 'the context of [knowledge's] application, framed by the problem rather than its disciplinary components, and negotiated between the academics, users and stakeholders according to commercial viability and social acceptability'.[24] The currency of this theory encouraged policies indifferent and even hostile to disciplines, supporting a shift, criticised by Stuart, 'from merit to utility, from intellectually self-propelled activity guided by peer judgement to predetermined projects chosen for their practical applications'.[25] Insofar as public policy (and, by extension, university policy) is informed by this problem-focused view of the rationale for research, the social sciences continue to be the poor relation, suffering in competition with the physical and biological sciences. It is easier for governments and the public to appreciate the instrumental efficacy of research in the physical and biological sciences; and this is reinforced by perceptions of the epistemological superiority of 'Science' over social science.

Stuart insists on the legitimate epistemological diversity of disciplines. He gives a sympathetic account of Paul Bourke's 1996 defence of the social sciences from the scientistic expectation that, as they mature, they should converge in method and theory.[26] In other writing, as I will show, he defends History and other HASS disciplines whose value is not that they produce technical solutions to particular problems (although at times they might) but that they reproduce a civic capacity for reflective and subtle public discourse.

But there is, on the other hand, a more negative account of disciplinarity in *The Poor Relation* and aligned papers. In their quest for relevance to governing elites, Stuart suggests, social scientists have sometimes been held back by a government perception that social scientists are excessively encased in their disciplines.[27] Disciplines deploy their own endogenous scales of honour, so that even sincere academic claims that their knowledge is of 'practical import' have been 'always secondary to their academic ambitions'.[28] And, as he says, social scientists vary in their hunger for practical relevance: to some it does not matter at all, and their careers are no worse for that. Stuart expounds Nugget Coombs's lament in 1982 that 'academic specialism' had subverted the reformist vision of the Australian National University's founders.[29] That two of the four founding schools were Social Sciences ('devoted to the core disciplines') and Pacific Studies ('applying them to Australians' regional circumstances') had seemed to Coombs a way to put social science knowledge 'at the service of national policy'.[30] Stuart seems sympathetic to Coombs's retrospective. The tendency towards 'academic specialism' is more than once rendered by Stuart's metaphor 'disciplinary undertow'—a phrase implying guild habit and intellectual inertia.[31] Stuart is disappointed in the routinisation of disciplinarity in Australia, finding social scientists 'conspicuously unreflective on developments in their disciplines': this has left them with little to challenge the utilitarians' policy assertion since the 1980s.[32] Projects that sought to combine disciplines, such as the Commonwealth-funded Botany Bay Project (1972–76), also set managerial tests for which distinguished social scientists were under-prepared by their experience of leading university departments.

We see Stuart's ambivalence towards the disciplinary formation of the social sciences when he writes that university teaching consolidated social scientists' organisation in separate disciplinary departments and 'shaped their research along disciplinary and professional lines, weakening commitment to the *social science project*'.[33] But what is/was the 'social science project'? Mundanely, it has been SSRC/ASSA lobbying governments for research funds. A more interesting answer invites us to follow a thread running through Stuart's work: the 'social science project' is to enable the modern state to know society as governable.

Social science and political agency

Let us consider, more fully than Stuart in *The Poor Relation* allows himself to do, the politics of social science. In the rest of this chapter, I take the term 'social science' to include not merely the research and teaching done by salaried academics in university departments bearing the name of a particular discipline but also the intellectual work—of many kinds, by many kinds of agent—that creates representations of 'society' as a governable object.

'Social science' in this broader sense of practically useful representations of 'society' began to arise in the late eighteenth century as a function of the fiscal–military state.[34] Networks of producers of such knowledge began to formalise their collection and analysis of social data.[35] Defined in this broad sense as *knowledge of the social as governable*, 'social science' has been in Australia since British authorities began to discuss how to manage an experiment: a new society composed of convicts, ex-convicts and free immigrants.

Stuart gives a vignette of this nascent 'social science' when, in the opening chapter of *Winners and Losers*, he draws attention to the principle of 'less eligibility' guiding the British government's penal policy in New South Wales and Van Diemen's Land. How to make a 'society' in what was still a penal colony was a question of public policy by the 1810s, and the answer included applying a concept from the ruling class's extant stock of social knowledge: 'less eligibility'. It meant that convicts were distinctly liable to such harsh treatment that free men and women of the lowest class—no matter how desperate in their poverty—would be able to distinguish their free condition from the convict lot.

The concept 'less eligibility' conveys the governing elite's useful conception of how the poor think, how they reckon their risks, duties and fortunes; it summarised experience of the exercise of authority over stratified configurations of property and labour in the British Isles—in particular, the management of the poor. 'Less eligibility' plausibly represented the reasoning of the poor: that to observe convicts living under 'salutary terror' would encourage good behaviour by the free. On the pertinence of this principle to authority, the authorities Stuart quotes are: Commissioner J.T. Bigge, Governor George Arthur, Sydney Smith and Robert Peel.[36] None of them 'social scientists', they each deployed practically tested and plausible knowledge of how a hierarchical social order could be reproduced.

Governing colonies necessitates the experimental application of social knowledge. In much of Stuart's work he shows Australian colonies giving scope to liberals who had to become practically competent in the knowing and doing of government. Lacking an 'equivalent Tory tradition' that conceived of governing in paternalist hierarchical terms, in continuity with 'tradition', the colonies' liberals took responsibility for mediating 'social justice' demands, devising institutional solutions consistent with maintaining prosperity in a market-based, capitalist settler colony. 'Hence their departures from the orthodoxies of political economy on the tariff question, their circumscription of the labour market and their willingness to alter the outcome of free competition.'[37] He quotes Deakin declaring that 'permanent prosperity can only be based upon institutions which are cemented by social justice'.[38] A governing elite guided by this belief must commit to social inquiry, for the identification and measurement of injustice is not only an effect of political agitation but also of intellectual effort to represent 'the social' and to promote policy solutions that plausibly pertain to the agreed social realities.

In *A Colonial Liberalism* Stuart discusses the 'moral economy of colonial liberalism' in writings by David Syme—an inductive antipodean social theorist with a reputation 'as an original thinker of international repute'.[39] Syme combined concerns for land tenure reform and industry protection 'into a coherent liberal discourse'.[40] Seeing Australia as vulnerable because of its dependence on a few exports, Syme questions the 'free trade imperialism' that had been popularised 'in countless texts and tracts' based on the classical economists and deployed as common sense. Its social imaginary postulated

> economic man with a natural propensity to barter and accumulate wealth; the liberty and autonomy that the possession of wealth conferred, and the corresponding necessity of self-reliance; the notion of the self-regulating market, its participants simultaneously pursuing their own advantage and advancing the common interest; the extension of the market across national boundaries so that trade ran in natural channels and producers maximised their comparative advantages.[41]

Syme's critique of this liberalism absorbed much from mid-century European political economy, and he studied the economic history of his times. His political economy upheld community and equitable dealings between social classes (although not between men and women and not between coloniser and colonised). Postulating moral community as a necessary brake on self-interest, Syme's 'economic writings conceived the social as primary and emphasised the importance of the ties of the family, community and nation'.[42]

Stuart's colonial liberals, such as Syme, idealised themselves as 'men of goodwill mediating between master and man'.[43] But what did 'man' think? An organised labour movement supported a socialist intellectual tradition that included a 'social science' pedagogy based on Marxist political economy. Stuart examined this culture of socialist knowledge in *A Proletarian Science*.[44] British labour militants studied Marxist political economy in classes led by 'working-class autodidacts' produced by 'a wider working-class intellectual culture', which included Ruskin College (founded as Ruskin Hall in 1899) and which led to the formation of the Plebs League and its journal

Plebs and then the Central Labour College, flourishing before and during World War I.[45] 'The most common subjects were industrial history, evolution and economics', but the curriculum extended to the study of English, Esperanto and public speaking.[46]

The 'heyday' of these labour colleges was the turmoil that preceded and helped to give birth in 1920 to the Communist Party of Great Britain. The Workers' Educational Association (founded in 1903) saw itself as a counter to 'Marxist education', providing 'remedial civic education'.[47] If we count labour movement educational activity as 'social science' (in pedagogy, at least) we echo these activists' self-conception: Stuart cites a British pamphlet, probably published in 1917, titled 'How to start a social science class'.[48]

Stuart has devoted less attention to parallel socialist knowledge formations in the Australian labour movement. In *The Reds* he relates that Bill Earsman, a member of the Amalgamated Society of Engineers and of the Victorian Socialist Party, persuaded some trade unions to support a labour college in 1917; the founders of the Communist Party of Australia were steeped in a tradition of working-class education that cherished writings from the eighteenth and nineteenth centuries by 'Paine, Carlyle, Ruskin, Darwin and Huxley' as well as Marx and Engels—an emancipatory social science lineage—as well as Romantic and socially descriptive fiction. Australia had its labour colleges and Plebs League that, in the years either side of 1920, 'fostered an autonomous and politically pointed curriculum in opposition to the reformist Workers' Educational Association and other university extension initiatives'.[49]

Vignettes of this alternative social science remind us that the creation and propagation of 'social science' knowledge is inescapably political, an object of class contention. Indeed, Stuart's understanding of 'capital' itself is an example of radical political economy. In *The Labour Experiment* (1989) he contrasted two understandings of 'capital'. It refers to 'assets such as land, factories and machinery (sometimes known as fixed capital), and used to pay for materials and labour (working capital)'; and 'profits … are commonly taken as the measure of productivity of … capital'. But can 'capital' be quantified, as 'textbook economics' would have us believe? Stuart encourages doubt. 'While labour's contribution can be quantified by counting heads (or hours worked), capital has no obvious inputs of measurement … Critics of economic orthodoxy would therefore argue that the distribution of income between capital and labour has to be understood not as the outcome of formal economic laws but of class struggle.'[50] Acknowledging Marxist political economy without necessarily endorsing it, this passage was anticipated by the Workers' Educational Association itself: its 'liberal pluralist' approach took Marxist theory seriously but 'made no effort to impart an explicit doctrine, Marxist or otherwise'.[51]

Extending the dimension of citizenship

If the knowledge deployed as social sciences and humanities has a range of political affinities, then we can ask of *The Poor Relation*: does it examine the political range of Australian social science? Only implicitly. In that book, as in other works by Stuart, the political matter at stake in Australian social science is Australians' vision of citizenship—that is, of entitled belonging to the nation. Stuart admires social science that has enlarged Australians' understanding of the national community. He reports that the SSRC's hope to 'contribute expertise to national tasks' began to bear fruit in the late 1950s when '… the council embarked on major projects of its own. The subjects it chose, women, Aboriginals and migrants, identified particular components of Australian society that were undergoing change, as well as the fiscal basis of the national government as it responded to new expectations. In extending the dimension of citizenship, gender, race and ethnicity complicated the nation-building project.'[52] And this intellectual and political creativity fed into the reformist public policies of the Whitlam government (which also boosted funding to the SSRC).[53] In 2004, he had sketched the 'contribution of the humanities and social sciences to national life'.

Educational research informed the changing school curriculum; urban studies improved the cities. Demographers and sociologists guided the acceptance of ethnic diversity; scholars of literature, art and music helped us to read, see and hear Australian work; lexicographers assisted us to appreciate its distinctive speech; historians enable recognition of a binding past. The causes that animate us— human rights, the green movement, feminism—all draw on the work of scholarship in the humanities. Economics developed the levers for steering the economy through the expansive years of full employment, and then led the turn back to the market.[54]

Stuart thus pointed to what the 'social science project' can and should be: multidisciplinary study of the dynamics of Australian society so as to grasp its potential to be more socially equitable. This version of the social science project is far from the emancipatory vision of social science held by the autodidacts of the radical labour movement—those convinced by Marxism that capitalist societies would collapse from their own deep contradictions, enabling a new class to rise and to rule in the interests of all people. Stuart's vision for social science is emancipatory, but within a liberal tradition of inclusive nation-building.

And then there is History

Stuart's writing on and within the liberal lineage of social science conveys his particular respect for History's combination of empirical rigour and moral sensibility. Max Crawford hoped to see students 'infusing public life with the wisdom of history', and Stuart also traces the actualisation of this possibility in the institutionalisation of academic History.[55] He depicts universities' public role.

Universities were established and developed in this country along with parliamentary democracy from the middle of the nineteenth century as a particular kind of public corporation, autonomous but accountable, state-funded yet fee-charging, open to all yet selective, enjoying special privileges but expected to fulfil a range of functions for the public good.[56]

History became another such 'function' when the University of Sydney initiated History as a discipline in 1891 by appointing G. Arnold Wood to the Challis chair. That the teaching of History strengthened universities' civic function by ethically training a governing elite is a theme of *A History for a Nation*. At Melbourne University in the 1920s, History eclipsed its only rival for that important task—Sociology ('an eclectic stew of history, economics, politics and international relations').[57]

Consistent with Stuart's ambivalence towards disciplinarity in *The Poor Relation*, his admiration of his own discipline is made clear: History's capacity to integrate to itself the tasks performed severally by other social science and humanities disciplines. In his 1992 lecture 'History, the university and the nation', Stuart distinguished two intellectual configurations in the teaching of History in the first two decades of the twentieth century. In one 'the study of the past was pursued as a branch of the humanities, while elsewhere it had closer affinities to the social sciences'.[58] The two strands were eventually to fuse, but meanwhile,

> As an established university subject, history was well placed to provide a beach-head for the new forms of social inquiry that rose to prominence between the wars: economics and economic history, political science and public administration, international relations and sociology. For as long as the boundaries between these branches of knowledge remained fluid, the students of [Ernest] Scott [Melbourne University] and [Edward] Shann [University of Western Australia] could play an active role in contemporary social inquiry and Australian social science could in turn be informed by an appreciation of the complexities of time and space.[59]

This intellectual formation was broad in its political affinities, as Stuart noted:

> We might understand the Melbourne school of history and political science as providing a repertoire of knowledges and skills that would assist the local elite in the temporary national capital to shape the country's future. And not only the governing elite: among Scott's honours students we may

note Brian Fitzpatrick, the civil libertarian and freelance radical historian; Esmonde Higgins, brother of Nettie Palmer and a key figure in the early history of Australian communism; and Lloyd Ross, another interwar communist intellectual.[60]

Conclusion: History and liberal culture

In *A History for a Nation* and other writings Stuart is fascinated by what connects him with and disconnects him from the founders of academic History in Australia. Continuing to believe in History as a training in worldly judgement about human affairs, he sees three threats to it. One is the too eager instrumentalisation of knowledge (knowledge as a solution to a problem). Another is the epistemological insecurity of the disciplines that are least like the physical and biological sciences. Stuart has noted 'the way that the research grant system enshrines a scientistic model of scholarship':

> The applicant proposes a project that is designed to create new knowledge, outlines the methodology, the data to which it will be applied, the expected outcomes, and the national benefit. This suits researchers in the laboratory disciplines, and many researchers in the humanities adapt it to their needs; but it is less well adapted to reflection, reinterpretation, critical inquiry, and other forms of scholarship. Humanists have imitated that form of research, but it is an approximation of their fundamental purpose.[61]

A third threat to (or modulation of) History as a training in worldly judgement comes from developments within the humanities—receptive, as they must be, to the radical politics of our times.

The assumption that History discloses order and value, or that past events disclose a coherent pattern, a grand narrative of progress towards a realisable goal, are now seen as Enlightenment illusions that one must now surrender. The stable meaning that the historian sought in mastery of the past yields to multiple, temporary, shifting meanings that are always conditional, inescapably discursive, necessarily constrained by the indeterminacy of the text. The autonomous individual of liberal humanist scholarship is dissolved into a site of subjectivities, speaking and acting positions in layers of text upon text. Disciplinary knowledge is itself arraigned as deeply complicit in the hierarchies of power.[62]

If knowledge of humanity is intrinsic to governing, our histories of such knowledge should ask not only about the strength of social science *vis à vis* other disciplines but also about the ideological textures of the social sciences—their contribution to governing.

Notes

1   Stuart Macintyre, *The Poor Relation: A History of the Social Sciences in Australia*, Melbourne University Press, Melbourne, 2010, pp. 9, 5.
2   Stuart Macintyre, *The Oxford History of Australia*, vol. 4: *1901–1942: The Succeeding Age*, Oxford University Press, Melbourne, 1986, pp. 238, 320.
3   Ibid., p. 239.
4   Ibid., p. 240.
5   Stuart Macintyre, *Winners and Losers: The Pursuit of Social Justice in Australian History*, Allen & Unwin, Sydney, 1985, p. 68.
6   Ibid., p. 69.
7   Stuart Macintyre, 'Equity in Australian history', in Patrick Troy (ed.), *A Just Society?* George Allen & Unwin, North Sydney, 1981, p. 37.
8   Stuart Macintyre, 'The poor relation: Establishing the social sciences in Australia, 1940–1970', *Australian Historical Studies*, vol. 40, no. 1, 2009, p. 53.
9   Ibid., pp. 53–4.
10   Ibid., p. 59.
11   Macintyre, 'Equity in Australian history', p. 37.
12   Ibid., p. 44.
13   Macintyre, *Winners and Losers*, p. 138.
14   Stuart's use of 'underdogs' in 'The social sciences in Australia: An unrequited instrumentalism' (*Thesis Eleven*, no. 95, 2008, p. 14) gestures towards such a reading.
15   Macintyre, *Winners and Losers*, pp. 145–6.
16   *The Poor Relation* includes a history of the Botany Bay Project, pp. 195–202.
17   Ibid., p. 260.
18   Ibid., p. 24.
19   Ibid., pp. 5–6.
20   Macintyre, 'An unrequited instrumentalism', p. 10.
21   Macintyre, *The Poor Relation*, p. 260.
22   Ibid., p. 28.
23   Ibid., pp. 337–8.
24   Ibid., p. 28.
25   Ibid., p. 302.
26   Ibid., pp. 275–6.
27   Ibid., p. 24.

28 Macintyre, 'An unrequited instrumentalism', p. 18.

29 Macintyre, *The Poor Relation*, p. 229.

30 Macintyre, 'The poor relation: Establishing', p. 51.

31 Macintyre, 'An unrequited instrumentalism', pp. 15–16; Macintyre, *The Poor Relation*, p. 100.

32 Macintyre, *The Poor Relation*, p. 224.

33 Ibid., p. 326; emphasis added.

34 For an account of the British state's growing capacity for social knowledge, see John Brewer, *The Sinews of Power War, Money and the English State, 1688–1783*, Unwin Hyman, London, 1989, in particular chapter 8.

35 Lawrence Goldman describes the British instance in *Science, Reform and Politics in Victorian Britain: The Social Science Association 1857–1886*, Cambridge University Press, Cambridge, 2002.

36 Macintyre, *Winner and Losers*, pp. 5–6.

37 Ibid., p. 141.

38 Ibid., p. 141.

39 Stuart Macintyre, *A Colonial Liberalism: The Lost World of Three Victorian Visionaries*, Oxford University Press, Melbourne, 1991, p. 95.

40 Ibid., p. 88.

41 Ibid., p. 90.

42 Ibid., pp. 93–4.

43 Ibid., p. 186.

44 Stuart Macintyre, *A Proletarian Science: Marxism in Britain 1917–1933*, Cambridge University Press, Cambridge, 1980.

45 Ibid., p. 73.

46 Ibid., p. 74.

47 Ibid., p. 76.

48 Ibid., p. 77.

49 Stuart Macintyre, *The Reds: The Communist Party of Australia from Origins to Illegality*, Allen & Unwin, Sydney, 1998, p. 122.

50 Stuart Macintyre, *The Labour Experiment*, McPhee Gribble, Melbourne, 1989, p. 7.

51 Macintyre, *A Proletarian Science*, pp. 88–9.

52 Macintyre, *The Poor Relation*, pp. 171–2.

53 Ibid., pp. 175–6.

54 Stuart Macintyre, 'The humanities in the knowledge economy', in Jane Kenway, Elizabeth Bullen and Simon Robb (eds), *Innovation and Tradition: The Arts, Humanities and the Knowledge Economy*, Peter Lang, New York, 2004, p. 26.

55 Stuart Macintyre, *A History for a Nation: Ernest Scott and the Making of Australian History*, Melbourne University Press, Melbourne, 1994, p. 207.

56 Stuart Macintyre (with Simon Marginson), 'The university and its public', in Tony Coady (ed.), *Why Universities Matter: A Conversation About Values, Means and Directions*, Allen & Unwin, St Leonards, 1999, p. 53.

57 Macintyre, *A History for a Nation*, p. 83.

58 Stuart Macintyre, *History, the University and the Nation*, Trevor Reese Memorial Lecture, Sir Robert Menzies Centre for Australian Studies, London, 28 April 1992, p. 15.

59 Ibid., p. 15.

60 Ibid., p. 17.

61 Macintyre, 'The humanities in the knowledge economy', p. 30.

62 Macintyre, *A History for a Nation*, p. 208.

Chapter 17

Labour colleagues

Phillip Deery and Julie Kimber

Other contributors have spoken of Stuart's astonishing productivity, the quality and importance of his publications, and his prolific contributions to public discussions and debates. This external public role as historian is matched by his immense contribution to the internal architecture of his profession. For those of us involved in the many professional associations and organisations that underpin the scholarship of history, Stuart's prolific activity is legendary. His membership of professional organisations speaks to his involvement, as does his editorship of numerous historical journals and his board membership of many more. This activity also extends to participation on numerous library councils, judging panels, government authorities, fellowship committees and reference groups and to his patronage of causes. It is a formidable and extraordinary level of commitment to his profession. As impressive as this activity was, there is yet a further layer: his behind-the-scenes encouragement and support given to legions of academics and postgraduate students over the years, as well as the myriad daily requests on his time—the last-minute calls to review a neglected paper, to help navigate a disagreement among referees, or to provide context for a long-forgotten historiographical dispute. Stuart was not known for saying no.

It is perhaps no surprise, then, that Stuart was called on to lead the Australian Society for the Study of Labour History (ASSLH) at a critical time after it had lost its institutional funding. He, of course, said yes. Stuart's commitment to the labour movement and the history of the working classes was genuinely felt, and its foregrounding of social justice ran deep, both in Stuart's own writing and in his dealings with his colleagues. It is this commitment that saw him successfully navigate the society through a tumultuous period when it relied on donations from members and the journal's operations were moved to Liverpool University Press. Fittingly, Stuart's formative years as historian were in part influenced by his friendships with the founders of the society, Edward Thompson and Eric Hobsbawm in the United Kingdom, and Bob Gollan and Eric Fry, among others, in Australia. Generational divisions between the old and New Left and an Althusserian detour aside, Stuart's historical curiosity ensured that his work burrowed between narrow historical 'tunnels' (to borrow from J.H. Hexter and later Ken Inglis). In the process, it has enlivened the field and entwined labour and social history with politics, policy and intellectual history.

Such entwining is especially evident in his authoritative two-volume history of Australian communism: *The Reds: The Communist Party of Australia from Origins to Illegality* (1998), and *The Party: Communism in Australia from Heyday to Reckoning, 1940–1970* (2022). The first is well known and widely reviewed; the second confirms his deep understanding of Communist Party history. Both are the product of prodigious scholarship and sophisticated analysis, and both are variously empathetic and critical. Neither is a celebratory history—he writes that 'the communist project itself was deeply flawed [and] nurtured tyranny within its emancipatory scheme'— but each recognises the contributions and achievements of communists in cultural as well as political and industrial spheres.[1] In *The Party*, the portraits of individual members—evidenced earlier in his *Militant: The Life and Times of Paddy Troy* and the *Australian Dictionary of Biography* entry on Lance Sharkey—are nuanced, compelling and memorable. These volumes will shape the way labour and social historians interpret the meaning and impact of communism and will stand as lasting monuments to Stuart's contribution to seventy years of Australian communist history.

Stuart's three pages of acknowledgements in *The Reds* are indicative of his generous acknowledgement of the scholarship of others and his exceptionally wide network. As the ASSLH's federal secretary and federal treasurer, we have both been grateful for his counsel and experienced leadership. Stuart also joined us as book review editors for *Labour History* in 2011. In the decade that followed, the journal's book review section benefited significantly from his knowledge and connections, which extend outside the academy into the labour movement. Stuart's leadership of the ASSLH, which brings together a wide community of people in branches across most states in Australia, demonstrates an egalitarian vision of history, beyond the 'historical establishment'. This vision fosters the study of history as a rigorous yet inclusive and collegiate project.

We should note that there are limits to Stuart's sense of collegiality. At a noisy pub in Stirling, Scotland, during a British–Australian Studies Association conference in 1996, he declined to participate in karaoke. When his name was chosen from a hat, the assigned song was Helen Reddy's 'I Am Woman'. He quietly slipped out to eat his haggis.

Despite this shortcoming, Stuart carried none of the conceit or hubris associated with his role and institutional home. He was instead a colleague who inspired and bolstered those around him. He always remained sympathetic to those of us in non-Group of Eight universities, as his sympathetic review of Faculty of Arts programs at Victoria University testified. At a time when academic citizenship is in retreat due to increasing demands on workloads and the use of pernicious performance metrics and rigid workload formulas, Stuart's achievements and length of service to his disciplinary community and to academic citizenship shows us what will be lost if the push to an 'academic capitalism' is realised. The internal architecture of our profession depends on the goodwill of each of us. That it has not yet crumbled is in part due to Stuart's sustained commitment and collegiality.

Notes

1   Stuart Macintyre, *The Reds: The Communist Party of Australia from Origins to Illegality*, Allen & Unwin, Sydney, 1998, p. 413.

Part 5

General histories

Chapter 18

Writing the Cambridge 'Australia'

Alison Bashford

Stuart Macintyre's *Concise History of Australia*, first published 1999, stands as an enduring sophisticated textbook through which much of the world first appreciates Australian history as one story and in several languages. Reliably updated, it stands as the Macintyre vision of the nation's past, the most recent edition incorporating changes from the early twenty-first century, including a mineral export boom enabling prosperity and capacity to withstand the financial crisis in 2007–08.[1] It points again to Australian historical prosperity and analysis of debates about how that prosperity could and might be shared, and how it sometimes is and often is not.

The inclination towards a foundational economic history of Australia is signature Stuart, one that nestled amongst other approaches and lines of inquiry, necessarily, in a larger collaborative venture with Cambridge University Press, *The Cambridge History of Australia*.[2] In two chronological volumes, sixty-eight historians from across the nation and beyond came together to rethink what was old and what was new, and whether and how they deserved to be incorporated. The politico-economic tradition that was Stuart's great strength needed to be conjoined with the great ascendance of cultural history in the years after his *Concise History* first appeared, with the centrality of Indigenous politics to Australia's past and to the geographically outward-looking trend so marked in Australian history writing in the new millennium. These elements are all there in the *Concise History*, but now there were the views and opinions and wisdoms of three-score-and-ten, counting various Cambridge editors, to incorporate and sometimes to adjudicate. Stuart's diplomacy was a key ingredient alongside his status in the profession, and perhaps especially his unsurpassed historiographical knowledge of what had and had not been said before.

The *Cambridge History of Australia* reached back and forward across generations of historians, schooled in different historiographies, with varying geographical investments as well. In designing the volumes, Stuart and I decided early to try to pair younger and more senior historians, to catch established and fresher visions of Australian history. With only modest ambition to temporary intellectual matchmaking, it is nonetheless the case that some of those pairs have gone on to form scholarly marriages of the finest order.

Was there a generational difference, or perhaps a geographical difference, between our approaches to a history of Australia? The geographical difference perhaps was less about Melbourne and Sydney emphases or historiographical traditions than about visions of Australia looking inwards and Australia looking outwards. My own sense is that these were highly complementary, Stuart the specialist of the former, myself inclined to the latter. From our first discussions in the middle of 2009—perhaps because I was then teaching Australian history outside the country—I was struck by the scholarship then linking Australia's past to different historical geographies, across the various seas, across the Tasman, across Torres Strait, across the Pacific and Indian oceans. Naturally, Stuart had read and appreciated all this new work, and to my mind a kind of inward and outward conversation unfolded. We even tried to persuade Cambridge to publish a three-volume set, the third a suite of essays on Australia's relations with different parts of the world, and other specific polities: chapters with a long historical view of Australia and China, Australia and South Asia, Australia and New Zealand, for example. Perhaps a bold Cambridge editor will consider this for future editions.

Many of us know the work of editing only too well. In this project, many of us were deeply appreciative of Stuart's capacity to scale out and scale in, simultaneously to hold a large vision on the one hand and to intervene in sentence structure and sequence on the other. I learned from Stuart the benefit of the occasional well-placed single-clause sentence. Powerful it is. I followed with interest his line-by-line edits of others' work, his own and of mine, and privately came to think of him as Stuart 'Syntax' Macintyre. And what a workhorse! For a time he led our daily contact morning, noon and night, wrestling the whole into order, Stuart rereading, resequencing and redrafting. And we did not need a fact-checker. Stuart knew it all, historical and historiographical, the most minute detail about publication dates and landing dates, about territorial journeys and intellectual journeys, about wool clips and coal exports, about parliaments and governments and self-government. Everyone in that wonderful enterprise benefited from his years of reading, that monumental library, plus the massive detail already distilled for the *Concise History*. It seemed to be—it was—all mentally filed, organised and accessible. And correct.

Inevitably, almost a decade on, there are things to add and things one would change about the 2013 *Cambridge History of Australia*, historians to include, and temporal reach to think through: what we then called the 'new millennium', now just the plain twenty-first century, can be considered in longer retrospect; and the genealogy of transnational Black Lives Matter requires integration into a longer outward- and inward-looking Australian history. Perhaps we also need a new long vision of the Australian economy weathering global crises of different orders. The *Cambridge History of Australia* will likely sit on our shelves as a marker of our profession and our conversations, circa 2013. How wonderful those conversations were, a gathering of our kind! Its multiple entries into the nation's past, its ecumenical discipline-wide appeal and reliability, is down to Stuart's own discipline.

Notes

1   Stuart Macintyre, *A Concise History of Australia*, 5th edn, Cambridge University Press, Melbourne, 2020.
2   Alison Bashford and Stuart Macintyre (eds), *The Cambridge History of Australia*, vol. 1: *Indigenous and Colonial Australia*, and vol. 2: *The Commonwealth of Australia*, Cambridge University Press, Melbourne, both 2013.

Chapter 19

Things as they are

Kate Darian-Smith

In 1979 Stuart Macintyre became an Australian historian. Returning to Australia from Cambridge, where he had been a doctoral student and then a research fellow working on histories of class struggle and experience in Britain, Stuart briefly joined the history department at the recently established Murdoch University. With no access to British records, Stuart recalled that when he began lecturing in Australian history, he 'was struck also by the opportunities to apply my enthusiasms to Australian material'.[1] When Geoffrey Bolton, foundation professor in history at Murdoch, invited Stuart to collaborate on *The Oxford History of Australia* there was no turning back.[2]

The Oxford History of Australia was an ambitiously conceived series, under the general editorship of Bolton, with the initial aim to produce five volumes, each sole-authored, spanning the history of the continent from Aboriginal Australia up to the 1980s. Stuart's volume 4: *1901–1942, The Succeeding Age* was the first in the series to be published, appearing at the end of 1986, and was subsequently issued in paperback and reprinted for more than two decades.[3] The subtitle drew upon the words of essayist and critic Nettie Palmer ('this is the succeeding age and a difficult one …'), and covered Federation, the impacts of World War I, economic collapse and

Depression, ending somewhat abruptly with the fall of Singapore and the onset of the Pacific War.

In the Preface, Stuart reflected on how the traditional understanding of a general history as being both synthesised in its coverage and holistic in its approach was threatened by the fragmentation of the discipline. The shift in inquiry to 'histories from below', whereby the experiences of those previously omitted from the grand historical narratives—women, Aborigines, the working class—were given voice and visibility, and the increasing autonomy of subdisciplines such as urban, educational or military history called into question older models of national history. It was simply no longer possible, Stuart wrote, to view 'history as made by the public endeavours of influential men', a stance 'beloved of an earlier generation of Oxford historians'. Nor could Australia's past be presented as 'a record of national achievement, a people moving towards self-realisation'. These challenges, he continued, 'should be regarded as less an impediment to the work of the general historian than as its justification'.[4] Central to this endeavour was recognising the 'structures of power', a perspective that built upon his recent book *Winners and Losers* and located politics 'as not an end in itself but a response to social relationships'.[5]

The *Oxford History* opened with a Prologue describing how the Western Australian goldfields community at Kalgoorlie celebrated the inauguration of the Commonwealth on 1 January 1901.[6] A crowd of 10 000 gathered to cheer a procession and to hear speeches that simultaneously celebrated national unification while confirming the exclusion of the 'white man's Australia' and thinly papering over the fissures of race, ethnicity, gender, class, capital and place that shaped the nation and its peoples. This relatively dramatic opening (described by one reviewer as a 'little flirtation with Annales-style writing')[7] was followed by the first chapter, where five short and diverse biographical sketches of Australians in very different circumstances set up the key strand running throughout the volume: the extremes of wealth and poverty, geographic and social mobility, and the webs of communities, interests and beliefs. Several chapters then covered Australian life, social and political allegiances and the making of the Commonwealth Government in the years leading up to the outbreak of World War I, the moment at which the narrative is more directly driven by political and economic events.

As the Bicentenary of the European colonisation of Australia loomed, it was a heady time for the writing of history and—so it seemed to me as a then postgraduate student—to be a member of the history profession. History mattered in ways that were immediate and tangible; looking to the past was also about the possibilities of the future. The expansion of higher education after World War II resulted in new and enlarged history departments, and as the teaching about Australia's past grew, so too did the number of honours and postgraduate history theses on Australian topics. There was also an explosion of popular interest in history, demonstrated by the enthusiastic collection, preservation and exhibition of the material culture and the folklore of Australia's settler heritage, the invigoration of community museums and historical societies, and the advocacy of the National Trust and urban activists to halt the destruction of nineteenth-century streetscapes and buildings.[8]

Within and outside universities, the practice of writing history was increasingly informed by contemporary political activism and discourses of feminism, multiculturalism, human rights, postcolonialism and decolonisation. Historians were also more widely embracing such techniques as oral history and bringing cross-disciplinary approaches, including ethnography and the analytical frame of cultural studies, to their understanding of the past and its current cultural representations and legacies.

The responses from the historical profession to the Bicentenary were varied and jostling. Some rejected what was billed the 'Celebration of a Nation' as a simplistic affirmation of nationhood that overlooked the brutalities of European invasion and the injustices of the past, both expressed more aptly in the powerful slogan of Indigenous protest: 'White Australia has a Black History'. Others were more welcoming, even if lukewarmly so, of the public elevation of history's role in strengthening social connections and national identity. There was funding available through the Australian Bicentennial Authority and other sources for a multitude of historical activities in local communities, and at the national level there were official and unofficial events including the 'Australia Live' telecast on New Year's Eve and a tacky First Fleet re-enactment in Sydney Harbour on Australia Day. As it unfolded before their eyes, historians were active participants but also documented and critiqued what the Bicentenary commemorations meant for the practice of history. Stuart co-edited what still stands as the most significant collective record from a wide-ranging group of historians on 'Making the Bicentenary', the title of a special issue of *Australian Historical Studies* published during 1988—and was in many later writings to situate the Bicentenary within the politics of the 'History Wars'.[9]

The *Oxford History of Australia* was not the only multivolume history underway in the 1980s. The Bicentennial spurred two important collaborative projects of history writing within universities that drew upon fresh research and aimed to appeal to a broad readership. The first, conceived in the late 1970s and led from ANU, was *Australians: A Historical Library* and involved more than four hundred scholars contributing to ten volumes of histories and reference works.[10] The histories were distinctive in employing a 'slice' methodology, which examined key years (1838, 1888, 1938) spaced at fifty-year intervals. Illustrated in full colour, the large-format volumes were lavishly produced and sold in a full set by subscription.[11] Stuart contributed a short entry on 'social justice' and a longer essay on Australian historiography to the reference texts.[12] A second collaborative project was very different in tone and structure, and its contributors were mainly early career historians and commentators, including a good proportion of women. *A People's History of Australia since 1788* tackled the past through a perspective more critical than celebratory, focusing on the nuances of everyday experience, and tapping into new research undertaken in labour and social history. Its four edited volumes, available in affordable paperback, were arranged by theme rather than chronology, with short essays in accessible prose organised around the core ideas of economy, society, politics and culture.[13]

In late November 1986, Stuart's volume of the *Oxford History of Australia* was launched by the Governor-General, Ninian Stephen, hitting the bookshops in time for Christmas and just ahead of the rush of history books, popular and scholarly, that were to be published over the next two years. Writing in the *Sydney Morning Herald* in December 1986, an early review by Manning Clark laboured a cricket metaphor when he described how Oxford University Press had been 'shrewd and very wise' in choosing 'a promising young Australian named Stuart Macintyre' as the 'opening batsman'—not only of its series but also of 'the Test matches of Australian historians' and their publishers as the Bicentennial approached. (Looking ahead, Clark's volume 6 of *A History of Australia*, covering the years 1916–35, was to be published later in 1987, and during the bicentennial year *Manning Clark: The Musical* attracted much discussion.)[14]

Stuart had published a lengthy historiographical essay in the literary journal *Meanjin* in 1982 on 'Manning Clark's critics', tracing how Clark was established as Australia's 'foremost historian' and the phases of critical response to his work.[15] Clark was enthusiastic about the *Oxford History*: its style was 'jaunty and engaging', its section on class likely to stir 'the self-appointed guardians of intellectual standards in Australia', and its examination of the politics of the period was 'judicious and sensible'. But, he warned readers, 'Those who believe the historian should be like God and impose an order on the chaos will probably be disappointed. Stuart Macintyre's eye is on things as they are.'[16]

A survey of the reception of the *Oxford History* highlights the concerns about history at the time, as well as the limitations on who could speak with authority about history in academic circles and in the public sphere. Overall, responses were positive, and the book was awarded the A.A. Phillips Prize for Australian Studies at the Victorian Premier's Literary Awards. One point of widespread discussion was its narrative format, notably conventional in contrast to the slice and thematic approaches taken by other multivolumed histories tied to the Bicentenary. As a 'Publisher's note' explained, the Oxford authors 'held firmly to the conviction that history needs to interpret the past as an intelligible whole', writing the volumes 'as narrative history with a clear and dramatic thread'.[17] Stuart argued in the press that narrative addressed 'what the public wants from history'. That history, he stated, 'should involve economic life, class associations, religion' while 'politics should be understood not as something that happens in Canberra, but a much wider process where power is exercised by one on another'.[18] The journalist Maurice Dunlevy agreed: the book will 'grip the common reader', offering 'history from both above and below'.[19] From London, Tom Millar's review for *History Today* praised the 'sensible narrative' and Stuart's 'determination to write history in the round'.[20]

Left-leaning academic colleagues writing in scholarly journals were a little sharper but ultimately congratulatory. Ken Buckley in *Labour History* pointed to the inevitable omissions of the genre but placed more emphasis on the volume's 'coherence, accuracy and thoughtfulness'.[21] In *The American Historical Review*, Terry Irving asked: 'What strategy should a general historian adopt in an age of historical specialisation?', concluding that Stuart's attempt to 'provide a new model' and his 'affinity with our age' made his book 'a resounding success'.[22]

Ann Curthoys, as the only woman and the only cultural historian among the reviewers I have examined, was more expansive and probing. Her robust review appeared in the special issue of *Australian Historical Studies* co-edited by Stuart. Curthoys found that the attempts to include the latest historical research on feminist history and Aboriginal history were insufficient but reserved her sharpest critique for the volume's lack of engagement with cultural history and the media. Yet the difficulty, she conceded, was that the task of general history was in some ways unrealisable, as new conceptual approaches disrupted the totality of synthesis. Despite such tensions, Curthoys concluded that in bringing together his radical concerns with class with the liberal traditions of the Melbourne School, Stuart had written a book that was 'eminently successful as a study of class and politics in early twentieth-century Australia'.[23]

My copy of Stuart's *Oxford History* is now battered and worn, with faint pencil markings in the margin (occasionally a question or exclamation mark) whose relevance is long forgotten. It accompanied me on my first appointments as a lecturer in Australian history, initially teaching at Ballarat in regional Victoria, and then at the Menzies Centre for Australian Studies at the University of London. I taught courses at both places on twentieth-century Australia and in particular on the world wars and the depression. Books were important tools in those predigital days, useful to the teacher and student alike at the most basic level for checking a date or a name. The *Oxford History*'s detailed Bibliographical Essay and fulsome endnotes were of great assistance, too, in my efforts to design course reading lists and photocopied 'readers', as well as guiding my own preparatory research. For the successive classes of British undergraduates I taught in London whose vision of Australia was bedazzled by the perpetual sunshine and seeming egalitarianism prevalent in the Australian television soaps that were so popular then, Stuart's arguments on the place of class and the hierarchies of power and capital in a reachable past served as a sobering antidote.

Stuart's second general history, *A Concise History of Australia*, was issued in 1999 as part of a new series from Cambridge University Press intended for use as tertiary textbooks, as well as providing, in the words of the Press, a historical introduction for the interested reader, 'travellers and members of the business community'. Stuart recalled, when talking to a History Honours class at the University of Melbourne two decades later, that writing for an imaginary reader who had never been to Australia drew him to the project: 'I was going to draw their attention to things that might puzzle them, things that were different, or things that might appear to be different … [T]hat was my angle.'[24] This wide audience, encompassing locals and those overseas, and the more and less informed among them, presented opportunities and challenges when constructing a narrative of Australia from its human beginning at least 50 000 years ago through to the present. The deliberate intention to situate Australia within the world, drawing out points of historical comparison, needed to be balanced with sufficient detail and specificity.[25]

'I have endeavoured to assume little,' wrote Stuart in the opening pages of the *Concise History*, 'and to paint a broad-brush picture in which the detail is subordinated to the characteristic features.'[26] But this was no set narrative: 'The idea of an objective and universal record of the past exactly as it happened yields to the myriad interpretations of a disposable past.'[27] Nor was the historian an 'impersonal, unselfconscious narrator' but someone 'present in the story'.[28] Such framing departed from conventional general history and enabled the integration (or digression) of different historical perspectives into the narrative, as Stuart's emphasis and pithy concluding points are woven into his conversation with the reader. Written on the cusp of the new millennium, the *Concise History* not only narrated the key moments of a familiar settler past—convicts, explorers, the Eureka rebellion, the Anzac legend and so on—but also traced their historiography and evolving symbolic and political meanings. Stuart's preoccupations with political history and the economy were accompanied by current historiographical concerns, notably those of race relations and, to a lesser extent, multiculturalism. Historical experiences were threaded across the chronological chapters, with Aboriginal resistance on the frontier in the nineteenth century followed by the rise of Indigenous protest and activism in the twentieth. Reflection on the consequences of child removal and the Stolen Generations (the *Bringing Them Home* report had been published in 1997) and John Howard's refusal to apologise to Indigenous Australians brought past injustices into the present.

At the time of the publication of the first edition of the *Concise History*, the contestations that had surfaced in Australia during the Bicentenary over the consequences of European colonisation for the past and present lives of Indigenous peoples had become louder, shriller and more explicitly politicised. The 1992 Mabo decision in the High Court, which overturned the legal legitimacy of the doctrine of *terra nullius*, Prime Minister Paul Keating's 'Redfern' speech acknowledging that colonisation had led to the dispossession of Indigenous Australians, and the passage of the Native Title Act in 1993 were among the events that were reshaping the nation's engagement with its past. Nevertheless, when John Howard succeeded Keating as Prime Minister in 1996, he rejected what Geoffrey Blainey had called the 'black armband' view of history in favour of a narrative of 'heroic achievement' aligned with British settlement and Western values.[29] There was increasing media commentary and ideological polarisation over questions of history and national identity, including how Australia's past was represented in museum exhibitions and taught in the classroom. Conservative commentators attacked the professional and personal integrity of historians, including accusations that scholars had 'fabricated' evidence in their accounts of Indigenous–settler frontier violence.[30] Not only was Stuart a participant and a target in these factionalised exchanges but also he was to document their evolution and impact in *The History Wars*, first released in 2003.[31]

But to step back a couple of years, the reception of *A Concise History of Australia* occurred amid this swelling interest in the importance of Australian history and the contested meanings attached to foundational moments in the national story. There was praise for the book from historians, including Blainey, in the popular press. 'It's a splendid piece of work … It conveys throughout a joy in writing history, in mastering the detail of the past—joy especially in struggling with the soul of the country,' wrote Alan Atkinson in the *Sydney Morning Herald*.[32] Carl Bridge in the *Times Literary Supplement* claimed that 'Macintyre's book is the best short history of Australia since Manning Clark's classic of 1963'.[33] Then there were ideological detractors, whose mode was abuse rather than assessment.[34] Points of obfuscation and omission, inevitable in any general history, were respectfully raised in the academic journals: there was not enough coverage, for instance, of the arts, religion, sexuality, women, immigrants.[35]

The significance of the *Concise History*, and Stuart's standing, was reflected in a lengthy and rich set of reviews by Alan Atkinson,

Marilyn Lake and Xavier Pons that appeared in *Australian Historical Studies*. All commented on the 'mood' of the history, variously noting the tragic 'rise and fall' of the historical trajectory and the disillusionment and disquiet of the final chapter. Lake identified the 'unease' between white settlers and Indigenous people that underpinned the history's emotional structure, evident in the tensions 'between national pride and shame, sobriety and humour, in the honouring of a shared past which yet resists commemoration' and asked the crucial question: 'How does one reconcile incommensurate national narratives?'[36] In response to the discussion, Stuart admitted that while 'it was difficult to feel optimistic' in the late 1990s, the writing of the *Concise History* had brought him 'both solace and pleasure'.[37]

In 2004, a second edition of the *Concise History* was issued. Stuart had modified the earlier chapters, drawing on recent historical scholarship and addressing some points of criticism. There was more on the role of the states and on religion and a little more on culture and women. The most substantial additions related to the very recent past, with the narrative delving more deeply into political and economic changes from the 1980s, the failure of the referendum on the republic and the role of the Howard government in the History Wars. A second wave of reviews followed on predictable lines, including fresh academic affirmation for the book's value as a textbook and introduction to Australian history.[38]

Subsequent revised editions of the *Concise History* have appeared in 2009, 2015 and 2020, and included changes both superficial and substantial. Cambridge University Press has modernised its series design, with the cover of its Australian volume becoming lighter (from blue to red to cream), and the original image of Sidney Nolan's 'Ned Kelly in the bush' now replaced by Grace Cossington-Smith's buoyant 'Bridge in curve'. In each edition, new historical research has been incorporated into the text, with the comprehensive Guide to Further Reading serving as a handy barometer of Australian historiography over the past two decades. Comparisons between the 1999 and 2020 editions of the *Concise History of Australia* reveal tweaks to chapter titles and periodisation, and an entirely new final chapter on Australia in the twenty-first century that ends with the early months of the COVID-19 pandemic. The availability of the *Concise History* in digital form has certainly widened its accessibility, as has its translation into Chinese, Japanese, Italian, Russian and Czech. In my own teaching of Australian history and Australian studies during the 2000s, I used it successfully as a text and a guide for courses that I offered in the United States, China and Japan, as well as for international students at the University of Melbourne eager to understand how Australia's past has influenced its present state.

For close to forty years, Stuart's general histories—the *Oxford History*, volume 4 and the *Concise History*—have influenced generations of students and interested readers within Australia and around the world. They have answered and initiated questions about Australia's origins and global connections, the diversity of experiences within the nation and how historical legacies shape the politics and the everyday existence of our present and future. Both books were conceived of and written from their time, and this context was to determine their reception, scholarly and otherwise. Stuart's contribution to national history was, of course, much more extensive than his authored general histories, and includes the major collaborative project of reference and interpretation in *The Oxford Companion to Australian History* in 1998 and his co-editorship of the multiauthored two volumes of *The Cambridge History of Australia* in 2013.[39] He continued to reflect on the history of historical writing in Australia and elsewhere, the state of history departments in universities and national history curricula in schools, the value in thinking historiographically and the interplay between national and transnational approaches to the past.[40] Stuart's capacity to see 'things as they are' in the connections between historical experiences and the present and his enthusiasm and collegiality have shaped and enriched my own work as an historian—just as they have profoundly contributed to the evolving professional practice of Australian history and its complex place in our public culture.

Notes

1   Stuart Macintyre, 'Labour history and radical nationalism', in Anna Clark and Paul
     Ashton (eds), *Australian History Now*, NewSouth Publishing, Sydney, 2013, p. 45.
2   Stuart continued to teach British history after he came to the University of
     Melbourne in 1980, and I was among his students. I remember his assistance with an
     essay on British exploration in Africa, prompting my later interest in postcolonialism
     and the decolonisation of Empire.
3   Stuart Macintyre, *The Oxford History of Australia*, vol. 4: *1901–1942, The Succeeding
     Age* [1986], Oxford University Press, Oxford, reprinted 1990 (paperback edition
     1993, reprinted 2001, 2003, 2004, 2006, 2009, 2012). Stuart also assisted with the
     editing of other volumes, especially volume 5 by Geoffrey Bolton. See Papers of
     Stuart Macintyre, MS 9389, Series 20, *The Oxford History of Australia*, 1979–84, and
     Series 19, Files on postwar reconstruction 1986–90, File 12–17, National Library of
     Australia (NLA). The other volumes were Beverley Kingston, *The Oxford History of
     Australia*, vol. 3: *1860–1900, Glad, Confident Morning*, Oxford University Press,
     Oxford, 1993; Geoffrey Bolton, *The Oxford History of Australia*, vol. 5: *1942–1988,
     The Middle Way*, Oxford University Press, Oxford, 1993; Jan Kociumbas, *The Oxford
     History of Australia*, vol. 2: *1770–1860, Possessions*, Oxford University Press, Oxford,
     1995. Volume 1, which was to be on Aboriginal Australia, was never published.
4   Macintyre, Prologue, *The Succeeding Age*, p. x.
5   Stuart Macintyre, *Winners and Losers: The Pursuit of Social Justice in Australian History*,
     Allen & Unwin, Sydney, 1985; Macintyre, *The Oxford History of Australia*, Prologue,
     pp. ix–xi.
6   See Macintyre, Preface, p. xi, and Prologue, pp. xvii–xx, *The Succeeding Age*.
7   Brian Dickey, 'Review of Stuart Macintyre, *The Oxford History of Australia*, Volume 4,
     1901–1942', *Journal of Australian Studies*, vol. 12, no. 23, 1988, p. 104.
8   An incisive analysis of this at the time can be seen in Graeme Davison, 'The use and
     abuse of Australian history', in *Making the Bicentenary: Australian Historical Studies*, vol.
     23, no. 91, 1988, pp. 55–76.
9   Stuart Macintyre and Susan Janson (eds), *Making the Bicentenary: Australian Historical
     Studies*, vol. 23, no. 91, 1988; Stuart Macintyre and Anna Clark, *The History Wars*,
     chapter 6: 'Bicentenary battles', pp. 93–118. See also Stuart Macintyre, *A Concise
     History of Australia*, Cambridge University Press, Melbourne, 1999, pp. 271–2.
10   'Australia 1788–1988: A bicentennial history', *Australian Historical Studies*, vol. 18, no.
     72, 1979, p. 510. See Oliver MacDonagh (ed.), *Australians: The Guide and Index*,
     Fairfax, Syme & Weldon Associates, Sydney, https://socialsciences.org.au/australians-
     the-guide-and-index/ (viewed 6 September 2021).
11   Alan D. Gilbert, K.S. Inglis and S.G. Foster (eds), *Australians: A Historical Library*,
     Fairfax, Syme & Weldon, Sydney, 1987–89. All volumes of *Australians* can be found
     at https://socialsciences.org.au/australians/
12   Stuart Macintyre, 'Social justice', in Graeme Aplin, S.G. Foster and Michael
     McKernan (eds), *Australians: A Historical Dictionary*, Fairfax, Syme & Weldon
     Associates, Sydney, 1987, pp. 369–70; Stuart Macintyre, 'The writing of Australian
     history', in D.H. Borchardt and V. Crittenden (eds), *Australians: A Guide to Sources*,
     Fairfax, Syme & Weldon Associates, Sydney, 1988, pp. 1–29.
13   Verity Burgmann and Jenny Lee (eds), *Staining the Wattle: A People's History of
     Australia since 1788*, McPhee Gribble Penguin, Melbourne, 1988; Burgmann and Lee
     (eds), *Making a Life: A People's History of Australia since 1788*, McPhee Gribble
     Penguin, Melbourne, 1988; Burgmann and Lee (eds), *A Most Valuable Acquisition: A
     People's History of Australia since 1788*, McPhee Gribble Penguin, Melbourne, 1988;

Burgmann and Lee (eds), *Constructing a Culture: A People's History of Australia since 1788*, McPhee Gribble Penguin, Melbourne, 1988; Verity Burgmann and Jenny Lee, 'Australia deconstructed? Assembling a People's History of Australia since 1788', *Australian Historical Studies*, vol. 23, no. 91, 1988, pp. 153–61; Macintyre and Clark, *The History Wars*, pp. 117–18.

14   Manning Clark, *A History of Australia: 'The Old Dead Tree and the Young Tree Green'* 1916–1935, vol. 6, Melbourne University Publishing, Melbourne, 1987.

15   Stuart Macintyre, 'Manning Clark's critics', *Meanjin*, vol. 41, no. 4, 1982, pp. 442–52.

16   Manning Clark, 'Oxford bats: A bold one for 1988', *Sydney Morning Herald*, 13 December 1986, p. 43.

17   'Publisher's note', *The Succeeding Age*, pp. vii–viii.

18   Quoted in Richard Glover, 'Our historians jump on the bicentennial bandwagon', *Sydney Morning Herald*, 4 December 1986, p. 11.

19   Maurice Dunlevy, 'Writer's world', *Canberra Times*, 24 January 1987, p. 3.

20   Tom Millar, 'The Australian history boom', *History Today*, vol. 38, no. 3, 1988, pp. 56–7.

21   Ken Buckley, 'Reviewed work(s): *The Oxford History of Australia*, Volume 4, *1901– 1942, The Succeeding Age* by Stuart Macintyre', *Labour History*, vol. 53, no. 2, 1987, pp. 137–8.

22   Terence H. Irving, 'Review', *American Historical Review*, vol. 97, no. 3, 1992, p. 915.

23   Ann Curthoys, 'Reviews', *Australian Historical Studies*, vol. 23, no. 91, 1988, pp. 208– 10.

24   'Stuart Macintyre in conversation with History Honours students', https://blogs. unimelb.edu.au/shaps-research/2021/01/12/stuart-macintyre-in-conversation-with-history-honours-students/ (viewed 11 September 2021).

25   Stuart commented in 2005 that he had been 'sparing in my use of names, for I thought the foreign reader would only be distracted by a roll-call of incidental figures. The complaints of my local readers taught me that a national history is expected to make full acknowledgement of all the characters. The naming not only orients the narrative journey, it turns that journey into a pilgrimage of ritual homage.' See Stuart Macintyre, *Age*, 9 July 2005, p. 4.

26   Stuart Macintyre, *A Concise History of Australia*, Cambridge University Press, Melbourne, 1999.

27   Ibid., p. 5.

28   Ibid., p. 5.

29   Mark McKenna, 'Different perspectives on Black Armband history', *Parliamentary Library Research Paper, no. 5, 1997–98*.

30   Keith Windschuttle, 'The breakup of Australia', *Quadrant*, vol. 44, no. 9, 2000, pp. 8–16; Keith Windschuttle, *The Fabrication of Aboriginal History*, Macleay Press, Padddington, 2002; Keith Windschuttle, 'Whitewash confirms the fabrication of Aboriginal history', *Quadrant*, vol. 47, no. 10, 2003, pp. 8–16.

31   Anna Clark and Stuart Macintyre, *The History Wars*, UNSW Press, Sydney, 2003. In a second edition, published in 2004, Stuart addressed the controversy that surrounded the original publication.

32   Alan Atkinson, 'Historian's adventure into the not so clever country', *Sydney Morning Herald*, 22 January 2000, p. 9.

33   Carl Bridge, 'In brief', *Times Literary Supplement*, no. 5101, 2001, p. 28.

34   For instance Peter Ryan, 'Apologies', *Quadrant*, vol. 44, no. 3, 2000, p. 87.

35   See for example Michael Sturma, '*A Concise History of Australia* by Stuart Macintyre', *History*, vol. 86, no. 283, 2001, pp. 379–80; John Rickard, 'Review', *Journal of Australian Studies*, vol. 24, no. 65, 2000, pp. 219–20; Ross Fitzgerald, '*A Concise*

History of Australia (book review)', *Australian Journal of Political Science*, vol. 35, no. 2, 2000, p. 340; Alan Atkinson, Marilyn Lake, Xavier Pons, Stuart Macintyre, 'Discussion: *A Concise History of Australia* by Stuart Macintyre', *Australian Historical Studies*, vol. 31, no. 115, 2000, pp. 335–43, 335.

36   Atkinson et al., 'Discussion', p. 338.

37   Macintyre, 'Discussion', p. 343.

38   See Jenny Gregory, 'Book reviews', *Commonwealth and Comparative Politics*, vol. 43, no. 3, 2005, pp. 419–45; Charlie Fox, *Pacific Affairs*, vol. 79, no. 1, 2006, pp. 163–4.

39   Graeme Davison, John Hirst and Stuart Macintyre (eds), *The Oxford Companion to Australian History* [1998], Oxford University Press, Melbourne, rev. edn 2001; Alison Bashford and Stuart Macintyre (eds), *The Cambridge History of Australia*, two vols, Cambridge University Press, Cambridge, 2013.

40   'Historical writing in Australia and New Zealand', in Stuart Macintyre, Juan Maiguashca and Attila Pók (eds), *The Oxford History of Historical Writing*, vol. 4: *1800–1945*, Oxford University Press, Oxford, 2011, pp. 410–27; 'Reading postwar reconstruction through national and transnational lenses', in Anna Clark, Anne Rees and Alecia Simmonds (eds), *Transnationalism, Nationalism and Australian History*, Palgrave Macmillan, Singapore, 2017, pp. 133–45; Stuart Macintyre, 'Historiography and history', in 'What is history? Historiography roundtable', *Rethinking History*, vol. 22, no. 4, 2018, pp. 500–24.

Chapter 20

Companions

Graeme Davison

Early in 1993 Peter Rose, commissioning editor of Oxford University Press Australia, invited the historian John Hirst to edit *The Oxford Companion to Australian History*. 'This will be a durable and influential reference book, appealing to diverse markets within and without the academy,' Rose anticipated. 'Oxford hopes to draw on the expertise of the country's most capable historians.' Attracted to the project but reluctant to take it on alone, John asked if I would join him, a conversation that quickly enlarged to include Stuart Macintyre. A few weeks later we agreed to edit it together, the beginning of a venture that was to be companionable in more ways than one. Rose responded to our decision enthusiastically: '*Australian History* will be our most successful and influential reference publication in the Nineties.'[1]

The Oxford Companion to Australian History (OCAH—'ocker' for short) appeared at an opportune moment in the lives of its editors and our discipline. It tapped the expertise of the historical profession at its apogee and drew fruitfully on wider debates about the public purposes of Australian history in which we, and Stuart especially, would play a part. In reflecting on that happy collaboration—perhaps the happiest in the author's experience—I seek to follow his lead as our foremost historiographer by reflecting on the project's place in the longer conversation we call 'Australian history'.

In co-editing an Oxford companion we were joining a well-established publishing tradition. The word 'companion' as the name for a concise readable reference volume dates from the seventeenth century. It anglicised an older idea denoted by the Latin word *vade-mecum*, meaning literally 'go with me'. Many early companions were designed for travellers, providing a portable source of commercial, scholarly or geographical information. A companion was friendlier and more concise than other reference volumes. The name conjured up a picture of the reader seated comfortably in an armchair rather than upright at a desk. It was designed to satisfy the browser as much as the scholarly researcher. While not forsaking accuracy or catholicity, it was less encumbered by the assumptions of universality, sobriety and authority associated with the dictionary and encyclopedia. It promised enjoyment as well as instruction. It aimed to stimulate curiosity as much as to satisfy it and to spark debates as well as settle them.

Sir Paul Harvey's *Oxford Companion to English Literature* (1932) popularised the companion genre in the English-speaking world. The illegitimate son of a French aristocrat and an English sculptress, Harvey was educated at Rugby School and Oxford University, where he studied classics before joining the British Civil Service. After a distinguished career as a financial adviser to the Egyptian government, he retired with a knighthood. With time on his hands, however, he agreed with a director of Oxford University Press, Kenneth Sisam, in return for a fee of £500, to produce a substantial A–Z reader's guide to English literature, containing biographies of English authors, synopses of major works and explanations of literary allusions. He wrote almost the entire 800 pages, a *tour de force* of scholarly omniscience, economy, industry and neutrality. 'Contemporary judgment is notoriously fickle,' he wrote in justifying his decision to exclude all but a very few living authors and to provide only 'a conventional view' of their works.[2]

The *Companion to English Literature* was a publishing phenom-
enon. My own copy, purchased by my grandfather from the
Booklover's Bookshop in Collins Street, comes from the fourth
reprint in 1934. Harvey doubled up with an *Oxford Companion to
Classical Literature* in 1937. More than seventy Oxford Companions
have since been published. The *Oxford Companion to American
Literature* (1941) appeared almost half a century before the first
Australian companion, Bill Wilde, Joy Hooton and Barry Andrews's
Oxford Companion to Australian Literature (1985).

In the 1990s, companions proliferated as never before. 'The
world of reference volumes has undergone a revolution more
profound than any in living memory,' an American sociologist
observed.[3] When Rose approached Hirst, Oxford Australia had
already published Bruce Johnson's *Australian Jazz* (1987) and Wray
Vamplew's *Australian Sport* (1992) and was soon to publish Gwenda
Davey and Graham Seal's *Oxford Companion to Australian Folklore*
(1993) and a revised and expanded edition of *Australian Literature*
(1994). A team at the Australian Defence Force Academy was
contracted to produce *Australian Military History* (1995), and Rose
was about to engage Warren Bebbington to edit *The Oxford
Companion to Australian Music* (1997). While we were at work, he
was also negotiating companions to Aboriginal studies, *Australian
Film* (1999) and *Australian Gardens* (2002). OCAH would fill an
obvious gap in the company's Australian list.

The *Companion to English Literature* was born in the twilight of
the scholarly amateur. 'Why don't you hire some leisured highbrow
to collect systematically?' a colleague suggested to Sisam when he
floated the idea of another reference volume, an *Oxford Book of
Quotations*. '£50 should buy a heap of quotations.'[4] The companion
was reborn in the 1990s into an age of academic specialisation and
mass higher education. The pen and typewriter were giving way to
the word processor, and the printed page to the electronic screen.
Instead of leisured highbrows working alone in the well-stocked
library of a country house, the editors of the new companions were

usually professors leading teams of salaried academics who worked for a token fee or a copy of the book.

Although Stuart, John and I knew each other well, OCAH would be the first project we had undertaken together. We came from different universities—Melbourne, La Trobe and Monash—and our interests and political viewpoints differed, sometimes strongly. From the first we regarded these differences as an asset. John and I were the eldest, state school students from Methodist families, who graduated in the early 1960s, from Adelaide and Melbourne respectively, while Stuart, grandson of a Congregationalist clergyman and educated in a Presbyterian private school, was a product of the radical early 1970s. 'Conservative', the label often applied to John, hardly did justice to the complicated mix of social egalitarianism, democratic liberalism and cultural conservatism in his outlook. Stuart, the *enfant terrible* of the Melbourne History School in the early 1970s, was the historian of the Australian Communist Party and of a series of books exploring the class dimension of Australian history. Also a product of the Melbourne School, I was usually described, accurately enough, as a political moderate, although my main historical interests were social and cultural rather than political.

If our perspectives differed, however, we had much in common. For more than two decades we had participated in the scholarly networks based on the journal *Australian Historical Studies*, the learned academies, the Australian Research Council and the Australian Historical Association. We had contributed to other collaborations, such as the bicentennial history project, and to national debates over school history, citizenship, heritage, libraries, archives and museums. If Rose wanted to tap the overlapping networks and collaborations of the discipline, we were probably a strong team. We were all middle-aged, middle-class men, conscious of some—but perhaps only some—of our biases. But far from imposing a scholarly orthodoxy, our aim was to encompass the widest range of subjects and views. We were each critics, from different standpoints, of the standard interpretations of Australian history, none more than Stuart.

In his 1972 article 'Radical history and bourgeois hegemony', the young Marxist historian, soon to leave for Cambridge, attacked the liberal empiricism ('document fetish') and 'bourgeois ideology' of Melbourne University's School of History, personified in different ways by its founding fathers, Ernest Scott and Max Crawford. Crawford's remark that Marxism offered a 'clue' to historical explanation but nothing more drew Stuart's particular scorn. He was just as critical of his forerunners on the Left, whose writing, he asserted, remained trapped within the 'same flawed problematic'. 'The primary task of any Marxist historian', he declared in what was evidently meant as a statement of intent, 'should be the analysis of the full complexity of class oppression.'[5] The word 'complexity' was important for here, as in later essays such as 'The making of the Australian working class', written soon after his return to Australia, Stuart was reacting against vulgar or mechanistic Marxism as much as bourgeois empiricism.[6]

Pervading Stuart's critique was his sense of a discipline in crisis. By the 1970s, he suggested, academic historians had become more numerous but less sure of their bearings. 'The rapid growth of the discipline', he wrote in a review for the Australian bicentennial history series, 'was not wholly beneficial and ... its practitioners [had] lost much of their earlier confidence and authority.' While Manning Clark and Geoffrey Blainey still played the prophet's role, their successors were 'no longer sure that they had anything to say'.[7] The splintering of the profession into the subfields of women's history, labour history, urban history and Aboriginal history left him wondering, in the introduction to his 1986 volume in *The Oxford History of Australia*, whether 'the project of a holistic representation of the [Australian] past' was possible any more.[8] The historians seemed to be talking to each other rather than to their fellow Australians.

The rebel son returned to the Melbourne History Department and in 1990 was appointed to the chair named for its founder Ernest Scott. In *A History for a Nation*, Stuart reviewed Scott's professorial role and career as a prologue to his own. 'Scott stood at the beginning of this [professional] order,' he concludes. 'I witness its decline, possibly even its supersession.' While Scott had 'narrated a knowable past with the authority of a narrator who stood outside that past and read its remains', his own generation of historians were more aware of 'the contingent, the might-have-been, the lines that peter out'.[9] In 1994, the year of Stuart's book and Peter Rose's invitation, voices were already calling for a more confident telling of the Australian story. While OCAH was being researched and written, they grew louder.

Travelling by different routes, John and I had also come to question the received versions of Australian history. In 'Changing my mind' John describes how he came to reject the views of his 'left-leaning, progressive' teachers at the University of Adelaide. Family influences, his studies of early New South Wales politics and his growing unease with the progressive politics of his own day led him to question the dominant leftist view of Australian history. It gave too much weight to rights and conflict, he suggested, and too little to responsibilities and social cohesion. While we were co-editing OCAH John was writing *Sentimental Nation*, a challenge to the leftist view that Federation ('the greatest political achievement in Australian history', he wrote in OCAH) was nothing but a business arrangement.[10] He found an outlet for his role as public controversialist in *Quadrant* magazine during Robert Manne's editorship, but his republican and egalitarian sympathies set him apart from the conservative mainstream. His insistence that history should encourage citizens to ask difficult questions made him uneasy company for those, including Prime Minister John Howard, who looked for rousing narratives of national progress.[11]

My own path to OCAH through urban and public history had led me to look at Australian history from yet another angle. In 1978, in the issue of *Historical Studies* that also carried John's essay on 'The pioneer legend' and Stuart's on 'The making of the Australian working class', I turned Russel Ward's 'Australian Legend' on its head by viewing it from Sydney rather than the bush.[12] Later, as a volume co-editor in the bicentennial history, I defended its distinctive 'slice' approach as a challenge to the teleological bias of narrative history. There and later I experimented with concepts such as time, climate, energy and mobility as correctives to the political emphasis of most national histories.[13] In my teaching and writing I had begun to engage with the old/new forms of history flourishing outside the academy, such as heritage, museums and family history.[14]

Our differences would have been enough to show that a companion to Australian history written on Harvey's model, as though by a single author dispensing only 'conventional opinions', was no longer possible or even desirable. From the first we resolved that OCAH should 'show how Australian history has been interpreted as well as how it has been made'.[15] Rather than a factual compendium of events, people, movements and ideas, it would show how writers, painters, filmmakers and museums, as well as historians, had shaped our views of Australia's past. By taking the reader inside the history workshop and showing how its products were made, we hoped the readers would be better able to exercise their own judgement about the historical questions now insistently arising in the public sphere.

OCAH was an answer to the gap we had each observed between academic knowledge and the wider society. 'Despite the great and growing interest in Australian history, historical consciousness in this country is still weak,' we wrote in applying for research funding. The project would require a critical re-examination of the ways in which knowledge of Australian history had been conceived and organised and attention to the new understandings conveyed by feminist and Aboriginal scholarship.[16]

During 1994 we began meeting on Tuesday evenings once a fortnight around the dining room table at John and Christine Hirst's house in North Balwyn, roughly halfway between Stuart's house and mine. We were all busy with other projects and public commitments, so these regular meetings were a way of holding each other to account for the progress of the project. But they quickly became something more creative and enjoyable. While planning the volume—refining the list of headwords, selecting contributors, reviewing draft entries—our conversation ranged into the state of our profession and the universities, news of mutual friends, our public engagements and our views of current events. Occasionally the political world reached into our own deliberations as, on one memorable occasion, John was called out of the room to take a telephone call from Prime Minister John Howard. The convivial atmosphere of these meetings cemented our friendship and permeated the making of the book itself.

'A *Companion* should be companionable,' we wrote in introducing OCAH. At the beginning our companions included commissioning editor Peter Rose. Previous Australian companions were about 400 000 words in length. Rose originally proposed a similar word length for OCAH, but by the time contracts were signed early in 1995 it had expanded to 600 000 words, roughly one-third to be biographical entries. (The final volume neared 800 000 words.) In 1994 Kim Torney, a secondary teacher who had taken family leave to complete a Master's degree at La Trobe, was recruited by John, her supervisor, as an assistant editor; she was soon joined by Helen Doyle, who had completed a Master's degree in Public History at Monash and worked on the *Monash Biographical Dictionary of Twentieth Century Australia*. As well as managing correspondence, smoothing difficulties and undertaking research, Kim and Helen eventually drafted most of the short entries. They became wry but tolerant observers of the foibles of the editors, noticing, for example, how John and I tacitly ceded the chair to Stuart in deference to his executive capacity and apparently encyclopedic knowledge of books, people and institutions.

There were few models in Australia or elsewhere for the book we imagined. *The Oxford Companion to British History* (1997), edited by John Cannon, acknowledged the uncertainties of selection and interpretation, and encouraged authors 'to express their own opinions rather than offer bland and lifeless summaries', but took no account of national historiography.[17] *A Reader's Companion to American History* (1991), edited by Eric Foner and John Garatty, came closer to our ideal, especially in its emphasis upon readability and preference for biographical entries that offered 'an expert's assessment of the person's significance rather than a dry recitation of dates and facts'.[18] In Australia, the bicentennial volume, *Australians: A Historical Dictionary* (1987) attempted to fill a similar gap but its 1000 short entries made it less comprehensive than our proposed 1600 entries, its coverage and quality were uneven, and it did not attempt to show how the national past had been interpreted.[19]

We drew up head lists of possible entries and whittled them down, before dividing them between long (1000-word), medium (500-word) and short (200-word) categories. Biographical subjects, drawn from the *ADB* and other biographical dictionaries, were ranked according to their historical significance but modified to take account of gender, region and ideology. Serious researchers, we assumed, would always refer to the *ADB*; this released us to make a selection of lives that reflected the breadth of Australian experience. We ransacked the *Australian National Dictionary* and Wilkes' *Australian Colloquialisms* for catchphrases from 'bunyip aristocracy' to 'walkabout', and pooled suggestions based on our own reading for historical concepts ranging from 'fair and reasonable' and 'foundations' to 'frontier thesis' and 'fragment thesis'. In the end, our most difficult choices were often budgetary—whether topics could be accommodated within our word limit—rather than of relative historical importance.

The question of whether OCAH should include a chronology of key events provoked lively discussion. Was such a list desirable or possible, or were chronologies a relic of the canonical accounts of Australia's past that we were leaving behind? We pondered alternatives that might help readers to navigate Australia's past while signalling the subjectivity of any selection of signposts. Perhaps each of the editors could contribute a chronology. Alternatively, should the list be arranged in parallel columns according to Aboriginal, feminist, socialist or conservative points of view? Could we just have an entry on Chronologies, I suggested. As he watched OCAH listing towards historical relativism, Peter Rose looked dubious. With deadlines approaching and the word count increasing, the chronological table was quietly dropped from our agenda and from the book.

A guide to the interpretation of Australian history obviously needed to include entries on notable historians. But how many? A book without entries on Manning Clark and Geoffrey Blainey would look incomplete, but a Who's Who of Australian historians could appear self-indulgent. One option was to follow Harvey's example and include only historians who were safely dead, together with a few of the most eminent retirees. That drew in Geoffrey Blainey, Geoffrey Bolton, Miriam Dixson, Ken Inglis, John Mulvaney, Michael Roe and Allan Shaw. In the end, we stretched the net a little further to include some, still active, whose key works had endured, such as Humphrey McQueen, Henry Reynolds and Anne Summers.

Poets, novelists, journalists and critics presented a similar dilemma. There was no point in duplicating the *Companion to Australian Literature*, yet Henry Lawson, Les Murray, Donald Horne and Judith Wright, for example, had shaped understandings of Australia's past as profoundly as any historian. So we made a selection and instructed our contributors to write about their historical influence rather than their literary merit. Some of our omissions puzzled Joy Hooton, co-editor of *Australian Literature*: 'Why Hal Porter and not Peter, why Les Murray and not Gwen Harwood, why George Johnson and not Charmian Clift?' We made a start on ranking historic places—Barcaldine, Glenrowan and Lambing Flat—before realising that we simply did not have words to include them; the massacre sites Myall Creek and Waterloo Creek were rare survivors. Diagrams and pictures—our contract had allowed 150 B&W illustrations—were other casualties of our battle with the word limit.

By stressing historiography as well as history, we had created another dilemma, for the experts were also potentially subjects. So rather than selecting the leading authority to write the entry we often preferred a writer who could review it from a fresh angle—a younger scholar, like Frank Bongiorno on Labour History, or an outsider, like Jay Winter on the Anzac Legend. David Fitzpatrick, an expert on Irish history, reviewed the Scots in Australia, while Eric Richards, a Scottish historian, took on the Irish. Some invitations passed like hot potatoes from hand to hand until a willing contributor was found: Judith Brett, Don Watson, Graham Little and Brian Matthews all passed up Autobiography until John Rickard nobly took it on. Several experts passed up Aboriginal Resistance and Aboriginal Massacres before Andrew Markus and Richard Broome bravely agreed and wrote admirably judicious entries. Geoffrey Blainey declined Sport but accepted Inventions. The prodigious Barry Jones declared the topic of 'Prodigies' impossible and wrote on Biography instead. After querying the word 'companion' ('Should be mate—where do you Anglophiles think you are?'), Hugh Stretton declined Social Justice and urged Kim and Helen to 'bully, blackmail, cajole, trick or seduce' John or Stuart to take it on. They failed. At the end of the first round, a gratifyingly high proportion of our first invitations had been accepted. 'The celerity of these acceptances and the quality of the growing list of contributors augurs well for the quality and punctuality of the Companion,' Peter Rose reported.

As editors we naturally hoped to put our personal imprint on the book. We circulated drafts of the kind of entries we wanted: lively miniature essays rather than compendiums of factual information. We shared the writing of about a third of the longer biographical and interpretive entries, almost half the historiographical ones, and a smaller proportion of the rest. We each had our beat—John in colonial politics, Stuart in twentieth-century politics, and me in social and cultural history—but took the opportunity to range into unfamiliar territory. In his shrewd thumbnail portraits of six prime ministers, Stuart captured the 'practical idealism' of Deakin, the lonely heroism of Curtin, the 'inordinate ambition' of Menzies and the 'indomitable' will of Whitlam—'the last great politician to follow his convictions'—but he left the 'domineering' and 'vituperative' Billy Hughes to John. Stuart also took the lion's share of the -isms— Liberalism, Communism and Socialism and so on—but left Conservatism to John, who also wrote fresh and perceptive entries on Constitutions, Bureaucracy and Democracy. I patrolled the hinterland of social and cultural history with long entries on Lawson and Paterson, Heritage and National Identity, Motor Cars, Museums and Suburbs. We each took one of the four 'big' historians: Keith Hancock (Stuart), Russel Ward (John) and Geoffrey Blainey (me), leaving Carl Bridge with Manning Clark.

Our selection of contributors inevitably reflected the strengths and weaknesses of our network. A Canberra reviewer accused OCAH of a 'Melbourne bias'.[20] A breakdown of the 416 invited authors showed 120 from Victoria, 62 from New South Wales, 38 from the ACT and smaller contingents from the other states. If entries by the editorial team are included, a Melbourne bias is apparent, although no more pronounced than the Canberra–Sydney bias of the ANU-sponsored *Historical Dictionary*. A similar 'bias' might be detected in gender composition. 'We're seriously down in the area of female entry writers,' Kim wrote to me urgently in 1995 while I was on leave at ANU. Could I find some more in Canberra? Our recruitment drive produced an increase from 72 to 94 (or 22 per cent of the total), but it was hard to increase the proportion when only 18 per cent of the historical profession, according to a contemporary survey, was female.[21] Counting the location and gender of authors, in any case, is a crude and imperfect measure of bias.

By mid-1996, with the word count nearing 650 000 and many entries still to arrive, it was time to take stock and raise the tempo of activity. Peter Rose, who had loosened the reins during the middle stages of the project, now tightened them. Contributors were held to their allotted word lengths and told to keep the historiography brief. Some planned entries were dropped: Surfing and Lifesaving were among the casualties. Stuart declared Friday a 'day of action' when the editors each pledged to write as many short entries as they could before arriving at the Hirsts' house at five o'clock with their homework hot in hand. No prizes for guessing who was awarded the elephant stamp.

Thanks largely to the dedication and efficiency of Kim and Helen, OCAH was completed on schedule and launched by Senator John Button at Parliament House, Melbourne in September 1998. The *Weekend Australian* published a generous three-page spread based

on interviews with the three editors who posed, without apparent
irony, beside a monument commemorating the ill-fated Burke and
Wills expedition.[22] In the years since we signed up, much had
changed in the academic and political worlds. John Howard had
replaced Paul Keating as Prime Minister. The History Wars had
hotted up.[23] Stuart and I participated in a Melbourne University
debate on the proposition 'That Historians should wear Black
Armbands'.[24] Yet reviews of the book from historians of all persua-
sions were generally positive. 'Fair, competent, comprehensive [and]
remarkably free from the biases of political correctness or economic
innocence,' declared Robert Murray in *Quadrant*.[25] *Time*'s Tom
Dusevic praised its 'lively, lucid and thoughtful essays on the
mundane topics most histories play down or neglect'.[26] 'It is a very
ambitious book,' Geoffrey Blainey observed in the *Times Literary
Supplement*, commending the originality, 'clarity and pithiness' of
many entries and the editors' ability to 'comment with insight on
fields that are not their own'.[27]

The only sour notes came from perennial critics of academic
history like Maurice Dunlevy and Peter Ryan. Dunlevy craved a
historical dictionary of the traditional kind with a chronological
table, index and impersonal factual entries.[28] Ryan's gripe was more
personal and ideological. All was not well with Australian history, he
declared, and the main trouble was with the historians who had
'vanished into the worm-holed woodwork of interpretation'.[29] His
criticism would have been more telling if interpretation was something historians or critics could avoid. Only later, as the History Wars
reached a climax, did the figment of an '*Oxford Companion* School'
lodge in the imagination of some right-wing warriors.[30] Our book,
according to *Quadrant* editor Paddy McGuinness, was a 'compendium of every wild allegation advanced for political purposes against
earlier generations of white Australians'.[31] At least he thought it was
comprehensive!

We view OCAH now from the other side of a great divide. We
were children of the great age of print. Well into our project we
were still circulating draft entries in hard copy, annotating them in

handwriting and returning them through the inter-university mail to Helen and Kim. (Stuart's work, they recall, was instantly recognisable by the coffee stains and scent of pipe tobacco.) The History Wars were fought out with pen and paper in the pages of books, quality broadsheets and monthly reviews. But the age of print and paper seemed to be waning. Stuart concluded his entry on Books with gloomy reflections on the 'inability of the book to hold the attention of students habituated to other forms of information and entertainment'.

Some perceptive reviewers recognised OCAH as a bridge over the digital divide. 'Roaming through the diligently cross-referenced *Companion* is like surfing the Internet—only faster, more reliable and more rewarding,' Tom Dusevic remarked.[32] It stimulated 'a kind of postmodern reading practice, inveigling us down unintended paths and alleyways', noted Mat Trinca.[33] Dusevic wondered whether OCAH might be reincarnated as a fully interactive CD-ROM. In 2001 Oxford published a revised print edition, which allowed us to correct some errors and update our entries on Keating and Howard, but it was the last. In 2003 OCAH went out of print and joined Oxford's other Australian companions in the searchable online Oxford Reference library.

The arrival of Google and Wikipedia signalled the end of the golden age of big printed reference books like OCAH. Scholarly reliability could no longer prevail against the attractions of instant access. 'The notion of "trudging" to the "brick and mortar" library, "hauling down" a "fat tome" which claimed when published to offer authoritative overviews of a given topic, is as alien to today's students as learning Latin and Greek,' an American professor observed.[34] Once the revenue stream from book sales was cut off, there was no financial incentive for publishers or editors to revise old volumes or produce new ones. So OCAH now sits unrevised on the shelf in Oxford's electronic library, accessible in a few keystrokes but frozen in the historiography of the 1990s.

I look back on OCAH now, very fondly, as the swan song of my generation of Australian historians. It reminds me of a time when disagreement, political and otherwise, within the circle of good scholarship and mutual respect, could enlighten rather than divide. When traditions of scholarly collaboration and civic responsibility were strong and historians contributed to projects of public value with little thought of international rankings or managerial imperatives. Such traditions are not dead—witness, for example, the continued health of the *Australian Dictionary of Biography*—but they seem weaker than they were.

Sadly, many of our contributors are now dead and most, if not all, have retired from the academy. As I turn its pages, I meet old friends, members of a 400-strong circle of companions who joined our virtual conversation about the nation's past. They were not members of some imaginary 'school', parroting lessons from an ideological textbook, but lively conversationalists, each with their own voices and insights into the Australian story. On page 421 I meet Ken Inglis, ever alert to shifts in the way his fellow Australians speak, pondering the future of Mateship: 'Guy as a gender-neutral term may ease out mate,' he predicts. On page 379 the historian of Landscape George Seddon reminds me that 'the coast remains central to our consciousness because that is what "the outback" and "the inland" are measured from'. On page 365 I smile as I read Bill Gammage's assertion that Ned Kelly 'was only a fair bushman and horseman' and remember that the editors prevented him calling the sainted outlaw a 'bad' one. On page 250 I read Marilyn Lake's parting words on Feminism: 'Women still dream of sweet freedom', and I wonder whether the dream is any closer. Friends and scholarly companions, I salute them all, none more fondly than my co-editors John Hirst, who brought us together, and Stuart Macintyre, who kept his eye on the big picture and held us to our task. Both, alas, are gone too soon, but their intelligence, integrity and generosity continue to shine.

Notes

1   I have supplemented and corrected personal memories of the project by reference to files of the correspondence, minutes, headwords and other documents in my papers at Monash University Archives, MON 1208/79–85, and from recollections of our assistants Kim Torney and Helen Doyle. Oxford University Press Australia was unfortunately not able to retrieve sales records or other archives of the project.

2   Jason Tomes, 'Harvey, Sir (Henry) Paul (1869–1948)', *Dictionary of National Biography*; A. Banerjee, 'Oxford Companions', *Sewanee Review*, vol. 120, no. 4, 2012, pp. 658–67.

3   Alan Sica, 'Encyclopedias, handbooks, and dictionaries', *International Encyclopedia of the Social and Behavioral Sciences*, 2nd edn, vol. 7, 2015, p. 585.

4   Simon Eliot (ed.), *The History of Oxford University Press*, Oxford University Press, Oxford, 2014, vol. 3, p. 343.

5   Stuart Macintyre, 'Radical history and bourgeois hegemony', *Intervention*, no. 2, 1972, pp. 47–73.

6   Stuart Macintyre, 'The making of the Australian working class: An historiographical survey', *Historical Studies*, vol. 18, no. 71, 1978, pp. 233–53.

7   Stuart Macintyre, 'The writing of Australian history' in D.H. Borchardt (ed.), *Australians: A Guide to Sources*, Fairfax, Syme & Weldon, Sydney, 1987, pp. 1–29.

8   Stuart Macintyre, *The Oxford History of Australia*, vol. 4: *The Succeeding Age*, Oxford University Press, Melbourne, 1986, pp. ix–x.

9   Stuart Macintyre, *A History for a Nation: Ernest Scott and the Making of Australian History*, Melbourne University Press, Carlton, 1994, pp. 205–11.

10   John Hirst, 'Changing my mind', in Stuart Macintyre (ed.), *The Historian's Conscience: Australian Historians on the Ethics of History*, Melbourne University Press, Melbourne, 2004, pp. 84–93.

11   John Hirst, 'How best to write—narrative or theme?' in *Looking for Australia— Historical Essays*, Black Inc., Melbourne, 2010, pp. 15–27; and his *Australian History in 7 Questions*, Black Inc., Melbourne, 2014.

12   Graeme Davison, 'Sydney and the bush: A context for the Australian Legend', *Historical Studies*, vol. 18, no. 71, 1978, pp. 191–209; Davison, *History as a Vocation*, School of Historical Studies, Monash University, Clayton, 2006.

13   Graeme Davison, 'Slicing Australian history: Reflections on the bicentennial history project', *New Zealand Journal of History*, vol. 16, 1982, pp. 3–20; Davison, *The Unforgiving Minute: How Australia Learned to Tell the Time*, Oxford University Press, Melbourne, 1993.

14   Graeme Davison, 'The use and abuse of Australian history', *Australian Historical Studies*, vol. 23, no. 91, 1988, pp. 55–76; Davison, *The Use and Abuse of Australian History*, Allen & Unwin, Sydney, 2000.

15   This formulation appeared first in our applications for ARC Infrastructure Funding in 1995.

16   Application for Research Cooperative Infrastructure Development Grant Mechanism C, June 1995.

17   John Cannon (ed.), *The Oxford Companion to British History*, Oxford University Press, Oxford, 1997, p. viii.

18   Eric Foner and John A. Garatty (eds), *The Reader's Guide to American History*, Houghton Mifflin, Boston, 1991, p. xix.

19   This is the judgement of Mandy Paul in the substantial review of other reference works we commissioned her to write during the planning phase of the project.

20   Maurice Dunlevy, 'History with a Melbourne bias', *Canberra Times*, 10 October 1998.

21   Terry D. Bilharz, 'Academic historians in Australia: A profile of a profession', *Australian Historical Association Bulletin*, no. 68, 1991, pp. 31–7.

22   'Past masters', *Weekend Australian*, 12–13 September 1998.

23   Stuart Macintyre and Anna Clark, *The History Wars*, Melbourne University Press, Melbourne, 2003.

24   Graeme Davison, 'The inaugural Melbourne debate: That historians should wear black armbands', *Melbourne Historical Journal*, vol. 26, 1998, pp. 11–16.

25 Robert Murray, 'The Oxford Companion to Australian History', *Quadrant*, vol. 42, no. 12, 1998.

26 Tom Dusevic, 'History in the details', *Time*, 23 November 1998.

27 Geoffrey Blainey, 'Brave new themes', *Times Literary Supplement*, no. 5035, 1 October 1999.

28 Dunlevy, 'History with a Melbourne bias'.

29 Peter Ryan, 'Odd socks of our history', *Sydney Morning Herald*, 17 November 1998.

30 Editorial, *Quadrant*, vol. 44, no. 11, 2000, pp. 2–4. Macintyre and Clark, *The History Wars*, p. 147.

31 Paddy McGuinness, *Sydney Morning Herald*, 14 September 2000; editors' (Davison, Hirst, Macintyre) reply, 20 September 2000.

32 Dusevic, 'History in the details', p. 92.

33 Mat Trinca, 'Voices from our past', *Australian*, 2 December 1998.

34 Alan Sica, 'Encyclopedias, handbooks, and dictionaries', *International Encyclopedia of the Social and Behavioral Sciences*, 2nd edn, vol. 7, 2015, p. 587.

Chapter 21

The making of a trans-Tasman bubble

Len Richardson

My introduction to Stuart Macintyre came in the late 1970s and was shaped by the debates taking place within the Australian historical community about the state of labour history. In 1971 I had taken up a PhD scholarship at the Australian National University with Bob Gollan as my supervisor. Thus I first began to grapple with Australian history just as the generation of Australian historians (Brian Fitzpatrick, Ian Turner, Bob Gollan, Russel Ward) whose work attracted me to Australia was being dubbed the 'Old Left' and a 'New Left' critique was emerging. Nowhere was this characterisation more colourfully present than in Humphrey McQueen's lively and provocative *New Britannia*.[1] New Zealand's pre-eminent, radical-nationalist historian of the day, Keith Sinclair, found it amusing. In a rollicking review he wondered whether *A New Britannia* was a 'send-up or put-on or spoof-out' and asked whether 'Humphrey McQueen was the pseudonym of Barry Humphreys'.[2] Sinclair found it hard to believe that McQueen could envisage a body of readers for whom the notion that Australian society was racist and capitalist would prove shocking. In the spirit of trans-Tasman banter in which he revelled, Sinclair suggested that such innocence might reside in the fact that most Australian historians were 'parsons' sons (like M. Clark)'.[3]

Australian historians rightly took *A New Britannia* more seriously. It was as this general debate developed that Stuart first defined his position within the Australian labour history community. In 1976, after having completed a doctoral thesis, subsequently published as *A Proletarian Science: Marxism in Britain 1917–1933*, he almost joined us in the History Department at the University of Canterbury as a postdoctoral fellow, but sadly preferred the attractions of the recently founded Murdoch University in Perth.[4] Stuart's 1978 article, 'The making of the Australian working class: An historiographical survey', with its review of the development of Australian labour history, in many respects became a foundation piece for an MA honours course I was in the process of mounting on the Australasian labour movements of the late nineteenth and early twentieth centuries.[5] At the heart of the article was a critique of McQueen's assertion in *A New Britannia* that Australian workers did not a working class make but were part of a 'petit-bourgeoisie'.[6] At issue, as I saw it, was the nature of class relations in the antipodes. E.P. Thompson's dictum, that class happened and was constructed in different places and at different times in historically unique ways, pointed a way ahead. In the words of Stuart's 1978 article, E.P. Thompson had 'redefined class for labour historians'.[7]

Armed with Stuart's historiographical essay, Thompson's definition and John Rickard's *Class and Politics*, I set out teaching my labour history Honours course.[8] A path-breaking account of a class-based party system in New South Wales, Victoria and the early Commonwealth, *Class and Politics*, creatively fused labour, social and political history in a manner that, in the words of Stuart's 1978 survey, moved beyond the 'ambit of Old Left'.[9] Australian labour historians had already produced a substantial body of institutional studies that provided a framework for understanding the working-class lives that shaped them. In New Zealand, such writing lagged noticeably behind its Australian counterpart, and it was partly with this in mind that a posthumous celebration of Jim Holt's *Compulsory*

Arbitration in New Zealand: The First 40 Years took place at a Stout Centre Conference in Wellington.[10] I can therefore, in unlikely fashion for an historian, be precise about my first meeting with Stuart: 7 November 1987. His paper that day presented an Australian perspective on the establishment of arbitration in New Zealand and was informed by a study of colonial liberalism in Victoria that he was then pursuing. A year later, as a visiting Canterbury Fellow, he completed and published the work as *A Colonial Liberalism: The Lost World of Three Victorian Visionaries*.[11]

The unfolding reassessment of the pioneering work produced by Australian labour historians continued to offer the most relevant road map for developments in New Zealand. The 1980s were dark times for the New Zealand labour movement as workers confronted a brutal neoliberal assault launched by the Labour Party they had created. For labour historians the arrival of free market economics and the disruption of the social fabric that inevitably followed brought into even sharper relief injustices that resided in race and gender as well as class. The debate among Australian scholars about the role labour history might play in progressive thought was instructive for New Zealand's labour historians and enabled them to see, in advance and in sharper focus, the contours of their own circumstances.

These were not the only ideas that bobbed about in the trans-Tasman bubble in which Stuart was an active participant. And the creative exchanges that ensued at the University of Canterbury and elsewhere from the 1980s found expression in many spheres. Not the least of Stuart's challenges while in New Zealand was to find a way of countering the absence of Saturday afternoon at the 'G' in support of the Hawthorn Hawks. The best we could offer was the opportunity to give one solitary lecture on the origins and early history of the AFL and Saturday afternoons watching Christchurch club rugby in somewhat less salubrious circumstances than were available in 'Marvellous Melbourne'. Together with an Oklahoma 'Sooner', a Fulbright Visitor in American Studies, some three-way analyses of play ensued that startled onlookers given to casting the football preference of Melburnians as an unfathomable variant of 'aerial ping-pong'.

Such is the ebb and flow of deep historical forces shaping affairs within the Australasian bubble that the sporting pendulum soon swung in Stuart's favour. In 2012, as his mighty Hawks stood on the cusp of three successive AFL Grand Final triumphs (2013–15), I found myself sitting at the 'G' taking instruction in the finer arts of the game Victorians had made their own. Not that labour history was ever far from mind. Nothing could make the point better than Stuart's unbelievable conjuring up of a meeting with a student contemporary at Ormond College whose British family had owned the Blackball coal mine, the acknowledged spiritual home of the New Zealand Labour Party. Like much else in the histories of Australia and New Zealand, teasing out the fusion of people and ideas that lay behind the socialist thinking shaping events at Blackball in the early twentieth century is a reminder of the interwoven threads that inform our past. Understanding the making of that connected but different past owes much to the insights Stuart Macintyre injected into the trans-Tasman bubble.

Notes

1　Humphrey McQueen, *A New Britannia: An Argument Concerning the Social Origins of Australian Radicalism and Nationalism*, Penguin, Melbourne, 1970.

2　Keith Sinclair, review of *A New Britannia: An Argument Concerning the Social Origins of Australian Radicalism and Nationalism*, by Humphrey McQueen, Penguin, Melbourne, 1970, *New Zealand Journal of History*, vol. 5, no. 1, 1971, pp. 95; 94–7; http://www.nzjh.auckland.ac.nz

3　Ibid., p. 95.

4　Stuart Macintyre, *A Proletarian Science: Marxism in Britain 1917–1933*, Cambridge University Press, Cambridge, 1980.

5　Stuart Macintyre, 'The making of the Australian working class: An historiographical survey', *Historical Studies*, vol. 18, no. 71, 1978, pp. 233–53. DOI: https://doi.org/10.1080/10314617808595589.

6　Stuart Macintyre, 'Introduction—The making of the Australian working class: An historiographical survey', in Penny Russell and Richard White (eds), *Pastiche I: Reflections on Nineteenth-century Australia*, Allen & Unwin, Sydney, 1994, p. 122.

7　Ibid., pp. 123, 134.

8　John Rickard, *Class and Politics: New South Wales, Victoria and the Early Commonwealth 1890–1910*, ANU Press, Canberra, 1976.

9　Macintyre, 'Introduction—The making of the Australian working class', p. 134.

10   James (Jim) Holt, *Compulsory Arbitration in New Zealand: The First 40 Years*, Auckland University Press, Auckland, 1986.

11   Stuart Macintyre, *A Colonialism Liberalism: The Lost World of Three Victorian Visionaries*, Oxford University Press, Melbourne, 1991.

Chapter 22

Oceanic connections

Philippa Mein Smith

Stuart was my colleague through reading his work as well as academic connections. The first book of his I read was his *Oxford History of Australia* volume, when seeking a broader context for my PhD thesis research in the 1980s.[1] That history surveyed key patterns of politics, the economy and Australian society from Federation until the fall of Singapore in 1942, which dashed faith in defence by the British Empire. What struck me then were Stuart's focus on class relationships and boundaries between the vulnerable and the power holders, or labour and capital, and how the reformers I was studying sought to regulate class relationships.

No doubt the experience of writing the Oxford history helped finesse Stuart's approach to his Cambridge *Concise History of Australia*, published in four editions from 1999 to 2015.[2] So did ventures such as *The Oxford Companion to Australian History*, edited with Graeme Davison and John Hirst.[3] Stuart noted wryly how History as a discipline was fragmenting around him as he wrote his concise national history. Fortunately for students around the world, including mine in New Zealand, he crafted a narrative that explained the forces shaping modern Australia in ways they could relate to and understand.

When Cambridge University Press asked me to write *A Concise History of New Zealand*, Stuart's volume proved the ideal model for structuring my work. I was already using his first edition in teaching a comparative course on Australian and New Zealand history. Imagining the two concise histories side by side on a bookshelf fired my thinking. The aim seemed obvious: to write a book that both sat beside Stuart's and was complementary in its sweep of structure and content. Conceptually this made sense since Australia and New Zealand shared a history of colonisation.

Ten chapters navigating major themes in chronological sequence provided a practical (if inevitably conventional) framework that helped much in resolving the problem of selection. Further, engagement with Stuart's analytical narrative involved appraisal and assessment of his concise history. 'How and when did Australia begin?' he asks in opening his volume. 'How and when did New Zealand begin?' I echo in mine, gesturing to a wider debate.[4] While I would not commence with European versions of foundation stories increasingly discredited by new understandings of the past, I understand why Stuart did.[5] His first and second editions coincided with Australia's 'History Wars', a viciousness from which he emerged a public intellectual. 'The question of national origins has never been so fiercely contested,' he wrote mildly when publicly he was under personal assault.[6] Later editions show that Australia has begun to grasp how the Australian landscape is an artefact of Aboriginal practices over eons, to cite one example of recently detonated colonial epistemologies; and Stuart turns to the long past once he has introduced the key idea of Australian history as contingent and in flux.

Aboriginal Australia in deep time initiates the passage of the book: power and appropriation follow. Power structures feature throughout, as when Stuart applies the theme of 'coercion' both to Indigenous Australians and transported convicts. On stolen children, he could not be more concise: the 'tears' of Indigenous women 'flowed well into the present century'.[7] Through the convict system he explains the transition from the imperial garrison state to colonial development resting on free settlers. Pastoralism flourished, violence intensified against Indigenous Australians and conditions for convicts grew harsher, laying the groundwork for a power contest between settlers, former convicts and the governors in Sydney (and from the 1820s in Hobart). The development of political systems in the Australian colonies and an empire of trade are thus explained, released from a bog of detail.

There is the odd droll swipe at cultural studies: 'We hardly need to deconstruct the writings of Thomas Mitchell', he states, 'to appreciate that his exploration was a conquest.'[8] The Black War—or wars, since frontier violence characterised the whole of Australia—receive their due: readers learn what happened in Tasmania's Black War, where Tasmanian Aboriginal survivors were driven off the island despite the failure of the infamous Black Line, and about the massacre at Myall Creek, which recent research exposes was a pattern of massacres around the continent.[9] Hunger for land drove the killings and, as Stuart explains so deftly, fed calls for democratic institutions of government.

Whereas Stuart labelled the era 1889–1913 'National reconstruction', I preferred 'Managing globalisation' in addressing parallel themes.[10] His chapter title is but one instance of a remarkable ability to express complex ideas cogently, as it alludes to far more than the Federation of the six Australian colonies in 1901. Identifying links that others miss between colonial feminism and the Maritime Strike that pitted the new unionism of worker solidarity against capital, Stuart argues that socialism and feminism helped spur the creation of a 'binding Australian nationhood' through their challenge to the nation as an imagined community.[11] Such insights spurred me to think harder about parallel dynamics in New Zealand, which aspired to a grander future within the empire than one achieved by joining Australia (that alternative was suspected to mean takeover). Nonetheless the features of the 'Australian Settlement' likewise characterised New Zealand's emergent modern state.[12]

Mindful of the locus of power, Stuart locates the two world wars in one chapter to highlight Australia's 'strategic dependence on Britain'.[13] That reliance until the 1960s was economic and financial as well as strategic. The 'Sacrifice' chapter's concluding sentence is another model of succinctness: 'From the tragic sacrifice of the First World War, and rancorous discontent that followed, a sufficient unity was created in the Second World War to make the sacrifice seem worthwhile.'[14] Every chapter ends with a wrap-up sentence. Students take note!

Harder to constrain in one chapter are the upheavals from the 1980s that saw governments demolish once-defining institutions, not least since the Howard government and its successors embedded the swing to economically and socially conservative policies. It is obvious that Stuart found this trend disillusioning. Conversely, two chapters were necessary to consider Rogernomics and related Treaty claims and politics in New Zealand.[15] Closing with the question 'What next?', Stuart contemplates the 'unfinished business' of Aboriginal self-determination, when Australian governments have thus far refused to decolonise themselves.[16]

Stuart did more than his bit as a fine historian in his life of scholarship. While he excelled as the observer, the interpreter and communicator, he wrote history that made a difference. His concise history is gently and elegantly activist in the way it makes sense of Australia, its past, present and what might be. Thank you, Stuart, for your example, your clarity and steadiness.

Notes

1   Stuart Macintyre, *The Oxford History of Australia*, vol. 4, *1901–1942: The Succeeding Age*, Oxford University Press, Melbourne, 1986.

2   Stuart Macintyre, *A Concise History of Australia* [1999], Cambridge University Press, Melbourne, 2nd edn, 2004, 3rd edn, 2009, 4th edn, 2015. There are also five foreign-language editions.

3   Graeme Davison, John Hirst and Stuart Macintyre (eds), *The Oxford Companion to Australian History*, Oxford University Press, Melbourne; my contribution was 'Health', pp. 304–6.

4   Macintyre, *Concise History*, 3rd edn, p. 1; Philippa Mein Smith, *A Concise History of New Zealand* [2005], Cambridge University Press, Melbourne, 2nd edn, 2011, p. 1.

5   The 'new understanding of the Australian past' is first made explicit in Macintyre, *Concise History*, 3rd edn, p. 5. Henceforth all references to his *Concise History* are to the 3rd edn.

6   Ibid., p. 6.

7   Ibid., p. 50.

8   Ibid., p. 57.

9   Lyndall Ryan and her project team at the University of Newcastle have compiled a
    digital map of colonial massacre sites that shows the massacres that accompanied the
    spread of pastoralism around Australia. The completed map will provide an accurate
    record of the Frontier Wars from 1788 to 1930. See for example Lyndall Ryan,
    'Mapping the sites of frontier massacres', 13 February 2020, National Library of
    Australia, www.nla.gov.au/stories/audio/mapping-the-sites-of-frontier-massacres
    (viewed June 2021). Macintyre's *Concise History* drew on Ryan's earlier work, *The
    Aboriginal Tasmanians* [1981], Allen & Unwin, Sydney, 2nd edn, 1997, and her
    updated *Tasmanian Aborigines: A History since 1803*, 2012.
10 See also ch. 11, 'Capital and labour: Resisting globalization', in Donald Denoon and
    Philippa Mein Smith, with Marivic Wyndham, *A History of Australia, New Zealand
    and the Pacific*, Blackwell Publishers, Malden MA, 2000.
11 Macintyre, *Concise History*, p. 136.
12 I agree the Australian (or Australasian) Settlement was not a settlement.
13 Macintyre, *Concise History*, p. 156.
14 Ibid., p. 199.
15 Mein Smith, chs 9 and 10, *Concise History*. 'Rogernomics' refers to neoliberal
    reforms driven by New Zealand finance minister Roger Douglas in the later 1980s.
16 Macintyre, *Concise History*, p. 304.

Part 6

Public works

Chapter 23

The sentimental deficit

Australians and their Constitution

Carolyn Holbrook

Stuart Macintyre once told me that historians tend to choose to research subjects about which they have an inner conflict or question. The process of historical research and writing becomes a means through which they seek to resolve that dilemma. If I were to apply Stuart's logic to his own work, I would conclude that he possessed an abiding concern about civic society. Over the course of six decades, Stuart's intellectual inquiries roved across political ideologies, civic institutions and the principles that guide the regulation of labour and the allocation of wealth. Stuart's work in history was a civic mission.

This civic mission became explicit during the 1990s. In his own telling, Stuart had grown increasingly concerned about the capacity of Australians to fulfil their civic duties. His disquiet emerged while researching Australian intellectual history and intensified after working on a project that compared Australian citizenship and civic arrangements with those of other countries.[1] Stuart also confessed to a 'professional concern as a professor of history with the decline of the humanities in the school curriculum and the retreat of higher education from its earlier civic mission'.[2] He expressed his anxieties about the 'civic deficit' in a short paper to Prime Minister Paul Keating in April 1994, which concluded that government was neglecting the civic education of Australians.

While the precise sequence of events remains unclear to me, Stuart's concerns squared with Paul Keating's desire to enhance Australians' civic literacy before he began in earnest the campaign to make Australia a republic. Two months after Stuart wrote to the prime minister, Keating asked him to lead two senior educationists, Sue Pascoe and Ken Boston, in a Civics Expert Group, tasked with devising a strategy for a non-partisan scheme of public education and information about civics and citizenship. The goal of the education program was to equip Australians with the knowledge to 'participate fully in decision-making processes'.[3] Stuart and his fellow experts were appointed in June 1994 and embarked on a series of consultations around the country with educational bodies, political parties and other relevant organisations. My minor role in the secretariat that supported the Civics Experts Group was my first introduction to Stuart, who would become my PhD supervisor fifteen years later. As a young policy adviser, fresh from university, I was oblivious to the broader political context in which the civics program was conceived. I certainly do not remember the republic ever being mentioned during my time on the secretariat.

The bulk of the recommendations for a program of school-based civics education in the group's report, *Whereas the People: Civics and Citizenship Education*, were accepted by the Keating government. Its introduction was delayed by the change of government in 1996. The Coalition led by John Howard tweaked the program, placing greater emphasis on the historical development of Australian democracy, and less on enhancing the active citizenship skills that were designed to encourage engagement with contemporary civics issues. The implementation of the renamed *Discovering Democracy* program proceeded in 1997.[4]

By his own measure, Paul Keating's program of civics education failed to achieve its goal. The emphatic 'No' vote in the 1999 republic referendum accords with Australians' longstanding resistance to changing the Constitution. Since 1901, only eight of forty-four referendums have passed. Most of those successes have pertained to technical or process-related issues that have benefited from bipartisan support. The most emphatic 'Yes' vote was registered in the 1967 referendum in which the Commonwealth was given authority to legislate in relation to Indigenous Australians. After the failure of the republic referendum in 1999, Commonwealth governments appear to have lost their appetite for constitutional reform.

Australians' referendum hesitancy has spawned much speculation and conjecture. Is it a sign of our innate conservatism or our distrust of politicians? Does it indicate that we are content with the constitutional status quo?[5] Prime Minister Paul Keating made the reasonable assumption in his push for a republic that our readiness to vote 'No' was a symptom of ignorance, best medicated with knowledge. In this chapter I argue that Keating's great misjudgement was in appointing a Civics Experts Group to *educate* Australians about their Constitution, rather than employing a marketing agency to *propagandise* about it. I examine the limits of education and the significance of sentiment (or its absence) in seeking to fill the civic deficit. First, I will show that Australians suffer from an 'original cynicism' about civic matters, which stems from the failure of our founding political moment to become sacralised in the collective imagination. Second, I will use the case study of the ambitious attempt to alter the Constitution by the Curtin Labor government in 1944 to substantiate my contention that knowledge is no match for emotion in the pursuit of constitutional reform.

Historians and Federation

In seeking to account for Australians' civic indolence, many scholars have nominated the prosaic nature of our nation-making moment. In the absence of a blood-stained altar around which to effuse, Federation was driven by pecuniary self-interest and achieved by pragmatic compromise.[6] This interpretation of 1901 was promoted by left-leaning intellectuals, many of whom were disillusioned by the social and economic inequities of the capitalist system. This disenchantment became acute once the limitations of the post-World War II reconstruction project were apparent. Far-reaching proposals for social and economic reform were stymied by conservative interests in state legislatures, which blocked plans to extend the Commonwealth's legislative powers.

An influential account of Federation was contained in a political science textbook published by L.F. Crisp in 1949. Crisp had been the speechwriter for the Attorney-General and Minister for External Affairs, H.V. Evatt, during the failed referendum campaign in 1944 to give the Commonwealth expanded powers. Crisp wrote that Federation was forged principally by 'the big men of the established political and economic order, the men of property or their trusted allies'; those who were successful in their mission to make the Commonwealth 'a splendid bastion of property'.[7] A subsequent variation of the 'top-down' explanation suggested that people voted in the Federation referendums according to local economic interests, although this view was soon challenged.[8] Critical interpretations were compounded by later scholarship highlighting the state-led sexism and racism that were embedded in the Federation moment.[9]

These 'top-down' interpretations of 1901 were not seriously challenged until the 1990s, when the republic campaign provided some incentive for its champions to find inspiration in our civic history. Indeed, it is possible to read John Hirst's history of the Federation movement, *The Sentimental Nation* (2000), as a mighty intellectual effort to enthuse Australians about their foundational moment. Together with Helen Irving's *To Constitute a Nation* (1997), Hirst's book rejected the notion that Federation was a pragmatic commercial settlement. If Irving encouraged us to see both pragmatism and romanticism in the Federation movement, Hirst sought to convince readers that it had been nothing less than a sacred cause. Using sources including poetry, convention debates, correspondence, public rhetoric and memoirs, Hirst describes how its proponents were propelled by a belief that 'God wanted Australia to be a nation'.[10] All those 'petty and provincial concerns of colonial politics—the struggle over roads and bridges; the endless deputations to ministers begging favours—would be replaced by a politics that dealt with a national life and the fate of a whole people'.[11]

Hirst did not claim that the nationalist idealism of the founders awakened a mass movement or that Federation was achieved by a popular groundswell. In its 'first, creative phase', he argues, nationalism possesses a minority of intellectuals, while the mass of the people 'remain attached to their chiefs, villages, or provinces and can see no benefit in creating a new government'.[12] He did, however, contend that voting patterns in the referendum on the draft constitution were influenced not merely by economic self-interest but also by a belief that the 'making of a nation' would be a good thing.[13] And he claims that there existed a 'widely known and accepted' foundation myth that the Commonwealth was the people's Federation—that it had come 'from the people by the people to the people'.[14]

Hirst is oddly cursory in accounting for the failure of Federation to lodge in the national imagination. He cites the democratic nature of the inauguration festival in Sydney, in which none of the founders except Parkes were lionised, with the implication that this explains why the leaders of the movement were forgotten. He also notes the veneration of the British royal family at the opening of parliament in Melbourne on 9 May 1901 but does not contrast that emotion with the dearth of admiration for Edmund Barton and his peers.

Stuart published an essay about Federation historiography in 2000, in which he observed that 'Sometime between the early part of the century and the present, Federation lost its following'.[15] The explanation could be found, Stuart claimed, in 'the teaching of history in schools, the forms of public memory and the profoundly ambiguous place of politics in the national culture'.[16] I am not convinced that this explanation is sufficiently autochthonous. In my reading of public attachment to Federation, the 'Good Ship Commonwealth' did not sink in the decades *after* it set sail but rather it failed ever to launch.

Failure to attach

The most persuasive illustration of the limitation of Hirst's argument in *The Sentimental Nation* is the near-universal apathy about Federation in the years immediately following 1901. If the idealism of the founders was so compelling, why did it expire so quickly and completely? Why was the undisputed leader of the Federation movement and the Commonwealth's first prime minister, Edmund Barton, so uninterested in commemorating his 'sacred cause'? The press became curious in the closing months of 1901 about the apparent lack of preparations for the approaching first anniversary of Federation. Barton confirmed in late December 1901 that 'nothing has been done' to mark the occasion.[17] He equivocated about which date was most suitable for the celebration: 'The 1st of January is the anniversary of the actual inauguration, but there are other days, which, like certain sites for the Federal Capital, have equal claims to choice.'[18] Barton listed the alternatives as 1 July—by which he meant 9 July, the anniversary of the date on which Queen Victoria assented to the Constitution bill; 1 May—by which he meant 9 May, the anniversary of the date on which the Commonwealth parliament first sat, and 30 September—actually 19 September, the anniversary of the date on which Queen Victoria's proclamation of the Constitution Act appeared in the London *Gazette*. The Prime Minister expected that one of those dates would 'probably be chosen to mark the federation of the Australian state', but he showed no inclination to do the choosing.[19]

Unlike Barton, Alfred Deakin felt sure that 1 January was the appropriate date for the commemoration of Federation. While debating the Public Service bill in federal parliament in mid-1901, he told members that New Year's Day should be renamed 'Commonwealth Day' and celebrated as the anniversary of Federation. The impossibility of reaching consensus was apparent when the proposal was discussed by a Senate committee in early 1902. Some senators complained that 1 January was entirely unsuitable for a national day and would always be overshadowed by New Year's celebrations. Others thought that 'the Federal Parliament should adhere to the day which possesses an historical significance'.[20] The impasse was in part an indication of the limits of federal power and authority. While the federal government could determine public holidays for Commonwealth employees, overall responsibility remained with the states. To declare a new date on which to celebrate Commonwealth Day would risk upsetting both commercial interests and states that were jealous of their post-Federation autonomy.

In January 1903, the Melbourne *Herald* reported that no Commonwealth celebration day had been officially decided upon because the 'Government and the Parliament have been too busy with matters of more practical concern'.[21] Barton told the press that, while he did not propose to take any special steps to celebrate the second anniversary of Federation, 'If the people feel inclined to celebrate the anniversary, they can do so without the Government taking the initiative'.[22] The people showed as much interest as the Prime Minister. A regional newspaper in Victoria remarked on the lack of patriotic sentiment: 'He would have been a bold man indeed who in 1901 would have ventured to predict that in two short years the patriotic fervor (we had almost said fever) and imperialistic rejoicings with which the inauguration of the Commonwealth was celebrated would have been practically non-existent.'[23]

There was a brief push from Launceston City Council to establish Commonwealth Day, supported by the local newspaper, but this effort quickly receded. The *Examiner* contrasted the feebleness of Australian national feeling with the sentiment attached to the Fourth of July in the United States:

The fact that the Commonwealth was inaugurated on New Year's Day should make it the great national holiday of Australia. So far, however, we have not been able to get away from the old surroundings. We have hardly come to realise our new nationality, and hence it sits lightly on our shoulders. In the United States the Fourth of July is regarded as the day of the year, but then they won their independence

after a protracted struggle, while ours was a free gift from
the dear old motherland.[24]

Despite the deficit of attachment to the nascent Commonwealth,
Australians had other loyalties with which to satisfy and comfort
themselves. Colonial allegiances lingered. Physical isolation—a trans-
continental railway was not completed until 1917—meant that
citizens of the outlying states often felt closer to Britain than to the
rest of Australia. The British royal family and British imperialism
continued to animate Australians. Both were propagandised in
pageantry and ritual, and disseminated to young Australians through
school textbooks, magazines, adventure stories and toys. Whatever
national sentiment existed was directed by the Australian Natives'
Association towards commemoration of 26 January, the anniversary
of the arrival of European settlers at Sydney Cove in 1788. It would
not be until Australian soldiers rushed the cliffs at Gallipoli in April
1915 that an Australian creation myth equal to the demands of early
twentieth-century nationalism was forged.

The failure of what John Hirst called that 'first, creative phase'
of nationalism to trickle down through the community suggests that
it was never as potent as Hirst hoped. While the idealism of Barton,
Alfred Deakin and others was no doubt genuinely held, Federation
might have owed more to the 'series of miracles' that Deakin
perceived than to the momentum of a group of righteous activists.[25]
Unlike the tales spun by Joseph Conrad's Marlow in *Heart of
Darkness*, the kernel of Federation was not enveloped by greater
meaning. It spawned no mythology that inspired people to cooperation, sacrifice and extraordinary endeavour. The fact that Australians
cared so little about 1901, their tendency to weigh Federation prag-
matically and according to their pecuniary interest, was to have
profound consequences for our national civic culture. Among the
most pervasive of these consequences has been the reluctance of
Australians to engage cooperatively in the processes necessary to
achieve constitutional reform.

The limits of education

When the Labor Party assumed office in October 1941, it took over and invigorated existing plans begun by the Menzies government for postwar reconstruction. Prime Minister John Curtin appointed the Treasurer Ben Chifley as Minister for Post-War Reconstruction in December 1942, and H.C. Coombs became Director General of a new department charged with coordinating the reconstruction effort. Labor's aspirations were bold. It sought not to replace, remodel or recondition 'the old systems that have proved so detrimental to the people's welfare', rather to build 'a new world with materials not worked and faded but with fresh plans that will give happiness and security to the people'.[26] Foremost among the government's priorities was a desire to avoid the cycle of economic boom and bust that followed World War I and led to the immense suffering of the Great Depression. If the government were to remake the postwar world, it would need an extension of the sweeping authority it exercised during the war under the defence power in the Constitution.

Curtin would have been wise to resolve the question of reconstruction powers imminently, to capitalise on the prevailing spirit of sacrifice and cooperation. A Gallup Poll held in May 1942 confirmed impressions that the Commonwealth Government was widely admired for its management of the war effort. Sixty per cent of respondents (including 72 per cent of those in New South Wales) favoured abolition of the states, while 19 per cent (and majorities in Tasmania and Western Australia) opposed it. Twenty-one per cent either held no opinion or failed to answer.[27] Polling in August 1942 suggested that 'about three out of four people expect great changes in our way of life after the war'. Most important among these changes were the eradication of unemployment, improvement in the living standards of working people and social security. Others referred to housing, education, inequality, improved morality and 'no more wars'.[28] A Gallup Poll in November 1942 found similar support for the abolition of the states. There was trepidation, however, about the centralisation of power in a national government. Among those who believed the states should be abolished, two in every three thought power should be given to regional councils rather than concentrated in a central authority.[29]

When Evatt introduced a bill to parliament seeking an extension of wartime powers, he was met with protests not only from the opposition but also from senior Labor figures in the states. In an effort to broker a compromise, Curtin convened a Constitutional Convention attended by state and federal parliamentarians from the major parties in December 1942. An agreement was reached wherein the states undertook to transfer controls over rationing, wages, employment, prices and a range of other reconstruction powers to the Commonwealth for the duration of the war and five years afterwards. Simultaneous Gallup polling revealed that all states except Western Australia strongly supported the principle of transferring extra powers to the Commonwealth.[30] Sixty-four per cent were in favour, 13 per cent were opposed, 10 per cent were undecided and 13 per cent could not answer. In Western Australia, 44 per cent favoured the transfer and only 32 per cent opposed it. The remaining 24 per cent comprised people who were undecided and unacquainted with the issue. More than a third of women did not offer an opinion. Of those women who did, five out of six favoured the transfer of powers.[31]

Despite the agreement that was reached at the Constitutional Convention in December 1942, Western Australia, Victoria, South Australia and Tasmania failed to transfer powers to the Commonwealth. While Curtin lashed out at the states for breaking their promises, Labor backbenchers urged him to hold a referendum while public opinion remained in the government's favour. Ignoring these appeals to act quickly, Curtin preferred to wait until after the election in August 1943. When Labor was returned to government with a convincing mandate, Curtin still hesitated.[32] For reasons that Stuart judges in *Australia's Boldest Experiment* to be impossible to pin down, the Prime Minister appeared to have lost enthusiasm for seeking expanded Commonwealth powers. He commented in the margin of a draft of the bill in November 1943 that only banking, trade and commerce powers were 'absolutely necessary'. Others would be 'useful but not indispensable'.[33]

Curtin finally set the process in motion for holding a referendum in October 1943. Stuart deduces in *Australia's Boldest
Experiment* that Curtin decided to act in order to circumvent calls
for even stronger reform measures, such as the socialisation of
industry, which were likely to be made at the approaching Federal
Conference of the ALP.[34] Although the threat of Japanese invasion
had subsided, there was still reason for supporters of an expansion of
Commonwealth power to be optimistic. A Gallup Poll in November
1943 indicated that there was a sound majority in support of the
Commonwealth power to legislate on employment and unemployment.[35] Gallup polling also suggested that the referendum would be
successful if it had been held in January 1944.[36] Support had declined
by March, with a majority of Tasmanians now opposed to the
transfer of powers, but there remained a solid margin in favour of
increased Commonwealth power overall.[37]

Planning had begun in 1943 for a large-scale education program
about the proposed changes. The process was overseen by a joint
committee of officers from the Departments of Post-War
Reconstruction, Attorney-General's and Information, chaired by the
Director General of Information. In December 1943, the
Department of Information's chief publicity officer, Norman
McCauley, wrote to his regional deputies asking them to 'quietly
sound out public opinion' and seek to ascertain the likely quarters of
opposition and their lines of attack. McCauley acknowledged that
there was 'very little awareness of the referendum issue' and charged
his officers with finding out 'the angles of the problem that the man
in the street is most interested in'.[38] While the employment question
would clearly concern this everyman, the department needed to find
ways to show him that he also had a stake in such issues as the
proposed commerce and financial powers.

The Victorian deputy director, T.P. Hoey, convened a discussion
group of about twenty people and reported back to McCauley a
nuanced range of views. The idea that the Commonwealth should
be the coordinating authority had intuitive appeal, but there were
many caveats. State public servants were likely to vote 'no' for fear

that their jobs would be imperilled. And 'the man-in-the-street, at first approach', favours state retention of employment powers for fear that 'remote control will offer him less personal security'. 'The average woman has given little thought to the subject of Commonwealth powers, and will probably be swayed by her husband or relatives who are better informed,' Hoey reported. He added: 'Even more than on political issues, women are likely to be guided by their more socially minded leaders.' Hoey estimated that approximately a third of Victorians favoured a 'yes' vote, a third a 'no' vote and a third 'have no opinion because they have never thought about it'.[39]

In February 1944 the Adelaide branch of the Information Department reported fears among the public that wider Commonwealth powers might lead to 'socialisation in terms of regimentation, bureaucracy, and curtailment of individual liberties. This involves religious influences'. South Australians were also concerned that any relinquishment of powers to the Commonwealth would 'play into the hands of larger and more securely established concerns in the Eastern States'. The unnamed author of the briefing note reported a conversation with J.F. Walsh, President of the state ALP, who said that 'the Referendum would have been carried without a doubt had it been held last August'.[40]

The education campaign was launched in early 1944, with the expectation that the referendum would be held in the third week of May. Curtin's absence in Britain, Canada and the United States from early April until late June 1944 delayed the process, the success of which would depend on using the Prime Minister's 'personal standing to reassure doubters'.[41] The education campaign had begun by the time Curtin finally announced in July that the referendum would be held on 19 August 1944. The campaign was thorough and far-reaching. The Information department released a range of booklets, with titles including 'We Can Do Better', 'You and the Referendum' and 'For This We Fight'. Postwar discussion groups, facilitated by trained leaders, were formed around the nation, and a series of two-minute radio spots entitled 'Post-War Messages' was broadcast.

As the education campaign intensified, support for the referendum declined. Gallup polling showed that only 41 per cent of men and 33 per cent of women would have voted 'Yes' in May 1944.[42] Polling in July 1944 underlined how steady and consistent the erosion of support had been. The 'Yes' vote now sat at 35 per cent for men and 33 per cent for women.[43] Once the campaign proper began in July 1944, ill-health prevented Prime Minister Curtin from fulfilling all but two of his speaking engagements. Chifley was similarly inactive. Evatt did the bulk of campaigning, assisted by Crisp as his speechwriter.

Curtin was 'disappointed but not surprised' when the referendum proposal was defeated. He had learned from the failure of Labor's referendums in 1911 and 1913 that opportunities for major constitutional reform were rare. As the apprehension of Japanese invasion diminished, so did the public's tolerance for sacrifice and its trust in government. The window of opportunity to pass such a wide-reaching alteration to the balance of the Constitution had been in 1942, in the midst of the crisis. As Stuart writes in *Australia's Boldest Experiment*, 'With every month that followed the desperate days of 1942, the spirit of sacrifice faded, while the emergency powers measures became increasingly irksome.'[44]

Knowledge about the fourteen powers referendum and support for it moved along opposite trajectories in 1944. The dwindling of the centrifugal force unleashed by external threat was not the only factor that made people less inclined to vote for radical change and place unprecedented trust in a central authority. Opponents of the referendum, including the opportunistic United Australia and Country parties, sought to instil fear in the electorate that an expanded Commonwealth might lead the country down the authoritarian path of nazism or communism; the threats were invoked alternately. The history of the fourteen powers campaign suggests that sentiment—initially the fear of Japanese invasion and later fears about tyranny—rather than reasoned appraisal of the merits or otherwise of the referendum proposals guided voting intentions.

The sentimental deficit

Stuart's legacy is profound. He perceived a deficit in Australians' civic knowledge in the 1990s and proceeded to remedy it. The civics and citizenship education program initiated by the work of the Civics Expert Group has weathered the buffeting winds of the culture wars and the jostling within a crowded curriculum. Civics and Citizenship currently sits within one of the eight key learning areas in the Australian curriculum. Despite the fact that civics is implanted in the national curriculum, we still face a major challenge in raising informed and active citizens. The most recent review of the civics curriculum indicates that only 38 per cent of Year 10 students—the level at which the curriculum finishes—are proficient in civics and citizenship knowledge.[45]

The need to produce informed and active citizens is even more pressing than when Stuart sent his missive of concern to Paul Keating in 1994. Stuart began his civic mission at the end of the Cold War when influential commentators were proclaiming the triumph of Western liberal democracy. Inevitably, events have made a mockery of that declaration—not least the storming of the United States Capitol building on 6 January 2021. Trust in democratic institutions across Western nations has fallen sharply in the past two decades, although the COVID-19 pandemic has reversed the trend in some countries. Loss of faith in democracy is particularly noticeable among young people.[46]

In order to safeguard our democratic institutions, we need to redouble our efforts to raise civically engaged citizens and to welcome immigrant populations into the civic community. Australians are capable of furnishing themselves with detailed and technical information pertaining to significant civic issues. The COVID-19 pandemic has produced a wave of lay epidemiologists and experts on the intricacies of mRNA vaccinations, the advantages of Pfizer over AstraZeneca and the aetiology of blood clots. Clearly, it is the apprehension of danger that has impelled citizens to arm themselves with knowledge. Equally, many people have proved vulnerable during the pandemic to misinformation, in forms including self-serving political messages, biased media reportage and conspiracy theories. Information, draped in sentimental clothing, can be a dangerous weapon.

As Stuart, John Hirst and many others have observed, Australians are apathetic about the history of their democratic institutions and practices.[47] Federation was not forged on an anvil of existential threat or physical danger, of the kind that neuroscience clearly indicates spurs emotional attachment.[48] Australians are not inclined to learn about their institutions of government because they feel little attachment to them. This is an emotional deficit that cannot be satisfied by a campaign of civics education. It could, however, be filled by a concerted effort by government to enthuse Australians about our democratic system: our pioneering of the secret ballot, for instance, and our system of compulsory voting. These are vital signs of civic health that can be celebrated in ways that include *all* Australians— we are all democrats. Imagine if the Commonwealth showed the same commitment to fanning a mythology of Australian democracy as it does to propagandising the Anzac legend.[49] A $1 billion campaign to mythologise the democracy sausage—that could work.

Notes

1   Stuart Macintyre, 'An expert's confession', *Australian Quarterly*, vol. 67, no. 3, 1995, p. 3; Stuart Macintyre, 'Rethinking Australian citizenship', Cunningham Lecture, Academy of the Social Sciences in Australia, Canberra, 1992.
2   Macintyre, 'An expert's confession', p. 3.
3   Ibid., p. 4.
4   Stuart Macintyre and Noel Simpson, 'Consensus and division in Australian citizenship education', *Citizenship Studies*, vol. 13, no. 2, 2009, p. 125.
5   This is argument is made by Brian Galligan, *A Federal Republic: Australia's Constitutional System of Government*, Cambridge University Press, Melbourne, 1995, pp. 110–32.
6   See for example Ronald Norris, *The Emergent Commonwealth*, Melbourne University Press, Melbourne, 1975, and W.G. McMinn, *Nationalism and Federalism in Australia*, Oxford University Press, Melbourne, 1994. For an example of the sentiment that nations needed a martial event around which to cohere, see Alfred Buchanan, *The Real Australia*, T. Fisher Unwin, London, 1907, p. 308.
7   L.F. Crisp, *Australian National Government*, Longman Cheshire, Melbourne, 1978, p. 14, originally published as *The Parliamentary Government of the Commonwealth of Australia*, Longmans, Green, London, 1949. See also McMinn, *Nationalism and Federalism in Australia*, and Norris, *The Emergent Commonwealth*.
8   R.S. Parker, 'Australian Federation: The influence of economic interests and political

pressures', *Historical Studies*, vol. 4, no. 13, 1949, pp. 1–24; Geoffrey Blainey, 'The role of economic interests in Australian Federation', *Historical Studies*, vol. 4, no. 15, 1950, pp. 224–37; John Bastin, 'Federation and Western Australia', *Historical Studies*, vol. 5, no. 17, 1951, pp. 47–58; Patricia Hewett, 'Aspects of campaigns in south-eastern New South Wales at the Federation referenda of 1898 and 1899', pp. 167–84, in A.W. Martin (ed.), *Essays in Australian Federation*, Melbourne University Press, Melbourne, 1969.

9   For example Patricia Grimshaw, 'Federation as a turning point in Australian history', *Australian Historical Studies*, vol. 33, no. 118, 2002, pp. 25–41; Patricia Grimshaw, Marilyn Lake, Ann McGrath and Marian Quartly, *Creating a Nation*, McPhee Gribble, Melbourne, 1994; Marilyn Lake, *Getting Equal: A History of Australian Feminism*, Allen & Unwin, Sydney, 1999.

10   John Hirst, *The Sentimental Nation: The Making of the Australian Commonwealth*, Oxford University Press, Melbourne, 2000, p. 4.

11   Ibid., p. 7.

12   John Hirst, 'Federation: Destiny and identity', *Papers on Parliament*, vol. 37, 2001.

13   Hirst, *The Sentimental Nation*, p. 265.

14   Ibid., p. 297, quote from *Advertiser*, Adelaide, 2 January 1901.

15   Stuart Macintyre, 'The fortunes of Federation', in David Headon and John Williams, *Makers of Miracles: The Cast of the Federation Story*, Melbourne University Press, Melbourne, 2000, p. 7.

16   Ibid.

17   *Evening News*, Sydney, 26 December 1901, p. 4.

18   Ibid.

19   Ibid.

20   Commonwealth *Hansard*, 29 January 1902, p. 9323.

21   *Herald*, Melbourne, 1 January 1903, p. 1.

22   *Sydney Morning Herald*, 19 December 1902, p. 5.

23   *Numurkah Leader*, 9 January 1903, p. 2.

24   *Examiner*, Launceston, 1 January 1903, p. 4.

25   Alfred Deakin, *The Federal Story: The Inner History of the Federal Cause, 1880–1900*, Melbourne University Press, Melbourne, 1963, p. 173.

26   'Referendum 1944', Prime Minister's Department, Referendum, Alteration to Constitution, Part 2, National Archives of Australia (NAA), A461, L342/1/2 PART 2.

27   *West Australian*, 10 June 1942, p. 2.

28   *Advertiser*, Adelaide, 15 August 1942, p. 7.

29   Ibid., 26 November 1942, p. 6.

30   *West Australian*, 30 December 1942, p. 2.

31   Ibid.

32   Stuart Macintyre, *Australia's Boldest Experiment: War and Reconstruction in the 1940s*, NewSouth Publishing, Sydney, 2015, p. 255.

33   Cabinet minutes, 23 November 1943, NAA, A2703, 53, quoted in ibid., p. 255.

34   Macintyre, *Australia's Boldest Experiment*, p. 257.

35   *Courier Mail*, Brisbane, 16 December 1943, p. 4.

36   *Sun*, Sydney, 16 January 1944, p. 5.

37   Ibid., 5 March 1944, p. 3.

38   'Department of Information, referendum matters', Memorandum from McCauley to Deputy Directors, 13 December 1943, NAA: M44, SP112/1.

39   Letter from Hoey to McCauley, 30 December 1943, loc. cit.

40   'South Australia Campaign Report undated ? February 1944', loc. cit.

41   Macintyre, *Australia's Boldest Experiment*, p. 259.

42   *Sun*, Sydney, 11 June 1944, p. 7.

43   *Advertiser*, Adelaide, 5 August 1944, p. 11.

44   Macintyre, *Australia's Boldest Experiment*, p. 254.

45   'National Civics and Citizenship Report released', *ACER Discover*, 22 January 2021.

46   Edelman Trust Barometer 2021; 'Trust in government hits all-time low', ANU Election Study, 9 December 2019; Lowy Institute Poll 2019.

47   Macintyre, 'The fortunes of Federation'; John Hirst, *Australia's Democracy: A Short History*, Allen & Unwin, Sydney, 2002.

48   For example, Miranda Olff, 'Bonding after trauma: On the role of social support and the oxytocin system in traumatic stress', *European Journal of Psychotraumatology*, vol. 3, no. 1, 2012; DOI: 10.3402/ejpt.v3i0.18597.

49   Paul Daley, 'A \$500 million expansion of the War Memorial is a reckless waste of money', *Guardian Australia*, 8 April 2018; Richard Flanagan, 'Our politics is a dreadful black comedy', *Guardian Australia,* 18 April 2018.

Chapter 24

Stuart Macintyre and the 'History Wars'

Compassionate histories and compassionate historians

Anna Clark

The 'History Wars' have arguably been *the* defining image of Australian history since the 1990s. Fought over the contents and interpretation of Australia's past, these disputes confirm the contestability and politicisation of national memory. They reveal how competing historical discourses play out in politics, in the media, in communities and education. In turn, such contests demonstrate how historical debates also reflect Australian politics, cultures and beliefs in the present.

The most striking aspect of the History Wars is the lines of division they explicitly demarcate. Every outbreak of historical dispute—a museum exhibit here, a history syllabus there, a political speech or public commemoration—is immediately positioned onto one side or the other of an ideological fence-line. The historical choices are stark: colonisation is either 'settlement' or 'invasion', Australians are apologists for the past or proudly stand by it, the nation's historians either don black armbands or white blindfolds.

There is no grey. Such contests have polarised the community and left historians in the difficult position of attempting to analyse this historical disagreement without somehow being enveloped by its stark political divisions.[1]

At their heart, such debates play out over the history and moral legitimacy of the settler colonial state, focusing on the extent of frontier violence in Australia's past and how that past is remembered in the present. Indigenous communities never ceded sovereignty, yet the 'dispersal' of their cultures and peoples was actively undertaken or tacitly authorised by a succession of imperial, colonial, state and federal governments. Australia might be a largely peaceful, diverse and successful democracy in the present, but to what extent were its origins morally ambiguous? Meanwhile, the question of how contemporary Australians face up to and reckon with the consequences of that past are also up for grabs. How do we judge from today's perspective the colonial project that settled the Australian continent? Indeed, to what extent does Australia's relative national wealth derive precisely from the forced expropriation of Indigenous lands, waterways and resources? What 'actually happened' in the colonial past and how those 'happenings' reverberate into the present form the crux of this historical contest.

We can see the emergence of dispute most clearly during the 1988 Bicentenary, when the challenges of Australia's settler-colonial beginnings were unmissable. Framed by a growing movement for Indigenous land rights, political representation and historical revision, 'celebrations' of the continent's colonisation were always going to be problematic. And as thousands of Indigenous demonstrators and their allies marched through Sydney on 26 January 1988 to protest the nation's historical 'progress', the 'Australian Achievement' looked increasingly shaky. Even the Labor Prime Minister Bob Hawke declared that 'All of us have a guilt and a responsibility for many of the injustices that occurred in those 200 years'.[2] Not everyone agreed. In an article for the conservative *IPA Review*, the mining executive Hugh Morgan claimed that any sort of apology was simply the work of a 'Guilt Industry', which 'campaigned' to 'delegitimise the settlement of this country'.[3] That sense of division mounted in the 1990s, as alternative readings of Australian history were increasingly ascribed to and advanced by opposing political parties.[4]

In December 1992, for example, when the Labor Prime Minister Paul Keating gave a speech to mark the coming International Year for the World's Indigenous Peoples, he famously reflected on the cleavages wrought on Indigenous Australians by colonisation. And he framed the critical importance for non-Indigenous Australians to undertake an 'act of recognition', as he insisted that 'it was we who did the dispossessing': 'We took the traditional lands and smashed the traditional way of life. We brought the disasters. The alcohol. We committed the murders. We took the children from their mothers. We practised discrimination and exclusion.'[5]

Only months after Keating's speech, the historian Geoffrey Blainey provided the History Wars its most powerful imagery to date when he suggested that Australian history had become overly apologetic and unbalanced. While the damage by colonists on the frontier had tended to be ignored in the past, Blainey acknowledged, historians had recently swung away from that triumphalist perspective to an approach that had overcompensated and was overly negative, Blainey surmised, ignoring what he understood to be the 'Australian Achievement'. With his instinct for a catchy metaphor, Blainey called this form of history 'Black Armband'.[6]

His imagery was adopted by a number of conservative political figures, who appropriated the categorisation of Australian history writing into negative and positive, black and white. Keating's prime ministerial opponent and eventual successor, the Liberal politician John Howard, championed the 'Black Armband' label. His belief that an intellectual elite had silenced more positive perspectives of Australian history was evidently influenced by Blainey's ideas. Outlining his views to parliament soon after he was elected prime minister in 1996, Howard maintained that 'I do not take the black armband view of Australian history. I believe that the balance sheet of Australian history is overwhelmingly a positive one'.[7]

Given the history that the previous Labor government had advanced, and the High Court's renunciation of the fiction of *terra nullius* through its Mabo decision in 1992, such a historical realignment by Howard was a conscious move to wrest control of the national narrative. In his well-publicised 1996 Menzies Lecture, Howard articulated that act of historical reimagining. 'A year or two ago, we witnessed one of the high-water marks in the attempt to rewrite important parts of Australia's political history,' he outlined, in a tacit critique of Keating's account of the Australian story. 'It was an assault without substance, without honour and without success,' Howard continued, which 'failed because the facts of history simply did not sustain it.'[8]

Such interventions showed that Australian history was political, it was contested, and it mattered. In turn, the History Wars enveloped sites of national historical memory across the country, beyond the political arena. This is oversimplifying, of course. For one thing, despite its inherent parochialism, the History Wars have actually been thoroughly transnational. Just look at those debates over whether Japan should apologise for its role in World War II, how Germany should commemorate the Holocaust, how the Troubles in Northern Ireland can be constructively studied, or what legacies of slavery and colonisation should feature in US history textbooks.[9] The focus of contest shifts slightly across national borders, but the historical 'wars' themselves all exhibit the same characteristics, including the same rhetoric: the battlefield metaphors, polarised discourse and partisan appeals to the national past.[10]

There are also aspects of the History Wars that confound its politicising and polarising terms of debate. Some conservative commentators were profoundly affected by the 'Bringing Them Home' report, which detailed the forced removal of generations of Aboriginal children from their families and demanded an official government apology.[11] Many conservative politicians and public commentators openly supported the processes of Indigenous reconciliation, redress and recognition, as well as the belated 2008 apology to the 'Stolen Generations'. Meanwhile, some Labor politicians, such as the New South Wales Premier Bob Carr, aligned with Howard in critiquing history teaching that had become too divorced from chronology and content. Both examples show the fluidity of public debate.[12]

Such discourse reflects the inherent diversity of opinions, political affiliations and historical consciousness, rather than opposing poles of an ideological compass. But in practice, that spectrum of views was funnelled into partisan camps of what became a bitterly contested public debate over the nation's past. The very structure of the History Wars meant that any intervention was reduced to its lines of division.[13]

That is not to say that certain distinctions are unimportant. Historians revise and disagree as part of their practice: each generation asks questions that reflect their own times and context.[14] Yet those iterative processes of historical revision and changing understandings of historical practice were sidelined in the History Wars, despite being central to the debate itself.

Understanding the political potency of national history and the ways certain historical narratives are grafted to alternative visions of the nation's present and future can be clarifying. Yet historiographical awareness of history's inherent subjectivity, nuance and complexity has been largely overlooked in these partisan disputes over the past. When the conservative literary scholar and public commentator Keith Windschuttle published a series of articles for *Quadrant* magazine in 2000, for example, he accused politically progressive historians of actively fabricating Australian history in order to bolster their ideological assumptions. Revision was not a process—it was the problem. 'Over the past twenty years, Australian historians have conducted a story of widespread massacres on the frontier of the expanding pastoral industry,' Windschuttle contended. 'However, when it is closely examined, the evidence of these claims turns out to be highly suspect.'[15]

These attacks culminated in the 2002 publication of Windschuttle's first volume of *The Fabrication of Aboriginal History*, focusing on colonial Tasmania, in which he reiterated the accusations in more detail and admonished historians such as Lyndall Ryan and Henry Reynolds for exaggerating the extent of frontier violence. A cabal of progressive revisionists, he wrote, had formed a new sort of historical orthodoxy at the expense of 'truth and objectivity'.[16]

Windschuttle's assessment was emphatic but not unexpected: he insisted that the history discipline's methods of empirical objectivity and pursuit of the truth had been undermined by postmodern ideas of relativity and critical discourse theory. It is a view he had earlier outlined in *The Killing of History: How Literary Critics and Social Theorists are Murdering Our Past*.[17] But it is too simple. Windschuttle's history of 'history' conflated motivations to rewrite Australian colonial history with bias. And his intervention confirmed how the blunt instrument of this debate has tended to preclude any complex discussion about the function of history, the process of historical revision and the role of the historian that the History Wars might also have prompted.

So when Stuart was asked (or rather cajoled) by the Melbourne University publisher Louise Adler to write about the History Wars, it was always going to be a near-impossible task to keep out of the firing line. Inevitably, this intervention would not be a mapping exercise but a view from the trenches. Given its reception, I would add now that entering the fray also required a certain sort of bravery: Stuart accepted that his argument would inevitably be consigned to one camp, whether he intended it to be or not, *and*, that understood, he would come under attack for his assessment of the History Wars.

I distinctly remember that sense of being 'labelled' with considerable frustration. I was in the middle of my PhD at the time, researching the contested space of history education in Australia, and Stuart had invited me to include some of that research in his *History Wars* book. It was an act of characteristic generosity on his part: giving a student a national platform for an emerging idea. But seeing my work immediately placed into one of two opposing factions, and the judgement that accompanied such a narrowly prescriptive reading of my research, was unnerving, to say the least.

That frustration was not simply because I did not share Stuart's bravery (although it was certainly a factor in my reluctance to get involved!). It was also a realisation that the politics and simplicity of these historical disputes overshadowed the methodological questions of doing frontier history in a settler colonial society. As Ann Curthoys intimated, the History Wars are a series of arguments not only over what happened and what we remember as a nation but also how we *do* history.[18] Pressure to include Indigenous perspectives in Australian history, for example, confounded any belief that Australia's national narrative was one of 'continuous progress', as T.A. Coghlan and T.T. Ewing had expounded in their 1902 economic history of Australia.[19] Moreover, historians were increasingly pondering the ethics of their field; namely, the problematic status of a discipline founded in the 'age of Enlightenment' and used to advance ideas of colonial expansion, 'progress' and 'civilisation'.[20] When categories of truth, objectivity and progress had been defined by a discipline that had largely silenced Indigenous perspectives, the ethical obligation upon historians to revise was paramount. The question was how.

In response, writing histories of the colonised, the oppressed and the silenced was not simply a process of historical addition, as the postcolonial historian Dipesh Chakrabarty explained, but required new methodologies that questioned the 'status of historical truth'.[21] Around the world, Indigenous scholars similarly wondered whether Western epistemologies could even accommodate their histories and identities.[22] This was 'an era in which historical truth came to be widely recognised as being necessarily partisan', Chakrabarty noted.[23]

While Windschuttle's assessment of a politically biased and divided discipline ramped up the debate, like the History Wars more broadly it left deeper methodological questions raised by that revision unanswered. Such questions were not even about Left or Right but sought to unpack deeper ideas about the ethics and practice of history in a settler-colonial society: for example, how is it possible for Australians to recollect, read and reflect on the past when historical methods have been part of the architecture and logic of colonisation? How should historians engage with such a troubling past? What are the ethical obligations to empathise with the past or judge it according to our own changing moral code?

In other words, what is the historian's conscience?

That question was made clear during a panel discussion hosted by the journalist and broadcaster Phillip Adams after the launch of Stuart's *History Wars* in 2003. On the panel, alongside Stuart sat Keith Windschuttle, the sociologist John Carroll, the historian and Keating's former speechwriter Don Watson, and the Indigenous writer and historian Tony Birch. I have written about this occasion elsewhere, in a longer study of Australian historiography, but I want to examine the panel discussion again here because it reveals precisely the methodological issues at stake in the History Wars, which were overshadowed by superficial and divisive partisanism.

After Adams asked each of the panellists to describe briefly what they thought the role of the historian should be, Windschuttle was characteristically resolute. History should provide a faithful account of the past. This 'ancient discipline' was founded as a means of 'pursuing the truth', he insisted. Historians 'were supposed to be as objective as possible, to stand outside their political and religious system and comment at a distance on their own society'. It is a view that good history is synonymous with objectivity and truth; revision is politically motivated bias. 'My complaint about history in Australia over the last two decades, certainly academic history, is that it has been too politicised,' Windschuttle explains.[24]

But when Adams read out an excerpt from an official report by the colonist John Batman, about a Tasmanian roving party he led in a raid on an Aboriginal community in winter in 1829, the disconnect between the political and ethical implications of the History Wars was made clear. Batman described how his party followed a group of sixty or seventy Aboriginal people along the eastern side of Ben Lomond mountain in north-eastern Tasmania. After eventually catching up with the Tasmanian tribe, they waited in ambush, close enough to 'hear the Natives conversing distinctly'. They crouched, undetected, until dark. But when they crept up to attack the families sleeping in their huts, one of Batman's men loudly knocked his musket and the Tasmanians' dogs barked loudly into the night.

Once the alarm was raised, 'The natives arose from the ground', Batman recounted,

> and were in the act of running away into the thick scrub, when I ordered the men to fire upon them, which was done, and a rush by the party immediately followed, we only captured that Night one Woman and a Male Child about Two Years old, the party was in search of them the remainder of the Night, but without success, next morning we found one Man very badly wounded in the ankle, and knee, shortly after we found another 10 Buck shot had entered his Body, he was alive but very bad, there were a great number of traces of Blood in various directions and learned from those we took that 10 Men were wounded in the Body which they gave us to understand were dead or would die, and Two Women in the same state had crawled away, besides a Number that was shot in the legs. The whole of Thursday we kept up the pursuit, but without any further success [...] on Friday morning we left the place for my Farm, with the Two Men, Woman and child, but found it quite impossible that the two former could walk, and after trying them by every means in my power, for some time, found I could not get them on I was obliged therefore to shoot them.[25]

In his volume on the Tasmanian frontier, Windschuttle had counted just two deaths from that conflict—it is all Batman's report confirmed, after all. I found his interpretation of that colonial source, exhibiting a direct literalism that allowed no intuitive reading between the lines or imagination, utterly confounding.[26] Adams was also baffled by Windschuttle's logic: 'Why don't the others get counted?' he wondered. 'The wounded ones?' asked Windschuttle. He then explained how Batman had looked for them all night and the next day, but did not find any. If 'he'd found the bodies, I would have put them in my table and recorded it', he contended. But 'unless you actually know they die you can't actually say, "Well, that's definitely a kill". You have to go on what the evidence tells you. A number of people probably did die but they never found the bodies.'[27]

I remember squirming in my seat. Windschuttle's insistence on the word-for-word interpretation of Batman's report was horrifying and seemed determined to remove the humanity from this frontier encounter. Even the Colonial Secretary John Burnett, who read Batman's report in 1829, was troubled enough by the raid to scribble anxiously in the margins of his report, 'Shoots wounded Natives because they could not keep up'.[28]

On the panel, Tony Birch was appalled, and voiced his outrage to the audience:

> I think it just shows what a disgusting, crude debate it is if that's the level you sink to. This is about an act of violence committed against a people and if you can say, 'Well, there was only *one kill* or *two kills*', I think context is everything, and to think that you can equate the atrocities committed against a people by the number of dead bodies you can count I think is ludicrous, and it's an insult to people.[29]

Later, he was even more forceful, criticising the History Wars for how they objectified Indigenous people while largely excluding Indigenous voices, and for skewing the debate away from the 'interests of Indigenous people'.[30]

Don Watson also wondered how you could listen to Adams's reading of Batman's account and not be horrified. 'Compassionate understanding or empathetic understanding seems to me right at the heart of the question' Adams has asked of them, he said. If 'you can't imagine your way into a rough number of dead, or what the trauma might have been of that, then you probably shouldn't be practising history'.[31]

Stuart similarly implored a compassionate reading of this history. 'The thing that most alarms me about Keith's handling of this issue is his lack of compassion for the events that occurred,' he insisted.

> I mean, however you want to see the story and however many body-counts you want to make, if you want to make body-counts, you're dealing with a quite traumatic [history]—of occupation and dispossession and death—and it does alarm me that this is a history that doesn't seem to show a quite crucial component of historical scholarship and that is empathy and compassion.[32]

But Windschuttle was unmoved. 'In my view, the responsibility of the historian is not to be compassionate,' he explained to Phillip Adams and the audience. 'The responsibility of the historian is to be dispassionate.'[33]

That one brief exchange revealed much about the limitations of the History Wars—where a horrifying night of bloodshed in colonial Tasmania might be reduced to a dispassionate form of accounting, without any sense of the ethical responsibility required to tell that story. And in a follow-up volume edited by Stuart, *The Historian's Conscience*, those questions of ethics, practice and approach framed the responses by contributing historians.

It is in this conversation, prompted by Stuart, that there was finally a productive lens to deliberate on the impact of the History Wars. As he noted in the introduction to the collection, '... many historians are loath to join the History Wars. They feel uncomfortable with the martial metaphor, and its adversarial implications of two opposing forces in combat with each other to control the past'.[34] But that frustration had also provoked historians to think about and articulate *what* they were doing and *why*. After all, history 'is a means of exploring, and also extending, the dimensions of humanity', he continued.[35] And in that realisation, the conversation about historians' conscience and approach allowed practitioners to ponder their discipline in a way that took the History Wars to a more complex and useful discursive terrain rather than reinforcing its familiar and uncomfortable partisan trenches.

In that collection, the contributors grasped and grappled with the histories they researched and wrote. They admitted to self-doubt, as well as being captivated by the past. They moved beyond the politics of contested national memory to consider the ethical dimensions of history-making and historical consciousness. And they pondered whether the History Wars had been worth it.

In particular, the chapters showed that historians do not view truth-telling of Australia's colonial history as incompatible with compassion and empathy. As Marilyn Lake explained in relation to her own historical practice, being connected to the past, being moved by it, did not mean foregoing her critical faculties as an academic historian. 'As their self-appointed interpreters, we must try to understand what our historical subjects were about, to grasp their intended meanings and unintended effects, to comprehend their contexts and subjectivities, to enter the world,' she articulated. 'But we need to write about our subjects in this world.'[36] Penny Russell was similarly careful in her articulation of how historical fidelity did not preclude connection with her subjects and the lives they led: 'As historians, we must tell what we find. But what we find is inevitably distinctive, individual, political and personal.'[37]

Being faithful to the past does not mean foregoing compassion but depends upon it, Alan Atkinson surmised. In fact, compassion 'is good history's main motive', he insisted.[38] And while you could hardly accuse John Hirst of revisionist extremism, even he was adamant about the need for historians to peer into the past and feel moved by what they encountered: 'I hesitate to condemn the past, but I recognise that I run the danger of not seeing horror when it is truly there.'[39]

That conversational turn towards compassion did not end the History Wars by any means, but it did confirm the original terms of debate had been unproductive and beleaguered. In one sense, politicised contests over the past provided great copy, filling pages of politicians' speeches, opinion pieces and vociferous letters to news editors. Analysing that content in turn generated literally millions of words in theses (my own included), books and articles, as well as providing hours of media coverage. But such analyses also tended to reproduce the terms of debate, however unwittingly. By shifting the discussion away from the tallies of dead on the frontier, by reflecting on historical revision and empathy as part of the process of historical practice, the History Wars could become more than a political contest over the past. As Stuart insists in his introduction to *The Historian's Conscience*, studying the history of humanity requires a degree of humanity—something the History Wars desperately needed.

Notes

1   Andrew Bonnell and Martin Crotty, 'Australia's history under Howard, 1996–2007', *ANNALS of the American Academy of Political and Social Science*, vol. 617, no. 1, 2008, p. 150.

2   Cit. Hugh Morgan, 'The guilt industry', *IPA Review*, vol. 42, no. 1, 1988, p. 18. See also Peter Spearitt, 'Celebration of a nation: The triumph of spectacle', *Australian Historical Studies*, vol. 23, no. 91, 1988, pp. 3–20; Tony Bennett, Pat Buckridge, David Carter and Colin Mercer (eds), *Celebrating the Nation: A Critical Study of Australia's Bicentenary*, Allen & Unwin, St Leonards, 1992.

3   Morgan, 'The guilt industry', p. 17.

4   Anna Clark, 'Politicians using history', *Australian Journal of Politics and History*, vol. 56, no. 1, 2010, pp. 119–30.

5   Paul Keating, 'Redfern Park speech', 10 December 1992, www.austlii.edu.au/au/journals/ILB/2001/57.html (viewed 6 September 2021).

6   Geoffrey Blainey, 'Drawing up a balance sheet of our history', *Quadrant*, vol. 37, no. 7–8, 1993, pp. 10–15.

7   John Howard, *Weekly House Hansard, 29 October 1996*, House of Representatives, Canberra, 1996.

8   John Howard, 'The Liberal tradition: The beliefs and values which guide the Federal Government, 1996 Sir Robert Menzies Lecture', 12 February 1996, https://pmtranscripts.pmc.gov.au/release/transcript-10171 (viewed 6 September 2021).

9   Josef Joffe, 'The battle of the historians', *Encounter*, vol. 69, no. 1, 1987, pp. 72–7; Burton Bollag, 'A confrontation with the past: The Japanese textbook dispute', *American Educator*, vol. 25, no. 4, 2001, pp. 22–7; Gary Nash, Charlotte Crabtree and Ross Dunn, *History on Trial: Culture Wars and the Teaching of the Past*, Alfred A. Knopf, New York, 1997; Vincent O'Malley and Joanna Kidman, 'Settler colonial history, commemoration and white backlash: Remembering the New Zealand wars', *Settler Colonial Studies*, vol. 8, no. 3, 2018, pp. 298–313; Melissa Nobles, *The Politics of Official Apologies*, Cambridge University Press, New York, 2008; Edward Linenthal and Tom Engelhardt, 'Introduction', in Edward Linenthal and Tom Engelhardt (eds), *History Wars: The Enola Gay and Other Battles for the American Past*, Metropolitan Books, New York, 1996, pp. 1–8.

10   Ann Curthoys, 'Thinking about history', *AHA Bulletin*, no. 83, 1996, p. 25; Peter

Seixas, 'CHR Forum: Heavy baggage en route to Winnipeg', *Canadian Historical Review*, vol. 82, no. 3, 2002, pp. 396–7.

11   'Bringing Them Home', Report of the National Inquiry into the Separation of Aboriginal and Torres Strait Islander Children from Their Families, Parliamentary Paper, no. 128 of 1997, Human Rights and Equal Opportunity Commission, Sydney, 1997.

12   Robert Manne, *Left, Right, Left: Political Essays 1977–2005*, Black Inc., Melbourne, 2005; Bob Carr, 'Carr on history', *Teaching History (NSW)*, vol. 29, no. 4, 1995, pp. 18–19.

13   Mark McKenna, 'Different perspectives on Black Armband history', *Parliamentary Library Research Paper*, no. 5, 1997–98.

14   Stuart Macintyre, 'Historical writing in Australian and New Zealand', in Stuart Macintyre, Juan Maiguashca and Attila Pók (eds), *The Oxford History of Historical Writing*, vol. 4: *1800–1945*, Oxford University Press, Oxford, 2011, pp. 410–27; Stuart Macintyre, 'Australia and the Empire', in Robin Winks (ed.), *Historiography*, Oxford University Press, Oxford, 1999, pp. 163–81; Bain Attwood, 'Settler histories and indigenous pasts: Australia and New Zealand', in Axel Schneider and Daniel Woolf (eds), *The Oxford History of Historical Writing*, vol. 5: *Historical Writing since 1945*, Oxford University Press, Oxford, 2015, pp. 594–614; Rob Pascoe, *The Manufacture of Australian History*, Oxford University Press, Melbourne, 1979; Marnie Hughes-Warrington, *Revisionist Histories*, Routledge, London, 2013, p. 1.

15   Keith Windschuttle, 'The myths of frontier massacres in Australian history (Part I)', *Quadrant*, vol. 44, no. 10, 2000, pp. 8–21. See also Windschuttle, 'The myths of frontier massacres in Australian history (Part II)', *Quadrant*, vol. 44, no. 11, 2000, pp. 17–24; Windschuttle, 'The myths of frontier massacres in Australian history (Part III)', *Quadrant*, vol. 44, no. 12, 2000, pp. 6–20.

16   Keith Windschuttle, *The Fabrication of Aboriginal History*, vol. 1: *Van Diemen's Land 1803–1847*, Macleay Press, Paddington, 2002, p. 403.

17   Keith Windschuttle, *The Killing of History: How Literary Critics and Social Theorists are Murdering Our Past*, Macleay Press, Paddington, 1994.

18   Ann Curthoys, 'Disputing national histories: Some recent Australian debates', vol. 1, no. 1, 2006, *Transforming Cultures eJournal*, p. 16; DOI: https://doi.org/10.5130/tfc. v1i1.187.

19   T.A. Coghlan and T.T. Ewing, *The Progress of Australasia in the Nineteenth Century*, Linscott Publishing Company, London, 1902, pp. 309–10.

20   John Gascoigne, *The Enlightenment and the Origins of European Australia*, Cambridge University Press, Cambridge, 2002.

21   Dipesh Chakrabarty, 'The politics and possibility of historical knowledge: Continuing the conversation', *Postcolonial Studies*, vol. 14, no. 2, 2011, p. 247. See also Durba Ghosh, 'Another set of imperial turns?', *American Historical Review*, vol. 117, no. 3, 2012, p. 782; Edward Said, *Culture and Imperialism*, Vintage, London, 1994; Gayatri Chakravorty Spivak, 'Can the subaltern speak?', in Cary Nelson and Lawrence Grossberg (eds), *Marxism and the Interpretation of Culture*, University of Illinois Press, Champaign, 1988, pp. 280–1.

22   Michael Marker, 'The "realness" of place in the spiral of time: Reflections on indigenous historical consciousness from the Coast Salish territory', in Anna Clark and Carla Peck (eds), *Contemplating Historical Consciousness: Notes from the Field*, Berghahn Books, New York, 2019, pp. 185–99; Krim Benterrak, Stephen Muecke and Paddy Roe, *Reading the Country: Introduction to Nomadology*, Re.Press, Melbourne, 2014; Martin Nakata, *Disciplining the Savages, Savaging the Disciplines*, Aboriginal Studies Press, Canberra, 2007; Aileen Moreton-Robinson, 'Introduction',

in Aileen Moreton-Robinson (ed.), *Sovereign Subjects: Indigenous Sovereignty Matters*, Allen & Unwin, Crows Nest, 2007, pp. 1–11; Linda Tuhiwai Smith, *Decolonizing Methodologies: Research and Indigenous Peoples*, 2nd edn, Zed Books, London, 2012; Epeli Hauofa, *We are the Ocean: Selected Works*, University of Hawai'i Press, Honolulu, 2008, p. 69; Tracey Banivanua Mar, *Decolonisation and the Pacific: Indigenous Globalisation and the Ends of Empire*, Cambridge University Press, Cambridge, 2016, p. 15.

23   Dipesh Chakrabarty, 'Empire, ethics, and the calling of history: Knowledge in the postcolony', in Sebastian Jobs and Alf Lüdtke (eds), *Unsettling History: Archiving and Narrating in Historiography*, Campus Verlag, Frankfurt, 2010, p. 69.

24   Phillip Adams, 'The History Wars', *Late Night Live*, ABC, 3 September 2003. See also Keith Windschuttle, 'The fabrication of Aboriginal history', *Sydney Papers*, 2003, p. 29.

25   John Batman, 'CSO1-320-7578 Batman to Anstey 7-09-1829', 7 September 1829, TA151, Colonial Secretary's Office. My sincere thanks to Nicholas Brodie for sharing his knowledge and archival nous of this event.

26   Keith Windschuttle, 'Inventing massacre stories', *Quadrant Online*, 29 April 2011.

27   Adams, 'The History Wars'.

28   Batman, 'CSO1-320-7578 Batman to Anstey 7-09-1829'. See also Nick Brodie, *The Vandemonian War*, Hardie Grant, Richmond, Vic, 2017, pp. 96–103.

29   Adams, 'The History Wars'.

30   Tony Birch, '"The invisible fire": Indigenous sovereignty, history and responsibility', in Aileen Moreton-Robinson (ed.), *Sovereign Subjects: Indigenous Sovereignty Matters*, Allen & Unwin, Crows Nest, 2007, p. 108.

31   Adams, 'The History Wars'.

32   Ibid.

33   Ibid.

34   Stuart Macintyre, 'Introduction', in Stuart Macintyre (ed.), *The Historian's Conscience*, Melbourne University Press, Melbourne, 2004, p. 4.

35   Ibid., p. 5.

36   Marilyn Lake, 'On history and politics', in Macintyre, *The Historian's Conscience*, p. 95.

37   Penny Russell, 'Almost believing: The ethics of historical imagination', in Macintyre, *The Historian's Conscience*, p. 116.

38   Alan Atkinson, 'Do good historians have feelings?', in Macintyre, *The Historian's Conscience*, p. 18.

39   John Hirst, 'Changing my mind', in Macintyre, *The Historian's Conscience*, p. 89.

Chapter 25

Universities

Simon Marginson

'Universities are steeped in tradition but they live in the present', as Stuart Macintyre says.[1] This coupling of a received past with day-to-day realities, which helps to explain the longevity of the Euro-American university as a form, leads to a balanced temporality, one that seems almost Sinic when universities are compared with other modern Western institutions. It makes universities an interesting object for historians, and more so given that, if they work in a university, that institution is also a subject. It also means that there is more than one temporal lens through which Australian universities can be viewed.

On one hand, the present Australian university is an accumulation of norms and practices with universal and colonial foundations. Those foundations are instructive because, as Stuart shows[2] and Glyn Davis[3] also argues in a recent book, the Australian university is both homogenous and path dependent, still reproducing early features of the University of Sydney (1850) and University of Melbourne (1853). On the other hand, the past of the universities, much of it still present, is a poignant basis for reflexivity. The corporate institution of the period after 1990 can be contrasted with the university of the professors. This move is specific to universities. We do not discuss banks or unions or government departments this way—we do not invoke their earlier practices as an active comparator. However, using the older university as a template can deteriorate into a golden age lament (which is satisfying for some and grating for others) that is detached from both past and present experience and leaves no more to be said. Stuart avoids this. He does not idolise the pre-massification university, and his criticism of the current utilitarian university is grounded in an empirical alternative. His basis for reflexivity, a torch passed on, combines norms, systems and practices that are critical, liberal and democratic. This assemblage is desirable, feasible, active and living: continuous to the university but always under threat.

Stuart generated writing of both kinds on universities: historical works that discuss the Australian institutions from their foundation to the present, and current commentary on their issues and predicaments. As would be expected, norms are more apparent in the commentary whereas the historical work is bounded by narrative logics. However, the two kinds of work are written in the same spare, clear explanatory style and embody similar preoccupations, and there is reciprocity: the historical works explain the contemporary university whereas the commentaries draw on historical evidence. As Stuart remarks when comparing Australian and American universities,[4] policy discussion of Australian universities typically neglects their history and therefore fails to understand the features that distinguish them from their British and American counterparts: their utilitarianism and uniformity, their continuous nesting in government and their weak civic presence. Stuart's unique and indispensable contribution has been to ground Australian universities for us, explaining the distinctive features of their traditions, forms, norms and practices. His secondary contribution, shared with others, is his public advocacy of the life of the mind, amid the oscillations between public instrumentalism and public indifference.

Sameness under different skies

Discussing the Dawkins Labor reforms in higher education in 1991, Stuart recalls the optimism of the colonial period. 'Australians liked to think of themselves as the coming nation.' They believed they could realise the potentials of the European legacy 'because they had escaped its constraints and were accordingly freer, more equal, less cynical, better able to invent the future'.[5] 'A fixed social hierarchy had yielded to a different form of stratification, one that allowed for a degree of social mobility and a measure of parity of esteem.' How would learning, knowledge and universities contribute? In schooling 'the absence of a stable social hierarchy, an established church and halls of learning left a vacuum of authority: the educationists accordingly fell back on a highly centralised form of state provision'.[6] Government filled the gap. It was the same in the universities.

Unlike the schools, the universities were self-governing, but in implementing British university traditions (which did not always work) they found themselves wholly dependent on government. Unfortunately, this sense of a common public interest was not shared by their funders. The main pattern, until deep into the twentieth century, was neglect.

The derived tradition was expressed in the mottos of the first universities. Sydney's '*Sidere mens eadem mutato*' appears below a coat of arms with the open book of Oxford and the royal lion of Cambridge, and the stars of the southern cross. The literal translation is 'though the constellation has changed, the mind remains the same'. This is mostly reworked as 'the same under different skies'.[7] Nevertheless, from the beginning colonial conditions shaped a distinctive model. Unlike Oxford and Cambridge, the universities were largely secular, located at the edge of city centres and primarily non-residential, with students living at home. Some attended evening classes on a part-time basis. The universities were more accessible than those in Europe and North America. Despite attempts after World War II to develop greenfields universities with student residences, this pattern persisted.

The characteristic utilitarianism was also a product of starting conditions, and while it suited government, it was essential to the universities. Sydney, Melbourne and Adelaide began with a liberal curriculum in the classics, philosophy and mathematics. Almost no one was interested. The *Bildung* idea had few adherents; amid goldrushes and pastoral booms and the endemic labour shortage, there was no economic need for a university degree, and wealthy families could send their sons to England. The early Australian universities shrewdly secured their future through vocational training in law, medicine and engineering, gaining a control over professional accreditation that their English counterparts had not achieved. 'The converse of this ease of access was a vocational orientation: the Australian university had little concern with the intellectual and moral cultivation associated with a full-time residential experience since its chief concern was training the professions. It sacrificed liberality for equity and utility.'[8]

From very early the proportion of the enrolment in liberal disciplines was lower than in Europe and North America, and in contrast with Germany, for the first century there was little research science. The first federal government research grants came late, in 1936, and totalled only £30 000.[9] Science was taught as science and was as derivative as the humanities. Local manufacturing imported its technology and did not need help. The important innovations in mining and agriculture, like the combine harvester, occurred inside those industries.[10]

The larger power of universities derives from each student's reflexive immersion in knowledge, the more open ontology that this brings, and the double potentials for self-formation and social formation that follow.[11] Emerging Australian society was indifferent to this. Universities were understood in deductive and demographic terms: birth, graduation, marriage, death. Here there was a chicken-and-egg problem. A vibrant civil society conditions an exciting university— yet civil societies depend partly on universities for their ongoing formation. How to begin? Universities and their personnel have agency. They are not wholly locked in. Nevertheless, it takes decades of enthusiasm and energy to build a civil constituency, swimming against the stream. Many of the land grant American universities were able to do it but not the Australian universities. They were tepid advocates for science, culture and themselves. It was easier and more fruitful to nestle up to government.

It was not because of government largesse. There seemed to be no alternative. The universities had little income aside from student fees and inadequate public grants, their constituency outside government was weaker than in Britain and the United States, and their governance kept them close. Their ultimate authority was not the professors, as in the collegial institutions in Britain, nor the university president as in the United States. It was the external councils, including the government appointees. Perpetually worried about the reception of the university in government, polite society and the press, the councils were unreliable defenders of university autonomy and, at times, suppressed academic freedom.[12]

The early prototype proved to be remarkably potent. Beginning with Queensland and Western Australia, successive new universities set out to carve their own paths—in some cases, later, in the 1960s and 1970s foundations at Macquarie, La Trobe, Murdoch, Flinders and Griffith, with dazzlingly original epistemological designs. Yet all were legislated and financed by colonial, then state and later federal governments, and government was intrinsically committed to standardised services across the country.[13] Further, while the new universities claimed equality of status they had to make it stick. Each one found itself pulled back towards the structures, internal roles, research systems and professional disciplines of the stronger early foundations, although they varied in the extent to which the non-vocational sciences and humanities were sustained. The process of homogenisation was quickened when the higher education system was normed as a competitive market after 1987, and research became administered as a performance economy, but the 'striking uniformity'[14] of Australian universities was custom built from the nineteenth century onwards.

This then is Stuart's account of the Australian university. British roots in Cambridge, Oxford, London, Edinburgh and Ulster, with pragmatic adaptations. Secular and public. A local urban student body. Vocational and utilitarian. Accessible but socially and politically isolated, lacking a constituency, and closely tied to government despite day-to-day operational autonomy and chronic state indifference. Modest in its intellectual and cultural demands on its communities and for long, marginal to them.[15] Profoundly isomorphic.

The foundational prototype explains much of what has happened in Australian higher education. Consider the continued hold of central policy and the one-size-fits-all framework, which extends beyond financial power, and the inability of the Australian universities to call up influential support in business, politics and civil society when their autonomy is at risk, by comparison with often successful defences of the universities in Britain and the United States.[16] Consider the persistent policy emphases on utilitarian studies in business and technology, and on applied rather than basic research. Above all, consider the failure of every attempt, whether through public planning or competitive settings, to foster diversity of mission, institutional shape and educational contents. The foundational utilitarianism, the logic of both government and market, decisively shapes expectations and behaviour. As long as the centripetal driver is in place, and 'higher education' is defined in instrumental, standard and hence deductive terms, and that mechanical reasoning is sealed off from heretical knowledge bubbling up from below, this homogenisation will persist.

That is not to say that everything is unchanged since 1850. In the era of larger social participation and national system-building that began with the 1957 Murray report,[17] the Australian universities retained most of their foundational features, but like universities all over the world they moved to a more central position in economic and social life and in government policy. They also built a research infrastructure.[18] Looking beyond Stuart's account we find that while the liberal humanities are still embattled, Australia has developed strong scientific communities with excellent worldwide networks. This is a break with the colonial and neocolonial eras. Further, material growth and research cultures, in post-1990 settings of neoliberal government and networked globality, have led in many cases to robust and confident institutions, prolific (and sometimes grandiose) facilities and an enterprising university leadership. Some (not all) universities as institutions have flourished; educational immersion in knowledge, and scholarly inquiry as an end in itself, have travelled less well. Many Australian universities have followed the 'World-Class University' path, securing upward trajectories in international education and in global university rankings.[19]

Yet the in-your-face corporate achievements overshadow the heterogenous intellectual serendipity, and prizes have more cachet than great works, except perhaps in medicine and the life sciences. With Australia never having broken with Britain, despite being in Asia, a distinctive Australian intellectualism remains far off. The Australian university prototype marches down history alongside its British equivalent. In fact, the mature Australian universities are more convergent with universities in Britain than was the case in colonial times, although contemporary British universities exhibit much greater institutional variety.

'An alert and self-critical awareness'

Underpinning Stuart's critiques of top-down policies and university managerialism are social democratic commitments to the democratisation of opportunity, including gender equity[20] and public culture,[21] and collegial commitments to institutional autonomy and academic freedom. Some of the commentary, from spoken papers, slips into polemic and invective. He lampoons the economistic claims of 'the evangelists of the enterprise university',[22] and the absurdities of university marketing, and trains sharp fire on interventions in 2004 and 2005 by federal Liberal minister Brendan Nelson. The minister overturned peer review-based decisions of the Australian Research Council, and nominated the conservative commentator P.P. McGuinness to one of the council's committees. 'The narcissistic former minister for education is not an ideologue but an opportunist who will say or do whatever brings praise,' states Stuart.[23] Take that!

In 'Academic freedom' in the 2010 Elsevier *International Encyclopedia of Education*, Stuart grounds institutional autonomy and academic freedom with a larger measure of gravitas. Academic freedom rests on two assumptions: 'the pursuit of knowledge is dependent on freedom of inquiry', and the university can best perform its function in civil society 'if it is able to conduct its own affairs'.[24] Stuart nests academic freedom in institutional autonomy, the classical collegial view. Yet he also notes that the modern university is shaped by government, and the mass university is no longer a place apart.

Universities are now expected to meet much greater expectations of public accountability. If they were once neglected, they are now of direct interest to a mass clientele and a constant source of news and media commentary. As they become central to the operations of government, economy and society, much of their older immunity has been withdrawn. The university is a public institution that depends on public support and is expected to serve its public, but in order to do so it requires respect for its distinctive nature. The shifting boundaries of institutional autonomy are formed by this interrelationship of dependence and interdependence.[25]

Academic autonomy is essential to knowledge practices, but for social democrats the university is engaged with its society. Stuart does not resolve the dilemma. Social democracy and collegiality are not necessarily opposed, but they are heterogenous and need to be deliberately stitched together. Arguably, this suggests a more nuanced kind of public regulation in which, while social inclusion and responsiveness are integral to the public university, part of its public remit is to provide conditions, positive as well as negative, for the 'agency freedom' of faculty and students so that the life of the mind can flourish.[26] Amartya Sen's capability approach may suggest a solution.[27] Stuart does not go there. He rarely cites social theory. Sometimes he hints at a larger infrastructure of interpretive ideas,[28] but he mostly prefers to let visible evidence do the talking and is slow to fill in the dots.

Nevertheless, Stuart identifies several specific junctions between social democracy and collegiality. First, his critique of those imaginings of higher education that follow a capitalist logic. Not only does this narrow what can be offered but also it is 'a belief of heroic proportions'.[29] While such a reduction can do much damage when applied, it is unworkable, incapable of becoming a coherent system. Most academics are not entrepreneurs. Many are competitive but for academic standing. The 'principal incentive' for many working in non-vocational areas is 'the opportunity to pursue their discipline'.[30] Second, his work on the contributions of university-based intellectuals to reforming Labor governments in Australia, as discussed in his wonderful study of postwar reconstruction, and in the volume on the social sciences in Australia (see chapters 14 and 16).[31] Third, his idea of non-utilitarian liberal education, which requires academic freedom, *Lernfreiheit*, in order to be practised and, according to the Kantian argument, is enlightening and enlarging of individuals and, through them, of society.

No End of a Lesson is dedicated to Davis McCaughey, 'who spoke with wisdom and humility on the vital importance of a liberal education'.[32] Stuart does not fully spell out what this means, but elsewhere he argues that 'our task is to discover educational practices that will promote an alert and self critical awareness'.[33] This says a good deal. The liberal mission, grounded in the engagement with knowledge, is foundational. Public universities can be made to serve many purposes, he states, and they can lose their way. But they 'remain places that support research and scholarship, places of intellectual awakening where students can still become committed to a life of the mind … [T]he pursuit of knowledge remains their core business'.[34] If the university has to be an enterprise, it is 'not beyond the national wit' to devise strategies that sustain 'the academic activities that constitute it'.[35]

This suggests that the primary problem is utilitarianism, not corporatism (and that we might be better served by partly separating institutional autonomy and academic freedom). In contrast with the colonial period, the utilitarian bias in Australia is primarily fostered on the supply side, not on the student demand side, and as much by universities as government. While undergraduate demand for vocational disciplines is a fact, student demand for the humanities is also fairly robust. However, generic arts and science degrees are 'cannibalised' by quasi-vocational offerings, like media and communications. Staff in philosophy and history are reduced in larger proportion than the small declines in student demand. Anthropology and languages are submerged in departmental mergers or closed.[36]

Stuart also knows that more than wrong-headed policy is entailed. Larger changes are afoot. Much of the older collegiality is gone beyond recall. Discussing the accumulation, intensification and speed up of academic work revealed in successive surveys, he states:

> Less often noticed and more difficult to measure is the effect of such busyness on the university as a workplace. The advent of email provided a powerful tool for internal communication, making it possible to transact business quickly and efficiently. It allowed wide dissemination, with no limit on the volume of information or requests for information, and it also provided a highly unsuitable medium for settling disagreements. Email dissolved the limits of the working day, so that academics could answer questions at any time of the day or night, from office or home. Time was when they had worked with their office doors open to all-comers, the corridor busy with the traffic of staff and students. Coming together for morning and afternoon tea was an important ritual in this collegiality. Now, with so much to do, they crouched alone over their networked computers. The door was shut ... Together with the changed conditions of employment and the increased use of casuals, these work patterns fragmented the profession.[37]

Stuart does not have a solution to the weakening of local bonds. No one does. There is a gain in global community, however, one that he does not discuss. It is not all bad.

The Dawkins reforms

Stuart Macintyre did not produce a comprehensive history of the Australian university. There are smaller studies, especially at the

University of Melbourne. However, *No End of a Lesson*, on the John Dawkins-led Labor remaking of higher education between 1987 and 1996, which Stuart wrote with some help from André Brett and Gwilym Croucher, is a major work and the definitive account. Here Stuart combines two interests: the reform projects of Labor governments, and the 'fundamental transformation' of collegial relations and disciplinary life in the universities during his time.[38] Dawkins expected the universities to adopt 'strong managerial modes of operation' and 'stream-lined decision-making'.[39] The main worth of the humanities, as the minister saw it, was not immersion in knowledge and creativity but 'broad and transferable skills'.[40] This marginalised the liberal disciplines. After Dawkins they survived better in older universities such as Melbourne, where intellectual cultures were protected by institutional prestige and social capital, than they did elsewhere.

Macintyre and his co-authors cover all the issues: Dawkins's closure of the university-friendly Commonwealth Tertiary Education Commission (CTEC) and remaking of the machinery of consultation, funding and administration, locating the higher education sector under his department; his unified national system design based on a single institutional mission, the massive institutional merger program; the growth of participation; finances and the introduction of tuition fees; management, governance and staffing; teaching, research and the effects in academic life. The book is more engaging than this list suggests. It tells the story of a higher education sector whose key organisations and personnel were continually wrong-footed by an able minister with a plan and a capacity to control the agenda. The narrative is carried by a fascination with the events, which were never certain to take the course that they did, and supported with delightful snippets from the archives that bring the reader close to the political process. Dawkins 'set the terms of debate', conducted in utilitarian fashion 'as an argument of how best the university should make itself useful as an instrument of national objectives'. He 'retained the initiative'.[41] He had the business organisations and unions onside, and his policy secured public acceptance.

He persuaded university executives that they had more to gain by individually investing in his system than by joining to oppose it. And, remarkably for such a large package of reforms, he achieved most of his detailed objectives. His system is still in place thirty years later.

Dawkins's policy in higher education was often critiqued as neoliberal marketisation, corresponding to Labor's deregulation of the currency and privatisation of Qantas and the Commonwealth Bank. Stuart shows that notwithstanding Dawkins's new public management rhetoric and introduction of tuition fees, his 'limited market mechanism was a highly regulated artefact'.[42] He used competition, markets in bounded areas, and enhanced managerial autonomy and financial responsibility as means of nesting universities more tightly in government and increasing his capacity for direct intervention. His tuition fees were not market prices regulating supply and demand, but income-contingent loans, which eliminated payment at point of entry and minimised the effect of price variations on behaviour. While they funded expansion at the expense of the graduate, they suppressed the trade-off between private costs and access, thereby maximising social inclusion. Although income-contingent loans were a Friedman idea, this was far from a neoliberal solution.

Dawkins's goal was not to install the disciplines of profit and bankruptcy, still less to achieve a market-based diversity of provision in higher education, but to secure homogeneous provision across Australia in institutions tethered to the regulator—within a policy framework that positioned universities not directly but ultimately as the servants of capital. It was government, not market forces operating directly, that was to be the arbiter in higher education of the needs of the economy. Notwithstanding all the talk about research as an engine of economic innovation, the main role of universities was not to startle the economy with off-the-wall ideas, market generated or otherwise, but to be efficient and predictable. 'Uniform funding formulae ... militated against specialisation.'[43]

The system settings secured standardisation of provision, while using competitive mechanisms to legitimate the unequal outcomes of internal sector distributions, such as resources to conduct research. 'The result was less diversity but more differentiation', as Croucher puts it in the chapter on finance.[44] Thus the Dawkins reforms normalised the large multidisciplinary university, sustained student numbers everywhere, strengthened the middle layer of institutions by guaranteeing their status as research universities and ensuring their sufficiency as exporters of international education,[45] and reproduced the top layer of older universities without allowing them to peel right away from the pack (and thereby compete with the leading Anglophone universities on the global plane).[46] Stuart does not say it, but this form of institutional stratification in higher education, fiercely competitive but moderated in outcome, levelling down at the top with a floor of minimum subsistence at the bottom, would not have been out of place in colonial New South Wales.

Rather than neoliberal, the reform package is best understood as characteristically Australian in its utilitarianism, its idea of equity as inclusion and standardisation, and its relation between government and the universities; even in its corporatism, as the public corporation was a longstanding Australian way of providing common services. It is not surprising that Dawkins was supported outside the universities. Labor's attitude to higher education had long been instrumental, more so than the Menzies Liberal government, which established national university policy.[47] As Labor saw it, the universities were a device for promoting equality, or educating citizens, or an adjunct of the economy, with 'little regard for intellectual and cultural endeavour as an end in itself'.[48] Dawkins was unconcerned to enlist the disciplinary loyalties of scholars. However, he needed their institutions. He shrewdly exploited the incentives driving the university manager-leaders who were the main winners in the new system. The vice chancellors found that they could do more rather than less without CTEC.[49] Dawkins knew that universities were impelled to grow their social roles, aggregating functions, although less good at shedding them.[50] Dawkins's Unified National System, minimum size requirements, incentives to merge and to market courses offshore 'imprisoned them in a growth trap, with significant implications for their size, scale and coherence'.[51] Thus the minister harnessed institutional logics to his objectives while celebrating university leaders for doing their public duty and serving the common good.

In a companion volume to *No End of a Lesson*, Brett, Croucher and Macintyre describe concurrent events at the University of Melbourne, where David Penington, a centralising vice chancellor with his own well-defined agenda, positioned himself as Dawkins's chief public critic—while using the structures and momentum for change triggered by Dawkins to implement his own (Penington's) internal changes. A feature of these books is the vivid warts-and-all portraits of the two leaders.[52] (It takes a special skill to do this in relation to living persons. The only defence is scrupulous authenticity and accuracy.)

Life after Dawkins: The University of Melbourne in the Unified National System of Higher Education concludes that as an institution, Melbourne was strengthened in the Dawkins years. The authors also suggest that it was relatively attuned to a post-collegial outlook and gained from conformity. 'Collegiality in some older universities such as Sydney allowed senior academics to resist change and made concerted action difficult. There was no such obstruction at Melbourne, where the professors functioned not so much as a fractious guild as members of a corporate profession.'[53] As Stuart notes elsewhere, 'each university has its own way of doing things'.[54] Local factors could modulate Dawkins's designer uniformity.

But only up to point. In the prescriptive Australian system, as ever, the single container held all of the universities in. The outcome for each could be better or worse but not fundamentally other. It can be argued that Stuart overestimates the extent to which Melbourne's changes were self-driven as well as the extent to which institutional resistance across the system reduced Dawkins's success.[55] Little on the minister's list was not secured.

It is true that Dawkins did not implement the planned performance-based funding system before stepping down in 1992, but this followed in the post-Dawkins years.[56] Although Labor was unable to generate a flourishing of university research for industry,[57] this indicates not the failure of higher education policy but the traditional indifference of Australian industry. Amid the equally traditional shortage of public funds, in universities that carried both expanded functions and the new costs of marketing, Dawkins successfully entrenched the hunger for private money, from almost any source. It is also true that his attempt to integrate universities closely with Vocational Education and Training (VET) was largely unsuccessful.[58] Joining the dots, this was an outcome of federal/state fracture, with VET stuck on the resource-poor state side of the divide. More fundamentally, it was conditioned by the global economic weakness of the Australian manufacturing sector, which Labor did not remedy.[59] There was little industry impetus for federal government-led funding and modernisation of high-skill training along German lines. As in the nineteenth-century colonies, it seemed that manufacturing was content to get by with imported technology.

Regardless, Stuart was sure about the overall impact of Dawkins. 'We still live with consequences of what he created, with the structural constraints, the financial pressures, the over-dependence on government, brash commercialism and micro-management.'[60]

Stuart did not compare the Dawkins reforms to the earlier Labor forays in social formation. We might do so, using what Stuart has given us. Although Dawkins brought informed intelligence and determined stamina to the task, this was not a social democratic transformation of the public machinery and redistribution of the possibilities of life, akin to Chifley's mighty reconstruction or Whitlam's uplifting expansion of citizenship. Dawkins went with the flow of mainstream OECD-defined 'structural adjustment'.[61] The rationale was not free democratic agency but the prosperity of the capitalist economy, leavened by OECD Europe's understanding that modern markets are underpinned by social inclusion. The top-down nature of the Dawkins reforms, and the way they reinforced rather than redistributed Australian relations of power, ensured their confirmation by conservative vice chancellors and the Liberal governments that followed—and left the next generation of scholars and students to salvage, if local conditions permitted, 'an alert and self-critical awareness'.[62]

Like all of Stuart's writings on universities, *No End of a Lesson* is exemplary in its clear-minded realism and its sense of what is at stake. Australian universities are hybrid institutions, dedicated both to unlimited knowledge and to a constraining utility, as they were from the beginning. Their problem is that the second strand, utilitarianism, became more sophisticated than the first. The intellectual mission remains partly derivative from stronger Anglo–American centres but, for better or worse, Australian utilitarianism is something more distinctive and developed. It is in utilitarian terms that the Dawkins system is world class.

Stuart tells us where the universities have come from and why they are as they are. This kind of inquiry, where the available material far outstrips the scarce time of the historian, is never finished, always becoming. But there has never been a better body of work on the antipodean university as an object of inquiry. Stuart's contribution is exemplary in another way, in the sense of the university as subject. He shows us that the lights have not all been turned off, by Dawkins or anyone else. Scholars are beleaguered, yet the possibilities, as ever, are open. When liberal social democratic scholarship is both critically minded and brilliant, as in the case of his work, it continues to enlighten and elevate us.

Notes

1   Stuart Macintyre, André Brett and Gwilym Croucher, *No End of a Lesson: Australia's Unified National System of Higher Education*, Melbourne University Press, Melbourne, 2017, p. 3. In the present chapter all cited material from this book is taken from chapters authored by Macintyre (p. ix), unless otherwise indicated.
2   Stuart Macintyre, 'The same under different skies: The university in the United States and Australia', *Journal of Australian Studies*, vol. 33, no. 3, 2009, pp. 353–69.
3   Glyn Davis, *The Australian Idea of a University*, Melbourne University Press, Melbourne, 2017, pp. 28–34.
4   Macintyre, 'The same under different skies', p. 353.
5   Stuart Macintyre, 'The meanings of the clever country', *Australian Universities Review*, vol. 34, no. 1, 1991, p. 34.
6   Stuart Macintyre, 'A sense of tradition: R.J.W. Selleck and the purpose of educational history', *Journal of Educational Administration and History*, vol. 41, no. 2, 2014, p. 119.
7   Macintyre, 'The same under different skies', p. 356.

8   Macintyre, Brett and Croucher, *No End of a Lesson*, pp. 19–20.

9   Macintyre, 'The same under different skies', p. 361.

10 Macintyre, 'The meanings of the clever country', p. 35.

11 Simon Marginson, 'Higher education as self-formation', in B. Cantwell, S. Marginson, D. Platonova and A. Smolentseva (eds), *The Contributions of Higher Education*, forthcoming.

12 Macintyre, 'The same under different skies', pp. 357–8; Stuart Macintyre and Simon Marginson, 'The university and its public', in T. Coady (ed.), *Why Universities Matter*, Allen & Unwin, Sydney, 2000, pp. 54–5.

13 Macintyre, 'The same under different skies', p. 363.

14 Ibid., p. 353.

15 Ibid., pp. 354, 357.

16 Stuart Macintyre, with Gwilym Croucher, Glyn Davis and Simon Marginson, 'Making the Unified National System', in G. Croucher, S. Marginson, A. Norton and J. Wells (eds), *The Dawkins Revolution 25 Years On*, Melbourne University Press, Melbourne, 2013, p. 32.

17 Simon Marginson, *Educating Australia: Government, Economy and Citizen since 1960*, Cambridge University Press, Cambridge, 1997.

18 Brendan Cantwell, Simon Marginson and Anna Smolentseva (eds), *High Participation Systems of Higher Education*, Oxford University Press, Oxford, 2018.

19 Simon Marginson and Mark Considine, *The Enterprise University: Power, Governance and Reinvention in Australia*, Cambridge University Press, Cambridge, 2000; Simon Marginson, 'Regulated isomorphic competition and the middle layer of institutions: High participation higher education in Australia', in Cantwell, Marginson and Smolentseva, *High Participation Systems of Higher Education*, pp. 266–94.

20 Gender inequity, especially in academic careers, is a recurring theme in Stuart Macintyre's writing on universities; for example Stuart Macintyre and R.J.W. Selleck, *A Short History of the University of Melbourne*, Melbourne University Press, Melbourne, 2003, pp. 91–3; Macintyre, Brett and Croucher, *No End of a Lesson*, p. 20.

21 See Macintyre and Marginson, 'The university and its public'.

22 Stuart Macintyre, '"Funny you should ask for that": Higher education as a market', in S. Cooper, J. Hinkson and G. Sharp (eds), *Scholars and Entrepreneurs*, Arena Publications, Melbourne, 2002, p. 84.

23 Stuart Macintyre, 'Universities', in C. Hamilton and S. Maddison (eds), *Silencing Dissent: How the Australian Government is Controlling Public Opinion and Stifling Debate*, Allen & Unwin, Sydney, 2007, p. 45.

24 Stuart Macintyre, 'Academic freedom', in E. Baker, P. Peterson and B. McGaw (eds), *The International Encyclopedia and Education*, 3rd edn, Elsevier, Oxford, 2010, p. 328.

25 Ibid., p. 332.

26 Amartya Sen, 'Well-being, agency and freedom: The Dewey Lectures 1984', *Journal of Philosophy*, vol. 82, no. 4, 1985, p. 203.

27 Amartya Sen, *Development as Freedom*, Penguin, London, 1999.

28 For example the discussion of the association of 'reform' and social solidarity in Macintyre, Brett and Croucher, *No End of a Lesson*, p. 23.

29 Macintyre, 'The meanings of the clever country', p. 36.

30 Macintyre, Brett and Croucher, *No End of a Lesson*, p. 39.

31 Stuart Macintyre, *The Poor Relation: A History of the Social Sciences in Australia*, Melbourne University Press, Melbourne, 2010; Stuart Macintyre, *Australia's Boldest Experiment: War and Reconstruction in the 1940s*, NewSouth Publishing, Sydney, 2015.

32 Macintyre, Brett and Croucher, *No End of a Lesson*, p. x.

33 Macintyre, 'The meanings of the clever country', p. 37.

34   Macintyre, Brett and Croucher, *No End of a Lesson*, p. 252.
35   Macintyre, '"Funny you should ask for that"' p. 89.
36   Ibid., p. 85.
37   Macintyre, Brett and Croucher, *No End of a Lesson*, p. 236.
38   Ibid., p. 214.
39   Ibid., p. 66.
40   Ibid., p. 62.
41   Ibid., p. 252.
42   Ibid., p. 23.
43   Macintyre, 'The same under different skies', p. 365.
44   Macintyre, Brett and Croucher, *No End of a Lesson*, p. 154.
45   Marginson, 'Regulated isomorphic competition and the middle layer of institutions'.
46   Macintyre, 'The same under different skies', p. 365.
47   Macintyre, 'Universities', pp. 53–4.
48   Macintyre, Brett and Croucher, *No End of a Lesson*, p. 53.
49   Ibid., p. 251.
50   Ibid., p. 238.
51   Macintyre, 'The same under different skies', p. 365.
52   For example Macintyre, Brett and Croucher, *No End of a Lesson*, p. 10; André Brett,
      Gwilym Croucher and Stuart Macintyre, *Life after Dawkins: The University of
      Melbourne in the Unified National System of Higher Education*, Melbourne University
      Press, Melbourne, 2016, pp. 16–17, 114–15.
53   Ibid., p. 114.
54   Macintyre, 'The same under different skies', p. 353.
55   Macintyre, Brett and Croucher, *No End of a Lesson*, pp. 10, 248–52.
56   Ibid., p. 249.
57   Ibid., p. 249.
58   Ibid., p. 249.
59   Ibid., p. 249.
60   Ibid., p. 252.
61   Ibid., pp. 42–4.
62   Macintyre, 'The meanings of the clever country', p. 37.

Chapter 26

Stuart Macintyre as colleague

Patricia Grimshaw

Stuart Macintyre and I were colleagues in History at the University of Melbourne from 1980 when he took up a lectureship in the department, where I had worked for some seven years as a research assistant, tutor and untenured lecturer. Although academics in the humanities for the most part gain entry to the profession by virtue of a demonstrated capacity for individual research, universities are in fact deeply dependent for the execution of many core responsibilities on the collegiality of their employees. The history community in Australia has rightly held Stuart in high esteem for his extensive research, his publications and his influential public advocacy for the discipline. Less generally known is how those of us in the department were witnesses to his capacity to combine this impressive performance with a close attention to the innumerable vital responsibilities expected of academics at the grass-roots level. Stuart was a very good colleague indeed, undertaking with understated efficiency the time-consuming and seemingly never-ending tasks of everyday academic work.

To work alongside Stuart was to witness with some considerable astonishment the extensive range of departmental tasks he was able to sustain year in and year out, all enriched by his deep research engagement and standing as a scholar. The history department Stuart entered was distinguished by notable senior staff, long-established disciplinary specialisms and a sound teaching program. A strong spirit of departmental collegiality endured despite lively recurrent disagreements grounded in the hierarchical career structure of the profession, and history's increasingly divergent disciplinary and theoretical approaches, alongside certain somewhat opaque personal feuds of apparent long standing. As a newcomer, I had been surprised at the extent to which what divided the department was, however, entirely secondary to its members' pervasive respect for the discipline they practised, for the notable achievements of its past key figures and its dedication to its students' scholarly advancement. All policy and practices were not subject to the behest of so-called god professors. By 1980 there were avenues for shared decision-making that enhanced collegiality, while senior staff adhered to admirable protocols of mentoring junior members, including assisting newcomers to master the idiosyncratic practices of wider university culture. Whatever the internal rumblings of discontent within history, its members by and large presented a united front in faculty, central university and intra-university affairs, from which junior members drew strength.

From February to November each year our working hours were dominated by undergraduate teaching: planning courses, writing lectures, taking classes, advising students, marking essays, evaluating results, conferring with co-teachers. Research and writing were commonly squeezed into late night hours, weekends and vacations, except during precious study leave. Overworked humanities staff suspiciously scrutinised very productive researchers' workloads surreptitiously, keen to discern whether they had found routes to escape routine teaching. Nobody could say that of Stuart. He was an enthusiastic and extremely able undergraduate teacher. An excellent communicator, he was consistently on top of his form whether delivering lectures to large crowded halls or facilitating discussion in tutorials and honours classes. To the gratitude of his co-teachers, he completed his subject evaluation and administrative tasks with admirable promptness. Stuart had a core area of preferred subjects dealing with social and political history but readily expanded his range to make good gaps in departmental offerings. A traditional educator, he displayed generosity towards novel approaches of colleagues to curriculum and subject delivery. This was particularly significant for those of us who, in the 1980s, trialled with his encouragement teaching in feminist history and women's (later gender) studies. Stuart's extensive postgraduate teaching was similarly exemplary. He supervised a prodigious number of postgraduate research students, a further important contribution of course to national research in Australian history. His impressive contingent of research students energised a lively supportive departmental postgraduate community. He generously continued to advise his ex-students as they entered their own careers.

Stuart also managed to combine his fruitful research endeavours with extensive administrative responsibilities, at departmental and faculty levels. If some academics differed from mainstream opinion by holding that undergraduate teaching invigorated rather than diminished their research, almost all were convinced that the assumption of administrative responsibilities spelt the death of personal scholarship. Academic administrators, we thought, dutifully took on the obligation of spending precious research days attending meetings to sort out the collective organisational lives of colleagues, the demands of which appeared at times to balloon out of control. Stuart, on the contrary, moved from participation in departmental committees to head of department to the deanship of the faculty without sacrificing his scholarly engagements. Academic collegiality became increasingly under threat through the decades of the 1980s, 1990s and early 2000s as the university adopted business management practices in which financial considerations began to outweigh the scholarly considerations to which we adhered. But the former regimen had not of course constituted any golden age, certainly not for women. The new practices that emerged were by no means uniformly negative, given that they dented, if they did not remove, the universities' male hierarchy of management and the conservatism of its entrenched curriculum. Stuart walked the tightrope with apparent ease. He strove to sustain the faculty's core values in the face of the concerns of successive senior administrators about the viability of the humanities and social sciences, while being alert to the advantages of new possibilities for the arts that were emerging.

The impact of Stuart's achievements rippled out to his colleagues, especially to those who shared his specialism in Australian history. All in history benefited, however, from a colleague who continued through thick and thin to increase his energising research profile, as he sustained his national and international scholarly network and increased his connections with the world of publishing. Stuart was a hard worker. He supported the department journal, *Australian Historical Studies*, serving spells as chair of the board and as editor. He read our drafts of articles and our research funding applications, commented on our published work, launched our books and offered co-workers who sought it judicious frank advice. Through his external membership of judging panels, journal boards, advisory bodies, governmental committees and, in time, his active fellowships of the learned academies (the Academy of the Social Sciences in Australia and the Australian Academy of the Humanities), he kept us in touch with intellectual shifts in the discipline and the implications of political decisions for the future of the profession. Through it all Stuart was a consistent advocate for progressive change in the university and nationally. We were fortunate indeed to have him as a colleague.

Part 7

Conclusion

Chapter 27

What true believers need

Understanding Labo(u)r

Liam Byrne

Historians are 'poor rememberers', but I remember the first time I saw Stuart Macintyre.[1] I was 18, and it was just a few weeks into my first semester at the University of Melbourne. The subject was Australian colonial history, and Stuart, the Dean of Arts, was guest lecturing on the labour movement. It was the first time I had heard someone, especially someone of such eminence and prestige, lecture specifically on the movement of working people, with all its faults and frailties, its excitement and accomplishments. It was an affirmation that the history of labour was worth telling; that there was still something we could learn from it. It mattered.

This chapter considers Stuart's work on one element of that movement, the Australian Labor Party. Stuart once noted that Labor has 'a concern for its past amounting almost to an obsession'.[2] I approach Stuart's work as one of the obsessed. I am not only an historian but also a 'true believer', an ALP activist seeking to use historical knowledge to intervene in debates over Labor's contemporary meaning and purpose. For the ALP, the past, present and future are not distinct and discrete stages on a linear progression—although there is certainly a narrative of progression in the party's mythos. Past, present and future are intertwined and dynamic, rebounding upon and transforming each other. In its best moments, the party has drawn upon its past as a reservoir of hope and knowledge to fuel its aspirations for a better future. How that past is received and experienced is conditioned by the imperatives of the present. Those imperatives themselves are shaped by intentions for the future.

To debate Labor's past is, implicitly or explicitly, to contribute to the never-ceasing contest over its potential futures. And so it matters how we understand the party's foundation and its record of thought and action. It matters how we historically engage today with not only those moments when it has made Australia a better, more equal place but also when it has failed in this mission and perpetuated inequality.

There is no serious engagement with Labor's past that does not involve a deep and meaningful consideration of the work of Stuart Macintyre. His full corpus, in all its complexity, cannot receive a complete exegesis in this chapter. So, instead, to consider the content and significance of his work, I tease out threads from Stuart's analysis of three interlinked periods of Labor's past: the context of its emergence, its early decades, and the reconstruction governments of John Curtin and Ben Chifley.

'the fu' course insteed': class and totality in Labor's emergence

By his own account, Stuart was drawn to history as a discipline through political engagement, and others in this collection have elucidated his journey into the New Left and the Communist Party. At a time of struggle and social turmoil, 'historical knowledge' allowed the young Marxist to deepen his comprehension of the issues that animated him: 'I discovered another dimension of history—its ability to comprehend.'[3] This was the essence of historical materialism, which is, as Georg Lukács explained, a 'scientific method' to grasp the 'true nature' of historic events within the

broader schema of class struggle and the project of proletarian liberation. But historical materialism is not a method for comprehension
alone; it is an 'instrument of war', its arena the 'field of action'.[4]

It seems wonderfully Stuartesque that his early published political interventions were historiographical. His 1972 article 'Radical
history and bourgeois hegemony', in *Intervention*, excoriated the
'liberal empiricist historiographical tradition' of the Melbourne
School.[5] The fervour of this denunciation would later be self-
described as an attempt to resolve the 'oedipal predicament' of his
own relationship to this department.[6] But its potency also derives
from conviction, the belief that it mattered who was producing
historical knowledge, from what standpoint and to what end. This
was not an intradepartmental quibble—a broader transformative
project was at stake.

History, Stuart explained, was integral to the attempts of radicals
to understand Australian society, all the better to change it.
Identifying the methodological deficiencies of the radical historians
who preceded him was part of the search for a more complete form
of historical knowledge that would unveil contemporary social relations and through this advance the struggle. To this end, the great
radical historians Brian Fitzpatrick and Ian Turner were criticised for
being immured in the liberal–empiricist historical tradition and for
sharing its assumptions, rather than critically interrogating the 'foundations of historical knowledge'.[7]

Their reliance on this bourgeois historical outlook, Stuart
contended, prevented a truly scientific understanding of class.
Because he lacked an appreciation for the specifics of class formation
(and how this changed across time due to transformations in the
mode of production) Fitzpatrick 'operated at the banal level of a
psychological insight into human motivation'.[8] Turner is marked out
for his 'economic mechanistic understanding' resulting from his
empiricism, and for a myopic view of the labour movement that
extracts it from the broader social context, obviating the relational
nature of social class. Both historians allegedly failed to grasp the
necessity of the 'Marxist concept of totality', based on 'specification

and differentiation of its particular social relations'.[9] 'It will be necessary', Stuart writes, 'not just to study and write Marxist history but to repeat over and over again that our history is based on a quite different problematic from that which is presently dominant.'[10] Or, as Lukács would have it, 'the whole of history really has to be re-written'.[11]

These ideas were developed in a more considered and extensive manner in an *Historical Studies* article from 1978, 'The making of the Australian working class'. In this piece, Stuart articulated his interest in the application of E.P. Thompson's insights into how a class creates itself historically to Australian scholarship on working-class formation. He queried how best to measure the working class's activities, organisations, specific cultural forms and accomplishments not against a pre-determined metric of an acceptable level of self-actualisation but as valid in themselves as part of the processes through which Australian labour created itself.

Ian Turner is characteristic of the 'Old Guard' who perceived the economic base to predominate over the superstructure, leading to a mechanistic representation of labour as 'purely a class in itself'.[12] On the other hand, the 'Young Turks', represented by Humphrey McQueen, are chided for going too far in divorcing ideas from the economic base in conceiving consciousness as an 'independent determinant' in the creation of class. Stuart took particular issue with McQueen's argument in *A New Britannia* that in late colonial Australia the labouring class had a 'petit-bourgeois consciousness', so, *ergo*, there was no working class at all.[13]

Stuart wanted to take consciousness seriously as a concept but not as a force independent of broader social relations and material conditions. He was critical of the tendency of some authors to raise consciousness to the 'ultimate criterion' of class.[14] He retained his earlier insistence on the importance of totality in comprehending the nature of a social class. No class is self-sufficient—and the existence of any one class is relational (this is true of all social categories, for nothing can be defined without its antithesis). And so labour cannot be understood outside the totality of class relations—the shape and tenor of its forms and mode of production, its specific industries and the particular professional cultures and rituals, and the imperial and racialised context in which the class arises (he would later explore the gendered aspect more explicitly). The working class's cultural production is its own and must be understood on its own terms, but this cultural production arises from a set of circumstances that labour does not control.

The creation of the working class in colonial Australia (and, *contra* McQueen, a working class it was) occurred in the context of a 'limited antagonism' between labour and capital. Stuart argued that a compact existed between the two great social forces leading to shorter hours and higher wages, the cost of which was borne by consumers. Until the depression of the 1890s, labour could satisfy its desire for "'a fair day's work for a fair day's pay'" without disrupting existing class relations.[15]

The ALP was constructed at this time as one of the institutions through which the class mediated the structural conflict 'over the social distribution' of what it produced. The character of the party was defined by this 'limited antagonism', an antagonism that at this point, and 'during most of the twentieth' century, was 'principally defensive'. The 'fortress' created by Labor and the unions was one beyond which 'the class infrequently ventures but which it has shown considerable determination to defend'.[16]

Stuart would move away from historical materialism as a key weapon in the class struggle, but his later works were influenced by the methodology forged in these earlier years. The emphasis on understanding historical subjects within their broader totality, the comprehension of class as relational, and the emphasis on the role economic structures play in creating and limiting the potentials for change would be enduring, as would be the emphasis on the 'limited' nature of Labor's antagonism to the social relations of Australian capitalism.

'Now show me in a vision for the wrongs of Earth a cure': Foundation and emergent decades

The Hawke–Keating ascendancy prompted a deep and uncomfortable questioning of Labor's meaning and purpose. Was this a 'hijack' of the party by a determined coterie of neoliberals or an attempt to implement the party's traditional values and aims in a new policy setting, driven by the exigencies of the time? This contemporaneous debate gave a new meaning to Labor's 'precocious political achievement' in the early twentieth century.[17] In such a context, Stuart's writings on Labor's emergence and early party life were inevitably a kind of intervention.

Writing in *Thesis Eleven* in 1986, Stuart classified Labor's early program as a '*masculine form of state intervention* in a *semi-mature capitalist economy*'.[18] Its function was to realise the political aspirations of the white men who dominated organised labour, seeking to enhance the standing of the wage-earning male whose relationship to production was in part mediated by state-based arbitration wage tribunals.[19]

This view was further elucidated in *The Labour Experiment* (1989), a volume marked by its brevity and precision in dissecting Labor's first decades: what were the circumstances of its rise, and to what extent was it able to actualise its program?[20] This is not a study that coheres to the strict principles of historical materialism, but it bears its inflection. It retains the insistence on totality, class as a central object and subject of history, and the relational nature of labour to other classes (predominantly, although not exclusively, to capital).

Stuart poses a basic definition of the working class, 'the class that has sold its labour', then immediately problematises it: what to make, for instance, of domestic labour? Instantly, he makes clear that the working class as constituted in the rhetoric and practices of the early movement, and subsequently bolstered in historical analysis, emphasised a certain variant of gender difference that 'confined the definition of labour to wage labour performed in the paid workforce'.[21]

But, he argues, the fundamental dynamic of the capitalist economy is that the labourer sells their labour power as a commodity to the owners of capital. Labourers both resist and accept this dynamic: combining to drive up the price of their labour and to seek control over aspects of the labour process, but doing so within the framework established by capital. This is not simply a workplace tension, for the commodification of labour is an affront to the labourers' innate human dignity, so the struggle over wages is also a struggle over the 'very basis of their life and community living standards'.[22]

Labour's mobilisation was a product of these tensions. Up until 1890, generally favourable conditions allowed labourers to bargain with employers. But the mass unemployment and industrial strife of the 1890s depression led to new tactics, foremost among them the creation of labour parties to win 'through political action what they could not win by industrial action'.[23] This mobilisation was imbued with collective values—but within tightly policed boundaries. Exclusion—by race, gender and professional status—was as crucial to the construction of labour solidarity as was inclusion. Labour as a movement therefore 'reflected the sectional interests of the organized white adult men who comprised it'.[24]

Labor's program reflected this dynamic. Men were presumed to be the primary supporter of the family unit, and their wage standards were expected to reflect this status. A plentiful supply of jobs was pursued to stave off the mass unemployment and dislocation experienced during the 1890s. Some welfare provisions were desired for those unable to work due to illness, accident or age.[25] The overarching emphasis of the party's program was on creating conditions that would make the (male) wage the 'principal means of meeting working-class needs'.[26] This was the essence of the 'wage-earners' welfare state'.[27]

These aims were not hegemonic. Socialists sought to direct Labor's ambitions in a more radical direction, without great success. The movement was inflected with regional, industrial and sectional differences.[28] Unions pushed for Labor to represent the movement's interests as starkly as possible—Labor Party parliamentarians sought a broader representation, all the better to secure the support of a wider electorate, creating tensions between the industrial and political wings.[29]

Both labourism and socialism were influential doctrines, disproving claims that Labor lacked theory. But neither on its own was capable of providing 'a coherent strategy for gaining and exercising power within a democratic parliamentary framework'.[30] Labor's 'precocious success' allowed the ambiguities created by these tensions to flourish. Its political appeal was also less than overwhelming—Labor governed for just eight years between Federation and the outbreak of World War II. Hence, to whatever extent Labor's political economy was actualised in this period, up to 1909 this often relied on support of other parties. After the 'Fusion' of non-labour parties in that year, 'there was little alteration of the essential pattern': conservative governments would cut welfare and wage protection, and Labor governments would improve them. But the established class relations persisted without further major alterations in social power.[31] And as for effects, Stuart doubts whether labour's share of the national wealth grew any faster than the general growth in output.[32]

In *The Labour Experiment*, Stuart captures many of the complexities of a mobilised class, in all its ambiguity, ambivalence and contradiction. His is a nuanced comprehension of how this mobilisation was shaped by particular actors within the organised labour movement to best represent their interests as white male wage-earners. This is an important qualifier on our understanding of the Labor Party's early advances.

The advances that Labor did achieve in this period pushed the bounds on what was deemed politically practical and acceptable. They placed the ALP in the vanguard of international social progress. The entrance of labour into politics was deemed a substantive threat by various powerful interests. This opposition was mobilised in right-wing populist campaigns, such as the Kyabram movement, and in the parliamentary sphere, with George Reid's short-lived Anti-Socialist Party an overt example (and 'Fusion' itself another). Labor's attempts to alter the balance of constitutional power through mass acts of democracy—the referenda campaigns of this era—were unsuccessful but indicated a stifled reforming ambition that had the potential to usher in even greater transformation. Within the party, organised socialists and groups of Labor women contested its political direction, which was set by the moderate leadership. These contests were frequently spurred by great social turmoil, such as the conscription campaigns of 1916 and 1917 and the militant upsurge at the end of World War I.

Politics, fundamentally, is about social power and competing interests. In this early period, the dominant moderate leadership of the party predominantly conceived of its mission as the pursuit of the interests of the organised worker—and the worker was assumed to be a white man. Labor is a party of many competing traditions, but this cannot be an alibi for excusing those actions of the party at its founding that perpetuated, rather than ameliorated, inequality. Stuart's history captures these aims and reminds us whose ambitions they ultimately represented.

Stuart's *Boldest Experiment*

Is it possible for Labor to achieve genuinely transformational reform through the institutions of Australian democracy? It is natural that the contemporary party would turn to reconstruction to answer this quandary. It is a period filled with Labor heroes, John Curtin and Ben Chifley foremost among them. It is an era of victory: victory in war and victory in peace. And it was sustained: although the Labor governments of this time lasted from just 1941 to 1949,[33] the governing consensus they established had a long half-life.

Stuart's history of reconstruction, *Australia's Boldest Experiment*, is not a direct intervention in contemporary debates on the possibility of change. It is not a *vade mecum* for a new generation of eager reformers. It is the history of the specific programs that were implemented and the reforming spirit that underpinned them amid an 'ethos of national endeavour'.[34] But it presents a compelling and extensive portrait of this epochal Labor government, situated within the broader social context of its time: the social totality pursued by the younger historian. It situates the party within the broader institutional and structural frameworks that governed the potentialities of reform and considers how, within this context, the substantial mobilisation of the war generated a brief window through which pent-up energies for change could find political expression.

Stuart's purpose is not to provide a recitation of Labor mythos but to chart the interrelated processes through which history was made. He presents the party's key figures in a much more ambivalent way than many true believers would otherwise find them. Curtin is frequently chided for recalcitrance in implementing reconstruction—even amid the pressures of wartime administration.[35] Chifley is described more favourably for translating the plans of progressive intellectuals 'into the idiom of Labor ideology', adapting 'them to the party's objectives' and using 'them to extend its policy repertoire'.[36] In Stuart's account, it is primarily 'progressive intellectuals' in the public service who propelled reconstruction and are credited with much of its design and implementation. H.C. Coombs is the particular hero of the piece.[37] It is noticeable, when considering the intellectual backdrop and influences on reconstruction, that the substantive debates among Labor intellectuals and power-brokers that took place in the decades preceding the war as to the shape of a possible new world order are largely elided.[38]

The 'fundamental goal' of reconstruction was full employment, a policy demonstrating both the opportunities for and restrictions on social transformation.[39] From an early stage, it was clear to avid reconstructionists that Australia's economy would struggle to maintain full employment without creating a demand for imports that would throw out its balance of payments. This was a serious challenge, and one that it is easy to imagine modern governments using to justify a lack of ambition.

But the Labor politicians and public service policy-makers of the reconstruction era did not use this as an excuse for inaction. Instead, fully aware of this danger, they pushed for something even more ambitious, eagerly promoting the embrace of full employment internationally: the 'positive approach'. This would alleviate the threat to the balance of payments by creating a demand for Australia's exports overseas.[40] This became the basis of a 'distinctively Australian approach' to postwar employment, 'pressed at every opportunity ... puzzling and exasperating those who listened to Australia's delegates expound it at international conferences'.[41]

The policy was beset with problems and threats to the general program of reconstruction. Pent-up consumer demand threatened to explode after the war. Labour was not in excess but shortage.[42] Full employment would require an element of discipline from labour, especially *sans* the ongoing constitutional power for the Commonwealth to control wages and prices.[43] A measure of austerity and continued rationing would have to be retained lest inflation spiral out of control.[44] The deterioration of productivity caused by the shift to the war economy threatened recession.[45] This precipitated a consistent problem for the postwar economy: an inability to increase the productivity of the basic industries upon which so much of the rest of the economy depended.[46]

Stuart does not allow a slip into easy nostalgia over epochal policies such as full employment. In his telling, the full challenges of affecting such change, and the inevitable limitations to far-reaching programs that must be overcome, are presented in sometimes daunting detail. But this makes the pursuit of this change all the more inspiring, its key players the more deserving of acclaim. For to propound the virtues of full employment was not just to advocate for a policy; it was to reject the entire economic orthodoxy that underpinned the pre-war governing consensus, a consensus itself backed by powerful interests.[47] War, economic calamity and structural change drive political transformation. Sometimes, in the right context, in the right conditions, so too can conviction and courage.

In true dialectical fashion, reconstruction contained its own negation. Weariness with regulation and bureaucracy turned the state into 'the eucalyptus that sheds its incendiary debris until a conflagration burns away the entire undergrowth'.[48] The popular acceptance of the need for restraint was gradually undermined by the government's opponents of the Right and Left, and its own discipline was often lacking. Failures in important postwar referenda (although not all), the campaign against Chifley's proposed bank nationalisation, and continued agitation in the mining industry gradually wore down Labor's support. It is a melancholy denouement, the sense of a missed opportunity at even more substantive transformation resonating through the concluding sections.

Perhaps this melancholia matches the moment in which it was written. By the point of the book's release, 2015, reconstruction had fallen from public consciousness. Since the electoral defeat of Paul Keating's Big Picture in 1996, it was the small target that had dominated Australian politics. Howard's chronic short-termism was followed by Federal Labor's uncivil wars, then the balatronic prime ministership of Tony Abbott. Where to look for hope of genuine vision and substantive reform?

Australia's Boldest Experiment is, at its core, a story of change—the change that was achieved, and the change that might have been. It spares few details in describing the many substantial blockages to reform within Australia's constitutional system. There is a palpable sense of opportunities lost, of a much more ambitious program of social betterment that could have been pursued. But, even with these qualifications, this is a book that charts a moment of hope. A time when eager and talented reformers believed social transformation not just possible but also necessary and were willing to dedicate themselves to its realisation. And realised it was. Reconstruction was not an abstract ideal but a lived reality for the nation, bringing 'benefits that before the war were scarcely imaginable'.[49]

The book is not a guide for our times—although we do now live at a point of national emergency caused by a global cataclysm. But one of the most powerful resources for those who prosper from an established social arrangement is the sense of cynicism towards change, the closing of possibilities that leads the subjugated to accept that what is, is all there can be.

Australia's Boldest Experiment is an important reminder, especially for Labor, that this is not the case. What exists around us has been created, and this is not the way it has always been. The story of reconstruction is not a simple heroic tale, but it is an important reminder that the reformers' élan, the spirit of change, is not foreign to Australia. Ambition can be matched with electoral success. A country that can throw up a moment of such transformation should remember it.

'The people who believe in things'

Labor has been transformed immeasurably since reconstruction. Laborism was largely 'exhausted' by the 1950s.[50] Gough Whitlam's rise saw a 'reforming wing' lead a concerted push to update the ALP's program with a new social democratic emphasis on matching full employment with a suite of social protections that pushed far beyond the male wage-earners welfare model.[51] The end of the postwar boom coincided with the collapse of Whitlamism and the embrace within the ALP of deflationary politics.

Stuart argued that the Hawke government's Accord with the ACTU demonstrated the residual influence of Laborism.[52] But residual was all it could be, as the institutional infrastructure of that traditional brand of Labor politics was disassembled: the economy was deregulated, the tariff reduced and substantial changes made to the public sector.[53] The fate of arbitration was more complicated, but the system was transformed fundamentally by Hawke and Keating (and later largely undermined by Howard). With these economic revolutions, the workforce changed. Labour transferred from primary production to the service and tertiary sectors.[54] The number of white-collar jobs grew faster than blue, women were entering the workforce in unprecedented numbers.[55] Labor was gripped by an identity crisis. In this fast-paced and transformed society, what was its purpose?

The party itself became more closed. The mechanisms through which the unions had historically intervened to command Labor's direction in key moments atrophied—conference, the platform and the pledge—were reduced in influence. A new form of party history, celebrating its *Cause for Power*, was spread by the New South Wales

Right faction. In a 1994 lecture at the ALP National Conference, Stuart concluded: 'To celebrate the Labor Party as a *Cause for Power* is not enough. True believers need beliefs.'[56]

Just what are those beliefs to be?

It is typical of Stuart that he does not offer a simple answer, as so many others would be tempted to do.[57] In his histories of the party, Stuart does not offer easy succour to the true believers. Rather, he challenges us to query the source of our beliefs and to reconsider the place and function of the party's mythos. This is not to dispel all hope for change or to dismiss the notion that the ALP has at times played a positive role in transforming Australia for the better. But it is to insist upon a deeper and more nuanced understanding of the nature of that change and of the people who made it.

It is an empathetic method of historical enquiry, filled with sympathetic renderings of real-world historical actors. His works are devoid of crude and condescending judgements and demonstrate an awareness of the imperfect nature of all who seek change. The point of progressive reform is the opening up of new possibilities, many beyond contemporary imagining, so that the future world will be so altered that those who inhabit it look back and wonder, how could they ever have believed that? The task of the historian is not to cast aside the flawed reformer, nor is it to excuse them. It is to understand them: their aspirations, their actions, their accomplishments and their limitations.

In its past, there are many moments when Labor perpetuated inequities, and this can neither be excused nor forgotten. In the party's history there are also many moments when, in often confused and contradictory ways, it has pushed against the barriers of the unjust and moved the country forward in a progressive direction. Labor is not just the sum of its actions; it is also the product of contest. Its history also includes many possible alternative pathways, many lost past futures. Labor's story is immense and often contradictory. Of course it is—Labor contains multitudes.

To learn from its past, Labor must understand its true lessons, which are often challenging. This necessitates a holistic approach, drawing together all the aspects of party life and situating Labor within the ever-changing social relations of the country that has shaped it and which it has shaped in turn. This requires a form of historical knowledge that is unflinching, comprehensive, immaculately researched and guided by an appreciation of how the seemingly discrete aspects of a society function as part of a greater totality. Australia has yet to see a greater practitioner of this than Stuart Macintyre.

Postscript

I was an overly eager undergraduate in 2005 when I first saw Stuart speak. I did not have a chance to meet him until 2012, when I undertook my Honours degree in History. Stuart led a subject on the writing of Australian history, and like others in the student group, the main reason I took the subject was because he was the one teaching it.

As a teacher, Stuart brought incredible wisdom as well as warmth and generosity to his classroom. He intellectually challenged you without ever making you feel as though *you* were being challenged. I remember well the feeling of being in full rhetorical flight making some polemical point or other just to see Stuart, arms folded, leaning back in his chair (is that a wry smile starting to curve the side of his mouth?), his eyebrow beginning to rise. Oh no, I would think. Here we go again, as Stuart asked a well-timed and perfectly honed question that stopped me in my tracks. Blast, I didn't think of that!

Never pernicious, never supercilious, slightly Socratic and with a wry sense of humour, always in command yet never dominating the discussion. Taking a class with Stuart was an exercise in critical analysis well beyond the content of the course. Each week we came together in that small conference room in the Old Quad Building (the eight-hour day building, soon to house the Menzies Institute, oh irony!) for discussions infused with his passion and enthusiasm for the historians we would consider, but more broadly, for the discipline and the learning process itself.

The subject finished, and my PhD began the following year. Stuart was not one of my supervisors, but I reached out to him frequently, asking for advice, a source, a critical eye over an unfinished thesis chapter. Send him a 10 000-word chapter and it would seemingly be back to you, fully noted, the page filled with red tracked changes and comments or suggestions, in under an hour. How? I have yet to learn his secret. Nothing ever seemed too much for Stuart. As a teacher, I respect and admire Stuart beyond measure. I caught myself, more than once, in my own classrooms, leaning back in the chair, arms folded, a wry smile beginning to appear, waiting for the moment to delicately interpose, 'But what if …?'

Stuart was not only an historian; he was also an educator. In the true sense of the word. And to understand his career and the influence he has had on the study of history in Australia, it is necessary also to appreciate the extraordinary contribution he has made to so many in this capacity. He taught us history, he taught us how to teach, and he taught us how to analyse and question. These lessons have been carried, well beyond the academy, by so many who had the good luck and the opportunity to have spent time in one of his classrooms.

We live in a time when the transformative effect of university education is being denigrated. Research locked behind paywalls is prized more highly by university administrations than the work of providing students with the critical faculties required not just to appreciate historical content but also to understand the world that they inhabit. Against this, Stuart's life stands as an enduring testament to the power of education, to the power of the teacher and to the transformative effects history can have on our society and the individuals who inhabit it. Just ask the kid in 2005, sitting in the theatre. Waiting for the lecture to begin.

Notes

1 Stuart Macintyre, 'True for the moment', in Bain Attwood (ed.), *Labour Histories: Robin Gollan, Stuart Macintyre, Verity Burgmann, Peter Beilharz, Raelene Frances*, Monash University, Clayton, Vic, 1994, p. 13.

2 Stuart Macintyre, 'Who are the true believers? The Manning Clark Labor History Memorial Lecture', *Labour History*, vol. 68, no. 1, 1995, p. 155.

3 Macintyre, 'True for the moment', p. 21.

4 Georg Lukács, *History and Class Consciousness: Studies in Marxist Dialectics*, MIT Press, Cambridge, 1971, pp. 223–4.

5 Sean Scalmer's chapter in this collection outlines the intellectual background and context to this piece.

6 Macintyre, 'True for the moment', p. 19.

7 Stuart Macintyre, 'Radical history and bourgeois hegemony', *Intervention*, no. 2, 1972, p. 59.

8 Ibid., p. 60.

9 Ibid., pp. 67–8.

10 Ibid., p. 72.

11 Lukács, *History and Class Consciousness*, p. 223.

12 Stuart Macintyre, 'The making of the Australian working class: An historiographical survey', *Historical Studies*, vol. 18, no. 71, 1978, p. 234.

13 Ibid., pp. 234–9.

14 Ibid., p. 248.

15 Ibid., pp. 249–51.

16 Ibid., pp. 252–3.

17 Stuart Macintyre, 'The short history of social democracy in Australia', *Thesis Eleven*, no. 15, 1986, p. 3.

18 Ibid., p. 4 (italicisation in original). Stuart had earlier proposed a similar definition in Stuart Macintyre, 'Early socialism and labor', *Intervention*, no. 8, 1977, pp. 81–2. He would further develop this with a more biographical frame, but fundamentally the same analysis, in his contribution to the centennial volume for the federal ALP: Stuart Macintyre, 'The first caucus', in John Faulkner and Stuart Macintyre (eds), *True Believers: The Story of the Federal Parliamentary Labor Party*, Allen & Unwin, Crows Nest, NSW, 2001, pp. 17–29.

19 Macintyre, 'The short history of social democracy in Australia', pp. 4–5.

20 Stuart Macintyre, *The Labour Experiment*, McPhee Gribble, Melbourne, 1989, pp. 4–5.

21 Ibid., p. 5.

22 Ibid., p. 6.

23 Ibid., p. 6.

24 Ibid., p. 6.

25 Ibid., p. 19.

26 Ibid., p. 27.

27 Ibid., p. 28.

28 Ibid., pp. 33–4.

29 Ibid., p. 35.

30 Ibid.

31 Ibid., pp. 36–7.

32 Ibid., p. 47.

33 'Just' is relative, as this was a record tenure of Labor government at the time and for a considerable period afterwards.

34   Stuart Macintyre, *Australia's Boldest Experiment: War and Reconstruction in the 1940s*, NewSouth Publishing, Sydney, 2015, p. 13.

35   Ibid., pp. 13, 471. The most significant critique is Curtin's approach to what would become the 1944 referendum, ibid., pp. 254–5, 268–70.

36   Ibid., p. 472.

37   Ibid., p. 470.

38   Ibid., p. 48.

39   Ibid., p. 237.

40   Ibid., pp. 117, 243.

41   Ibid., p. 239.

42   Ibid., p. 325.

43   Ibid., pp. 289, 343, 347–9.

44   Ibid., p. 343.

45   Ibid., p. 340.

46   Ibid., p. 341.

47   Ibid., pp. 287–8.

48   Ibid., p. 14.

49   Ibid., p. 5.

50   Macintyre, *The Labour Experiment*, p. 62.

51   Macintyre, 'The short history of social democracy in Australia', p. 8.

52   Ibid., p. 13.

53   Macintyre, *The Labour Experiment*, p. 65.

54   Macintyre, 'The short history of social democracy in Australia', p. 10.

55   Ibid.

56   Macintyre, 'Who are the true believers?', p. 166.

57   Liam Byrne, *Becoming John Curtin and James Scullin: The Making of the Modern Labor Party*, Melbourne University Press, Carlton, 2020.

Chapter 28

Response

Stuart Macintyre

My reaction when first presented with these essays was rather like that of Fred Daly, the Labor parliamentarian who served as Opposition Whip in the early 1950s and as minister in the Whitlam administration twenty years later. In 1953 this jesting cynic attended the funeral of Sol Rosevear, a parliamentary colleague, and listened to a fulsome eulogy of the former Speaker's devotion to duty and spotless character until he could stand no more. In a pause before the peroration Daly spoke in a clear voice heard by all: 'By God, we're burying the wrong man.'

The incident was recorded by Paul Hasluck in one of the acid pen portraits he composed to work off his contempt for lesser mortals. Rosevear, who served as Speaker from 1943 until the end of 1949, was widely regarded as the most shamelessly partisan of all presiding officers. It was his custom during Saturdays when Parliament House was closed to use its phone lines to place bets on horse races until sometime late in the afternoon when he would collect a generous parcel of food from the kitchen and leave from a service doorway at the back of the building. Hasluck, then writing the first volume of his official history of World War II, worked in Parliament House on Saturdays and was thus able to observe this routine, although his account did not appear in print until 1997. Nor did he attend Rosevear's funeral, and his account of it is open to challenge. (He attributed the eulogy to a young Methodist minister, whereas the funeral was conducted by an Anglican one.)[1]

There are a number of events in this account of my life and career set out in this volume that were new to me—or at least had no presence in my memory. This is perhaps especially the case with those essays recalling my first steps as a doctoral candidate—although it is fortunate there is no witness here to my shameful neglect of studies as an undergraduate, which I remember all too well. Both Geoff Eley and Kevin Morgan describe a confidence I did not feel as a newcomer to Cambridge in 1972, although I had the advantage of already completing an MA thesis at Monash, where I had acquired research skills and prior knowledge of my field. While those beginning their PhD after completing the Cambridge tripos were formidably intelligent, they had no previous experience of working in archives, and I recall explaining to them how to take notes, using Beatrice Webb's time-honoured method—except that I could no longer afford her notecards.

A number of the contributors express gratitude for my helping them make their way. Such is the nature of a project like this, although I was surprised by the implication that this was unusual. Throughout my career I have been the beneficiary of assistance from others. This began at Monash in 1969, where three supervisors of quite different disposition—Ian Turner, Alan McBriar and David Cuthbert—went well beyond the call of duty. It continued at Melbourne when I returned there as a full-time tutor in 1970 at the behest of Alison Patrick, then at Cambridge where Henry Pelling was a sketchy supervisor and generous patron. Geoff Bolton entrusted me, a newcomer to Australian history, with writing a whole volume of the prestigious *Oxford History of Australia*.

The term 'patron' carries connotations of favouritism, although patronage is not finite and can be shared among a number of beneficiaries. Some of the most powerful influences on our own behaviour come not from tutelage but from observation. As a junior member of the Melbourne history department, I was able to observe how Geoffrey Blainey chaired meetings in a timely manner without anyone feeling the pressure of a timetable. I was struck similarly as a member of the Council of the National Library by Ninian Stephen's capacity to win over the most prickly participants, and as a miscreant by Davis McCaughey's ability to deliver an admonition without rancour. I did not consciously imitate any of them. Rather, when faced with similar tasks I found my mind going back to their example.

The contributors deal with my work across a number of fields of study. It is an attraction of history as a discipline that it allows such movement: unlike, say, a geneticist, you are not restricted to work always on the same gene by the need for a fully equipped laboratory and funding for salaries, but can turn to a different topic. I have often availed myself of this freedom, partly I suspect because of a low threshold of boredom and partly because some topics lent themselves to the time constraints of my career. And I am conscious that I have enjoyed an unusual freedom: I have never sought permission to embark on a new topic. That freedom is now circumscribed by university research policies, performance measures, ethics committees, intellectual property rules and various other management tools.

A penalty for not knowing how to say no is that an opportunity can become an obligation with a deadline. But overwhelmingly I have had the better of the exchange, the consent creating a major new interest. Carolyn Holbrook writes here of how I approached Paul Keating in 1994 with the suggestion that he initiate an inquiry into civics and citizenship education. I certainly had an interest in civics, as my subscription to Hansard at the age of 14 attests, but even then I was conscious that my enjoyment of working out a Senate quota in the Year 10 civics class held after lunch on a Wednesday was not widely shared. And since Carolyn was a member of the secretariat that supported the inquiry, it speaks well of the discretion in the Department of Prime Minister and Cabinet that she was not aware of its genesis.

So far from proposing a civics inquiry to Keating, I was asked to do so by Don Watson, Keating's speechwriter, as part of their promotion of an informed and active citizenship that would embrace a republic. At their behest I wrote to the prime minister and then found myself criss-crossing the country in the company of two senior educationists, Ken Boston and Susan Pascoe, and an official of the Department of Education, Noel Simpson. The enthusiasm of Ken and Susan for civics education in and out of the classroom was strong. I was more reluctant. Among the amenities of citizenship, I found myself saying, was the right not to be an active citizen. Even so, the experience initiated a lasting interest and also introduced me to Carolyn, with whom I worked on her doctoral candidature and now the postdoctoral research project.

One final response. I have benefited particularly from the cogent criticism of my work exemplified in the contributions of Tim Rowse, Rob Watts and Simon Marginson. That they and others have given me so much to ponder only increases my appreciation of Peter Beilharz and Sian Supski for assembling the collection.

Notes

1   Frank Bongiorno was the first to bring it to notice, so that it was added to *ADB* entries for Rosevear and Hasluck.

What if?

Peter Beilharz and Sian Supski

In 2006 Stuart edited a novel book project, conceived together with Sean Scalmer. Entitled *What If?*, it brought together eminent historians to play counterfactuals.[1] It was a platform for the historical imagination, for the contemplation of contingency in history. What if France had colonised Tasmania? What if Gallipoli was a minor event? What if Whitlam had not been dismissed? and so on.

We close this volume with three such questions for Stuart Macintyre.

First, what if Stuart had joined the Liberal Party? Liberalism is, as we have seen, a constant concern for Stuart. His own path took him from the Communist Party to the Labor Party. But if he was to become a liberal, his was the social liberalism of Evatt, Chifley, Coombs, perhaps later Stretton. It is an old Left adage that, as Lenin had it in 1913, the Australian Labor Party were the liberals and the liberals our conservatives. This is a line that Stuart follows in a review of *A Liberal State*, the fourth volume of David Kemp's monumental history of liberalism in Australia. Stuart asks of Kemp, and of Menzies, 'But how liberal was he?'[2] That liberal consensus has always coexisted with the cultural presence of labourism and, differently, socialism in Australia; this brings an endless and open field of discussion. Here the issue is as much cultural as political—Stuart Macintyre has always been on the Left. His autobiography, like his written work, describes an arc, not a rupture. This, at least, is a non-question.

Second, what if Stuart had remained in England? Alternatively, what if he had remained committed to working on British history? What if he had moved to the USA like Geoff Eley or Sheila Fitzpatrick? What if he had stayed in Perth? This is not the place for a detailed discussion, but it is fair to say that just as Stuart is on the Left, so is he in and of Melbourne; although, as our contributors note, the view is not provincial. You might have bumped into him in an archive but more likely in an airport.

Third, what if Stuart had become a sociologist? This last is the real trick question, for as we have dared to suggest above, Stuart is indeed also a sociologist or at the very least an honorary sociologist. This is apparent in the way he thinks, seeking out patterns, discerning trends, individuals, classes, groups, puzzling over the nexus between culture and power, oriented to the present and to generality as well as to the particulars. Perhaps this is most apparent in the earlier work, such as *Winners and Losers* and *The Labour Experiment*; but there is also a driving interest in ideas and ideology, not least in the work on the colonial liberals and reconstruction, which follows throughout his work. More, there is the dual-track interest in and enthusiasm for social sciences, manifest in the mission to think history also as a social science and in the practical leadership given to both Australian academies, Social Sciences and Humanities alike. The point is not that the work of history is less than paramount. It is that a certain openness to the big world calls to all of us. Stuart knew how to look up but also sideways and out. What if the work of history could follow? In fact, it does. It moves.

As editors we are outsiders, fellow travellers of our friends who practise the work of history as a vocation. But we have also spent our lives arguing for the work of history, alongside Stuart and our collaborators here. What is outside history? Nothing. It is a lesson we must continue to learn and to teach.

Notes

1   Stuart Macintyre and Sean Scalmer, *What If? Australian History as it Might Have Been*, Melbourne University Press, Melbourne, 2006.
2   Stuart Macintyre, 'But how liberal was he?', *Inside Story*, 4 March 2021.

The work of supervision

Higher degrees completed under the supervision of Stuart Macintyre

Principal supervisor ★
Co-supervisor #
Unless otherwise stated, awarded in the Faculty of Arts

Name	Year	Thesis title	Degree
James Davidson	1993	Louise Hanson-Dyer of L'Oiseau-Lyre, 1927–1962: The career of a musical expatriate	PhD#
Donald Garden	1993	Teacher training in Carlton: The predecessors of the Institute of Education	PhD Education#
Margaret Glass	1993	Thomas Bent: The Survivor	PhD★
John Murphy	1993	The Australian intervention in the Vietnam War	PhD★
Christopher Healy	1994	The training of memory: Moments of historical imagination in Australia	PhD★
Mark Peel	1994	Making a home for workers: The building of Elizabeth 1955–1975	PhD★
John Chesterman	1995	Law and the New Left: A history of the Fitzroy Legal Service, 1972–1994	PhD#
James Humphery	1995	New worlds, familiar places – Supermarkets, consumption and cultural critique	PhD#

Name	Year	Thesis title	Degree
Cecile Trioli	1995	Brunswick during the interwar years: A social, political and economic study 1920–1939	PhD★
Velma Joynson	1996	Post-World War Two British migration to Australia 'the most pampered and protected of the intake'	PhD★
James Bennett	1997	Redeeming the Imagination: A transnational history of Australia and Aotearoa New Zealand, 1890–1944	PhD★
David Dutton	1998	Strangers and Citizens: The boundaries of Australian citizenship 1901–73	PhD★
Prudence Torney-Parlicki	1998	Somewhere in Asia: The Australian news media and conflict in the Asia–Pacific region, 1941–75	PhD★
Martin Crotty	1999	Making the Australian male: The construction of manly middle-class youth in Australia, 1870–1920	PhD#
Victoria Emery	1999	Reading and After: Literary community identity and practice in Melbourne circa 1886–1910	PhD#
Paul Jones	1999	Alien Acts: The White Australia Policy, 1901 to 1939	PhD★
Daniel Mandel	1999	Justice and Expediency: Dr H.V. Evatt and Palestine 1947–1949	PhD★
Sara Wills	1999	A Reasonable Share in the Beauty of Earth: William Morris' culture of nature	PhD★
Fay Woodhouse	2001	A Place Apart? A study of student political engagement at the University of Melbourne 1930–39	PhD★
Adam Carr	2002	An Age of Certainty: Three generations of Melbourne radicals 1870–1988	PhD★
Michael Liffman	2002	Uncommon Good: Seventy-five years of Myer family philanthropy	PhD★
Helen MacDonald	2002	Human Remains: Episodes in nineteenth-century colonial human dissection	PhD#

Name	Year	Thesis title	Degree
Anne Sunter	2002	Birth of a Nation: Constructing and de-constructing the Eureka Legend	PhD★
Fay Anderson	2003	Max Crawford: Necessity and freedom	PhD★
Robin Lucas	2003	Nettie Palmer and Fourteen Years	MA Australian Studies#
Charles Parkinson	2003	Sir William Stawell and the Victorian Constitution	MA History#
Jonathan Ritchie	2003	'Making their own law': Popular participation in the development of Papua New Guinea's constitution	PhD★
Kim Torney	2003	From 'babes in the wood' to 'bush-lost babies': The development of an Australian image	PhD#
Elizabeth Prest	2004	The Political Career of Sir John Langdon Bonython, 1848–1939	PhD★
Anna Clark	2005	Teaching the Nation: Politics and pedagogy in Australian history	PhD★
Jacqueline Dickenson	2005	Renegades and Rats: Betrayal and the remaking of radical organisations in Britain and Australia, 1840–1940	PhD★
Donald Given	2007	Transits of Empires: Ernest Fisk and the worldwide wireless	PhD★
Joan Gravina	2007	Turbulent Flow: The origins and early days of chemical engineering at the University of Melbourne, 1950–1970	MA-History★
Simon Booth	2008	Picturing Politics: Cartoons of Melbourne's labour press, 1890–1919	PhD★
Michael Cathcart	2008	The Water Dreamers: How water and silence shaped Australia	PhD#
Peter Johnston	2008	Who's Playing Our Song? The development of the Australian musical 1900–2000	PhD#
Danielle Thornton	2008	Factory Girls: Gender, empire and the making of a female working class, Melbourne and London, 1880–1920	PhD#

Name	Year	Thesis title	Degree
Edward Waghorne	2008	Defending Democratic Rights: The Australian Council for Civil Liberties, 1936–1965	PhD#
Ai Kobayashi	2009	William Macmahon Ball: The public life of a political scientist	PhD★
Claire McLisky	2009	Settlers on a Mission: Faith, power and subjectivity in the lives of David and Janet Matthews	PhD#
Vivienne Nicholson	2009	Grassroots Activism: Cost or benefit?	PhD#
Ronald Sulman	2009	Does History Have a Future? An inquiry into history as research	PhD#
John Waugh	2009	Diploma Privilege: Legal education at the University of Melbourne 1857–1946	PhD★
Stephen Hills	2010	Power, Purpose and Politics: A history of the Jervis Bay Nuclear Project	MA History#
Sarah Martin	2011	A Passionate Commitment: Davis McCaughey, the Australian years (1953–2005)	PhD★
Iain McIntyre	2011	The AIDEX '91 Protest: A case study of Obstructive Direct Action	MA History★
Ruth Dick	2012	Ellen Mulcahy: A study of her work and life in the context of her times	PhD★
Jennifer Hibben	2012	Shirley Andrews: A prismatic life	PhD★
Elizabeth Kleinhenz	2012	La Primadonna: The life of Kathleen Fitzpatrick	PhD★
Robert O'Shea	2012	The Australian Governor-Generalship: Sources of authority and identity	MA History★
Janice Friedel	2013	Left-wing Melbourne artists and the Communist Party during the early Cold War period	PhD#
Dino Hodge	2013	Pink, Red and Vermilion: Homophobia in the life and times of Don Dunstan	PhD#
Carolyn Holbrook	2013	The Great War in the Australian Imagination since 1915	PhD#

Name	Year	Thesis title	Degree
Mira Adler–Gillies	2014	Collectivism or Cooperation? The contest for meaning in the French socialist movement, 1870–1890	PhD#
André Brett	2014	Acknowledge No Frontier: The creation and demise of New Zealand's provinces, 1853–76	PhD★
Thomas Rogers	2014	The Civilisation of Port Phillip	PhD#
Douglas Wilkie	2014	1849 The Rush that Never Started: Forgotten origins of the 1851 gold discoveries in Victoria	PhD#
Alex Burston–Chorowicz	2015	Labour Victories: A comparative study of the British Labour Party and the Australian Labor Party and their electoral success in the immediate post-war period	MA History#
Bronwyn Lowe	2015	'The right thing to read': Australian girl-readers in history and text, 1910–1960	PhD#
Kate Rogers	2015	Providing for Perfection: Welfare eugenics in Australia, 1901–2000s	PhD#
James Tierney	2015	Protest and Patient Care: Employing theories of organising and mobilisation to explain the growth of the Victorian Nurses' Union	MA History#
Timothy Gassin	2016	Canada and Australia: Federation and nationhood	PhD★
Tanya Josev	2016	The Changing Meanings of 'Judicial Activism' in the United States and Australia, 1947–2008	PhD★
David Llewellyn	2016	Australia Felix: Jeremy Bentham and Australian colonial democracy	PhD#
Caitlin Mahar	2016	The Good Death: Historicising euthanasia in Australia	PhD#
Sarah Midford	2016	From Achilles to Anzac: Classical receptions in the Australian Anzac narrative	PhD★

Name	Year	Thesis title	Degree
Tyson Retz	2016	The History and Function of Empathy in Historical Studies: Re-enactment and hermeneutics	PhD★
Joel Barnes	2017	The Tragedy of the Common Law: The ancient constitution in the Age of Reform, 1830–1909	PhD★
Kenneth Barelli	2019	The Voice of Methodism: Temperance policy in Victoria, Australia 1902–1977	MA#
Shane Murray Cahill	2019	Visions of a Mutual Pacific Destiny: The Japan-Australia Society, 1896–1942	PhD#
Katherine Davison	2020	Sex, Psychiatry and the Cold War: A Transnational History of Homosexual Aversion Therapy, 1948–1981	PhD★
Phoebe Kelloway	2020	Three Major Industrial Disputes 1928–30, Rank-and-File Action and the Communist Party of Australia	PhD★
Andrew Murray Black	2020	The Victorian Farmers' Union, Country, and National Party, 1916–2000: Survival, adaptation, and evolution	PhD#
Susan Reidy	2021	Glorious Gardens and Exuberant Grounds: The history of urban public parks in Australia	PhD—to be conferred#
Kenneth Barelli		The Methodists in Victoria: 1902–1977	PhD—enrolled#
Melanie Brand		Out of Sight, Out of Mind? The development of intelligence oversight in Cold War Australia	PhD—enrolled#
Claire Marika Deery		The Teaching of History in Australian Primary Schools	PhD—enrolled#
Daniel Rule		Sir John Latham: A Biography	PhD—enrolled#
Neville Yeomans		A History of Australia's Immigrant Doctors, 1788–2017: Contributions, contestations and controversies	PhD—enrolled#

Bibliography

Publications of Stuart Forbes Macintyre

Books

A Proletarian Science: Marxism in Britain 1917–1933, Cambridge University Press, Cambridge, 1980. Reissued Lawrence & Wishart, London, 1986; paperback, Cambridge University Press, 2011

Little Moscows: Communism and Working-class Militancy in Inter-war Britain, Croom Helm, London, 1980

Militant: The Life and Times of Paddy Troy, Allen & Unwin, Sydney, 1984

Winners and Losers: The Pursuit of Social Justice in Australian History, Allen & Unwin, Sydney, 1985. Reprinted 1988, 1990; ebook edition 2009

The Oxford History of Australia, vol. 4: *1901–1942: The Succeeding Age*, Oxford University Press, Melbourne, 1986. (Awarded A.A. Phillips Prize for Australian Studies, Premier's Literary Awards, 1987) Reprinted 1990. Paperback edition, 1993; reprinted 1997, 2001, 2003, 2004

The Labour Experiment, McPhee Gribble Penguin, Melbourne, 1988

A Colonial Liberalism: The Lost World of Three Victorian Visionaries, Oxford University Press, Melbourne, 1991

A History for a Nation: Ernest Scott and the Making of Australian History, Melbourne University Press, Melbourne, 1994

The Reds: The Communist Party of Australia from Origins to Illegality, Allen & Unwin, Sydney, 1998. (Awarded *Age* Non-Fiction Book of the Year Award, 1998) Paperback edition, 1999

Concise History of Australia, Cambridge University Press, Cambridge, 1999. Reprinted 2000, 2002. Second edition, 2004, third edition, 2009, fourth edition, 2015, fifth edition, 2020. Chinese edition, Shanghai Foreign Language Education Press, 2007; Orient Publishing Center, 2009; Italian edition, Clueb, 2007; Japanese edition, 2008, Russian edition, Cambridge University Press, 2011; Czech edition, Nakladatelstvi Lidove Noviny, 2013

Stuart Macintyre and R.J.W. Selleck, *A Short History of the University of Melbourne*, Melbourne University Press, Melbourne, 2003

Stuart Macintyre and Anna Clark, *The History Wars*, Melbourne University Press, Melbourne, 2003. (Awarded Queensland Premier's Literary Award for Best Work Advancing Public Debate, New South Wales Premier's History Award) Reprinted 2003. Revised edition 2004

The Poor Relation: A History of the Social Sciences in Australia, Melbourne University Press, Melbourne, 2010

James Waghorne and Stuart Macintyre, *Liberty: A History of Civil Liberties in Australia*, UNSW Press, Sydney, 2011

Australia's Boldest Experiment: War and Reconstruction in the 1940s, NewSouth Publishing, Sydney, 2015. (Awarded Ernest Scott Prize, 2015–16; New South Wales Premier's Australian History Prize, 2016)

Graeme Powell with Stuart Macintyre, *Land of Opportunity: Australia's Post-war Reconstruction*, National Archives of Australia, Canberra, 2015. (Awarded Mander-Jones Award for best finding aid to an archival collection, 2015)

André Brett, Gwilym Croucher and Stuart Macintyre, *Life After Dawkins: The University of Melbourne in the Unified National System of Higher Education*, Melbourne University Press, Melbourne, 2016

Stuart Macintyre, André Brett and Gwilym Croucher, *No End of a Lesson: Australia's Unified National System of Higher Education*, Melbourne University Press, Melbourne, 2017

The Party: The Communist Party of Australia from Heyday to Reckoning, Allen & Unwin, Sydney, 2022

Edited books

Ormond College Centenary Essays, Melbourne University Press, Melbourne, 1984

R.M. Crawford, Manning Clark and Geoffrey Blainey, *Making History*, McPhee Gribble Penguin, Melbourne, 1985

(With Susan Janson) *Making the Bicentenary*, Australian Historical Studies, Melbourne, 1989

(With Richard Mitchell) *Foundations of Arbitration: The Origins and Effects of State Compulsory Arbitration, 1890–1914*, Oxford University Press, Melbourne, 1989

(With Susan Janson) *Through White Eyes*, Allen & Unwin, Sydney, 1990

Max Crawford, *Old Bebb's Store and Other Poems*, History Department, University of Melbourne, Melbourne, 1992

(With Beverley Symons and Andrew Wells) *Communism in Australia: A Resource Bibliography*, National Library of Australia, Canberra, 1994

'And Be One People': Alfred Deakin's Federal Story, Melbourne University Press, Melbourne, 1995

(With Julian Thomas) *The Discovery of Australian History 1890–1939*, Melbourne University Press, Melbourne, 1995

(With Graeme Davison and John Hirst) *The Oxford Companion to Australian History*, Oxford University Press, Melbourne, 1998. Reprinted 1998, 1999. Revised edition 2001

(With Peter McPhee) *Max Crawford's School of History*, History Department, University of Melbourne, Melbourne, 2000

(With Helen Irving) *J.A. La Nauze. No Ordinary Act: Essays on Federation and the Constitution*, Melbourne University Press, Melbourne, 2001

(With John Faulkner) *True Believers: The Story of the Federal Parliamentary Labor Party*, Allen & Unwin, Crows Nest, NSW, 2001

(With Beverley Symons) *Communism in Australia: A Supplementary Resource Bibliography*, Sydney Branch, Australian Society for the Study of Labour History, Sydney, 2002

(With Deborah Gare, Geoffrey Bolton and Tom Stannage) *The Fuss That Never Ended: The Life and Work of Geoffrey Blainey*, Melbourne University Press, Melbourne, 2003

The Historian's Conscience: Australian Historians on the Ethics of History, Melbourne University Press, Melbourne, 2004

(With Joe Isaac) *The New Province for Law and Order: 100 Years of Australian Industrial Conciliation and Arbitration*, Cambridge University Press, Cambridge, 2004

(With Sean Scalmer) *What If? Australian History as it Might Have Been*, Melbourne University Press, Melbourne, 2006; reprinted 2006

(With Fay Anderson) *The Life of the Past: The Discipline of History at the University of Melbourne*, RMIT Publishing, Melbourne, 2006

(With Gordon Boyce and Simon Ville) *How Organisations Connect: Investing in Communication*, Melbourne University Press, Melbourne, 2006

(With Kate Darian-Smith and Patricia Grimshaw) *Britishness Abroad: Transnational Movements and Imperial Cultures*, Melbourne University Press, Melbourne, 2007

(With Sheila Fitzpatrick) *Against the Grain: Brian Fitzpatrick and Manning Clark in Australian History and Politics*, Melbourne University Press, Melbourne, 2007

(With Juan Maiguashca and Attila Pók) *The Oxford History of Historical Writing*, vol. 4: *1800–1945*, Oxford University Press, Oxford, 2011. Paperback edition, 2015; Chinese edition, 2014

(With Alison Bashford) *The Cambridge History of Australia*, vol. 1: *Indigenous and Colonial Australia*, Cambridge University Press, Cambridge, 2013; paperback 2014

(With Alison Bashford) *The Cambridge History of Australia*, vol. 2: *The Commonwealth of Australia*, Cambridge University Press, Cambridge, 2013, paperback 2013

(With Lenore Layman and Jenny Gregory) *A Historian for All Seasons: Essays for Geoffrey Bolton*, Monash University Publishing, Melbourne, 2017

Minor publications

Imperialism and the British Labour Movement, CPGB Our History, no. 64, 1975

(With Vivienne Jackson) *T.A. Jackson: A Centenary Appreciation*, CPGB Our History, 73, 1979

Knowing and Possessing: Ernest Scott's Circumnavigation of Australian History: An Inaugural Lecture, History Department, University of Melbourne, 1991

History, the University and the Nation, Trevor Reese Memorial Lecture, Sir Robert Menzies Centre for Australian Studies, Institute of Commonwealth Studies, University of London, 1992

Rethinking Australian Citizenship, Cunningham Lecture for 1992, Academy of the Social Sciences in Australia, Canberra, 1993

(With Anthony Day, David Goodman, Barry Hindess and David Marr) *Perceiving 'Citizenship'*, Australian–Asian Perceptions Project, Working Paper No. 1, Academy of the Social Sciences in Australia and the Asia–Australia Institute, University of New South Wales, Sydney, 1993

Civics Expert Group (Stuart Macintyre, Kenneth Boston, Susan Pascoe), *Whereas the People: Civics and Citizenship Education*, Australian Government Publishing Service, Canberra, 1994

History for the Homeless: Kathleen Fitzpatrick's Vocation and Ours, Public Lecture, History Department, University of Melbourne, 1995

What Happened to Compassion, Fourteenth Sambell Memorial Oration, Brotherhood of St Laurence, Fitzroy, 1995

The Necessity of History, Inaugural History Lecture for the History Council of New South Wales, History Council of New South Wales, Sydney, 1997

(With Robert Pascoe, John Ainley and Jim Williamson) *The Lettered Country*, Australian Universities Teaching Committee, Canberra, 2003

National History Curriculum: Draft Framing Paper, National Curriculum Board, Melbourne, 2008

Chapters of books

Australian Dictionary of Biography, entries for William McLellan, Sir John Latham, J.L. Rentoul, William Somerville, Eric Harrison, J.B. Miles, Lance Sharkey, P.L. Troy, Ralph Gibson, Ted Laurie, J.J. Brown, J.A. La Nauze, ADB, Melbourne University Press, Melbourne, 1966–

'Equity in Australian history', in P.N. Troy (ed.), *A Just Society? Essays on Equity in Australia*, Allen & Unwin, Sydney, 1981, pp. 37–50

'Labour, capital and arbitration', in Brian Head (ed.), *State and Economy in Australia*, Oxford University Press, Melbourne, 1983, pp. 98–114

'War and peace: A history of the college initiation', in Stuart Macintyre (ed.), *Ormond College Centenary Essays*, Melbourne University Press, Melbourne, 1984, pp. 79–102

'Australian responses to unemployment in the last depression', in Jill Roe (ed.), *Unemployment: Are There Lessons from History?*, Hale & Iremonger, Sydney, 1985, pp. 22–35

'The making of a school', in R.M. Crawford, Manning Clark and Geoffrey Blainey, *Making History*, McPhee Gribble Penguin, Melbourne, 1985, pp. 3–33

'The short history of social democracy in Australia', in D.W. Rawson (ed.), *Blast, Budge or Bypass: Towards a Social Democratic Australia*, Academy of the Social Sciences in Australia, Canberra, 1986, pp. 133–45

'Rusden, Turner and the lessons of the past', in Jeff Leeuwenburg (ed.), *The Writing of Victoria's History 1835–1985*, Baillieu Library, University of Melbourne, 1986, pp. 11–18

'Social justice', in Graeme Aplin, S.G. Foster and Michael McKernan (eds), *Australians: A Historical Dictionary*, Fairfax, Syme & Weldon Associates, Sydney, 1987, pp. 369–70

'Australia 200 years', *Collier's Encyclopaedia Yearbook 1988*, Macmillan, New York, 1987, pp. 74–85

'The writing of Australian history', in D.H. Borchardt and V. Crittenden (eds), *Australians: A Guide to Sources*, Fairfax, Syme & Weldon Associates, Sydney, 1988, pp. 1–29

(With Verity Burgmann) 'Divided we fell', in Verity Burgmann and Jenny Lee (eds), *Staining the Wattle: A People's History of Australia Since 1788*, McPhee Gribble Penguin, Melbourne, 1988, pp. 109–31

'Writing for the Oxford History of Australia', in George Shaw (ed.), *1988 and All That*, University of Queensland Press, St Lucia, 1988, pp. 45–9, 118–23

'Neither capital nor labour: The politics of the establishment of arbitration', in Stuart Macintyre and Richard Mitchell (eds), *Foundations of Arbitration: The Origins and Effects of State Compulsory Arbitration,*

Oxford University Press, Melbourne, 1989, pp. 178–200

Longman's Encyclopedia, thirty-nine entries on Australian history, Longman, London, 1989

'Introduction', in Stuart Macintyre and Susan Janson (eds), *Through White Eyes*, Allen & Unwin, Sydney, 1990, pp. x–xvi

'A renewed citizenship', in Michael Dugan (ed.), *Furious Agreement*, Penguin Books in association with the Australian Institute of Management, Melbourne, 1991, pp. 3–7

'Decline and fall', in David Burchell and Race Matthews (eds), *Labor's Troubled Times*, Pluto Press, Leichhardt, NSW, 1991, pp. 18–25

'Exploring the cultural and educational impediments to Australia becoming a "clever country"', in John Anwyl (ed.), *CSHE 1990 Spring Lectures on Higher Education*, Centre for the Study of Higher Education, University of Melbourne, Melbourne, 1991, pp. 67–76

'Josef Dietzgen', in Tom Bottomore (ed.), *A Dictionary of Marxist Thought*, 2nd edition, Blackwell, Oxford, 1991, pp. 152–3

'A view from the council', in Peter Biskup and Margaret Henty (eds), *Library for the Nation* (special issue of *Australian Academic and Research Libraries*), Canberra, 1991, pp. 14–20

'A user's perspective', in Peter Clayton and Russell McCaskie (eds), *Priorities for the Future: Proceedings of the First National Reference and Information Service Conference*, Australian Library and Information Association and D.W. Thorpe, Port Melbourne, 1992, pp. 147–9

'Social democracy: Australia's record', in Peter Vintila, John Phillimore and Peter Newman (eds), *Markets, Morals and Manifestos: 'Fightback' and the Politics of Economic Rationalism in the 1990s*, Institute for Science and Technology Policy, Murdoch University, 1992, pp. 13–20; reprinted as 'Radicals and conservatives', *Australian Left Review*, no. 144, 1992, pp. 26–31

'"The blessed reign of mobocracy": George Higinbotham and the Maritime Strike', in Jim Hagan and Andrew Wells (eds), *The Maritime Strike: A Centennial Retrospective. Essays in Honour of E.C. Fry*, University of Wollongong Labour History Research Group in conjunction with the Australian Society for the Study of Labour History, Wollongong, 1992, pp. 59–67

'Ever new, my after fame shall grow', in *Change and Tradition: A Portrait of the University of Melbourne*, University of Melbourne, Melbourne, 1993, pp. 46–51

'Cultural and intellectual changes', in John Mulvaney and Colin Steele (eds), *Changes in Scholarly Communications: Australia and the Electronic Library*, Australian Academy of the Humanities, Canberra, 1993, pp. 175–8

'People's treasures, people's history: Using and interpreting the national collection', in John Thompson (ed.), *The People's Treasures: Collections in the National Library of Australia*, National Library of Australia, Canberra, 1993, pp. 6–13

'Les syndicalismes d'Oceanie: Une importation européenne', in Jean Sagnes (ed.), *Histoire du Syndicalisme dans le Monde: Des Origins a Nos Jours*, Editions Privat, Toulouse, 1994, pp. 375–85

'The making of the Australian working class: An historiographical survey', in Penny Russell and Richard White (eds), *Pastiche I: Reflections on Nineteenth-century Australia*, Allen & Unwin, Sydney, 1994, pp. 121–39

'The new republican temper', in David Headon, James Warden and Bill Gammage (eds), *Crown or Country: The Traditions of Australian Republicanism*, Allen & Unwin, Sydney, 1994, pp. 107–17

'True for the moment', in Bain Attwood (ed.), *Labour Histories*, Monash Publications in History, Clayton, Vic, 1994, pp. 13–27

'Always a pace or two apart' in Carl Bridge (ed.), *Manning Clark: Essays on His Place in History*, Melbourne University Press, Melbourne, 1994, pp. 17–29

'Australia 1901–1939', in Susan Bambrick (ed.), *The Cambridge Encyclopedia of Australia*, Cambridge University Press, Cambridge, 1994, pp. 102–9

'History', in Ken Inglis (ed.), *Geoffrey Serle: In Tribute*, National Library of Australia, Canberra, 1994, pp. 1–4. Reprinted 1998

'Australasia and Oceania', in Mary Beth Norton and Pamela Gerardi (eds), *The American Historical Association's Guide to Historical Literature*, 3rd edition, Oxford University Press, New York, 1995, pp. 1526–46

'Introduction' to Stuart Macintyre (ed.), *'And Be One People': Alfred Deakin's Federal Story*, Melbourne University Press, Melbourne, 1995, pp. vii–xxviii

'Ernest Scott: "My history is a romance"', in Stuart Macintyre and Julian Thomas (eds), *The Discovery of Australian History 1890–1939*, Melbourne University Press, Melbourne, 1995, pp. 71–90

'After social justice', in Peter Saunders and Sheila Shaver (eds), *Social Policy and the Challenges of Social Change. Proceedings of the National Social Policy Conference, Sydney, 5–7 July 1995*, University of New South Wales, Sydney, 1995, vol. 1, pp. 1–13

'Teaching citizenship', in Lyn Yates (ed.), *Citizenship and Education*, special issue of *Melbourne Studies in Education*, La Trobe University Press, Bundoora, Vic, 1995, pp. 7–20

Anthony Day, David Goodman, Barry Hindess, Stuart Macintyre and David Marr, 'Perceiving citizenship', in Anthony Milner and Mary

Quilty (eds), *Australia in Asia: Comparing Cultures*, Oxford University Press, Melbourne, 1996, pp. 224–52

'Diversity, citizenship and the curriculum', in Kerry Kennedy (ed.), *New Challenges for Civics and Citizenship Education*, Australian Curriculum Studies Association, Belconnen, ACT, 1996, pp. 23–8

'Citizenship and education', in S. Rufus Davis (ed.), *Citizenship in Australia: Democracy, Law and Society*, Constitutional Centenary Foundation, Melbourne, 1996, pp. 225–40

'Foreword' to Manning Clark, *Speaking Out of Turn: Lectures and Speeches 1940–1991*, Melbourne University Press, Melbourne, 1997, pp. vii–xi

'Preface' to Wayne Hudson and Geoffrey Bolton (eds), *Creating Australia: Changing Australian History*, Allen & Unwin, Sydney, 1997, pp. ix–xiii

'A federal commonwealth, an Australian citizenship', *The Constitution Makers. Papers on Parliament*, No. 30, Senate, Canberra, 1997, pp. 19–32

'History', in Reference Group for the Australian Academy of the Humanities, *Knowing Ourselves and Others: The Humanities in Australia into the 21st Century*, Australian Research Council, National Board of Employment, Education and Training, Canberra, 1998, vol. 2, pp. 139–50; and modified version in Academy of the Social Sciences in Australia, *Challenges for the Social Sciences and Australia*, Australian Research Council, National Board of Employment, Education and Training, Canberra, 1998, vol. 1, pp. 129–40

'The present state of labour history', in Jim Hagan and Andrew Wells (eds), *Australian Labour and Regional Change: Essays in Honour of R.A. Gollan*, Halstead Press and University of Wollongong, Rushcutters Bay, NSW, 1998, pp. 23–30

'The idea of the people', in *The People's Conventions: Corowa (1893) and Bathurst (1896). Papers on Parliament*, No. 32, Department of the Senate, Canberra, 1998, pp. 76–9

'Did the people make laws?', in Ian Copland and John Rickard (eds), *Federalism: Comparative Perspectives from India and Australia*, Manohar Publishers, New Delhi, 1999, pp. 209–14

(With Simon Marginson) 'The university and its public', in Tony Coady (ed.), *Why Universities Matter: A Conversation about Values, Means and Directions*, Allen & Unwin, St Leonards, NSW, 1999, pp. 49–71

'Australia and the Empire', in Robin Winks (ed.), *The Oxford History of the British Empire*, vol. 5: *Historiography*, Oxford University Press, Oxford, 1999, pp. 163–81

'The fortunes of Federation', in David Headon and John Williams (eds), *Makers of Miracles: The Cast of the Federation Story*, Melbourne University Press, Melbourne, 2000, pp. 3–17

(With Fay Anderson) 'Crawford as controversialist', in Stuart Macintyre
    and Peter McPhee (eds), *Max Crawford's School of History*, History
    Department, University of Melbourne, Melbourne, 2000, pp. 89–112
'History in a new country: Australians debate their past', in Rolf
    Torstendahl (ed.), *An Assessment of Twentieth-century Historiography*, Royal
    Academy of Letters, History and Antiquity, Stockholm, 2000, pp. 70–88
'Alfred Deakin', in Michelle Grattan (ed.), *Australian Prime Ministers*, New
    Holland Publishers, Sydney, 2000, pp. 36–53
'The library and the political life of the nation', in Peter Cochrane (ed.),
    *Remarkable Occurrences: The National Library of Australia's First 100 Years,
    1901–2001*, National Library of Australia, Canberra, 2001, pp. 123–44
(With John Faulkner) 'Introduction', in John Faulkner and Stuart
    Macintyre (eds), *True Believers: The Story of the Federal Parliamentary Labor
    Party*, Allen & Unwin, Crows Nest, NSW, 2001, pp. xx–xxxi
'The first caucus', in John Faulkner and Stuart Macintyre (eds), *True
    Believers: The Story of the Federal Parliamentary Labor Party*, Allen &
    Unwin, Crows Nest, NSW, 2001, pp. 17–29
'"Full of hits and misses": A reappraisal of Hancock's *Australia*', in D.A.
    Low (ed.), *Keith Hancock: The Legacies of an Historian*, Melbourne
    University Press, Melbourne, 2001, pp. 33–57
'Traditions', in *Position Papers: National Humanities and Social Sciences
    Summit*, ANU, Canberra, 2001, pp. 65–74
'The Communist Party as publisher', in Martyn Lyons and John Arnold
    (eds), *A History of the Book in Australia 1891–1945*, University of
    Queensland Press, St Lucia, 2001, pp. 51–4
'"Temper democratic, Bias Australian": One hundred years of the
    Australian Labor Party', in Peter Craven (ed.), *The Best Australian Essays
    2001*, Black Inc., Melbourne, 2001, pp. 161–76
'Alfred Deakin: His "sacred service"', in Marian Simms (ed.), *1901: The
    Forgotten Election*, University of Queensland Press, St Lucia, 2001,
    pp. 41–56
'Federation and the labour movement', in Mark Hearn and Greg Patmore
    (eds), *Working Life and Federation 1890–1914*, Pluto Press, Annandale,
    NSW, 2001, pp. 11–28
'Introduction', in Helen Irving and Stuart Macintyre (eds), *J.A. La Nauze.
    No Ordinary Act: Essays on Federation and the Constitution*, Melbourne
    University Press, Melbourne, 2001, pp. 1–23
'"Funny you should ask for that": Higher education as a market', in
    Simon Cooper, John Hinkson and Geoff Sharp (eds), *Scholars and
    Entrepreneurs*, Arena Publications, North Carlton, Vic, 2002, pp. 79–90
'Introduction' to Beverley Symons, *Communism in Australia: A*

Supplementary Resource Bibliography, Sydney Branch, Australian Society for the Study of Labour History, Sydney, 2002, pp. v–vii

'The nation-building project in the antipodes', in Arthur Grimes, Lydia Wevers and Ginny Sullivan (eds), *States of Mind: Australia and New Zealand 1901–2002*, Institute of Strategic Studies, Victoria University of Wellington, Wellington, 2002, pp. 3–14

'Blainey and the Australian historical profession', in Deborah Gare, Geoffrey Bolton, Stuart Macintyre and Tom Stannage (eds), *The Fuss That Never Ended: The Life and Work of Geoffrey Blainey*, Melbourne University Press, Melbourne, 2003, pp. 1–14

'Safeguarding Australia', in *The Humanities and Australia's National Research Priorities*, Australian Academy of the Humanities, Canberra, 2003, pp. 30–4

'The new line in the antipodes: Australian communists and class against class', in Matthew Worley (ed.), *In Search of Revolution: International Communist Parties in the Third Period*, I.B. Tauris, London, 2004, pp. 247–69

'Humanities in the knowledge economy', in Jane Kenway, Elizabeth Bullen and Simon Robb (eds), *Innovation and Tradition: The Arts, Humanities and the Knowledge Economy*, Peter Lang, New York, 2004, pp. 23–34

(With Joe Isaac) 'Introduction', in Joe Isaac and Stuart Macintyre (eds), *The New Province for Law and Order: 100 Years of Australian Industrial Conciliation and Arbitration*, Cambridge University Press, Cambridge, 2004, pp. 1–16

Stuart Macintyre, 'Arbitration in action', in Joe Isaac and Stuart Macintyre (eds), *The New Province for Law and Order: 100 Years of Australian Industrial Conciliation and Arbitration*, Cambridge University Press, Cambridge, 2004, pp. 55–97

'Introduction', in Barry Howarth and Ewan Maidment (eds), *Light from the Tunnel: Collecting the Archives of Australian Business and Labour at the Australian National University 1953–2003*, Friends of the Noel Butlin Archives Centre, Canberra, 2004, pp. 1–8

'The History Wars', in *Chasing Shadows: The Use and Abuse of History, 2003 Independent Scholars Association of Australia Annual Conference Proceedings*, ISAA, Canberra, 2004, pp. 66–70

'Alfred Deakin: A centenary tribute', *The Distinctive Foundations of Australian Democracy*, Papers on Parliament, No. 42, Senate, Canberra, 2004, pp. 1–12

'Universities and the idea of quality', in Rob Carmichael (ed.), *Quality in a Time of Change: Proceedings of the Australian Universities Quality Forum*

2004, Adelaide, 7–9 July 2004, Australian Universities Quality Agency, Melbourne, 2004, pp. 19–25

'Australia: History', in *The Far East and Australasia,* Europa Publications, London, 36th edition, 2004, pp. 52–9; revised for subsequent editions, 2005–16

'Introduction' to Melissa Reeves, *The Spook,* Currency Press, Sydney, 2005, pp. vii–xii

'History wars and the imperial legacy in the settler societies', in Philip Buckner and R. Douglas Francis (eds), *Rediscovering the British World,* University of Calgary Press, Calgary, 2005, pp. 381–98

'1880–1914', in Peter Beilharz and Trevor Hogan (eds), *Sociology: Place, Time and Division,* Oxford University Press, Melbourne, 2006, pp. 168–174

'What if Australia's baptism of fire had occurred at Cocos Islands?', in Stuart Macintyre and Sean Scalmer (eds), *What If? Australian History as it Might Have Been,* Melbourne University Press, Melbourne, 2006, pp. 115–37

(With Fay Anderson) 'History in the headlines', in Fay Anderson and Stuart Macintyre (eds), *The Life of the Past: The Discipline of History at the University of Melbourne,* RMIT Publishing, Melbourne, 2006, pp. 355–76

(With Fay Anderson) 'The honours graduates, 1967–2002', in Fay Anderson and Stuart Macintyre (eds), *The Life of the Past: The Discipline of History at the University of Melbourne,* RMIT Publishing, Melbourne, 2006, pp. 395–422

(With Gordon Boyce and Simon Ville) 'Investing in the inter-organisational domain', and 'Conclusion: Building collaborative capabilities', in Gordon Boyce, Stuart Macintyre and Simon Ville (eds), *How Organisations Connect: Investing in Communication,* Melbourne University Press, Melbourne, 2006, pp. 1–7, 198–208

'Universities', in Clive Hamilton (ed.), *Silencing Dissent,* Allen & Unwin, St Leonards, NSW, 2007, pp. 41–59

'Communist Party History', in David Clune and Ken Turner (eds), *Writing Party History: Papers from a Symposium Held at Parliament House, Sydney, May 2006,* New South Wales Parliamentary Library, Sydney, 2007, pp. 65–74

'Introduction', in Stuart Macintyre and Sheila Fitzpatrick (eds), *Against the Grain: Brian Fitzpatrick and Manning Clark in Australian History and Politics,* Melbourne University Press, Melbourne, 2007, pp. 1–11

'The radical and the mystic: Brian Fitzpatrick, Manning Clark and Australian history', in Stuart Macintyre and Sheila Fitzpatrick (eds),

Against the Grain: Brian Fitzpatrick and Manning Clark in Australian History and Politics, Melbourne University Press, Melbourne, 2007, pp. 12–36

'Foreword' to reissue of L.A. La Nauze, *Alfred Deakin: A Biography*, Miegunyah Press, Melbourne, 2009, pp. v–xii

'Whatever happened to Deakinite liberalism?', in Nick Dyrenfurth and Paul Strangio (eds), *'Con/Fusion: The Making of the Australian Two-party System*, Melbourne University Press, Melbourne, 2009, pp. 227–47

'Political history', in Rod Rhodes (ed.), *The Australian Study of Politics*, Palgrave Macmillan, London, 2009, pp. 84–96

'Academic freedom', in Eva Baker, Penelope Peterson and Barry McGaw (eds), *The International Encyclopedia of Education*, 3rd edition, Elsevier, Oxford, 2010, vol. 4, pp. 328–33

(With Juan Maiguashca and Attila Pók) 'Introduction', in Stuart Macintyre, Juan Maiguashca and Attila Pók (eds), *The Oxford History of Historical Writing*, vol. 4: *1800–1945*, Oxford University Press, Oxford, 2011, pp. 1–15

'Historical writing in Australia and New Zealand', in Stuart Macintyre, Juan Maiguashca and Attila Pók (eds), *The Oxford History of Historical Writing*, vol. 4: *1800–1945*, Oxford University Press, Oxford, 2011, pp. 410–27

'Australia: A European nation in an ancient land', in Peter Furtado (ed.), *Histories of Nations: How Their Identities Were Forged*, Thames & Hudson, London, 2012, pp. 222–31

'The political landscape', in Michelle Hetherington (ed.), *Glorious Days: Australia 1913*, National Museum of Australia, Canberra, 2013, pp. 49–57

'It won't always be like this', in Ross Fitzgerald and Ken Spillman (eds), *Australia's Game*, Slattery Media Group, Melbourne, 2013, pp. 200–5

(With Alison Bashford) 'Introduction', in *The Cambridge History of Australia*, vol. 1: *Indigenous and Colonial Australia*, Cambridge University Press, Cambridge, 2013, pp. 1–13

(With Sean Scalmer) 'Colonial states and civil society, 1860–1890', in *The Cambridge History of Australia*, vol. 1: *Indigenous and Colonial Australia*, Cambridge University Press, Cambridge, 2013, pp. 189–217

(With Alison Bashford) 'Introduction', in *The Cambridge History of Australia*, vol. 2: *The Commonwealth of Australia*, Cambridge University Press, Cambridge, 2013, pp. 1–12

(With Sean Scalmer) 'Class', in *The Cambridge History of Australia*, vol. 2: *The Commonwealth of Australia*, Cambridge University Press, Cambridge, 2013, pp. 358–76

'Labour history and radical nationalism', in Anna Clark and Paul Ashton (eds), *Australian History Now*, NewSouth Publishing, Sydney, 2013, pp. 40–55

(With Gwilym Croucher, Glyn Davis and Simon Marginson) 'Making the unified system', in Gwilym Croucher, Simon Marginson, Andrew Norton and Julie Wells (eds), *The Dawkins Revolution 25 Years On*, Melbourne University Press, Melbourne, 2013, pp. 9–55

"More Scotch abroad than home": The Australian Scots', in *For Auld Lang Syne: Images of Scottish Australia from First Fleet to Federation*, Art Gallery of Ballarat, Ballarat, 2014, pp. 63–82

'The Post-War Reconstruction project', in Sam Furphy (ed.), *Seven Dwarfs and the Age of Mandarins: Australian Government Administration in the Post-war Era*, ANU Press, Canberra, 2015, pp. 31–51

(With Tony Taylor) 'Cultural wars and history textbooks in democratic societies', in Mario Carretero, Stefan Berger and Maria Grever (eds), *Palgrave Handbook of Research in Historical Culture and Education*, Palgrave Macmillan, London, 2017, pp. 613–35

'Bust and boom: What economic lessons has Australia learned?', in David Stephens and Alison Broinowski (eds), *The Honest History Book*, NewSouth Publishing, Sydney, 2017, pp. 167–80

'Geoffrey Bolton: A lifetime of history', in Stuart Macintyre, Lenore Layman and Jenny Gregory (eds), *A Historian for All Seasons: Essays for Geoffrey Bolton*, Monash University Publishing, Melbourne, 2017, pp. 1–39

'Labor reconstructs: The 1940s and 1970s', in Jenny Hocking (ed.), *Making Modern Australia: The Whitlam Government's 21st-century Agenda*, Monash University Publishing, Melbourne, 2017, pp. 181–210

'Reading post-war reconstruction through national and transnational lenses', in Anna Clark, Anne Rees and Alecia Simmonds (eds), *Transnationalism, Nationalism and Australia History*, Palgrave Macmillan, Singapore, 2017, pp. 133–45

'South Australia, the pivotal state', in Carolyn Collins and Paul Sendziuk (eds), *Foundational Fictions in South Australian History*, Wakefield Press, Adelaide, 2018, pp. 133–49

'Understanding the Australian curriculum', in Tim Allender, Anna Clark and Robert Parkes (eds), *Historical Thinking for History Teachers*, Allen & Unwin, Sydney, 2019, pp. 18–30

'Useful knowledge: The contribution of universities to government between the wars', in Kate Darian-Smith and James Waghorne (eds), *The First World War, the Universities and the Professions: The Rise of Knowledge and Expertise in Australia*, Melbourne University Press, Melbourne, 2019, pp. 235–48

Articles

'Radical history and bourgeois hegemony', *Intervention*, no. 2, 1972, pp. 47–73

'Joseph Dietzgen and British working-class education', *Bulletin of the Society for the Study of Labour History*, no. 29, 1974, pp. 50–4

'Socialism, the unions and the Labour Party after 1918', *Bulletin of the Society for the Study of Labour History*, no. 31, 1975, pp. 101–11

'British labour, Marxism and working-class apathy in the 1920s', *Historical Journal*, n.s. vol. 20, 1977, pp. 479–96

'The concept of class in recent labourist historiography: Early socialism and labor', *Intervention*, no. 8, 1977, pp. 79–87.

'The making of the Australian working class: An historiography survey', *Historical Studies*, vol. 18, 1978, pp. 233–53; reprinted in Penny Russell and Richard White (eds), *Pastiche I: Reflections on Nineteenth-century Australia*, Allen & Unwin, Sydney, 1994, pp. 131–39

'Class in Volume Four of Clark's *A History of Australia*', *Australia 1988*, no. 3, 1979, pp. 48–52

'Some recent labour history', *Historical Journal*, vol. 22, no. 3, 1979, pp. 729–30

'In my mind the next vivid scene was …', *Studies in Western Australian History*, n.s. no. 5, 1981, pp. 79–85

'Manning Clark's critics', *Meanjin*, no. 4, 1982, pp. 442–52

'Righteousness and the Right: Twenty-five years of *Quadrant*', *Overland*, no. 92, 1983, pp. 21–6

'*Historical Studies*: A retrospective', *Historical Studies*, vol. 21, 1984, pp. 1–10

'What is labour history?', *Time Remembered*, no. 6, 1984, pp. 1–20

'Can a general history embrace an inclusive curriculum?', *Agora*, no. 21, 1986, pp. 2–6

'The short history of social democracy in Australia', *Thesis Eleven*, no. 15, 1986, pp. 3–14

'Hughes and the historians', *Meanjin*, no. 2, 1987, pp. 243–8

'Work in society: The weight of history', *Australian Historical Association Bulletin*, no. 51, 1987, pp. 7–15

'Holt and the establishment of arbitration: An Australian perspective', *New Zealand Journal of Industrial Relations*, vol. 12, 1987, pp. 151–9

'Raymond Williams and history', *Southern Review*, vol. 22, 1989, pp. 149–51

'Paradise lost: Conditions for the workers', *Bulletin of the Centre for Tasmanian Historical Studies*, vol. 2, no. 2, 1990, pp. 62–71

'The meanings of the clever country', *Australian Universities Review*, vol. 34, no. 1, 1991, pp. 34–7

'Blood, sweat and fears', *Eureka Street*, vol. 1, no. 4, 1991, pp. 8–10

'S.W. Carey', *Australian Geologist*, no. 82, 1992, pp. 11–13

'Raymond Maxwell Crawford 1906–1991', *Australian Historical Studies*, vol. 25, no. 98, pp. 123–5

'Collected wisdom: Libraries and the national character', *Voices*, vol. 2, no. 2, 1992, pp. 29–40

'History, a school for statecraft: or, How shall we sing the Lord's song in a strange land?', 1992 Eldershaw Memorial Lecture, *Tasmanian Historical Research Association Papers and Proceedings*, vol. 39, no. 3, 1992, pp. 105–17

'Libraries, information management and cultural heritage', *Australian Public Libraries and Information Services*, vol. 5, nos 3–4, 1992, pp. 174–81

'Response', *Australian Historical Studies*, vol. 25, no. 100, 1993, pp. 398–402

'Foundation', *Overland*, no. 132, 1993, pp. 6–12

'Foundations: The early history of the Australian Communist Party', *Left History*, vol. 1, no. 2, 1993, pp. 51–62

'Why do the Tories hate Manning Clark?', *Evatt Papers*, vol. 1, no. 2, 1993, pp. 17–20

'Corowa and the voice of the people', *Canberra Historical Journal*, n.s. no. 33, 1994, pp. 2–8, reprinted in Patricia Clarke (ed.), *Steps to Federation: Lectures Marking the Centenary of Federation*, Australian Scholarly Publishing, Melbourne, 2001, pp. 39–54, and *The People's Conventions: Corowa (1893) and Bathurst (1896), Papers on Parliament*, No. 32, Department of the Senate, Canberra, 1998, pp. 76–9

'Traiter avec Moscou: Le Komintern at les premières années du Parti communiste d'Australie', *Le Mouvement Social*, no. 167, 1994, pp. 99–120; reprinted as 'Dealing with Moscow: The Comintern and the early history of the Communist Party of Australia', *Labour History*, no. 67, 1994, pp. 128–43

'Deakin and the sovereignty of the people', *Voices*, vol. 4, no. 2, 1994, pp. 8–18

'After Corowa', *Victorian Historical Journal*, vol. 65, no. 2, 1994, pp. 98–112

'"Whereas the people have agreed to unite": The Commonwealth and its makers', *Voices*, vol. 4, no. 4, 1994–95, pp. 5–16

'Who are the true believers? The Manning Clark Labor History Memorial Lecture', *Labour History*, no. 68, 1995, pp. 155–67

'What about the books?', *La Trobe Library Journal*, vol. 14, no. 55, 1995, pp. 1–9

'The legacy of Sir Robert Menzies', *Voices*, vol. 5, no. 2, 1995, pp. 6–11

'An expert's confession', *Australian Quarterly*, vol. 67, no. 3, 1995, pp. 1–12

'Visions for democratic process', *Social Educator: Journal of the Social Education Association of Australia*, vol. 14, no. 3, 1995, pp. 14–20

'Civics and citizenship education and the teaching of history', *Unicorn: Journal of the Australian College of Education*, vol. 22, no. 1, 1996, pp. 59–63

'Diversity, citizenship and the curriculum', *Crossings: The Bulletin of the International Australian Studies Association*, vol. 10, no. 1, 1996, pp. 13–21

'Civics education: A progress report', *Fine Print: A Journal of Adult English Language and Literacy Education*, vol. 19, no. 4, 1996, pp. 3–4

'The genie and the bottle: Putting history back into the school curriculum', *History Teacher: Magazine of the Queensland History Teachers' Association*, vol. 34, no. 4, 1996, pp. 12–18

'Discipline review: History', *Australian Historical Association Bulletin*, no. 83, 1996, pp. 1–13

'The genie and the bottle: Putting history back into the school curriculum', and 'Response', *Australian Journal of Education*, vol. 41, no. 2, 1997, pp. 189–98, 213–15

'Bloodstained wattle or red heather? The Scottish strain in the Australian labour movement', *Australian Studies*, vol. 12, no. 2, 1997, pp. 91–103

'The third time as rodomontade', *Overland*, no. 150, 1998, pp. 5–10; reprinted in *Labor Herald*, June 1998

'Some absentees from Adelaide', *New Federalist: The Journal of Australian Federation History*, no. 1, 1998, pp. 16–19

'Coming to the party', *EQ Australia*, no. 3, 1998, pp. 10–12

'Max Crawford: A casualty of the Cold War', *Overland*, no. 155, 1999, pp. 19–22

'The future of history', *Australian Quarterly*, vol. 71, no. 6, 1999, pp. 8–11

'Patrick Troy: Public good and the intellectual', *Urban Policy and Research*, vol. 18, no. 2, 2000, pp. 145–58

'Prologue', *International Journal of the History of Sport*, vol. 17, nos 2–3, 2000, pp. 1–8

'One hundred years of the Australian Labor Party', *Overland*, no. 162, 2001, pp. 4–12; reprinted in Peter Craven (ed.), *The Best Australian Essays 2001*, Black Inc., Melbourne, 2001, pp. 161–76

'A case against Parkes', *New Federalist*, no. 8, 2001, pp. 29–30

'The History Wars', *Sydney Papers*, vol. 15, nos 3–4, 2003, pp. 77–83

'Reviewing the History Wars', *Labour History*, no. 85, 2003, pp. 213–16

'The History Wars', *Journal of Australian Colonial History*, vol. 4, no. 2, 2002 [published March 2004], pp. 1–19

'An historian's perspective', *Australian Journal of Political Science*, vol. 39, no. 1, 2004, pp. 31–4

'History, politics and the philosophy of history', *Australian Historical Studies*, vol. 35, no. 123, 2004, pp. 130–6

'Robin Gollan (1917–2007)', *Labour History*, no. 94, 2008, pp. 7–10

'The social sciences in Australia: An unrequited instrumentalism', *Thesis Eleven*, no. 94, 2008, pp. 5–19

(With Noel Simpson) 'Consensus and division in Australian citizenship education', *Citizenship Studies*, vol. 13, no. 2, 2009, pp. 119–32

'The poor relation: Establishing the social sciences in Australia, 1940–1970', *Australian Historical Studies*, vol. 40, no. 1, 2009, pp. 46–61

'The same under different skies: The university in the United States and Australia', *Journal of Australian Studies*, vol. 33, no. 3, 2009, pp. 353–69

'The rebirth of political history', *Australian Journal of Politics and History*, vol. 56, no. 1, 2010, pp. 1–5

'The challenges for history in the new curriculum', *EQ Australia*, Summer 2010, pp. 21–2

'Gold, democracy and Eureka', *Tinte'an*, no. 15, 2011, pp. 22–7

'The poor relation', Keith Hancock Lecture for 2010, *Dialogue*, vol. 30, no. 1, 2011, pp. 11–20

'Family fortunes and the global financial crisis', *Dialogue*, vol. 30, no. 1, 2011, pp. 59–61

'What makes a good biography?', *Adelaide Law Review*, vol. 32, no. 1, 2011, pp. 7–16

'Women's leadership in war and reconstruction', *Labour History*, no. 104, 2013, pp. 65–80

'"A sense of tradition": R.J.W. Selleck and the purpose of educational history', *Journal of Educational Administration and History*, vol. 41, no. 2, 2014, pp. 117–24

'Tipped out of the cradle: The academic fortunes of political studies', *Australian Review of Public Affairs*, vol. 13, no. 1, 2015

'Owners and tenants: The Commonwealth Housing Commission and post-war housing, 1943–1949', *Australian Economic History Review*, vol. 58, no. 3, 2018, pp. 265–82

'History and heritage', *Victorian Historical Journal*, vol. 89, no. 2, 2018, pp. 214–26

(With Anna Clark, Stefan Berger and Marnie Hughes-Warrington) 'What is history? Historiography roundtable—History and historiography', *Rethinking History*, vol. 22, no. 4, 2018, pp. 500–24

(With Tyson Retz) 'The Honours conception of history', *History Australia*, vol. 15, no. 4, 2018, pp. 804–22

'From Bolshevism to populism: Australia in a century of global transformation', *ANU Historical Journal II*, no. 1, 2019, pp. 207–22

Index

Aarons, Sam, 73
Abbott, Tony, 346
ABC, 184
Aboriginal history, 159
academic authority, declining of, 160
academic autonomy, 317–18
academic citizenship, 226
'Academic freedom' (Macintyre), 317–18
Academy of Social Sciences in Australia, 211, 212, 214, 332
Adams, Phillip, 303, 304
Adler, Louise, 301
Against the Grain (Macintyre & B. Fitzpatrick), 122, 123–4, 156
Age (newspaper), 93, 94–5, 99–100
Ah Mouy, Louis, 97–9
Alexander, Fred, 144
ALP. *See* Australian Labor Party
ALP–ACTU Accord, 8, 52, 191, 347
Althusser, Louis, 4, 5, 21–2, 28, 35, 40, 200
Althusser and Marxist Theory (Macintyre & Tribe), 21, 34
Althusserian moment, 4, 23, 34, 49, 150
Althusserianism, 29, 34, 35, 49, 151, 154
Anderson, Perry, 35, 150, 151
Andrews, Shirley, 55
Anthropology, rise as university discipline, 207
anti-political politics, 116–17
arbitration, 109–14, 347
Arena (journal), 150–1
Argus (newspaper), 93
Arthur, George, 215
Atkinson, Alan, 78, 243, 307
Australia (Hancock), 155, 159
Australian Academy of the Humanities, 332

Australian American Education Foundation, 168
Australian communism
    and Australian radicalism, 56–7
    internationalist perspective, 7
    Macintyre's publications on, 1–2, 7–8, 47, 49, 53–6, 57–9
    non-party communism, 60, 70
    ordinary communists, 54
    Stalinism, 47–8
    Western Australian exceptionalism, 73
Australian Football League, 268–9
Australian historians, Macintyre's studies of, 149–55
Australian Historical Association, 162, 252
Australian Historical Studies (journal), 91–2, 238, 240, 244, 332
Australian Labor Party, 58, 59
    Accord with unions, 8, 52, 191, 347
    arbitration and, 111–12
    centenary history of Federal Parliamentary Party, 118
    deflationary politics, 347
    and democracy, 114–15
    education policy, 320–6
    emergence, 338–9
    and federal Constitution, 114–16, 117
    foundation and early decades, 340–3
    full employment policy, 344–5
    Hawke-Keating era, 108
    history of, 335–6
    ideological narrowness, 114
    Macintyre's membership, 48, 118
    nationalism, 116
    place and function of mythos, 336, 347–9
    precocity, 114

Australian Left Review (journal), 151
Australian liberalism, 203
Australian Liberalism and National Character
   (Rowse), 5
Australian nation, foundational values and
   institutions, 107
Australian National University, 213
Australian Natives Association, 286
Australian radicalism, 49, 56–7, 60–1
Australian Republican Movement, 117
Australian Research Council, 252, 317
Australian Research Grants, 209
Australian Society for the Study of Labour
   History, 65, 118, 162, 225, 226
Australian Unlimited, 9
Australians
   A Historical Dictionary, 257
Australians
   A Historical Library (Gilbert, Inglis &
   Foster, eds), 238

Barton, Edmund, 98, 117, 282, 284, 285, 286
Bashford, Alison, 13
Batman, John, 303–5
Bauman, Zygmunt, 192, 200
Beilharz, Peter, 15–16
Belich, James, 11
Benn, Tony, 24
Bicentenary, 237–9, 297
Bigge, J.T., 215
biography writing, 66, 68–9, 76–7, 134, 135,
   136, 137–8, 139
Birch, Tony, 303, 305
'black armband' history, 119, 243, 298
Black War, 273
Blackball coal mine, 269
Blackbourn, David, 23
Blackburn, Jean, 55
Blainey, Geoffrey, 133, 156–7, 160, 161, 243,
   253, 259, 260, 261, 298, 355
Bolshevism, 59
Bolton, Geoffrey, 11, 150, 235, 354
Bongiorno, Frank, 10, 180, 258
Boston, Ken, 280, 356
Botany Bay Project, 213
Bourke, Paul, 92, 213
Branson, Noreen, 45n23
Brett, André, 321, 324
Brett, Judith, 259
Brewster, Ben, 21, 25n1

'Brian Fitzpatrick and the world outside
   Australia' (S. Fitzpatrick), 123–4
Bridge, Carl, 243, 260
British communism
   histories of, 29
   Macintyre's publications on, 6, 27, 29,
      36–43
   See also Communist Party of Great Britain
      History Group
British imperial values, 141
British imperialism, 286
British Marxist historiography, 28–9, 30–5
Broome, Richard, 259
Bruce–Page government, 168
Bruley, Sue, 32
Buckley, Ken, 240
Burnett, John, 305
Button, John, 260
Byrne, Liam, 14

Cain Labor government (Vic), 191
Cairns, Jim, 48
Cambridge Communist Party, 21
The Cambridge History of Australia (Bashford
   & Macintyre, eds), 231–3, 245
Cambridge Marxism Seminar, 21, 23
Cambridge Social History Seminar, 23,
   25–6n4, 31
Cambridge University, 23–4
capital, 217–18
Carr, Bob, 300
Castles, Francis, 112, 191
Castoriadis, Cornelius, 5
Chakrabarty, Dipesh, 302
Cheong, Cheok Hong, 97–9, 100, 102
Chifley, Ben, 178–9, 180, 181, 287, 291, 342,
   344, 357
Chifley Labor government, 174
Childe, V.G., 4, 70
Chinese immigrants
   Chinese Australians' arguments against
      exclusion, 98–9, 100–1, 102
   government attempts to exclude, 95–6
   legal challenge to exclusion, 100–1
   liberals' arguments against exclusion, 101–3
   liberals' arguments for exclusion, 96–7,
      99–101
   treatment in Australian colonies, 98–9
   as unmanly, 96
   on Victorian goldfields, 95
Chinese Immigration Act 1955 (Vic), 95

Chinese Influx Restriction Act 1881 (Vic), 96
The Chinese Question in Australia (Lowe, Cheong & Ah Mouy), 97–8
Chung Teong Toy v. Musgrove, 100–1
citizenship, 218–19
civic deficit, 279–80
civics and citizenship education, 280, 292, 355–6
Civics Expert Group, 280, 292
civil liberties, 168–9
Clark, Anna, 159
Clark, Manning, 122, 123, 124–5, 134, 145, 146, 157–8, 159, 161, 239, 253
Class and Politics (Rickard), 267
class inequality, 50
Coastal Dock Rivers and Harbour Works Union, 71–2, 73, 77
Coghlan, T.A., 302
Cold War, 69
collegiality, 318–19, 320
colonial liberalism, 4
  Aboriginal peoples and, 102
  manliness, 94–5, 96
  moral economy of, 215–16
  national sovereign rights, 99, 100, 101
  nationalist liberalism, 103
  racial exclusion. *See* Chinese immigrants
  women's rights, 94, 101, 102
A Colonial Liberalism (Macintyre), 92–3, 94, 102–4, 215–16, 268
Commonwealth Court of Conciliation and Arbitration, 110
Commonwealth Employment Service, 182
Commonwealth powers, 287–9
Commonwealth Reconstruction Training Scheme, 182
communism
  differentiated from Marxism, 6
  See also Australian communism; British communism
Communist Party Dissolution Act, 167–8
Communist Party of Australia
  Carlton branch, 48–9
  Davidson's history of, 56–7, 58
  decline, 49
  dissolution, 52
  education, 217
  influence in national politics, 8
  internal strife, 82
  internationalist perspective, 7
  Left Tendency, 4

loss of revolutionary zeal, 58–9
Macintyre's membership, 48–9, 160
Macintyre's writings on, 7–8, 47, 49, 53–6, 57–9, 61–2
mainstreaming of, 52
membership numbers, 60
repression of communists in World War II, 70–1
Stalinism, 47–8, 52, 53–4, 57
during World War II, 70
Communist Party of Great Britain
  Communist University of London, 36
  first academic history of, 31
  sixtieth anniversary, 32, 43
Communist Party of Great Britain History Group
  conferences, 30, 32
  courses, 36
  membership, 30
  official historians, 30, 35
  Our History pamphlets, 28, 30, 39
  publications, 28, 30, 32, 43
  surveys of members, 27
Communist Party of Italy (PCI), 33
communist rhetoric, 56
companion genre, 250–2
compassion, 306–7
Compulsory Arbitration in New Zealand (Holt), 267–8
conceptual history, 193
A Concise History of Australia (Macintyre), 16, 128, 231–2, 241–2, 243–5, 271, 272–4
A Concise History of New Zealand (Mein Smith), 271
consciousness, 154, 255, 300, 307, 338
Constitution, 114–15
Constitutional Convention 1942, 288
Continent of Mystery (Knight), 128
Coombs, H.C., 5, 10, 177–8, 180, 181–2, 185, 186, 213, 287, 344, 357
cosmopolitanism, 98–9
COVID-19, 292
Cowen, Zelman, 101
Crawford, R. M. (Max), 145, 151, 153, 155, 159, 160, 161, 219, 253
Crisp, L.F., 282, 291
Croucher, Gwilym, 321, 324
cultural studies, 273
culture wars, 86, 292
Curthoys, Ann, 13, 81, 82–3, 240–1, 302

Curtin, John, 179–80, 181, 184, 259, 287, 288, 290, 291, 342, 344
Curtin Labor government, 287
Cuthbert, David, 354

Daly, Fred, 353
Damousi, Joy, 10, 13, 133–4, 146
Darian-Smith, Kate, 10, 241
Davidson, Alastair, 8, 56–7, 58
Davis, Glyn, 311
Davison, Graeme, 14, 249–50, 252, 254–5, 259
Dawkins, John, 128
Dawkins reforms, 128, 320–6
Deakin, Alfred, 10, 93, 100, 103, 117, 197, 202, 215, 259, 284, 286
Deery, Phillip, 14, 83
democracy in Australia, 114–18, 292–3
democracy of knowledge, 24
Dening, Greg, 91
Denoon, Donald, 110
Department of Post-War Reconstruction, 177
deradicalisation, 194–5
Devanny, Jean, 55
Dewey, John, 203–4
disciplinarity, 212–14
Discovering Democracy program, 280
Docker, John, 83
Doyle, Helen, 256, 259, 260, 262
Dunlevy, Maurice, 240, 261
Dusevic, Tom, 261, 262

Earsman, Bill, 217
economic rationalism, 4
Economics, rise as university discipline, 207–8
'Elegies of Australian communism' (Beilharz), 15
Eley, Geoff, 4, 21–5, 31, 354, 358
empathy, 306, 307, 308
equality, racial exclusion and, 99–100
equality of opportunity, 197–8
Ernest Scott Chair in History, 133–4, 137
ethics, 306, 307
Eurocommunism, 41
European Marxism, 150
European social democracy, 112, 114
Evatt, H.V., 5, 282, 288, 291, 357
Ewing, T.T., 302

The Fatal Shore (Hughes), 13
Faulkner, John, 118
federal movement, 116–17, 118
Federation
    apathy about commemoration, 284–6
    democracy and, 114–18
    historians' accounts of, 281–3
female historians, 137
feminism, 22, 91, 92, 112, 263
Finnis, John, 200
Fisher, Mark, 203
Fitzpatrick, Brian, 11, 13, 109, 122, 123–5, 145, 152, 156, 161, 181, 221, 266, 337
Fitzpatrick, David, 258
Fitzpatrick, Kathleen, 134, 137, 138, 143–4
Fitzpatrick, Sheila, 13, 123–4, 125–6, 358
Flinders University, 315
Forster, E.M., 118
Forster, John, 40
Fremantle, 66, 67–8, 75, 78
Freud, Sigmund, 5
frontier history, methodological questions, 302–3
Fry, Eric, 225
Fulbright awards, 168
full employment policy, 344–5
Furphy, Joseph, 106

Gallipoli landing, 286
Gammage, Bill, 263
gender, as category of political analysis, 91–2
Gollan, Robin (Bob), 49, 192, 225, 266
Goody, Jack, 5
Google, 262
Gourlay, Stephen, 44n8
Gramsci, Antonio, 7, 22, 33, 150
Griffith University, 315
Grimshaw, Pat, 14

Habermas, Jürgen, 203
Hall, Stuart, 5, 22
Hancock, Keith, 138, 144, 153, 155, 159, 260
Hart, H.L.A, 199
Harvey, Paul, 250, 255, 258
Hasluck, Paul, 180, 353–4
Hawke, Bob, 297
Hawke Labor government, 107, 177, 191, 203, 347
Hawke-Keating era, 176, 191, 340
Healy, Kevin, 71

Henderson, Gerard, 161
Higgins, Esmonde, 221
Higgins, Henry Bournes, 10, 110, 113, 117, 197
higher education policy, 128, 176, 312, 320–6
Higinbotham, George, 93–4, 95, 99, 100, 103
Hill, Christopher, 34, 35, 40
Hindess, Barry, 34, 35
Hirst, Christine, 255
Hirst, John, 92, 115, 117, 249, 252, 254, 255–6, 259, 263, 282, 286, 307
Hirst, Paul, 34, 35
The Historian's Conscience (ed. Macintyre), 77–8, 306–7, 308
historical materialism, 5, 336–7
Historical Studies. See Australian Historical Studies (journal)
historiography, 81, 92, 109, 152, 153–4, 242, 258, 260, 337
History (discipline)
  and liberal culture, 221–2
  Macintyre's views on, 219–21, 253
  politicisation, 303
  threats to, 221
'History, the university and the nation' (Macintyre), 220–1
A History for a Nation (Macintyre), 134, 135, 145, 146–7, 150, 220, 253–4
history from below, 9–10
A History of Australia (M. Clark), 124, 157, 159, 239
History of the Peloponnesian War (Thucydides), 83
History Wars, 86, 161, 238, 243, 244, 262, 272, 296–300, 302, 306–8
The History Wars (Macintyre & A. Clark), 86–7, 150, 156, 159–60, 243, 303
History Workshop movement, 30
Hobsbawm, Eric, 28, 30, 31, 40, 41, 192, 225
Hoey, T.P., 289–90
Holbrook, Carolyn, 355, 356
Holt, Jim, 267–8
Hooton, Joy, 258
Howard, John, 242, 243, 254, 256, 261, 298, 347
Howard Coalition government, 107, 244, 274, 280
Hughes, Billy, 259
Hughes, Robert, 13

human rights, 99
humanism, 34
humanist Marxism, 5
Humphrys, Elizabeth, 203
Hurd, Ron, 73

ideological state apparatuses, 22
immigration restriction, exclusion of Chinese immigrants, 95
Immigration Restriction Bill 1901, 98
Indigenous Australians
  apology to, 243, 297, 299
  cosmology and epistemology, 196–7
  frontier violence, 86, 243, 273, 275n9, 303–5
  historical representations, 141, 142
  protest and activism, 232, 237, 242, 297
  recognition of dispossession, 242–3
  referendum of 1967, 297
  Stolen Generations, 242, 272, 299
Indigenous perspectives, including in Australian history, 302
individualism, 5
industrialism, 194
Inglis, Ken, 150, 161–2, 263
Institute of International Affairs, 158
intellectual work, political action and, 24, 28, 85
intersectionality, 12
Intervention (journal), 4, 49, 112, 150
Irving, Helen, 282
Irving, Terry, 8, 240
Is History Fiction? (Curthoys & Docker), 83
Isaac, Joe, 113
Italian Communist Party (PCI), 32

Jackson, Tommy, 39
Johnson, Boris, 117
Jones, Barry, 259
Jones, Evan, 178

Kalecki, Michał, 195
karaoke, 226
Keating, Paul, 180, 242–3, 261, 280, 298, 299, 346, 355
Keating Labor government, 107, 191, 203, 280, 347
Kelly, Ned, 263
Kemp, David, 357
Keynes, John Maynard, 4
Keynesianism, 178, 190, 194

Kiernan, Victor, 34
The Killing of History (Windschuttle), 301
Kimber, Julie, 14
Kirkby, Diane, 14, 166–7
Klugman, James, 30, 32
Knight, Stephen, 14, 127–30
Kong, Lowe Meng, 97–9

La Nauze, John, 134
La Trobe University, 162, 167, 315
Labor Party. *See* Australian Labor Party
labour colleges, 216–17
The Labour Experiment (Macintyre), 8, 107, 175, 217–18, 340–3
labour history, 9–10
Labour History (journal), 226
labour movement history, 29, 30, 31, 36, 39, 41, 42, 50, 107, 267–8
labour socialism, 38
labourism, 8–9, 342, 347
Labour's Utopias (Beilharz), 15
Laclau, Ernesto, 22
Lake, Marilyn, 5, 244, 263, 307
Latham, John, 167–8
Latour, Bruno, 11
Lawson, Henry, 106
Leach, Edmund, 5
leftist history, practice of, 27
Lenin, Vladimir, 4, 357
Leninism, 59
'less eligibility' principle, 214–15
Levi-Strass, Claude, 5
Lewis, Essington, 9
liberal education, 313–14, 319
liberal hegemony, 4, 5
A Liberal State (Kemp), 357
liberalism
  Australian liberalism, 93, 203
  critiques of, 5
  individualism and, 5
  and Marxism, 3–6
  masculinism and, 5, 94–5, 103
  Macintyre's views on, 110
  nationalist liberalism, 103
  view of justice, 200
  See also colonial liberalism
Life after Dawkins (Brett, Croucher & Macintyre), 324
Little, Graham, 259
Little Moscow (Macintyre), 6, 23, 31, 40–3, 50

Love, Peter, 14
Lukács, Georg, 336–7, 338

Mabo decision, 242, 299
Macintyre, Martha, 5, 7, 24
Macintyre, Stuart
  academic career, 2, 48, 329
  as administrator, 128, 329, 331
  awards and honours, 86
  collegiality, 128–30, 329–32, 354
  early life and education, 2
  as grand storyteller, 15
  influence and legacy, 1, 16
  personal characteristics, 24–5, 125
  professional eminence, 86
  public engagement, 85–6, 332
  reputation, 1, 52
  supervision of higher degrees, 65, 331, 360–5
  as teacher, 330–1, 349–50
  voice and style, 12–14
  writings and lectures, 2–3, 165, 167. *See also titles*

MacCabe, Colin, 21
Macpherson, C.B., 5
Macquarie University, 315
'The making of a school' (Macintyre), 156, 162
'The making of the Australian working class' (Macintyre), 154, 253, 254, 267, 338–9
'Making the Bicentenary,' 238
manliness, 94–5, 96
Manne, Robert, 254
'Manning Clark's critics' (Macintyre), 159, 239
Marginson, Simon, 12, 14, 356
Maritime Workers Union of Western Australia, 73
Markus, Andrew, 259
Marshall, T.H., 195
Marx, Karl, 4, 6
Marxism
  base and superstructure dilemmas, 21–3
  humanist Marxism, 5
  liberalism and, 3–6
  Macintyre's understanding of, 38
  structuralism, 4, 5
Marxist political history, 56
masculinism
  arbitration and, 112

liberalism and, 5, 94–5, 103
  in postwar era, 181
masculinity
  history of, 91, 92
  nationalism and, 103
Matthews, Brian, 259
McBriar, Alan, 354
McCarthyism, 168
McCaughey, Davis, 319, 355
McCauley, Norman, 289
McGuinness, Paddy, 261, 317
McQueen, Humphrey, 266, 267, 338
media hostility, 160–1
Meeting Soviet Man (M. Clark), 124
Mein Smith, Philippa, 11
Melbourne Cup, 14
Melbourne History School, 1, 155, 161–2,
  185, 240, 252, 253
Menzies, R.G., 177, 259, 357
Menzies Liberal government, 323
Miles, J.B., 73
Militant (Macintyre), 6, 13, 50–1, 66–7,
  68–77, 78
Mill, J.S., 4
Millar, Tom, 240
Millions Club, 9
Milliss, Bruce, 9
misinformation, 292–3
Mitchell, Richard, 166
Monash University, 153
moral economy, 109, 114
moral entitlement, 199
Morgan, Hugh, 297–8
Morgan, Kevin, 4, 21, 23, 354
Morrison, Scott, 117
Mountjoy, Bill, 71
Murdoch University, 65, 66, 67, 78, 106, 235,
  267, 315
Murphy, Peter, 14, 15
Murray, Robert, 261
Murray Report, 316
Mysteries of the Cities series (Knight), 130

National Health Service, 26n5
national identity, 243
National Life and Character (Pearson), 93, 98
nationalism, 119
nationalist liberalism, 103
Native Title Act 1993, 243
Nazi-Soviet Non-Aggression Pact, 70
Nelson, Brendon, 317

neoliberalism, 4, 52, 191, 194, 268, 274, 322
neutrality of historians, 53
A New Britannia (McQueen), 266–7, 338
'new class' intellectuals, 177–8
New Left, 8, 34, 50, 107, 150, 266
New Left Party, 52
New Left Review (journal), 150, 151
New Right, 194
New Zealand labour movement, 268
New Zealand Labour Party, 268, 269
Nisbet, Robert, 194
No End of a Lesson (Macintyre), 319, 321
Normington Rawling, James, 70

O'Connor, C.Y., 67, 78
O'Connor, James, 203
Offe, Claus, 194
Oliver, Bobbie, 11, 14
Olssen, Eric, 11
ordinary communism, 54, 55, 63n26
ordinary Stalinism, 55, 63n26
Orwell, George, 12
Osmond, Warren, 140
The Oxford Companion to Australian History
  (Davison, Hirst & Macintyre, eds), 245,
  249–50, 252, 254–6, 257, 258–63, 271
The Oxford Companion to British History
  (Cannon, ed), 256, 271
Oxford Companion to English Literature
  (Harvey), 250–1
*The Oxford History of Australia
  1901–1942* (Macintyre), 52, 66, 154, 179,
  235–7, 239–41, 245, 271
The Oxford History of Historical Writing, vol 4
  (Macintyre, ed.), 153
Oxford Social History Seminar, 23

Palmer, Nettie, 235
Palonen, Kari, 193
Parkes, Henry, 116, 282
Parsons, Talcott, 194
The Party (Macintyre), 7, 8, 13, 47, 51, 54,
  55, 61, 82, 83–4, 225–6
Pascoe, Sue, 280, 356
Patrick, Alison, 354
Pearson, Charles Henry, 93, 95, 96–7, 99,
  100, 103
Peel, Robert, 215
Pelling, Henry, 31, 35, 354
A People's History of Australia since 1788
  (Burgmann & Lee, eds), 238

Phillips, Mary Willmott, 182
The Philosophy of Loyalty (Royce), 93
'The pioneer legend' (Hirst), 254
political action, and intellectual work, 24, 28, 85
political economy, 8, 57, 108, 114, 177
politics
  engagement with, 106–7
  popular prejudice against, 116–17
politics of knowledge, 24, 25
'The politics of respectability' (Lake), 91–2
Pons, Xavier, 244
The Poor Relation (Macintyre), 207, 208, 210, 211, 212, 213, 218, 220
populism, 10, 61, 116, 117
possessive individualism, 5
postmodernism, 142, 301
postwar reconstruction
  aspirations, 287
  creativity in work of, 180–1
  fading prospects for reform, 185–6
  gendered character, 181
  Labor Party and, 343–7
  lost promise of, 173–5, 345–6
  political economy of, 182
  training and employment schemes, 182–3
power, history and, 158
private health insurance, 26n5
A Proletarian Science (Macintyre), 6, 23, 34, 35, 36, 43, 50, 127, 216–17

Quadrant (magazine), 254, 261, 300
Quick, John, 117
Quinlan, Michael, 60

racial exclusion, 99–100, 103
See also Chinese immigrants
'The radical and the mystic' (Macintyre), 124
'Radical history and bourgeois hegemony' (Macintyre), 150, 151–3, 158, 253, 337
radical nationalist tradition, 49, 153
A Reader's Companion to American History (Foner & Garaty, eds), 256–7
Redfern Speech, 298
The Reds (Macintyre), 7, 13, 48, 49, 51, 53–4, 55, 57, 58, 59, 66–7, 225–6
referendums
  on expansion of Commonwealth powers, 289–91
  on republic, 282

voting patterns, 281
regimental history, 28, 32
Reid, George, 111, 116, 117, 342
republic referendum, 280–1, 282
Reynolds, Henry, 301
Richards, Eric, 258
Richards, Ron, 70–1
Richardson, Len, 11
Rickard, John, 259, 267
Roberts, Stephen, 144, 145
Rose, Peter, 249, 251, 256, 257, 259, 260
Rosevear, Sol, 353–4
Ross, Lloyd, 221
Round Table, 158
Rowse, Tim, 5, 178, 356
Royce, Josiah, 93
Rudkin, Arthur, 71
Russell, Penny, 307
Ryan, Lyndall, 275n9, 301
Ryan, Peter, 261

Samuel, Raphael, 5, 40
Sandel, Michael, 200
Sassoon, Donald, 32–3, 35, 40, 44n15
Saville, John, 34
Scalmer, Sean, 4, 357
Scott (nee Dyason), Emily, 139, 140, 144
Scott, Ernest
  ancestry, 137–8
  contribution to scholarship, 135, 140–3, 151, 155–6, 254
  contribution to teaching, 142–3
  emotional life, 139–40
  impact and legacy, 143–6
  milieu, 135
  networks and patronage, 179
  scholars' representations of, 134–5, 143–4
  students, 220–1
  as subject of biography, 136
  times and conditions compared to Macintyre's, 136–7
Scott, Mabel, 139
Scott, Muriel, 139
Seamen's Union, 168
Search Foundation, 52, 55
Seddon, George, 263
The Selling of the Australian Mind (Knight), 128
Sen, Amartya, 318
The Sentimental Nation (Hirst), 254, 282–3, 284

Serle, Geoff, 101, 192
Serle, Percival, 138
Shann, Edward, 11
Shiels, William, 101–2
Ship Painters' and Dockers Union, 73
Short History of Australia (Scott), 141–2
Simpson, Noel, 356
Sinclair, Keith, 266–7
Sisam, Kenneth, 250, 251
Sluga, Hans, 193
Smith, Bernard, 6
Smith, Sydney, 215
Snowy Mountains Hydro-Electricity
   Scheme, 181
social contact theory, 5
social democracy, 9, 112, 113, 114, 191, 318,
   347
social formations, 10–11, 27, 28, 29, 33, 35, 40
social history, 9
social history of ideas, 40
social justice history, 51, 190, 191, 192,
   195–204
social liberal triumphalism, 190
social liberalism, 4
Social Science Research Council, 211, 212,
   214, 218
social sciences, 11–12
   broad understanding of, 214
   disciplinarity, 212–14
   extending the dimension of citizenship,
      218–19
   and political agency, 214–18
   as the poor relation, 208–10
   social scientists' self-representation, 211–14
   studies of the welfare state, 193–5
socialism, 342
sociology, 11–12, 358
sovereign rights, and racial exclusion, 99,
   100, 101
Spence, W.G., 8
Spriano, Paolo, 32
Stalinism, 8, 47–8, 52, 53, 54, 55, 57
Stannage, Tom, 65
Stedman Jones, Gareth, 23, 31, 40, 151
Stephen, Ninian, 355
Stokes, Eric, 26n5
Stolen Generations, 242, 299
Strachey, John, 39
Strategy of the Italian Communist Party
   (Sassoon), 33
Stretton, Hugh, 259, 357

structuralist Marxism, 4, 5, 28
The Succeeding Age 1901–42 (Macintyre), 10,
   11, 207
Supski, Sian, 14–15
Syme, David, 93, 94–5, 99, 100, 103, 117,
   215–16
Symons, Beverley, 8, 57

Tawney Society, 24
Terre Napoléon (Scott), 140–1, 146
The Fabrication of Aboriginal History
   (Windschuttle), 300–1
Thesis Eleven (journal), 15
Thompson, E.P., 5, 9, 25n2, 29, 34, 35, 192,
   225, 267
Thucydides, 11, 83
Thucydidean history, 83
To Constitute a Nation (Irving), 282
Torney, Kim, 256, 259, 260, 262
trade unionism, 51, 59, 60
trade unions, membership, 73–4
Tribe, Keith, 21, 34
Trinca, Mat, 262
Troy, Mabel, 68, 70, 76
Troy, Paddy, 43, 49
   advocacy in Arbitration Court, 72–3
   biography. *See Militant* (Macintyre)
   contribution to history, 76
   death and funeral, 68, 76, 78
   family background, 69
   health problems, 75–6
   imprisonment, 70, 71
   on Liberals, 74–5
   personal records, 68
   place in community, 67
   as union secretary, 72
Troy, Patrick, 49–50, 67
Trumpism, 117
Turner, George, 117
Turner, Ian, 49, 152, 157, 158, 161, 192, 266,
   337, 354

universities
   collegiality, 318–19, 320
   corporate achievements, 316–17
   Dawkins reforms, 312, 320–6
   dependence on government, 313–15
   impact of foundational prototype, 316, 317
   liberal education, 313–14, 319
   Macintyre's writings on, 312, 317, 320–1,
      326

public accountability, 318
public role, 219, 316
sameness under different skies, 312–17
utilitarianism, 313–14, 315–16, 319–20, 323
The University is Closed for Open Day (Knight), 130
University of Adelaide, 313
University of Canterbury, 267, 268
University of Melbourne
  early years, 311, 313
  English Department, 127, 128
  Ernest Scott Chair in History, 133–4, 253
  History Department, 48, 52, 81, 92, 128, 133–4, 145, 146, 153, 166, 329–32
  Jessie Webb Library, 153
  Penington's changes, 324
  staff club, 128, 129
  'The working class in Literature and History' course, 128–9
  'The Writing of Australian History' course, 146
University of Queensland, 315
University of Sydney, 127, 219, 311, 313
University of Western Australia, 65, 315
utilitarianism, 313–14, 315–16, 319–20, 323

Victoria University, 226
Vocational Education and Training, 324

wage earners' welfare state, 112
Waghorne, James, 169
Wallace, Robert, 127
Wallerstein, Immanuel, 12
Walsh, J.F., 290
Ward, Russel, 49, 254, 260, 266
Waterside Workers Federation, 72
Watson, Don, 124, 259, 303, 305, 355

Watts, Rob, 356
Webb, Beatrice, 354
Webb, Jessie, 143, 153
welfare state, 112, 190–1, 193–5, 203
Wells, Andrew, 8, 52, 57, 62n17
What If? (Macintyre & Scalmer), 357
'What is history?' (Macintyre), 161
White Australia Policy, 104
White, Hayden, 12
whiteness, 5
Whitlam, Gough, 4, 9, 10, 15, 157, 158, 259, 347
Whitlam Labor government, 113, 157, 177, 186, 190, 197, 218
Whitlamism, 347
Wikipedia, 262
Williams, Raymond, 22
Windschuttle, Keith, 159, 300–1, 303, 304–6
Winners and Losers (Macintyre), 50, 51, 87, 109–10, 174, 176, 190–1, 197–204, 209–10, 214–15
Winter, Jay, 258
Wise, Bernard, 111
women's rights, 101, 102
women's suffrage, 94
Wood, G. Arnold, 219
Woolgar, Steve, 11
work of history, 1–2, 10, 25, 29
Workers' Educational Association, 217, 218
working class
  creation in colonial Australia, 154, 253, 254, 267, 338–9
  definition, 340–1
'The working class in Literature and History' (course), 128
World War II, 183
Wrixon, Henry, 101